Joe Habraken

Sams **Teach Yourself**

Windows®
Server 2008
in **24**
Hours

SAMS   800 East 96th Street, Indianapolis, Indiana 46240 USA

Sams Teach Yourself Windows Server® 2008 in 24 Hours

ISBN-13: 978-0-67232-3012-4
ISBN-10: 0-672-33012-1

Library of Congress Cataloging-in-Publication Data:

Habraken, Joseph W., 1954-

Sams teach yourself Windows server 2008 in 24 hours / Joe Habraken.

    p. cm.

ISBN 0-672-33012-1

1. Microsoft Windows server. 2. Operating systems (Computers) I.
Title.

QA76.76.063H3267 2008

005.4'476–dc22

2008014765

Printed in the United States of America

First Printing May 2008

Trademarks

Warning and Disclaimer

Bulk Sales

Sams Publishing offers excellent discounts on this book when ordered in quantity for bulk purchases or special sales. For more information, please contact

U.S. Corporate and Government Sales

1-800-382-3419

corpsales@pearsontechgroup.com

For sales outside of the U.S., please contact

International Sales

international@pearson.com

Editor-in-Chief
Karen Gettman

Executive Editor
Neil Rowe

Aquisitions Editor
Brook Farling

Development Editor
Mark Renfrow

Managing Editor
Patrick Kanouse

Senior Project Editor
San Dee Phillips

Copy Editor
Margo Catts

Indexer
Ken Johnson

Proofreader
Mike Henry

Technical Editor
Jeff Guillet

Publishing Coordinator
Cindy Teeters

Cover and Interior Designer
Gary Adair

Composition
Regina Rexrode

The Safari® Enabled icon on the cover of your favorite technology book means the book is available through Safari Bookshelf. When you buy this book, you get free access to the online edition for 45 days.

Safari Bookshelf is an electronic reference library that lets you easily search thousands of technical books, find code samples, download chapters, and access technical information whenever and wherever you need it.

To gain 45-day Safari Enabled access to this book:

▶ Go to http://www.informit.com/onlineedition

▶ Complete the brief registration form

▶ Enter the coupon code MGJA-EUDK-IMWT-WJK8-FZA7

If you have difficulty registering on Safari Bookshelf or accessing the online edition, please email customer-service@safaribooksonline.com.

Contents at a Glance

iv

Sams Teach Yourself Windows Server 2008 in 24 Hours

Table of Contents

Part II: Network Users, Resources, and Special Server Roles

HOUR 7: Working with TCP/IP Network Protocols   121

HOUR 8: Understanding and Configuring Active Directory Domain Services   141

About the Author

Joe Habraken is an information technology and new media professional with more than 15 years of professional experience in the information technology and digital media production fields. Joe is a best-selling author and his recent publications include *Home Wireless Networking in a Snap*, *Skinning Windows XP*, and *Sams Teach Yourself Networking in 24 Hours* (with Matt Hayden). Joe currently serves as an associate professor at the University of New England in Biddeford, Maine, where he teaches a variety of new media– and information technology–related courses. Joe is a Microsoft Certified Professional and a Cisco Certified Network Associate.

Dedication

To my wonderful wife, Kim; thanks for making my life so great and loving me. I love you, too!

Acknowledgments

Creating a book that covers a topic such as Microsoft Windows Server 2008 takes a team of dedicated professionals; information technology experts, highly skilled editors, proofreaders, and desktop publishers. First of all, I would certainly like to thank all the folks at Sams Publishing who were involved in the creation of this book. I would also like to specifically thank some of the folks who have made this book a reality.

First of all, I would like to thank the very hard-working Neil Rowe, my acquisitions editor, who assembled the team that worked on this project. Neil showed great enthusiasm for the project and has made my continued association with Sams a pleasant and productive one. I would also like to thank acquisitions editor Brook Farling who picked up this book in midstream and was very patient and helpful during the writing of the first draft of the manuscript.

A big thanks goes out to Mark Renfrow, the development editor, who worked extremely hard to make sure this was the best book possible. I would also like to thank Margo Catts, our copy editor, for cleaning up the text; Jeff Guillet, our technical editor; and finally, a big thanks to the project editor, San Dee Phillips, who ran the last leg of the race and made sure this book got into print (and into your local bookstore). Thank you all very much!

We Want to Hear from You!

As the reader of this book, *you* are our most important critic and commentator. We value your opinion and want to know what we're doing right, what we could do better, what areas you'd like to see us publish in, and any other words of wisdom you're willing to pass our way.

You can email or write me directly to let me know what you did or didn't like about this book—as well as what we can do to make our books stronger.

Please note that I cannot help you with technical problems related to the topic of this book, and that due to the high volume of mail I receive, I might not be able to reply to every message.

When you write, please be sure to include this book's title and author as well as your name and phone or email address. I will carefully review your comments and share them with the author and editors who worked on the book.

Email: consumer@samspublishing.com

Mail: Karen Gettman
             Editor-in-Chief
             Sams Publishing
             800 East 96th Street
             Indianapolis, IN 46240 USA

Reader Services

Visit our website and register this book at informit.com/register for convenient access to any updates, downloads, or errata that might be available for this book.

Introduction

Selecting and deploying a network operating system is one of the most important tasks shouldered by a network administrator. In this book, I wanted to put together a body of information related to the newest version of Microsoft's powerful network operating system platform—Microsoft Windows Server 2008—that would not only highlight the functions and capabilities of the network server software, but also provide a hands-on approach to deploying the product. The *Sams Teach Yourself in 24 Hours* format provides for both the subject matter coverage and a practical step-by-step look at important server features and tools.

Microsoft has spent a great deal of time and effort (and development money) to improve both the security and scalability of Windows Server 2008. *Sams Teach Yourself Windows Server 2008 in 24 Hours* provides you with all the information you need to get a Windows domain up and running. Coverage of network services and the ins and outs of supporting users on the network is also provided.

Material in the book is approached in a straightforward, step-by-step manner that makes it easy to digest the information. The hours in the book are arranged so that there is a building of information as you move from Hour 1 to Hour 24.

Who Should Use This Book?

This book is designed for people who have a basic knowledge of computer networking. The book is arranged in 24 self-contained hours. Each hour helps build your knowledge base of Windows Server 2008. Coverage includes many important Windows Server 2008 network services, such as the Active Directory Domain Services, Group Policy, DHCP, DNS, and file and print services. A hands-on approach, coupled with easy-to-read background information, will help you quickly enlarge your knowledge base of Microsoft's powerful network operating system platform.

The book is divided into four parts. Each part provides a grouping of hours that share a common theme.

Part I, "Server Installation and Configuration," includes hours that provide you with information on installing the Windows Server 2008 operating system and configuring a server running this network operating system for a variety of possible roles. The new Server Manager is also introduced in this part of the book. Part I also provides you with insight into using Windows Deployment Services to deploy domain clients and servers, and shows you how to configure hard drives and volumes on your servers.

Part II, "Network Users, Resources, and Special Server Roles," includes hours that help you expand your knowledge of data communications on the network through a discussion of the TCP/IP protocol and securing resources with share and NTFS permissions. You also learn how to bring your domain online by configuring a domain controller with the Active Directory Domain Services, and you learn how to use Group Policy and Network Access Protection to standardize and protect your domain. This part also provides information on how to provide file and printing services to your network users.

Part III, "Advanced Networking," provides information on a number of Windows Server 2008 roles, such as Routing and Remote Access, WINS, and Terminal Services. The hours in Part III help you deploy remote access in your domain and configure a server running Windows Server 2008 as a router. You learn how to install WINS on the network and supply network users access to tools and applications via the Windows Terminal Services role.

Part IV, "Network Security, Web Services, and Performance Monitoring," provides hours that help you tackle security and services related to data traffic on your network and help you provide web services to your user base. It covers securing the local network with the Windows Firewall and securing IP data packets with IPSec. It also looks at the use of advanced security strategies such as certificate services. Tools such as the Performance Monitor, Reliability Monitor, and the Event Viewer are explored in the context of keeping important domain servers up and running at peak performance.

Conventions Used in This Book

Certain conventions have been followed in this book to help you digest all the material. For example, at the beginning of each hour, you'll find a list of the major topics that will be covered in that particular hour. You will also find that icons are used throughout this book. These icons either are accompanied by additional information on a subject or supply you with shortcuts or optional ways to perform a task. These icons are as follows:

> By the Way elements include additional information related to the current topic, such as asides and comments.

> Did You Know elements contain shortcuts and hints on performing a particular task.

At the end of each hour, you will find both a Summary section and a Q&A section. The Summary section provides a brief encapsulation of the core information covered in the hour. The Q&A section provides a series of questions and answers that help cement important facts and concepts covered in the hour.

PART I

Server Installation and Configuration

Introducing Microsoft Windows Server 2008

What You'll Learn in This Hour:

▶ Introducing Windows Server 2008

▶ Improvements and Additions to Windows Server 2008

▶ The Different Flavors of Windows Server 2008

In this hour, you are introduced to the latest version of Microsoft's network operating system (NOS) platform: Microsoft Windows Server 2008. You'll learn about the features that Windows Server 2008 has inherited from its predecessors and some of the new features provided by this NOS. We also look at the different editions of Windows Server 2008.

Introducing Windows Server 2008

Microsoft Windows Server 2008 is the latest version of Microsoft's server network operating system. Windows Server 2008 builds on the features found in Windows Server 2003 and also offers a number of enhancements. Windows Server 2008 was part of the development cycle that produced Microsoft's Windows Vista desktop operating system.

During the development cycle, Longhorn, now known as Windows Server 2008, incorporated the best of what was found in the Windows Server 2003 environment and also adapted some of the new bells and whistles that are also found in the Windows Vista operating system. Windows Server 2008 also provides a number of improvements over Windows Server 2003, while still providing a scalable enterprise networking platform that can be easily expanded as a company or organization grows.

In terms of features adopted from Windows Vista, you will find that Windows Server 2008 shares a number of similarities with Windows Vista, including the Start Menu, desktop, and Windows Control Panel. Thanks to Windows Vista, Windows Server 2008 also now provides a better native backup utility: the Windows Server Backup snap-in (see Figure 1.1). This backup utility runs in the Microsoft Management Console (as do many other snap-ins available in Windows Server 2008) and enables you to back up and restore server files to backup media including DVDs.

FIGURE 1.1
The Windows
Server Backup
snap-in.

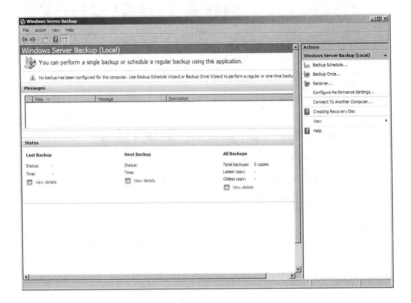

Windows Server 2008 also takes advantage of Windows BitLocker drive encryption, which is a new encryption feature that was created during the development cycle that produced Windows Vista and Windows Server 2008. BitLocker encrypts all the data on the volume. It can be used to encrypt all the data on the volume that contains the Windows operating system, including paging files, applications, and data used by applications.

Although Windows Server 2008 has adopted some Windows Vista features and also provides many new features of its own, you shouldn't find the Windows Server 2008 administrative environment totally alien if you have used other versions of the network operating system such as Windows Server 2003 (or even the earlier version of this product, Windows 2000 Server). Many of the features and tools that were made available in Windows Server 2003 are also found in Windows Server 2008, including these:

▶ **The Active Directory**—Known as the Active Directory for Domain Services (AD DS) in Windows Server 2008, this directory service provides the hierarchical directory of objects on the network (such as users, computers, and printers). AD DS also provides the logical hierarchy for your enterprise forests and child domains and the physical hierarchy for sites.

▶ **Group Policy**—Group Policy provides a way to control the user and computer environment found on the network. Application deployment, client desktop settings, and policies related to administrative controls such as auditing can all be configured in Group Policy (Group Policy is discussed in Hour 11, "Deploying Group Policy and Network Access Protection").

▶ **High-level security**—The same security options that you found in Windows Server 2003 are also available in Windows Server 2008, such as data encryption, certificates, and a number of other security enhancements, such as the IP Security Protocol. Windows Server 2008 builds on these security features and offers even greater security than its predecessor, including features such as BitLocker drive encryption and the new Network Access Protection service (discussed in Hour 11).

▶ **Web server capabilities**—Windows Server 2008 provides the newest version of Microsoft's Internet Information Server—version 7 (IIS7)—which incorporates content delivery platforms such as ASP.NET and SharePoint services into one easy-to-manage web platform. IIS7 also supplies a new management snap-in that can be run in the Microsoft Management Console or MMC (see Hour 23, "Using the Internet Information Service," for more about IIS7).

Windows Server 2008 builds on the security that was provided by Windows 2003 Server and now provides a way to limit network access based on health policies related to Windows Update and the configuration of the Windows Firewall. For more information see Hour 11.

By the Way

In addition to features gleaned from the development of Windows Vista and the solid foundation provided by Windows Server 2003, Windows Server 2008 provides many enhancements, more enhancements than can be covered in one book. Let's take a look at some of the improvements and new features provided by Windows Server 2008.

Improvements and Additions to Windows Server 2008

A number of improvements and additions have been made to Windows Server 2008. As already mentioned, Windows Server 2008 shares some of the look and feel provided by Windows Vista. Windows Server 2008 also supplies a number of new tools; one of the most dramatic of these new tools in terms of managing a Windows server is the Server Manager.

In Windows Server 2003, a number of the administrative tools ran as snap-ins in the MMC. As you added a role to the server, such as DNS or DHCP, a new snap-in would be available. The new Server Manager provides easy access to nearly all the configuration, monitoring, and troubleshooting snap-ins that you will need to use as you manage your Windows server (see Figure 1.2).

FIGURE 1.2
The Server Manager provides quick access to your server management tools.

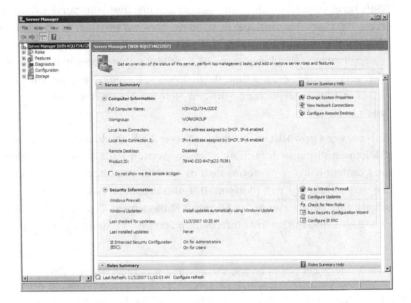

The Server Manager not only provides quick access to many of the management snap-ins, but it also includes quick access to the Add New Roles Wizard and enables you to view the services that are installed and running in association with a particular server role. The Server Manager is introduced in Hour 3, "Configuring Windows Server 2008 Basic Settings," and is used extensively throughout the book to manage the various roles provided by Windows Server 2008.

Another important change to Windows Server 2008 is how it approaches installing new roles and services on a server. When you boot the server, Windows Server 2008 loads the Initial Configuration Tasks window. This utility enables you to view the roles that are currently installed on the server and also provides easy access to settings such as the time zone, the computer name and domain membership, automatic updates, and the server's network interfaces.

More importantly, both the Initial Configuration Tasks window (and the Server Manager) provide quick access to the Add Roles Wizard. The Add Roles Wizard (see Figure 1.3) not only makes it easy for you to install a new role such as the domain controller role, DNS role, or the Active Directory Certificate Services role, it also makes sure that you install all the necessary services required for that role to function appropriately.

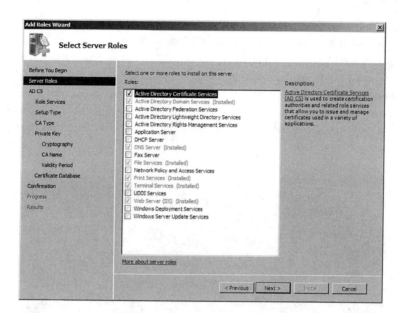

FIGURE 1.3
The Add Roles
Wizard enables
you to add roles
and also helps
to make sure
that required
services for the
role are
installed.

For example, if you are installing the Certification Authority Web Enrollment service (a web interface where users can request and renew certificates) as part of the Active Directory Certificate Services (a server role), the Add Roles Wizard alerts you to the fact that this service requires IIS7 and that it will be installed during the process of adding the role to your server.

Another improvement provided by Windows Server 2008 is that you can now deploy read-only domain controllers. This enables you to deploy a domain controller in a less secure environment such as a branch office. Read-only domain controllers contain a read-only copy of the Active Directory, which provides much more security in these environments.

Windows Server 2008 also enables you to perform a core installation of the network operating system. A core installation is a minimal or stripped-down installation of Windows Server 2008 that is managed from the command line (the Windows GUI interface is not installed) and can supply certain services and server roles to the client computers on your network. A core installation can provide services such as print services and file services. A server with a core installation can also function in roles such as a DHCP server and DNS server (Windows Server 2008 installations are discussed in Hour 2, "Installing and Configuring Windows Server 2008").

In Windows Server 2003, a number of new command-line tools were added, such as DiskPart (a disk partitioning tool) and the dfscmd Distributed File System utility that enables you to create DFS roots from the command line. Windows Server 2008 takes the command-line utility one step further with the Windows PowerShell (also available in Windows Vista), which provides a powerful set of command-line tools (called *cmdlets*) and a full-fledged scripting language. PowerShell (see Figure 1.4) is added to Windows Server 2008 as a feature, and although it is not covered in this book (we concentrate on the snap-ins that run in the Server Manager and the MMC), it provides you with an alternative to the various snap-ins and other GUI tools provided by the network operating system.

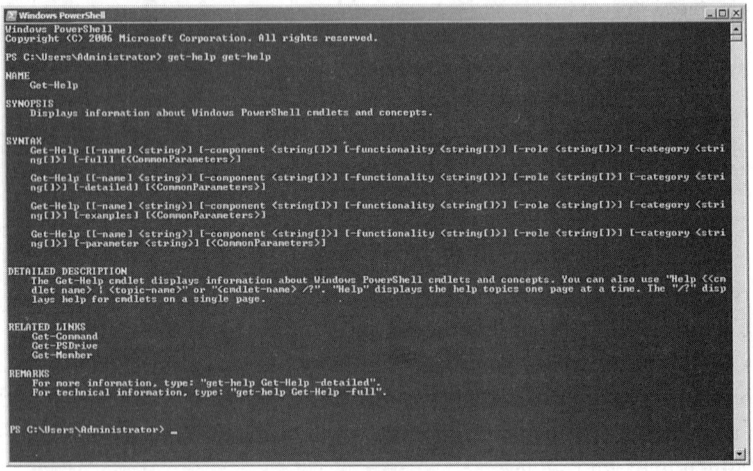

FIGURE 1.4
PowerShell is a new command-line and scripting tool.

Windows Server 2008 also makes the management of printers and print servers easier in your domain. The new Print Management snap-in (see Figure 1.5) enables you to view print servers and the printers that they provide for the domain. You can even locate (using filters) printers that currently have print jobs and printers that are not ready (meaning paused or offline).

The discussion here only scratches the surface of new features found in and the improvements made to the Windows Server 2008 platform. The lists that follow provide a quick look at some of the most important new features and the improvements found in the Windows Server 2008 network operating system platform.

New features:

▶ **Read-only domain controllers**—This feature enables you to deploy read-only domain controllers in your domain for added security and branch office or other remote location access to the Active Directory database.

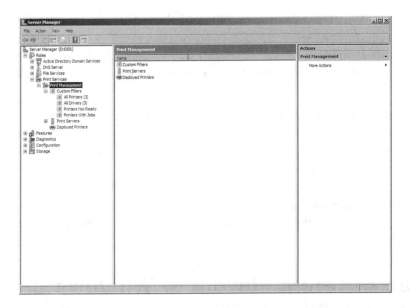

FIGURE 1.5
The Print
Management
snap-in.

▶ **Internet Information Services 7 (IIS7)**—IIS7 provides an easily managed platform for a number of web-based technologies, including ASP.NET and SharePoint services. IIS7 also enables you to manage your web servers, using a web browser.

▶ **Windows Server 2008 core installation**—The stripped-down core installation enables you to deploy server services and roles on server hardware that does not meet the hardware requirements (such as RAM) for a full Windows Server 2008 installation.

▶ **Internet Protocol version 6**—Windows Server 2008 installs IPv6 by default and allows you to run IPv4 and IPv6 in tandem on your network interfaces.

▶ **Server virtualization**—Windows Server 2008 provides Hyper-V, which is a software virtualization technology that enables you to run multiple virtual servers on a single server.

Improved features:

▶ **Windows Deployment Services**—Windows Deployment Services (WDS) replaces the Remote Installation Services (RIS) provided by Windows Server 2003. WDS allows you to install both Windows Server 2008 and client operating systems (including Windows Vista and Windows XP) using an image-based installation. WDS is discussed in Hour 5, "Implementing Windows Deployment Services."

▶ **Windows Firewall**—The new Windows Firewall with Advanced Security found in Windows Server 2008 offers you greater management control of the firewall in the new Windows Firewall with Advanced Security snap-in. IPSec has also been added to the Windows Firewall to provide greater IP traffic security.

▶ **Reliability and Performance Monitor**—The new Reliability and Performance Monitor enables you to monitor server performance in real time. You can monitor hardware and application performance and create threshold alerts and performance reports.

We will be working with a number of the new features and improvements found in the Windows Server 2008 operating system. These features are discussed throughout the book in the context of the appropriate subject matter.

The Different Flavors of Windows Server 2008

The Windows Server 2008 family consists of several different network operating systems that are designed to serve businesses of different sizes and different needs.

The members of the Windows Server 2008 family are listed here and discussed in the sections that follow:

▶ Standard Edition

▶ Enterprise Edition

▶ Datacenter Edition

▶ Web Edition

Standard Edition

Standard Server is considered the entry-level version of Windows Sever 2008 (if there is such a thing as "entry-level" with server platforms). It is suitable for smaller businesses and organizations ("smaller" meaning users in the hundreds, not thousands, although multiple standard servers in a tree or trees would certainly accommodate even the largest of companies).

Standard Server supplies all the features discussed in this hour, including Hyper-V virtualization, and IIS7. It also provides for Network Address Translation and multihomed servers (servers with more than one network interface) that allow multiple network clients to share the same Internet connection in a small business setting.

Standard Server supports multiple processors (four cores on both x86 and x64 systems) and up to 4GB of RAM on an x86-based server and 32GB of RAM on an X64-based server. Standard Server provides a maximum of 250 Remote Access connections and 250 Terminal Services connections.

> Because this book is an introduction to and survey of installing and administering a Windows network environment, we primarily cover the tools and features found in Windows Server 2008 Standard Edition. These features and server roles would also be available in the Windows Server 2008 Enterprise Edition. The Web Edition is intended as a web server product and does not contain many of the standard features for deploying a domain.

By the Way

Enterprise Edition

The Enterprise Edition supplies all the features and tools provided by the Standard Edition. The major difference is that the Enterprise Edition is considered a workhorse platform for very large enterprisewide networks.

To provide the processing power needed for larger networks, the Enterprise Edition can support up to eight processors and also supports server clustering (up to 16 cluster nodes, meaning that 16 servers can be tied together using the clustering feature and thus can act as one megaserver).

The Enterprise Edition on an x86-based server allows up to 64GB of RAM and up to 2TB on an x64-based system. This edition also provides for unlimited connections by Remote Access and Terminal Services clients.

Datacenter Edition

The Datacenter Edition provides all the features found in the other editions and allows you to deploy servers with a great deal of hardware muscle. The Datacenter Edition provides for multiple processors (32 x86 and 64 x64) and has the same potential RAM capacity as the Enterprise Edition (64GB on x86 and 2TB on X64).

The Datacenter Edition provides for unlimited Remote Access and Terminal Services connections. It also grants you unlimited deployment of virtual servers, whereas the limit with the Enterprise Edition is four and with the Standard Edition is one. The Datacenter Edition is considered the appropriate platform for very large-scale networks requiring access to large databases and real-time transaction validation.

Web Edition

The Web Edition is considered the ideal platform for web hosting; it is a scaled-down version of Windows Server and does not provide tools for deploying a domain-based network. The Web Edition provides IIS7 as its web platform.

The Web Edition supports multiple processors (four on both x86 and x64 systems) and up to 4GB of RAM on an x86-based server and 32 GB of RAM on an x64-based server. As a product intended for delivery of web-based content, the Web Edition does not support common server services such as Remote Access or Terminal Services.

> Microsoft also provides two additional versions of Windows Server 2008: Windows Server 2008 for Itanium-based systems and Windows HPC Server 2008. The Itanium version is designed for networks that require large databases and custom applications. The HPC version is designed for high-performance computing (thus the HPC) environments using server clustering. Bottom line: Both of these versions are for big, high-capacity networks.

All the versions of Windows Server 2008, except for the Web Edition, include the Hyper-V virtualization platform. However, you can also purchase the Standard, Enterprise, and Datacenter versions of Windows Server 2008 without the Hyper-V technology. Obviously, Microsoft provides enough flavors of Windows Server 2008 that you can select the edition that will work best for your networking needs.

Summary

This hour covered the latest version of Microsoft's network operating system: Windows Server 2008. Windows Server 2008 provides the services and featured offered in the previous Windows Server 2003 networking platform and also provides a number of improvements and new features.

Windows Server 2008 was developed in the same development cycle as Windows Vista and so shares some new features first seen at the release of Vista, such as the new desktop and Control Panel look. Windows Server 2008 now includes a new more robust backup utility called Windows Server Backup. Windows Server 2008 also includes the Windows PowerShell, first introduced with Windows Vista.

Windows Server 2008 provides new administrative tools such as the Server Manager, which supplies access to most of the role management snap-ins used to manage server roles and services. Windows Server 2008 also provides greater security possibilities than its predecessors, including a new Windows Firewall, IPSec, the BitLocker drive encryption, and the new Network Access Protection Service.

New server deployment possibilities such as read-only domain controllers and the Windows core installation provide you with flexibility for client access to the Active Directory Domain Services and services such as DHCP and DNS. The Hyper-V virtualization technology enables you to run multiple server deployments on a single computer.

The Windows Server 2008 provides a family of network server products, including the Standard, Enterprise, Datacenter, and Web Editions. The Standard Edition is considered the entry-level version of this powerful server platform and can be purchased with or without the new Hyper-V virtualization platform.

Q&A

Q. *What are some of the new tools and features provided by Windows Server 2008?*

A. Windows Server 2008 now provides a desktop environment similar to Microsoft Windows Vista and includes tools also found in Vista, such as the new backup snap-in and the BitLocker drive encryption feature. Windows Server 2008 also provides the new IIS7 web server and the Windows Deployment Service.

Q. *What are the different editions of Windows Server 2008?*

A. The entry-level version of Windows Server 2008 is the Standard Edition. The Enterprise Edition provides a platform for large enterprisewide networks. The Datacenter Edition provides support for unlimited Hyper-V virtualization and advanced clustering services. The Web Edition is a scaled-down version of Windows Server 2008 intended for use as a dedicated web server. The Standard, Enterprise, and Datacenter Editions can be purchased with or without the Hyper-V virtualization technology.

HOUR 2

Installing Windows Server 2008

This hour discusses the different types of Windows Server 2008 installations, such as upgrading an existing server or making a clean install on a server that is not currently configured with a network operating system. It discusses issues related to a Windows 2008 core installation as well as Windows Server 2008 hardware requirements, server licensing, and server activation.

Planning the Server Installation

Before you install Windows Server 2008 on a computer, particularly in cases when you are creating a new network infrastructure, you should create a map of what your network will look like (a good tool for creating a network map is Microsoft Visio). In particular, you should outline the servers and other resource devices, such as printers, that will provide your network clients with services. The role that a particular server will fill on the network should be determined long before you install the network operating system. The server's role, such as acting as a domain controller, a DHCP server, a multihomed router (a Windows Server 2008 configured with more than one network interface card), or a NAT server, dictates not only the server's hardware configuration, but also the configuration of that server (and the services it provides).

> Hour 4, "Understanding and Configuring Server Roles and Services," provides an overview on how to configure the various roles for a server, including such services as DNS, a file server, and a print server. Other hours in the book look at the specifics of configuring these various services. Hour 8, "Understanding and Configuring Active Directory Domain Services," looks at the Active Directory namespace and provides the steps for making Windows Server 2008 a domain controller.

Other issues related to the installation of Windows Server 2008 on a computer have to do with the computer's hardware configuration and its compatibility with Windows Server 2008. You must also be aware (before installation) of how you will configure client licensing on your network. Let's look at the Windows Server 2008 hardware requirements; then we can look at a quick way to check an existing server's upgrade compatibility and discuss server licensing issues.

Server Hardware Requirements

Windows Server 2008 requires a minimum hardware configuration to run. As with all software—particularly network operating systems—the more you exceed the minimum requirements in areas such as RAM, processor speed (even number of processors), and hard drive space, the faster the server supplies services to network users and the greater the number of roles one server can fill on the network. (For example, a server could be a domain controller and could provide the DNS and DHCP services.) DOMAIN CONTROLLER, DNS, DHCP

Windows Server 2008 throws a bit of a monkey wrench into the hardware requirement discussion because it provides a "low rent" core installation, which doesn't require the same hardware muscle as a typical server installation. Windows Server 2008 also provides network administrators with the option of deploying virtual servers that run in addition to the Windows Server 2008 NOS already installed on a server, and you will definitely need more hardware muscle (meaning exceeding the minimum hardware requirements quite a bit) on any server you will run that uses the Windows Server 2008 virtualization feature.

Microsoft's _minimum_ hardware requirements for a Windows Server 2008 installation are listed here:

- ▶ CPU speed: 1GHz (x86 processor) or 1.4GHz (x64 processor)
- ▶ RAM: 512MB
- ▶ Disk space: 10GB
- ▶ DVD-ROM drive
- ▶ Monitor: Super VGA capable of providing 800×600 resolution

You can see that the minimum hardware requirements for Wndows Server 2008 are considerably more than previous versions of the Microsoft NOS. (Windows Server 2003 minimum requirements needed only 128MB of RAM and a 133MHz processor.) Microsoft also provides a _suggested_ list of hardware requirements:

- ▶ CPU speed: 2GHz or faster
- ▶ RAM: 2GB or greater
- ▶ Disk space: 40GB or greater

A server core installation, which is a stripped-down version of Windows Server 2008, requires at least 512MB of RAM. But because it is designed to provide services such as DHCP with lower overhead, you don't need as much hard drive space and can get by with a minimum of 8GB. Windows Server 2008 core basically allows you to still get some mileage out of your older server hardware in cases where you want to move services off your "newer" servers, particularly those that would typically have to serve multiple roles such as domain controller, DHCP, and DNS server.

If you are going to run Microsoft's virtualization product, Windows Server Virtualization, your hardware requirements are even greater. You definitely need an x64-based processor, hardware-assisted virtualization (AMD-V or Intel VT), and hardware data execution protection. _VIRTUALIZATION_

Not only must you meet the minimum hardware requirements to successfully install and run Windows Server 2008, but you also must have a server that provides hardware that is proven to be compatible with the network operating system. If you intend to use the server in a true production environment where you must supply mission-critical services to network users, your server hardware must come right off the Microsoft Windows Server 2008 Hardware Compatibility List. A copy of the list is available at http://www.microsoft.com/whdc/winlogo/HWrequirements.mspx and you can also locate the list via the Microsoft Windows 2008 Server home page at http://www.microsoft.com/windowsserver2008/default.mspx.

It makes sense (considering that hardware costs are relatively reasonable at this time) to go with at least a 2GHz processor (I'm talking an x64 processor and multiple processors if your budget allows) and plenty of RAM and disk space. Consider going with a SCSI drive array with at least three 100GB drives, particularly if you are going to use RAID fault tolerance on the server and you want to run virtual servers (Microsoft or Linux). Remember that any server hardware configuration must address the capacity that will be required by the services you run on the server and any server-side applications that you will deploy, such as Microsoft SQL Server or Microsoft Exchange Server.

Understanding Server Licensing Issues

Another aspect of planning your Windows Server 2008 installation is determining how you will license the clients that log on to your network servers. There are two licensing modes in terms of network clients: per server and per seat. It's important that you choose the licensing mode that best suits your networking plan and the potential growth of your user base.

In *per server* mode, you are licensed for a certain number of concurrent connections to the server. If you have 50 licenses, 50 clients can connect to the server. Per server mode is the best choice when you have a small network consisting of only one domain (and one domain controller). It also works best for networks when only part of your client base is connected to the server at any one time. For example, if you run different shifts at your company, you need only a per server license that covers the number of users connected to the server at any one time (not your entire employee population).

In *per seat* mode, you purchase a license for each network user on the network. Each of these users can connect to any and all the servers on the network. As far as large networks go, per seat mode is probably the best licensing strategy, especially if network resources are spread across a number of Windows Server 2008 servers.

Microsoft has created some new licensing schemes for Microsoft Windows Server 2008. A new User Client Access license enables a user to connect to network services using any device, including computers and devices such as PDAs. (This does not replace the Device Client Access licensing scheme currently in use in Windows 2000 and Windows Server 2008.) External Connector licenses are also new and can be used by customers or partners to connect to licensed network services in the domain. Whatever licensing you use, you need to make sure that you have the appropriate number of licenses for your Windows Server 2008 domain. For more information on Microsoft licensing, check out http://www.microsoft.com/licensing/Default.asp.

Choosing to Upgrade or Make a Clean Installation

A major consideration related to a Windows Server 2008 installation is whether to upgrade in-place servers or do a clean install on a replacement server that is to take over the role of a server or servers already on the network. For example, you might be running Windows 2000 Server on a computer that you want to replace (it might have seen better days hardware-wise). You can install Windows Server 2008 on a new server and make it a domain controller in the Windows domain that already exists. This enables the new server to replicate all the information in the Active Directory on the current domain controller. You can then "retire" the Windows 2000 Server and use the Windows Server 2008 as the domain controller for the domain.

In cases where you are running Windows Server 2003 on domain controllers and domain member servers, you should take a look at each of these servers and determine whether you want to upgrade, replace, or leave the server in place. If you want to use all the new features available in Windows Server 2008 within the domain, you may want to upgrade or replace domain controllers. The upgrade option depends on individual server hardware. You are much more likely to be able to upgrade a server running Windows Server 2003 to Windows Server 2008 than a server that has been in operation for a longer period of time and is running an older version of Windows Server, such as Windows 2000 Server.

Whatever your strategy is for bringing new servers online on an existing network, you must deal with issues related to earlier versions of the Windows network operating system, such as Windows 2000 Server and Windows Server 2003.

Upgrading a server (even a domain controller) from Windows Server 2003 or Windows 2000 Server to Windows Server 2008 is a fairly easy process. Because Windows Server 2003, Windows 2000 Server, and Windows Server 2008 all embrace the Active Directory hierarchy and DNS namespace, the notion of forests, trees, and domains is common to these network operating systems. This means that a radical redesign of the network domain structure is not necessary.

An upgrade from Windows Server 2003 or Windows 2000 Server to Windows Server 2008, however, doesn't just depend on whether or not the server hardware will be suitable to run Windows Server 2008, particularly in the case of upgrading a domain controller.

In cases where you are upgrading a Windows Server 2003 or Windows 2000 domain controller or even adding a new Windows Server 2008 domain controller to the domain, you must prepare the forest for the Windows Server 2008 domain controller. This step should be done before you upgrade a domain controller to Windows Server 2008 or add the Active Directory Domain Services role to a server in the domain that has Windows Server 2008 installed on it.

First you must log on to the Schema Master for the domain as a member of the Enterprise Admins, Schema Admins, or Domain Admins group. The Schema Master is typically the first domain controller you brought online using Windows 2000 Server or Windows Server 2003 when you first defined your domain forest. It is the Schema Master because it defines the Active Directory schema for the domain (the *schema* being the actual definition of the objects contained in the Active Directory). There is only one Schema Master per Windows 2000 or Windows 2003 forest (which can hold many domains).

After logging on to the Schema Master, insert the Windows Server 2008 installation DVD. Copy the contents of the \sources\adprep folder from the Windows Server 2008 installation DVD to the Schema Master.

You then use the adprep command-line utility found in the folder that you copied to the Schema Master. Open a Command Prompt window, navigate to the Adprep folder (the place where you copied the items from the DVD), and run adprep /forestprep.

The second step of this process is required to prepare each of the domains in the forest. You must log on to the Infrastructure Master for a domain as a member of the Domain Admins group. The Infrastructure Master is charged with the task of upgrading group. It keeps track of the groups to which users belong. If group membership changes, the Infrastructure Master records this and then replicates it to the other domain controllers in the domain. When you create the first domain in a Windows 2000 or Windows 2003 forest, that domain controller is assigned the Infrastructure Master status.

> On smaller domains with only a limited number of domain controllers, the Schema Master and the Infrastructure Master can be the same domain controller.

On the Infrastructure Master, copy the contents of the \sources\adprep folder from the installation DVD to the Infrastructure Master. You then need to open a Command Prompt window, navigate to the Adprep folder, and run adprep /domainprep /gpprep. Again, you need to wait until these changes to the domain have replicated to the other domain controllers in the domain. If you plan to use read-only domain controllers on the network, you will need to run adprep /rodcprep as well.

Windows Server 2008–Supported File Systems

Windows Server 2008 supports FAT32 and NTFS partitions on your server's hard drives. FAT is not supported. In terms of installing Windows Server 2008 on a drive, you can install Windows Server 2008 only on an NTFS volume or partition.

▶ **FAT32**—FAT32 is an extension of the FAT file system. It uses disk space on a drive more efficiently than FAT and was designed for Windows 95/98.

▶ **NTFS**—NTFS 5 is the newest version of the NT file system (NTFS 5 was first introduced with Windows 2000 Server). It provides increased security for files on NTFS volumes and supports more robust file system recovery. Microsoft recommends that you use NTFS as your file system on your Windows servers. It is also required if you want to install Active Directory on a server to make it a domain controller.

Unless you have some legacy operating system issues, you should use NTFS volumes on your servers. NTFS provides the stability, the security, and other bells and whistles that make it the appropriate choice for your server drive implementations.

Windows Vista and Windows Server 2008 have really signaled the end of the FAT file system in the enterprise networking arena.

Performing a Clean Installation

To install Windows Server 2008 on a server that is not configured with a previous operating system, set up the system so that it boots to the DVD-ROM drive (using the computer's BIOS settings utility). Insert the Windows Server 2008 installation DVD and boot the system. Click Next after supplying your country and language information.

The Install Windows window opens. Click the Install Now button to begin the installation. The Product Key and Activation window opens (see Figure 2.1).

Enter your product key in the Product Key box. Note that the Activate Windows check box is selected by default. This means that your server product is activated automatically (a requirement) when the server goes online and is connected to the Internet. After entering the product key, click Next.

FIGURE 2.1
Enter the product key for Windows Server 2008.

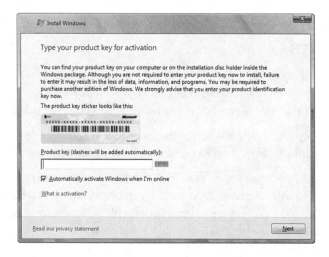

On the next installation page, you are provided with the option of installing Windows Server 2008 or installing a Windows Server 2008 core installation. The core installation (discussed later in this hour) is a stripped-down version of the Windows Server 2008 operating system and can be used to deploy network services on servers that have a less-than-optimal hardware configuration. In this case (for discussion purposes) select the Windows Server 2008 installation (not the core installation) and then click Next.

The next wizard page asks you to read the license terms for the server software. Click the I Accept the License Terms check box and then click Next to continue.

The next wizard page asks what type of installation you would like. In the case of a clean install, the Upgrade option is disabled (which it would not be if you were upgrading a previous version of the Windows Server NOS, such as Windows Server 2003). Click the Custom (Advanced) installation box.

On the next wizard page, you are provided with a list of the disks (and volumes or partitions if you placed them on the server with a utility such as `fdisk`) on the server (see Figure 2.2). Select the disk and or volume with unallocated space and then click Next.

The installation wizard copies files to the server drive and installs the Windows Server 2008 operating system files. After the installation is complete, the system boots to Windows Server 2008. You will need to configure a password for the Administrator account before you can log on for the first time. Set and confirm the password to log in (remember to use a strong password that includes different case characters and numbers).

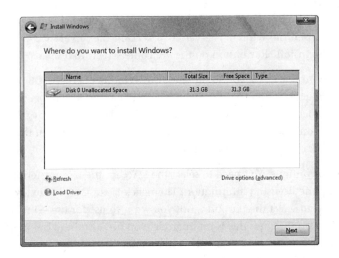

FIGURE 2.2
Select the location for the Windows Server 2008 installation.

You can then use the Initial Configuration Tasks window to begin the process of configuring the server for the roles it is to serve on the network. In terms of basic Windows Server 2008 settings, see Hour 3, "Configuring Windows Server 2008 Basic Settings."

Performing an In-Place Upgrade

If you are not in a position to do a clean install of Windows Server 2008, you can also upgrade an existing network operating system, such as Windows 2000 Server and Windows Server 2003. The actual upgrade process is very straightforward. But as already mentioned in this hour, the upgrade of a domain controller has consequences for the entire domain. Running mixed environments in which Windows 2000 or 2003 servers must interact with servers running Windows Server 2008 makes supplying important network resources in the domain more difficult (and quite confusing at times). In an ideal situation, you can upgrade all servers on the network to Windows Server 2008.

Windows Server 2008 is fairly flexible in terms of upgrading different versions of previous Windows Server operating systems such as Windows Server 2003. For example, if you are running Windows Server 2003 Standard Edition, you can upgrade to the Windows Server 2008 Standard Edition or to the Windows Server 2008 Enterprise Edition. A Windows Server 2003 Enterprise Edition can be upgraded to a Windows Server 2008 Enterprise Edition but cannot be downgraded to a Windows Server 2008 Standard Edition installation.

To perform an upgrade on a server running Windows 2000 Server or Windows Server 2003, insert the Windows Server 2008 DVD in the server's CD-ROM drive. Then click the Install Now button on the Welcome screen that opens.

The next wizard page asks you to provide your Windows Server 2008 product key. Enter the product key and then click Next. On the next wizard page, you are asked to select the operating system you want to install. Select the Windows Server 2008 (Full Installation) option. You cannot upgrade a previous version of the Windows Server network operating system to a core installation.

Click Next to continue. You need to select the I Accept the License Terms check box after reading the licensing information. Then click Next. On the next wizard page, you are asked to select the partition that you want to use for the Windows Server 2008 installation. Because this is an upgrade, you are installing the Windows Server 2008 files onto a volume that already contains the files for the previous version of the Windows server software. A warning box appears (when you select the partition for the installation) letting you know that you are installing to a partition that contains other operating system files (see Figure 2.3).

FIGURE 2.3
Click OK to install Windows Server 2008 on a volume containing an operating system.

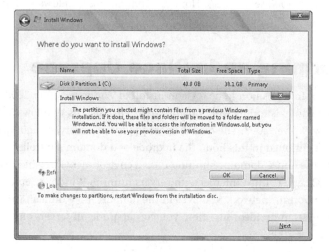

Click OK to close the information box. You can then click Next to proceed with the installation. The installation at this point requires little input from you. Files are copied to the server and the server restarts a couple of times. When the installation is complete, the upgraded server boots to Windows Server 2008.

> You can also use Windows Deployment Services to install multiple Windows Server installations. This enables you to install Windows 2008 Server on several computers from a server running Windows Deployment Services. This service can also be used to deploy client operating systems such as Windows Vista on your network. We discuss Windows Deployment Services in Hour 5, "Implementing Windows Deployment Services."

By the Way

Installing a Core Installation

A core installation is a minimal or stripped-down installation of Windows Server 2008 that can supply certain services and server roles to the client computers on your network. A core installation can provide services such as print services and file services. A server with a core installation can also function in roles such as a DHCP server and DNS server.

A server core installation should be made to a server that does not contain a previous network operating system (unless you plan on doing a dual-boot configuration). You will need at least 8GB of free space on a "free" volume to do the core installation.

As with the full or upgrade installation, insert the Windows Server 2008 installation DVD and then begin the installation from the Install Windows Wizard by clicking the Install Now button. You then need to enter your product key.

On the Select the Operating System You Want to Install page, select the Server Core option. Then click Next. You then need to accept the license terms and then continue the installation (such as selecting a clean installation and specifying where you want to install the operating system).

After the installation is complete, you need to log on to the server (after pressing Ctrl+Alt+Delete). You need to configure a password for the Administrator account before you can log on for the first time. Set and confirm the password to log in. When you are logged on to a core installation server, the Windows GUI is absent. A core installation requires that you work at the command line (this is one of the reasons why the core installation has less overhead than a full installation). Figure 2.4 shows the core installation command window.

FIGURE 2.4
A core installa-
tion is managed
from the com-
mand line.

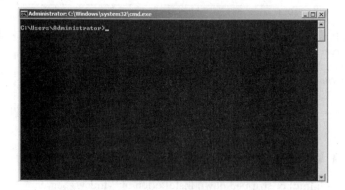

A complete reference for managing a core installation of Windows Server 2008 is beyond the scope of this book, but let's look at some of the possibilities. Remember you are working at the command line, so you can use commands that you are probably familiar with, such as ipconfig and hostname. *COMMANDS*

Let's say that you want to change the computer's name and then add the computer to a domain. Follow these steps:

1. At the command line, type **hostname**. This provides the computer name that was assigned to the computer during the server installation.

2. Now that you know the current hostname, you can type **netdom renamecomputer** *computer name* **/NewName:***new name*

   where *computer name* is the current name (found in step 1) and **new name** is the name you want to use for the server.

3. After executing the command, you are asked to proceed (type **y** and press Enter as shown in Figure 2.5). You then need to reboot the computer. Use the command **shutdown** **/r**. *REBOOT*

4. When the server reboots and you log on and return to the command prompt, type **netdom join** *computer name* **/domain:***domain name* **/userd:***username* **/passwordd:***password*

   where you provide the computer name, the domain name, and then a username and password with the administrative rights to add a computer to the domain.

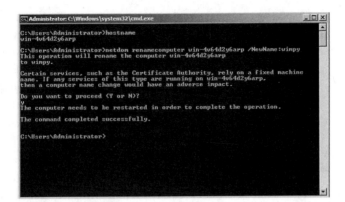

FIGURE 2.5
After changing
the computer's
name, you need
to restart the
server.

Obviously, working from the command line is not as easy as working with the Windows GUI and the various server tools. However, a server core installation can enable you to repurpose hardware that you might have otherwise abandoned.

You can activate the server from the command line; type **slmgr.vbs -ato** and press Enter. If the activation is successful over the Internet, you do not receive a message on the command line.

Did you Know?

Choosing Between a Workgroup and a Domain

One aspect of a server's configuration that you should have determined long before installing Windows Server 2008 is whether the server will be part of a workgroup or domain.

In a workgroup setting, Windows Server 2008 can supply services such as file and print services or function as an Internet gateway supplying IP addresses to the members of the workgroup using Network Address Translation. (For more about Network Address Translation, see Hour 22, "Using Network Address Translation and Certificate Services.")

In a domain, a server can be a domain controller, can supply services such as DNS and DHCP, or can serve as a router or remote access server. Windows Server 2008 is built to provide services on a domain, so deploying this server software on a domain really gives you more bang for your buck (as opposed to running a workgroup using the services that can be deployed by Windows desktop operating systems over an expensive server).

In terms of quickly adding a server to a workgroup or a domain (if this server will be the first domain controller on the domain, the domain doesn't exist until you add the Active Directory and Domain Services role discussed in Hour 8), you can access the System Properties dialog box by clicking the Provide Computer Name and Domain link in the Initial Configuration Tasks window. Click the Change button on the Computer Name of the System Properties dialog box and then use the Computer Name/Domain Changes dialog box to specify the workgroup or domain for the server.

Summary

This hour looked at installing Windows Server 2008. It is important to keep in mind that Windows Server 2008 requires a minimum hardware configuration and that you need to ensure that your server uses server hardware on the Windows Server 2008 Hardware Compatibility List.

To upgrade previous versions of the Windows server software to Windows Server 2008, make sure that you have installed the latest service packs for that version of Windows. Upgrading previous versions of Windows Server domains requires that the adprep utility be used to upgrade the Schema Master and Infrastructure Master on the domain.

The Windows Server 2008 installation DVD enables you to upgrade previous editions of Windows Server, to do a clean install of the operating system, and to install the Server core, a minimal installation of Windows Server 2008.

Q&A

Q. *What two hardware considerations should be an important part of the planning process for a Windows Server 2008 deployment?*

A. Any server on which you will install Windows Server 2008 should have at least the minimum hardware requirement for running the network operating system. Server hardware should also be on the Windows Server 2008 Hardware Compatibility List to avoid the possibility of hardware and network operating system incompatibility.

Q. *How does the activation process differ on Windows Server 2008 as compared to Windows Server 2003?*

A. You can select to have activation happen automatically when the Windows Server 2008 installation is complete. Make sure that the Automatically Activate Windows When I'm Online check box is selected on the Product Key page.

Q. *What are the options for installing Windows Server 2008?*

A. You can install Windows Server 2008 on a server not currently configured with NOS, or you can upgrade existing servers running Windows 2000 Server and Windows Server 2003.

Q. *How do you configure and manage a Windows Server 2008 core installation?*

A This stripped-down version of Windows Server 2008 is managed from the command line.

HOUR 3

Configuring Windows Server 2008 Basic Settings

What You'll Learn in This Hour:

- ▶ Working with the Server Start Menu
- ▶ Using the Control Panel
- ▶ Working with Printers and Other Hardware Devices
- ▶ Uninstalling a Program
- ▶ Scheduling Tasks
- ▶ Configuring Virtual Memory Settings
- ▶ Using the Server Manager
- ▶ Managing Local User Accounts and Groups

Windows Server 2008 has a slightly different look and feel when compared to the previous version—Windows Server 2003—of Microsoft's network operating system. It now embraces a somewhat similar desktop to Windows Vista. It also embraces a similar Start menu system and set of Control Panel applets.

Accessing administrative features for the local computer (such as local users and disk management) can still be accomplished through the Computer Management snap-in; however, Windows Server 2008 also provides a Server Manager console that enables you to work with both local computer settings and network server roles and features. This provides more of a "one-stop shopping" approach to managing a server running Windows Server 2008. In this hour, you'll look at the basic administrative environment for Windows Server 2008.

Working with the Server Start Menu

Windows Server 2008 began as part of the overall development process that resulted in Windows Vista for the desktop and now Windows Server 2008 for the network environment.

Windows Server has gone through a long development process known as "Longhorn," and is a complementary server environment to Window Vista's client desktop environment (particularly the Business Edition of Vista, designed for networks running Windows servers).

The Windows Server 2008 desktop provides a completely uncluttered workspace. The only icon provided by default is the Recycle Bin. The Start menu has also been updated as it has been with Vista (updated when compared to Windows Server 2003 and the versions of Windows XP).

In the first column, quick access icons to Server Manager, the command prompt, Windows Update, Internet Explorer, and Notepad are provided. Programs that you have used recently also are listed in this first tier of the Start menu. In addition, the first column of the Start menu provides access to all the programs on the computer via All Programs. When you click All Programs to access the Start menu, the list of available software appears in the first column. Clicking Back closes the list.

The Search feature has also been moved to the first column of the Start menu. Click in the Start Search box and type a search term. Results appear as you type. Click any of the links in the Search Results pane (in the first column of the Start menu) to access any of the "hits" that appear based on your search criteria (see Figure 3.1). You can close the Search Results pane by clicking the Close button to the right of the Search box.

FIGURE 3.1
The Start menu provides quick access to tools, search, and settings.

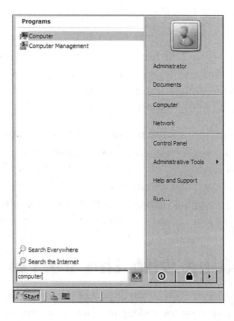

The second column of the Start menu provides access to other important tools, such as Computer (My Computer in previous versions of Windows), Network (the local network), Control Panel, Administrative Tools ,and Help and Support. A link for the current user (such as Administrator) also provides quick access to the folders that have been created for that user.

If you want to change the Start menu to the Classic Start menu (of previous Windows versions), right-click the Start button and select Properties. In the Taskbar and Start Menu Properties dialog box, select Classic Start Menu and then click OK.

The Start menu also provides easy access to the Shut Down and Lock commands and also provides single-button access to other commands such as Switch User, Log Off, and Restart. As with Windows Server 2003, the Shut Down command requires that you provide a reason for shutting down in the Shut Down Windows dialog box (see Figure 3.2).

FIGURE 3.2
You must provide a reason for shutting down the system.

Using the Control Panel

If you have worked with any version of Windows since the 95 desktop, you are familiar with the types of control utilities that are provided in the Windows Control Panel. Windows Server 2008 is no different. To access utilities (applets) that provide you with control over your computer's peripherals (and other hardware devices), installed software, and a number of other local computer and server settings, all you have to do is access the Control Panel.

To access the Control Panel's utilities in Windows Server 2008, select the Start button and then click the Control Panel icon. The Control Panel windows will open (see Figure 3.3).

FIGURE 3.3
The Windows
Server 2008
Control Panel.

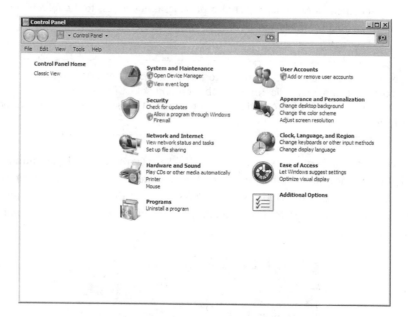

The Control Panel's main window is populated by several icons that are really categories of grouped commands and features. For example, the System and Maintenance icon provides access to the System window (showing the RAM and processor speed information), Windows Update, power options, indexing options, Device Manager, and administrative tools (such as the defragmenting tool, event logs, and task scheduling). To access a set of tools, click the category icon.

The Control Panel categories are similar to those found on any system running Windows Vista. So if you have rolled out Vista-based client computers, you will already be familiar with the new look of the Control Panel.

Let's take a look at the categories used to group the various tools. We can then take a look at some of the tools available in the Control Panel that you would typically use when configuring a server (as opposed to a client computer).

System and Maintenance

The System and Maintenance category provides quick access to system information and system tools. Much of the system information that was available from the System Properties dialog box in previous versions of Windows Server can now be reached directly from the Control Panel.

For example, you can check the RAM and processor speed of the server by clicking the View Amount of RAM and Processor Speed link. This provides the RAM and processor information and the version of Windows Server that is installed on the system (as well as the computer's name and workgroup or network name).

The System and Maintenance Control Panel window also provides access to the automatic update settings and the power options for the system. You can open the Device Manager from the System and Maintenance window and access other tools such as the Disk Defragmenter and the Disk Management snap-in.

Security

The Security window of the Control Panel provides access to Windows Firewall settings and Windows Update (as did the System and Maintenance window). The Security window also provides access to various Internet options (Internet Explorer options) such as security settings and the management of browser add-ons.

For example, selecting Change Security Settings under Internet Options opens the Internet Properties dialog box. This dialog box can also be opened directly from Internet Explorer. You will find that there is overlap between the various command and tool groupings or categories in the Control Panel. It also includes other options for accessing these various tools; as already mentioned, Internet options related to Internet Explorer can be accessed from Internet Explorer directly.

By the Way

You will find that the Control Panel categories or grouping windows provide a lot of redundancy in terms of accessing various Windows tools and settings.

Network and Internet

The Network and Internet window of the Control Panel provides access to the Network and Sharing Center. The Network and Sharing Center provides access to the computer's network status and sharing settings. It also enables you to connect to a network and view computers and devices on the network (we take a closer look at the Network and Sharing Center in Hour 24, "Monitoring Server Performance and Network Connections").

The Network and Internet window also provides access to change Internet options in the Internet Properties dialog box. This window also allows you to enable the server to store remote files locally for offline access and provides access to Windows Firewall settings.

Hardware and Sound

The Hardware and Sound window of the Control Panel provides access to printer settings, the default AutoPlay settings for CD-ROM and DVD-ROM devices, and sound settings. You will also find the adjustment settings for the computer's mouse and keyboard in the Hardware and Sound window.

The Hardware and Sound window also lets you access settings related to the screen settings such as screen resolution, and provides access to color management and dialing options for modems. As with other Control Panel windows, redundant access (redundant in the sense that you can access these tools from other Control Panel windows) is provided to tools such as the Device Manager and the power option settings.

Programs

The Programs window of the Control Panel enables you to view installed programs as well as to uninstall programs. It also makes it easy for you to turn Windows features on and off.

This window also enables you to set the default program for file types (the program that should open files of a certain type), as well as run the Program Compatibility Wizard, which is used if you want to attempt to install older (legacy) programs in Windows Server 2008. Programs that you install that contain their own utilities also typically install a set of icons in this Control Panel window for easy access.

User Accounts

The User Accounts window of the Control Panel enables you to add, edit, or delete local user accounts on the server. You can change account pictures and change your Windows password.

The User Accounts window also provides access to turn on the servers Guest account. In most cases, you don't use this account because you typically add local accounts that provide users varying degrees of access. Local user accounts are covered later in this hour in the section, "Managing Local User Accounts and Groups."

Appearance and Personalization

The Appearance and Personalization window of the Control Panel enables you to configure the various settings related to the overall look of Windows, including the desktop background, screen colors, and the Windows desktop theme. You can also access settings related to the Start menu and the taskbar.

This window also enables you to install and remove fonts and set folder options. The Ease of Access Center in the Appearance and Personalization window is where you can configure Windows to accommodate users with low vision by altering settings related to the screen contrast.

Clock, Language, and Region

The Clock, Language, and Region window of the Control Panel provides settings related to the clock and the installation of additional languages. You can set the time and date and you can change the time zone.

The window enables you to create additional clocks for different time zones. You can also install and uninstall screen languages as needed from this Control Panel window.

Ease of Access

The Ease of Access Center window enables you to optimize the Windows screen settings. Windows can actually optimize the visual display, based on your answers to a series of questions.

The Ease of Access Center also allows you to change mouse and keyboard settings. Sounds that are normally used as alerts or for other cues can actually be replaced by visual events in the Ease of Access Center (which can be useful in cases where you do not set up speakers for the server).

Now that you've had a general overview of the geography of the Windows Server 2008 Control Panel, let's take a look at some of the tools that you would commonly use. Let's begin by looking at printers and other hardware devices.

Working with Printers and Other Hardware Devices

Because a server offers services based on the hardware installed on it, such as a print server or file server, you need to access settings related to a printer (or printers) connected to a server and also access device settings for other hardware installed on the computer. Because Windows Server 2008 supports plug-and-play technology, hardware installation (in most cases) requires only that the new device (such as a backup drive or a printer) be attached to or installed on the server.

Windows Server 2008 should automatically install any printer that you connect to the server via a USB port (or any other USB or FireWire hardware for that matter). With some printers, you may have to supply the appropriate drivers for that printer during the installation process. If you are connecting a printer to a server via parallel port, or attempting to use a legacy printer, you may have to use the Add Printer command found in the Printers window of the Control Panel.

Let's take a look at how to access printer settings. You can then learn how to access the Device Manager, which provides a list of all installed hardware including printers.

To open the Printers window:

1. Select Start and then Control Panel.

2. In the Control Panel window, click the Printer link below the Hardware and Sound category link. The Printers window opens (see Figure 3.4).

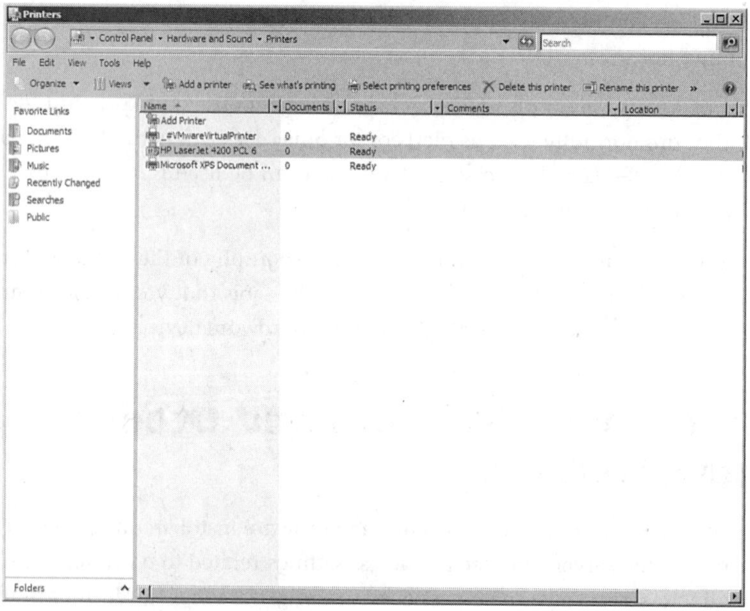

FIGURE 3.4
The Printers dialog box enables you to access printer settings.

3. To view the settings for a listed printer, select that printer and then click Select Printing Preferences.

The Preferences dialog box appears for the selected printer. The features and settings available vary, depending on the printer that is actually installed. When you have finished configuring the settings for the printer, click OK to close the printer's Preferences dialog box. In Hour 14, "Working with Network Printing," network printing and printers are covered in more detail.

The Device Manager is another of the hardware-related tools that you need to be able to access quickly. From the Control Panel, just click the Open Device Manager link below the System and Maintenance Category link. The Device Manager then opens (see Figure 3.5).

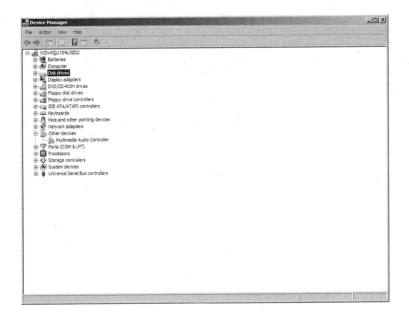

FIGURE 3.5
The Device Manager enables you to view and troubleshoot installed hardware.

The Device Manager enables you to view installed hardware and troubleshoot hardware problems, which are typically related to hardware drivers. You can expand each of the hardware categories (such as Disk Drives or Network Adapters) and then access information on a particular hardware device.

Right-click a device and choose Properties to view the properties for that device (see Figure 3.6). In the Properties dialog box for that device, you can update or reinstall the driver for the device. The Properties dialog box also enables you to view the resources used by the device, disable a device, or uninstall the current driver for the device.

FIGURE 3.6
Use the
Properties dia-
log box for a
device to
update or rein-
stall drivers.

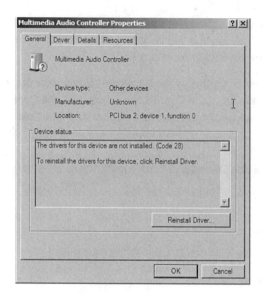

Uninstalling a Program

Although as a network administrator, your primary concerns relate to configuring server roles and services, you also have to deal with basic software and program settings. The Programs window of the Control Panel enables you to uninstall a program, view installed Windows updates, and turn Windows features on and off. You can also access the Program Compatibility Wizard (click Use an Older Program with This Version of Windows), which enables you to determine whether you can run a legacy software program in Windows Server 2008.

To uninstall a program, follow these steps:

1. Select Start and then Control Panel.

2. In the Control Panel window, click Programs. The Programs window opens (see Figure 3.7).

3. In the Programs windows, click Uninstall a Program under the Programs and Features link. The Programs and Features window appears, listing your installed software.

4. Select the software package you want to uninstall and then click the Uninstall button on the window toolbar.

5. Click Yes to uninstall the software. It will be removed from the computer.

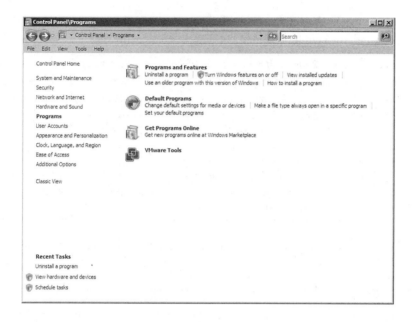

FIGURE 3.7
The Programs
window enables
you to uninstall
programs.

As already mentioned, the Programs window also provides access to Windows features. Because we are working with server software, the settings for items such as the firewall, the system, and other items such as Remote Desktop are so "tightly wound" with the basic purpose of the server—roles and services— that you will find that when you click Turn Windows Features On or Off (in the Programs window), the Server Manager opens. We will be spending a lot of time working with the Server Manager in subsequent hours, including Hour 4, "Understanding and Configuring Server Roles and Services."

Scheduling Tasks

The Task Scheduler enables you to schedule and automate the launching of applications or utilities on your server. For example, you could schedule the Disk Defragmenter to run at a particular time (perhaps late at night) or you could back up the system. Scheduling tasks allows you to automate the running of software, particularly in cases where you want to run tools when the server use is at a bare minimum.

Each task that you create must have a trigger—say, a certain day of the week and a time, and then an action, such as the running of Windows Server Backup. Tasks can also be configured with conditions. A condition must be met for the trigger to actually run the task. For example, you might want the trigger to be a certain time of day and the condition could be that the server must be idle for a certain amount of time. So, when the condition is met, the trigger can start the task.

The Windows Server 2008 Task Scheduler actually makes it very easy for you to create schedule tasks. Tasks that require only a trigger and an action can be created with the Create Basic Task Wizard. More complex tasks that also require a condition (or conditions) can be created in the Create Task dialog box.

By the Way

> The Task Scheduler also enables you to view the status of scheduled tasks. They can be viewed by timeframe, such as last 24 hours or last 7 days. Clicking a particular task in the task list enables you to see whether the task ran successfully and when the task began and finished.

To schedule a task using the Task Scheduler's Create Basic Task Wizard, follow these steps:

1. In the Control Panel, click the System and Maintenance link.

2. In the System and Maintenance window, click the Schedule Tasks link under the Administrative Tools heading. The Task Scheduler opens (see Figure 3.8).

FIGURE 3.8
The Task Scheduler enables you to configure tasks that will be carried out automatically.

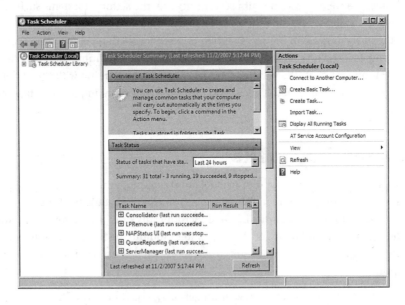

3. To create a new task with the Create Basic Task Wizard, click Create Basic Task in the Actions pane. The Create Basic Task Wizard opens.

4. Type a name and a description (optional) for the task. Then click Next.

5. On the Task Trigger screen, select a timeframe for the task, such as Daily or Weekly, or select an event such as When the Computer Starts or When I Log On. Then click Next.

6. If you choose a timeframe such as daily or weekly, the next screen asks you to specify other parameters for the task such as time, day, and recurrence (every day, every two days, and so on). Click Next. If you chose a task trigger such as when the computer starts or when you log on, you go immediately to the Action screen (step 7).

7. The next screen asks you to specify the action that the task will complete, such as start a program, send an email, or display a message. In many cases you will select Start a Program (see Figure 3.9) and then click Next.

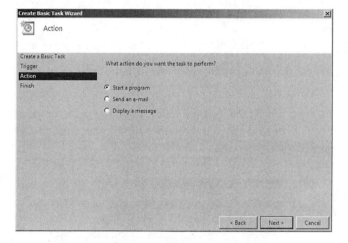

FIGURE 3.9
Specify the action for the task.

7. On the next screen, browse for the program (or script) that you want the task to start. You can also add optional arguments to this screen and then click Next.

8. The last wizard screen shows the name, description, trigger, and action for the new task. Click Finish.

To view your new task, click the Task Scheduler Library icon in the left pane of the Task Scheduler. Select the task you have created and you can use the tabs such as General, Triggers, Actions, and Conditions to review the parameters for the task. You can also edit any of the parameters on the various tabs. To delete a task, select the task and then press the Delete key. Click Yes to confirm the deletion.

You will find when you open the Task Scheduler Library that many default tasks are arranged in folders such as Active Directory Rights Management, Defrag, and Server Manager. You can edit any of these tasks or add additional tasks to the folders (or create your own folders) in the library.

Configuring Virtual Memory Settings

Virtual memory is fixed disk space that is reserved for the temporary storage of items that can no longer be held in the server's RAM. In the Windows Server 2008 environment, the virtual memory is referred to as the *paging file* (for a look at monitoring page file use, go to Hour 24.

Microsoft recommends that the virtual memory or paging file be equivalent to 1.5 times the RAM installed on the server (however, Windows Server 2008 sets the page-fule to System Manage Size, which could be less than the recommended size, particularly on a server with over 2GB of RAM). If you use programs that use large amounts of memory, you can increase the paging file size beyond the recommendation.

To view virtual memory settings (and other advanced settings in the System Properties dialog box), follow these steps:

1. In the Control Panel, click the System and Maintenance link.

2. In the System and Maintenance window, click the System link. The System window opens.

3. Click the Advanced System Settings task (in the Task pane on the left side of the window) to open the System Properties dialog box; select the Advanced tab (see Figure 3.10).

FIGURE 3.10
The Advanced tab of the System Properties dialog box.

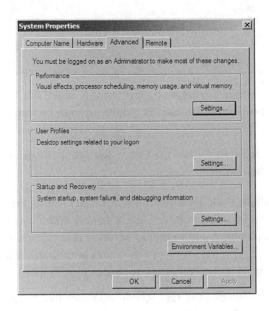

4. The Advanced tab provides access to memory settings, user profiles, and start-up and recovery settings. To access virtual memory settings, click Settings in the Performance box of the Advanced tab.

5. The Performance Options dialog box appears. Click the Advanced tab.

6. In the virtual memory box on the Advanced tab, click the Change button. The Virtual Memory dialog box appears (see Figure 3.11).

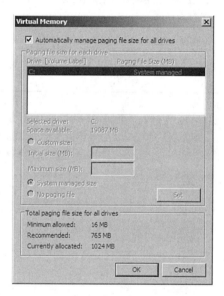

FIGURE 3.11
The Virtual Memory dialog box.

7. By default, the virtual memory or page file size is managed automatically. You can clear the Automatically Manage Paging File Size for All Drives check box and then specify a custom size by providing an initial size and a maximum size. After making your changes (or leaving everything as it was), click the OK button. You can close the other open dialog boxes by clicking OK on each.

In terms of optimizing the page file size and other performance settings, it probably makes sense to run your server with the default performance settings, including the virtual memory size. You can then use the Reliability and Performance tools in the Server Manager to track the server performance. You can then fine-tune settings as needed.

Using the Server Manager

Any discussion of the Windows Server 2008 administrative environment must include a look at the new Server Manager. In prior versions of Windows Server, most tools ran as snap-ins in the Microsoft Management Console (MMC), and you will still find that a few tools do run in the MMC. However, the Server Manager (by default) provides access to nearly all the configuration, monitoring, and troubleshooting tools you will need to use as you manage your Windows server. Figure 3.12 shows the new Server Manager.

Did you Know?

> You can launch the Server Manager from the Quick Launch toolbar next to the Start button.

FIGURE 3.12
The Server Manager provides quick access to many Windows Server tools.

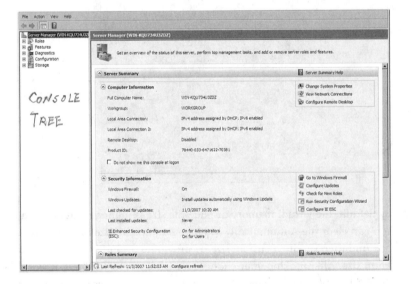

The left pane in the Server Manager window (the console tree) provides access to several categories of server management tools. The icons and various categories are

- ▶ **Server Manager**—When this icon is selected, you are provided an overview of the server's computer and security information. Server roles and features installed are also listed.

- ▶ **Roles**—When the Roles icon is expanded, the roles, roles status, and a list of all the available roles are listed in the Details pane (both installed and not installed). You can click a role link to load the snap-in for that role and then view the services installed for that role and view any events that have been

logged in relation to that role. Figure 3.13 shows the snap-in (in Server
Manager) for managing file services.

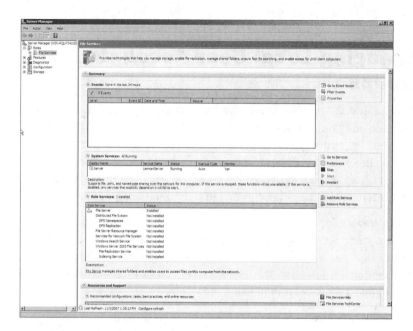

FIGURE 3.13
Select a role in
the Server
Manager and
the snap-in for
that role is
loaded.

▶ **Features**—When this icon is selected (or expanded), you are provided a list of
the services that have been installed on the server. A link, Add Features,
enables you to quickly add services to the server directly from the Server
Manager.

▶ **Diagnostics**—The Diagnostics category provides access to monitoring and
troubleshooting tools. You can expand the Diagnostics icon to access the Event
Viewer, the Reliability and Resource monitor, and the Device Manager. You
will be looking at issues related to monitoring your servers in Hour 24.

▶ **Configuration**—When you expand the Configuration icon, you can quickly
access the task scheduler, the Windows firewall, and other configuration settings, including local users and groups.

▶ **Storage**—The Storage category provides quick access to the new Windows
backup utility and local drive management. You'll learn more about drive
management in Hour 6, "Managing Hard Drives and Volumes."

We will be taking advantage of the new Server Manager as we work with Windows Server 2008 throughout this book. In the next section, we look at local user accounts and groups, which can be managed using the Server Manager.

Managing Local User Accounts and Groups

When you install Windows Server 2008 on a computer (as discussed in Hour 2, "Installing and Configuring Windows Server 2008"), an Administrator account is automatically created (you had to provide the password for the account before you could log in for the first time). This account is used to configure and administer the server. It is considered a local account. (However, after you install Active Directory Domain Services on the server, this account also has domain access privileges.)

You can create additional local user accounts that have varying degrees of access to the settings and service on the local machine. This is in contrast to the domain user accounts that you will create in Hour 8, "Understanding and Configuring Active Directory Domain Services." These types of accounts are designed to allow users to access different resources throughout the domain.

So, in a nutshell, local user accounts on a server are designed for people who will help maintain and administer the server. Local groups also exist on the local server and can be used to provide different access levels to your local users.

By the Way

> Creating local users and groups on Windows Server 2008—such as a member—is really no different than creating local users on a shared office computer running an operating system such as Windows Vista. You are creating the local accounts so that these users can access local resources on the computer.

You can create local user accounts by using the Server Manager on the local computer. To open the Server Manager window and access the user and group tools, follow these steps:

1. Select the Start menu, point at Administrative Tools, and then select Server Manager. The Server Manager window opens.

2. Expand the Configuration node in the tree and then expand the Local Users and Groups node. To view the current local users, click the Users folder.

The default local user accounts are Administrator and Guest. The Guest account is disabled by default.

Adding Local Users

You can add local users directly from the Server Manager. To add a local user to the computer with the list of local users showing, follow these steps:

1. Click the More Actions link in the Actions pane of the Server Manager. Select New User from the shortcut menu. The New User dialog box appears (see Figure 3.14).

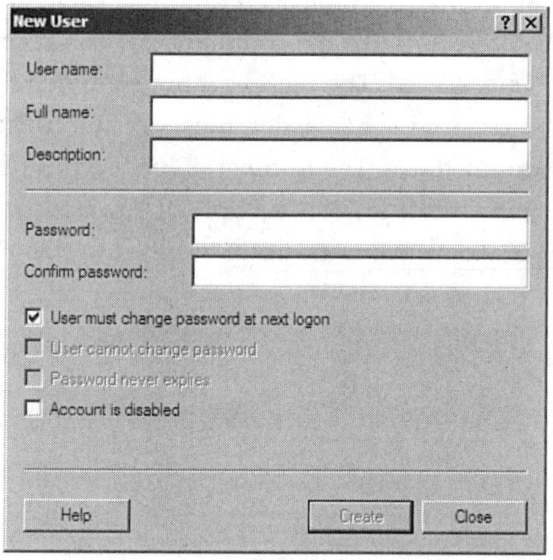

FIGURE 3.14
Set the user-name and pass-word for the new local user.

2. Enter a username, a full name, a description, and a password for the new account. You can also use the check boxes to set the following password options:

   ▶ User Must Change Password at Next Logon

   ▶ User Cannot Change Password

   ▶ Password Never Expires

   ▶ Account Is Disabled

3. After entering the various parameters, click the Create button. You can add other local user accounts if you want. Then click Close to close the dialog box. The new user (or users) appears in the user list in the Server Manager window.

The new user can now log on to the local computer. After you create a user, you can edit any settings related to the user, such as renaming the user and changing the user's password.

Local User Groups

On Windows Server 2008, computer local groups are typically used to impart certain access levels to the local users on the computer. For example, adding a local user to the Administrators group (a default group) grants that user all the administrative privileges on the local machine. This is also how you can create security equivalences for multiple users.

When you click the Groups folder in the Server Manager tree, a list of all the default local groups (this is before you make the computer a domain controller) appears in the Details pane (see Figure 3.15). The built-in groups provide special access levels and capabilities that make it easier to assign a user certain privileges without making the user a local administrator. The number of local groups shown depends on the services that you have installed. For example, if you have installed DHCP on the local computer, a DHCP Administrators group is added to the default group list.

FIGURE 3.15
Default local groups can be used to provide access levels to local users.

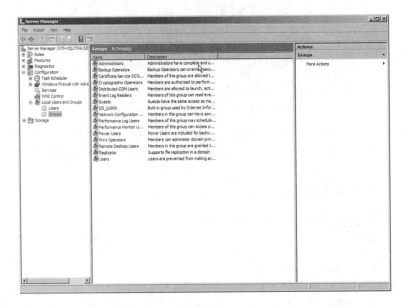

To add users to a local group, follow these steps:

1. Right-click a particular group (let's say you want to add users to the Administrators Group). Then select Add to Group from the shortcut menu. The group's Properties dialog box appears (see Figure 3.16). The current user members of the groups are listed.

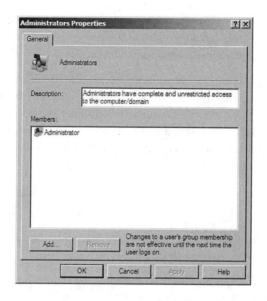

FIGURE 3.16
You can add local users to your local groups.

2. To add users to the group, click the Add button. The Select Users dialog box opens. Type the usernames that you want to add to the group in the Enter the Object Names box, and then click OK. The username (or names) is added to the group's list. Click OK to close the dialog box.

You can also create local groups, if you want. It probably makes sense to take advantage of the different access levels provided by the built-in local groups before you go to the trouble of creating special local groups.

To add a new group, right-click the Groups folder and then select New Group. The New Group dialog box opens. Enter a name for the new group. To complete the process, click the Create button. Your new group appears in the group list.

Remember that local users and groups are designed for the local server environment. Domain user accounts and groups are a different animal; they are discussed in detail in Hours 8 and 9, respectively.

Summary

In this hour, we looked at the Windows Server 2008 desktop, which embraces the user experience model found in Microsoft Windows Vista. As with previous versions of Windows, the Control Panel (either the menu or the window) provides access to a number of system utilities and tools, such as the system and maintenance tools, security tools, and the new Network and Sharing Center.

The new Server Manager provides administrative access to many of the tools used to manage your server. This includes managing server roles and services, monitoring the computer, and working with local users and groups.

Local user accounts are used to grant users access to the local computer. You can create local user accounts in the Computer Management snap-in. Local groups are used to provide access level to the local users. A number of default local groups, such as the Administrator's group, are provided by Windows Server 2008. Adding users to a group provides these users with the local access privileges afforded by the group.

Q&A

Q. *Which Control Panel tool enables you to automate the running of server utilities and other applications?*

A. The Task Scheduler enables you to schedule the launching of tools such as Windows Backup and Disk Defragmenter.

Q. *What are some of the items that can be accessed via the System Properties dialog box?*

A. You can access virtual memory settings and the Device Manager via the System Properties dialog box.

Q. *Which Windows Server utility provides a common interface for tools and utilities and provides access to server roles, services, and monitoring and drive utilities?*

A. The Server Manager provides both the interface and access to a large number of the utilities and tools that you will use as you manage your Windows server.

Q. *How are local user accounts and groups created?*

A. Local user accounts and groups are managed in the Local Users and Groups node in the Server Manager. Local user accounts and groups are used to provide local access to a server.

HOUR 4

Configuring Server Roles and Services

What You'll Learn in This Hour:

- ▶ Defining Your Network Infrastructure
- ▶ Determining Server Roles
- ▶ Understanding Windows Server 2008 Roles and Features
- ▶ Using the Initial Configuration Tasks Window to Add a Server Role
- ▶ Removing a Server Role
- ▶ Adding a Feature to Your Server Configuration
- ▶ Removing a Feature from Your Server Configuration

After you have installed Windows Server 2008 on a computer and configured some of the basic settings in the Control Panel and the Server Manager, the next step is to configure the server to fulfill its role (or roles) on your network. A single server can actually serve a number of different roles and offer a variety of services. However, the number of specialized servers that you will need depends not only on the services required by your users, but also the size of the network and the amount of traffic the network experiences. In this hour, you'll learn to identify different server roles and will look at how services are managed on the network.

Defining Your Network Infrastructure

The Microsoft networking model (going as far back as Microsoft LAN Manager and including the Windows NT and Windows Server 2003 environments) has always embraced the domain as the basic administrative container for the network. A *domain* is a logical grouping of computers and other devices that are managed as objects by a Windows domain controller. The domain maintains its own directory database of user accounts and controls all published resources within the domain, such as printers and shared files.

> Microsoft operating systems, including the network operating systems such as Windows Server 2008, enable you to share resources between computers without creating a domain. You can set up a workgroup and share resources between computers in what is termed a *peer-to-peer network*. Workgroups do not provide the security or scalability of the domain model and should be used only in small office settings or for home networks.

Although a domain could potentially serve thousand of users, there is often the need to go beyond the limitations provided by a single domain and expand the network's scale. The directory services provided by Windows Server 2008's Active Directory Domain Services (AD DS) provide you with a hierarchical structure in which domains can be nested within other domains.

Let's look at the domain hierarchy of Windows Server 2008. As already mentioned, the basic unit is the domain. The next largest unit is the tree. A *tree* is a collection of child domains. The tree itself is defined by a root domain, which serves as the parent domain for the child domains that branch from the domain root.

The largest administrative structure provided by the domain hierarchy is the forest. A *forest* is a collection of domain trees.

To truly understand how domains interact within trees and forests, you need to understand trust relationships. A *trust* is an electronic security agreement between domains. Users can log on to their domain but still get at resources in another domain if that domain "trusts" the user's domain.

When you create child domains within a domain tree with Windows Server, the child domains and the parent domain all are assigned transitive trusts. A *transitive trust* is a two-way street between the domains.

The domains trust each other, so they share each other's resources. This means that all the domains in a tree trust the other domains in the tree to use their resources (such as printers and DNS [Domain Name Service] server). So, the transitive trust relationships provide a reciprocating resource-sharing environment that flows down through the tree.

> This notion of a hierarchical directory services structure and how Active Directory Domain Services provides the infrastructure is discussed in more detail in Hour 8, "Understanding and Configuring Active Directory Domain Services."

You create a domain in the Windows Server 2008 environment by bringing the first domain controller online. The way to create a domain controller is by installing Active Directory Domain Services on a server running Windows Server 2008 (or an earlier version of Windows Server, such as Windows 2000 Server or Windows Server 2003). So, you will have to deploy at least one domain controller on your network for it to take advantage of the Active Directory hierarchy. Let's take a look at other server roles that often need to be filled on a network.

If you are deploying a new network (or for that matter adding to an existing network), it makes sense to put both a network map and an implementation plan together. Software such as Microsoft Visio enables you to create diagrams of the network. Creating a diagram can help you to visualize the number of servers and other devices that you need to implement the network.

Your implementation plan can be as simple as a to-do list or can provide more information such as costs, resources needed, and a timeline. If you have some familiarity with project management processes and want a very detailed plan, you can use software such as Microsoft Project, which enables you to create a timeline and manage resources (including employees) as you work through the implementation process.

By the Way

Windows Server 2008 also provides a new virtualization feature that allows you to deploy virtual servers on your network. These virtual servers have the same functionality as a physical server, however, any one physical server can actually be deployed as more than one virtual server on the network (provided its hardware configuration can handle running multiple instances of a network operating system). This opens up the possibilities for how server roles and services are provided on the network but also means that you will need to do more up-front planning and initial benchmarking if you want to take advantage of the virtualization role that Windows Server 2008 provides.

Determining Server Roles

The whole point of networking computers is to provide users with the ability to connect to network resources (and to each other). For resources to be available, a computer running a network operating system must be available to "serve up" the resource to the requesting client. A number of server roles exist, such as those of file, print, database, and application server. Let's look at some of the common server types you might have to deploy in your network.

Domain Controllers

As already mentioned, a Windows Server 2008 domain requires a domain controller. The domain controller authenticates users to the Active Directory as they attempt to log on to the network. The domain controller also provides the Global Catalog for the domain, which contains a subset of all the objects in the domains of the forest, such as users, groups, and printers.

Because domain controllers must validate users and devices, additional domain controllers are often deployed on a very large network. This enables user accounts to be validated more quickly because any domain controller in the domain can handle the authentication.

On large networks that consist of multiple forests or sites, a domain controller or controllers can serve as Global Catalog servers. These servers contain information on resources that span the domains in a forest, making it easier for users to find the resources that they need.

Windows Server 2008 also provides you with the option of creating read-only domain controllers (RODC). A read-only domain controller hosts a read-only copy of the Active Directory database. This type of domain controller is ideally used in environments where network security is an issue and also in environments where a limited number of users (such as in a branch office) need to access Active Directory resources. For more information about Active Directory, including installation, see Hour 8.

File Servers

A file server's job is to serve as a repository for the files that users need on the network. These files are typically held in what is called a *public folder*, which can include private folders that are specific for a particular user.

Windows Server 2008 actually makes it easy for you to package file resources that are held on any number of file servers so that users are not aware of (and don't need to know) the actual location of the resource files. This system is called the Distributed File System (DFS). DFS and the creation of network shares on a Windows Server 2008 file server are discussed in Hour 12, "Working with Network Shares and the Distributed File System."

Print Servers

A print server is used to host a network printer. It is basically the control conduit for the printer. Because print jobs are usually spooled (placed on the computer before they are sent to the printer) before they are printed, the print server supplies the hard-drive space needed.

The print server also queues up all the print jobs being directed to the printer. The network administrator can delete print jobs and change the queue order of print jobs by accessing the print server. Providing print resources in the Windows Server 2008 environment is discussed in Hour 14, "Working with Network Printing."

Web Servers

Web servers provide you with the capability to create a website that can be accessed by the general public via the World Wide Web. Web servers can also be used to create private web called *intranets* that enable employees to use web browsers to access internal company information.

Microsoft Windows Server 2008 provides Internet Information Service (IIS) 7.0, a full-featured web server platform that also provides other services such as FTP sites and NNTP newsgroups. IIS is discussed in Hour 23, "Using the Internet Information Service."

Application Servers

Application servers host various applications, such as specialized databases. Even typical desktop applications such as word processors and spreadsheet software can be stored on an application server. This makes updating software applications much easier because the software doesn't actually reside on every client workstation; users start these applications from their local computers, but the application software is actually stored on the server.

Although we typically look at the Internet Information Service provided by Windows Server as a web service, the addition of XML applications and other platforms for web applications (such as ASP.NET) has prompted Microsoft to consider IIS an application-server platform.

By the Way

Messaging Servers

A messaging server runs specialized software that enables users on the network to communicate and collaborate. It provides services such as electronic mail and discussion groups. Microsoft Exchange is an example of a communication server software package. It is installed on a server that is already running one of the Microsoft network operating systems, such as Windows Server 2008.

Understanding Windows Server 2008 Roles and Features

Our discussion so far has pointed out some of the more obvious server roles such as domain controllers and web servers. The Add Roles wizard, discussed later in this hour, is the tool for adding these roles to Windows Server 2008.

Windows Server 2008 does throw a slight curveball to network administrators who have deployed earlier versions of Windows server such as Windows Server 2003. When deploying network services on a server running Windows Server 2003 (and Windows 2000 Server), network services such as DNS, DHCP (Dynamic Host Configuration Protocol), and Remote Access were installed as network services. Windows Server 2003 provided a Services snap-in that ran in the Microsoft Management Console. Network services were not considered server roles.

However, most of these network services are now considered server roles in Windows Server 2008, and you use the Add Roles Wizard to install them. The Server Manager, also discussed later in the hour, is used to manage them (see "Managing Server Roles with the Server Manager").

Some network services, such as WINS (Windows Internet Name Service) and the Telnet Server, are now called *features*. You add these network services by using the Add Features Wizard. Let's take a look at some of the commonly deployed network services (and separate the roles from the features):

▶ The Domain Name Service is used to resolve "friendly" fully qualified domain names to IP addresses. DNS is the naming service used in the Windows Server 2008 environment. It must be deployed on the network for the Active Directory to function. DNS is now considered a server role and is discussed in detail in Hour 15, "Understanding the Domain Name Service."

▶ The Dynamic Host Configuration Protocol dynamically provides IP addresses, subnet masks, and other IP configuration options (such as the primary DNS server) to DHCP clients on the network. DHCP provides much more flexibility than static IP addresses, and it also negates the possibility of assigning the same IP address to two different nodes on the network. DHCP is now considered a server role and is discussed in Chapter 16, "Using the Dynamic Host Configuration Protocol."

▶ The Windows Internet Naming Service (WINS) resolves NetBIOS names to IP addresses. This allows down-level client operating systems such as Windows 9x to use WINS to help them identify resources on the network. In a network made up of client computers running Windows 2000 or later (Windows Vista working the best with Server 2008) and servers running Windows 2000 Server or later (with Windows Server 2008 providing the most secure environment), WINS would not be needed. Because many networks still use older client software, it is still often necessary to deploy WINS on the network. WINS is considered a feature and is discussed in Hour 20, "Understanding WINS."

▶ Remote Access enables your users to access network resources from a remote computer (a computer not directly connected to the physical network). Users can log in remotely using Remote Access and virtual private networking. Remote Access and VPNs are features in Windows Server 2008. We discuss these features in Hour 17, "Remote Access, Virtual Private Networking."

▶ Routing, considered a feature in Windows Server 2008, provides a method of breaking a large network into smaller logical IP subnets and connecting network subnets across WAN connections. Routing is typically handled by a dedicated hardware device called a *router* (routers also have their own proprietary operating systems). However, Windows Server 2008 configured with two or more network cards can be configured as a router. Routing is discussed in Hour 18, "Implementing Network Routing."

▶ Terminal Services allows a client computer to remotely connect to a terminal server and access Windows-based applications. The client computer actually functions as a terminal, and the terminal server provides the application and operating system environment. Terminal Services is a feature (as opposed to a role) and is discussed in Hour 19, "Implementing and Terminal Services."

▶ Network Address Translation (NAT) enables you to connect your network to the Internet using one public IP address (an IP address supplied by an Internet service provider). The computers on the internal network using NAT are assigned IP addresses from a private range (that does not conflict with outside or "real" IP addresses). NAT is still considered a service (obviously it didn't make the cut as a role or feature) and is configured in the Routing and Remote Access snap-in. Network Address Translation is discussed in Hour 22, "Using Network Address Translation, and Certificate Services."

The number of roles and features you want to run on any one server greatly depends on the size of your network. A server burdened with a number of network services (which we now call *roles* or *features*), such as DHCP, DNS, and Remote

Access, might soon become a performance bottleneck on your network as users access these services.

Let's take a look at how you can add and remove server roles from your server installation. We will then take a look at adding or removing a feature from a Windows Server 2008 installation.

By the Way

One way to test how well a server will run when providing a number of roles and features is to run a test server, enabling you to monitor server performance before deploying the server on the network. Information on creating server performance baselines is discussed in Chapter 24, "Monitoring Server Performance and Network Connections."

Using the Initial Configuration Tasks Window to Add a Server Role

Windows Server 2008 makes it very easy for you to configure a particular server for a role or roles. For example, on a small network, a domain controller could also function as a file server and a print server. The number of specialized servers that you have to deploy really depends on the size of your network (based on the number of users you must serve).

The Initial Configuration Tasks utility, which resides in its own window, provides you with the ability to quickly assign a particular role to your server. You will notice that as soon as you install Windows Server 2008 on your computer, the Initial Configuration Tasks window opens automatically when you reboot or start up the server.

Did you Know?

If you prefer, you can choose to not have the Initial Configuration Tasks window open when you boot the server. Click the Do Not Show This Window at Logon check box at the bottom left of the window. You can then do your server configuration using the Server Manager and its various snap-ins.

The Initial Configuration Tasks window (see Figure 4.1) also shows you the roles (and features) that have been configured on this server. This window also provides easy access to such as settings the time zone, the computer name and domain membership, automatic updates, and the Windows Firewall.

FIGURE 4.1
The Initial Configuration Tasks window makes it easy to configure your server for various roles.

Server roles can be added to a server directly from the Initial Configuration Tasks window:

1. Click Add Roles in the Customize This Server pane of the Initial Configuration Tasks window (in the bottom third of the window). The Add Roles Wizard opens. To bypass the initial wizard screen, click Next.

> If you don't want the first, informational screen of the Add Roles Wizard to appear when you use the wizard in the future, click the Skip This Page by Default check box on the first wizard screen.

Did you Know?

2. The next screen provides a list of server roles provided by Windows Server 2008 (see Figure 4.2). Any role that has already been assigned to the server is so noted by a check mark in its check box (the role is also "grayed out" and cannot be selected). To add a particular server role, such as File Services (to create a file server) or Web Server, click the appropriate server role in the list provided by the wizard and then click Next.

FIGURE 4.2
Select the server role that you want to add to the server.

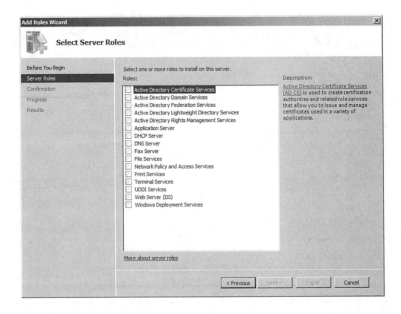

3. The next screen provides an overview of the role that you have chosen (for example, File Services help and information are provided on the screen if you have selected to install File Services). In some cases, an Add Features dialog box opens. It requires you to add features to your Windows server configuration so that the server can function in the role that you initially chose. For example, when installing the IIS web server, you are required to also install the Windows Process Activation Service (see Figure 4.3). Click Add Required Features. You are then taken to the overview screen for your chosen role; click Next to continue.

FIGURE 4.3
Some roles require that features to be added to your server's configuration.

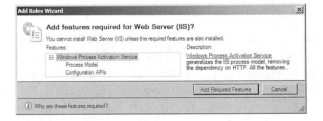

4. Most roles require that you select the services that will be provided by that role and so the next wizard screen requires that you select the role services to be installed for your new server role (see Figure 4.4).

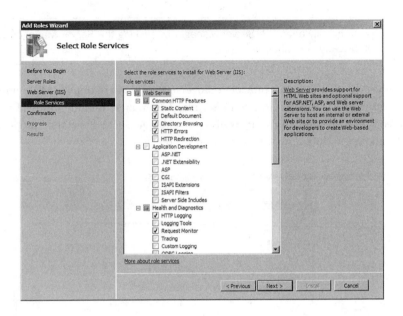

FIGURE 4.4
Select the role services for the role you are installing.

5. After selecting the services (using the provided check boxes), click Next. The next screen provides a confirmation list related to the role and associated services that you are about to install.

6. Click Install.

The role and associated services are then installed. In addition, the Windows Firewall is configured to allow network access for the new service, if necessary. When the installation is complete, the wizard provides a list of the role and role services that were installed. Click Finish to close the wizard window. After you have installed a particular role, you will find that it is listed in the Initial Configuration Tasks window.

Managing Server Roles with the Server Manager

When you want to go beyond the installation of roles and services and actually manage these additions to your server's configuration, you need to use the Windows Server 2008 Server Manager. It is a new addition to Windows Server 2008 and provides access to many of the snap-ins and tools that you had to load into the Microsoft Management Console in previous versions of Windows Server.

When you close the Initial Configuration Tasks window, the Server Manager opens automatically. You can also start the Server Manager from the Start menu: Click Start, point at Administrative Tools, and then select Server Manager.

You can also quickly open the Server Manager by clicking the Server Manager icon on the Quick Launch toolbar.

The Server Manager window provides an overview of server settings (such as name and workgroup or domain affiliation), security information, and the installed roles and features. This summary window also provides quick access to system properties, the Windows Firewall, and resources and support.

FIGURE 4.5
The Server Manager provides access to server information.

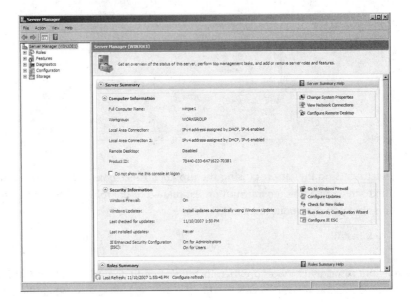

To view the installed server roles in the Server Manager window, click the Roles node in the node pane (the left pane of the window) of the Server Manager. A summary of installed roles and the status of those roles appears in the Server Manager Detail pane (the right side of the window) as shown in Figure 4.6.

To view the details related to a particular role, click that role in the detail pane. You can also select roles and services from the node tree in the node pane (expand any of the role nodes to view the associated snap-ins for that role).

You will find that the Server Manager not only provides the status of a current role or service but also enables you to quickly view events that have occurred related to that role (such as warnings or informational events).

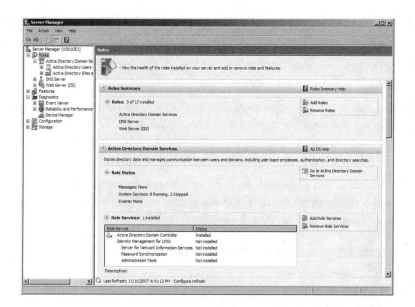

Server roles can be added to a server directly from the Server Manager. An Add Roles icon is available in the Roles pane and can be used to start the Add Roles Wizard. Services and tools related to a particular role can also be quickly added to your server configuration from the Server Manager window. We look at a number of server roles and services throughout this book and typically install these roles via Server Manager.

> If you have mapped out your network infrastructure carefully and determined the roles and services that will be provided by each server on the network, you can add roles to servers quickly by using the Initial Configuration Tasks window immediately upon booting up the system for the first time. Use the Server Manager to manage and maintain roles.

By the Way

Removing a Server Role

As you fine-tune your network and determine the capability of your servers to handle multiple roles through benchmarking, you may find that you want to remove a server role from a particular Windows Server 2008 installation. Server roles can easily be removed via the Server Manager by starting the Remove Roles Wizard.

1. Start the Server Manager (if it is not currently on the Windows desktop; select Start, Administrative Tools, and then Server Manager).

2. Select the Roles icon in the node tree; then in the details pane, click the Remove Roles icon. The Remove Roles Wizard opens.

3. The first wizard screen suggests administrative tasks related to removing a role, such as preserving role data, notifying users, and scheduling server downtime related to the removal of the role. After reading (and considering) the information on the wizard screen, click Next to continue.

4. The next screen provides a list of all server roles. Installed roles are in bold and have check marks in their check boxes (see Figure 4.7). Select the appropriate check box to remove the role (or roles). Then click Next.

FIGURE 4.7
Specify a server role to be removed.

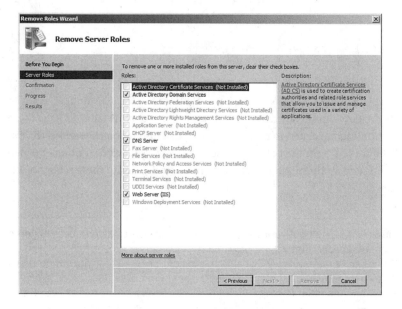

5. The wizard provides a list of the roles, role services, and associated features that will be removed based on your selection or selections in step 4. Click Remove.

The Remove Roles Wizard provides a progress bar that tracks the overall progress of the removal of the role and associated services and tools. A final wizard screen appears, noting that the role and associated services were removed. Click Close to close the Remove Roles Wizard.

Adding a Feature to Your Server Configuration

As already discussed in this hour, some server and network services are now collectively known as features (such as WINS, the Windows Backup utility, and the new BitLocker drive encryption feature). The Add Features Wizard is the tool for adding features. This wizard can be opened from the Initial Configuration Tasks window or from the Server Manager.

To add a server feature, follow these steps:

1. From the Initial Configuration Tasks window or the Server Manager (when Features is selected in the node pane), click the Add Features link. The Add Features Wizard opens (see Figure 4.8).

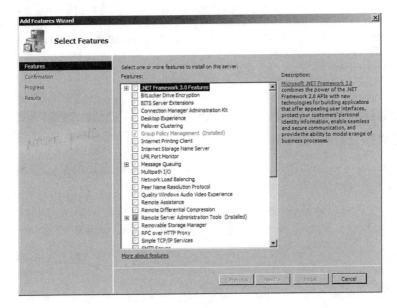

FIGURE 4.8
Select the feature or features you want to install.

2. Select the feature you want to add to the server's configuration from the list of features provided by the wizard (click the appropriate check box or check boxes). If the Add Features Wizard dialog box opens, requiring you to add additional features that support the feature you selected, click Add Required Features. Then click Next.

3. The next wizard screen lists the features you selected for installation (and any other features that must be installed to support it). Click Install to continue.

4. A progress screen appears, which keeps you apprised of the status of the feature installation. When the installation is complete, the results screen appears with a list of the features that were installed. Click Close to close the wizard window.

You can view and access installed features by selecting the Features node in the Server Manager node pane. To view available management snap-ins for installed features, expand the Features node and select the appropriate snap-in.

It may be a little disconcerting trying to find the tools to manage a particular feature after you install it. For example, you might install the Windows Server Backup feature and expect to see its feature node in the Features list in Server Manager. However, that's not the case and the Server Backup appears in the list of features under the Storage node (which does make sense). However, WINS, when installed as a feature, is not listed as a node in the Server Manager and must be managed from its own snap-in, which is started from the Administrative Tools menu (Start, Administrative Tools, WINS).

Removing a Feature from Your Server Configuration

You can also remove features from your server configuration as needed. The easiest way to start the Remove Features Wizard is via the Server Manager.

1. With the Features node selected in the Server Manager window, click the Remove Features link. The Remove Features Wizard opens (see Figure 4.9).

2. Deselect the check box for each feature you want to remove from the server installation. Then click Next.

3. The wizard provides a list of features that will be removed. Click Remove.

4. The wizard tracks the progress of the removal. When the feature removal is complete, click Close.

Remember that associated services are removed when you uninstall a particular feature. The removal of some features may require that you reboot the system, and a dialog box appears noting this fact when you attempt to close the Remove Features Wizard. You can click Yes in the dialog box to immediately reboot the server or click No to restart the server later. Remember that the feature and associated services won't be removed completely until the system has been restarted.

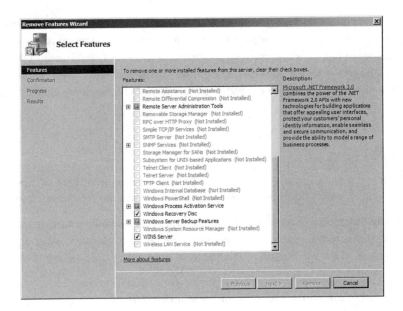

FIGURE 4.9
Select the feature or features you want to uninstall.

Summary

In this hour, we took a look at issues related to defining your network infrastructure using the Microsoft domain model. The administrative container for Microsoft server-based networks is the domain. A collection of domains resides in a tree. Each tree has a root domain; the other domains in the tree are child domains of the root. All the domains in a tree share transitive trusts, meaning that resources in any of the tree's domains are available to the users in the tree. A group of domain trees is called a forest.

Servers on the network serve specific roles. For example, the domain requires at least one domain controller. Files are made available to users by a file server, and print services are provided by a print server. A single server can serve multiple roles, but this greatly depends on the size of the network and the number of roles a single server is required to fill.

Windows Server 2008 divides most server roles, services, and other utilities into one of two categories: roles or features. The server role category includes obvious server roles such as domain controllers and file servers, and it also includes network services such as DNS and DHCP. Network services designated as features include Terminal Services, WINS and Rremote Access and Routing.

You can view and add roles and features by using the Initial Configuration Tasks window. The Server Manager enables you to view and manage server roles and features and also to add or remove roles and features as needed. You can start the Server Manager from the Start menu (Start, Administrative Tools, Server Manager). The Server Manager can also be started quickly from the icon on the Quick Launch toolbar.

Q&A

Q. *When a child domain is created in the domain tree, what type of trust relationship exists between the new child domain and the tree's root domain?*

A. Child domains and the root domain of a tree are assigned transitive trusts. This means that the root domain and child domain trust each other and allow resources in any domain in the tree to be accessed by users in any domain in the tree.

Q. *What is the primary function of domain controllers?*

A. The primary function of domain controllers is to validate users to the network. However, domain controllers also provide the catalog of Active Directory objects to users on the network.

Q. *What are some of the other roles that a server running Windows Server 2008 could fill on the network?*

A. A server running Windows Server 2008 can be configured as a domain controller, a file server, a print server, a web server, or an application server. Windows servers can also have roles and features that provide services such as DNS, DHCP, and Routing and Remote Access.

Q. *Which Windows Server 2008 tools make it easy to manage and configure a server's roles and features?*

A. The Server Manager window enables you to view the roles and features installed on a server and also to quickly access the tools used to manage these various roles and features. The Server Manager can be used to add and remove roles and features as needed.

HOUR 5

Implementing Windows Deployment Services

What You'll Learn in This Hour:

▶ Using Windows Deployment Services
▶ Configuring WDS
▶ Adding Images to the WDS Server
▶ Configuring WDS for Remote Installations
▶ Remotely Installing a Client Operating System

Hour 10, "Adding Client Computers and Member Servers to the Domain," looks at the process of adding client computers to the domain. We do not, however, tackle issues related to the actual process of installing client operating systems on those computers, which, depending on how you do it, can be quite time-consuming. An alternative to individual installations or third-party software solutions is the new Windows Deployment Services (WDS). This hour looks at the Windows Deployment Services and how you use it to install desktop operating systems on network client computers.

Using Windows Deployment Services

An alternative to installing client operating systems, such as Windows Vista, individually on desktop computers is to use the Windows Deployment Services. WDS replaces the Remote Installation Services (RIS) provided by Windows Server 2003.

WDS enables you to install a client operating system (including Windows Vista and Windows XP) during an image-based installation. The image for the client operating system is stored on the WDS server and WDS, by design, is used to install an operating system on a client that currently does not have an operating system installed on it.

WDS provides a couple important components that enable you to install an operating system over the network to a computer that has no operating system (and an unformatted hard drive). The Pre-Boot Execution Environment (PXE) server enables the WDS client to boot using Windows PE. The Trivial File Transfer Protocol (TFTP) server (of WDS) enables the operating system image to be installed.

By the Way

> WDS can also be used to configure multiple servers with the Windows Server 2008 network operating system. This can be useful when you are rolling out a number of new servers on a network.

To use WDS to deploy a client operating system, such as Windows Vista (or the Windows Server 2008 operating system to multiple servers), you must configure a WDS server on the network. The Active Directory Domain Services (AD DS) must also be available on the network, and you also need to have a DHCP server and a DNS server available. Because AD DS, DHCP, and DNS are all important services required for a domain, you basically need to have your domain infrastructure up and running before taking advantage of WDS.

Images used for installing operating systems to WDS clients must be stored on the WDS server on an NTFS volume. The first step in rolling out client operating systems (and server operating systems, if required) is to add the Windows Deployment Services role to a server on the network running Windows Server 2008.

Installing the Windows Deployment Services

You can install WDS on a domain member server or a domain controller. You cannot install WDS on a multihomed server (a server with more than one network card that may be functioning as a router or supplying a public connection to network clients using Network Address Translation [NAT] see Hour 18, "Implementing, Network Routing," for more about routing and Hour 22, "Using Network Address Translation and Certificate Services," for NAT).

It is important for any domain server that will function as a WDS server to also have enough dedicated hard drive space to hold the client images (and perhaps server NOS images) that you need to store. You can initiate the addition of the Windows Deployment Service role from either the Initial Configuration Tasks window or the Server Manager.

To add the Windows Deployment Services role to a server running Windows Server 2008, follow these steps:

1. From the Server Manager (with the Roles node selected) or the Initial Configuration Tasks window, select Add Roles. The Add Roles Wizard opens. Click Next to bypass the initial wizard page.

2. On the next wizard page, select the Windows Deployment Services check box (see Figure 5.1) and then click Next.

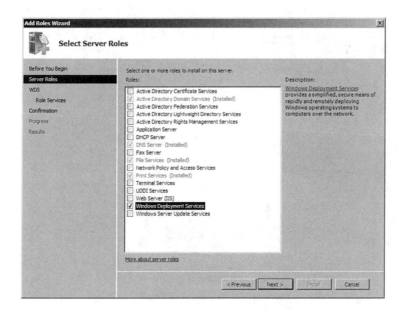

FIGURE 5.1
Select the
Windows
Deployment
Services role.

3. On the next page, you are provided a short introduction to the Windows Deployment Services and are also provided links to subject matter related to WDS. When you are ready to continue, click Next.

4. On the next page, the services related to WDS (Deployment Server and Transport Server) are listed and selected (see Figure 5.2). Make sure both services are selected and then click Next.

To deploy a "typical" WDS server you need to install both the Deployment Server and Transport Server services. You can deploy a standalone server that provides data via multicasting by installing the Transport Server only. This service uses a subset of the Deployment Server core networking components.

By the Way

---

5. The Confirmation page appears. To install WDS, click Install.

6. When the final wizard page appears (the Results page), click Close.

FIGURE 5.2
Install the
Deployment
Server and
Transport Server
for a complete
Windows
Deployment
Services
installation.

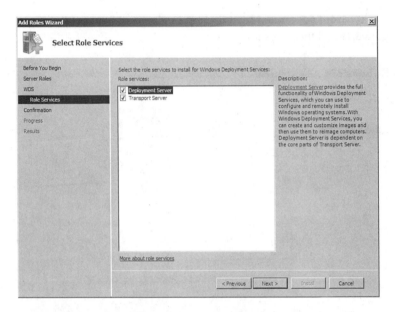

The WDS is added to the server's configuration. You can view the WDS role and
other roles installed on the server by expanding the Roles node in the Server
Manager.

Configuring WDS

Before you can use WDS, you need to configure it. You can configure WDS by using
the Windows Deployment Services snap-in. You can run the WDS snap-in in the
MMC or you can run it in the Server Manager. To access the WDS snap-in and configure WDS on the server, follow these steps:

1. In the WDS snap-in in the MMC (Start, Administrative Tools, Windows
    Deployment Services) or Server Manager (expand the Roles and WDS nodes),
    expand the Servers node (see Figure 5.3).

2. Right-click the server you want to configure and select Configure Server from
    the shortcut menu. The Windows Deployment Services Configuration Wizard
    opens.

3. Click Next to continue. On the next wizard page, provide the path to be used
    for the folder (RemoteInstall) that will contain the images you use to deploy
    operating systems with WDS (see Figure 5.4). Use the Browse button to specify
    another location. After specifying the path for the folder, click Next.

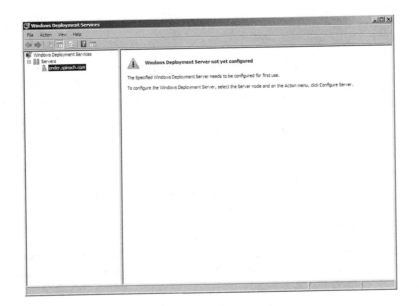

FIGURE 5.3
Expand the WDS and Servers nodes to access your server icon.

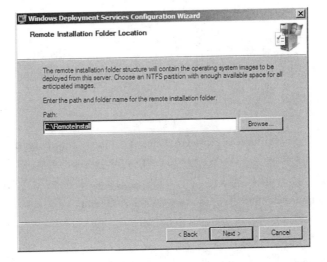

FIGURE 5.4
Specify the path for the folder that will hold the OS images.

It is recommended that you install the RemoteInstall folder on a volume other than the volume that contains the Windows Server 2008 operating system. It is also recommended that (if possible) the images (which are stored in RemoteInstall) actually be stored on a different disk than the Windows operating system.

Did you Know?

4. On the next screen you are asked to provide the PXE server settings. You are provided the following options:

- ▶ **Do Not Respond to Any Client Computer**—The default choice is designed to keep PXE clients from contacting the WDS server. This setting can be used to negate client contact before you have fully configured WDS or after you have completed all your client installations and do not wish unknown clients to contact the server.

- ▶ **Respond Only to Known Clients**—Selecting this option means that you need to "prestage" the client computers that will use WDS in the Active Directory Domain Services. You specify the MAC hardware address of the computer and identify it as a managed computer. You can also specify what WDS server the client computer is to use.

- ▶ **Respond to All (Known and Unknown) Client Computers**—This option allows any potential WDS client on the network to communicate with the WDS server.

Select one of the options (select the third option for discussion purposes) and then click Finish.

If you choose to allow unknown WDS clients to contact the WDS server, you can select the For Unknown Clients, Notify Administrator and Respond After Approval check box. This enables you to control whether the WDS server should respond to an unknown client on the network.

The configuration is complete. However, before you can actually use the WDS server, you need to add images to the WDS server that are then used by the WDS clients.

Two types of images are required: the boot image and the install image. The boot image is the image file that enables the WDS client to boot to the operating systme (via the network). The install image is the image file that contains the installation files for the OS.

The boot image and the install image files are found on the installation CD or DVD for the client operating system. Figure 5.5 shows the Select Windows Image File window (used during the installation of a boot or install image) during the installation of a boot image from a Windows Vista DVD. Note the selected file is `boot.wim`. The install image, `install.wim`, is also shown in the figure.

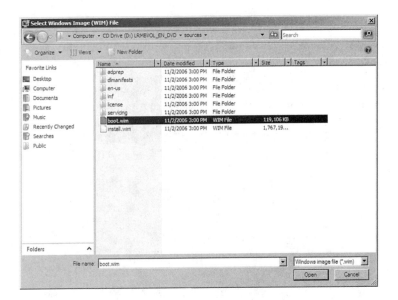

FIGURE 5.5
Boot and install
image files
(*.wim) must be
installed on
your WDS
server.

The next section looks at adding boot images to your WDS server. It looks also at
how to add the install images.

Adding Images to the WDS Server

The last page of the Windows Deployment Services Configuration Wizard can be
used to launch the Add Image Wizard (the check box is selected by default). You can
add images immediately to your WDS configuration or close the wizard and add the
images at a later time. To add boot and install images to the WDS server, you need
the installation CD (or DVD) for the Windows client operating system you want to
add.

It can be a little confusing in that the Add Image Wizard is used to add both boot
and install images. When you launch the Add Image Wizard via the Boot Images
node, the image added is a boot image. When you launch the Add Image Wizard
via the Install Images node, you are adding an install image. You need both for a
client operating system to be installed remotely.

By the Way

To add a boot image using the Add Image Wizard, follow these steps:

1. Insert the CD or DVD installation media for the client operating system (such as Windows Vista) in the removable media drive.

2. In the WDS snap-in, right-click the Boot Images node and select Add Boot Image. The Add Image Wizard opens (see Figure 5.6).

FIGURE 5.6
You must supply
the location of
the boot image.

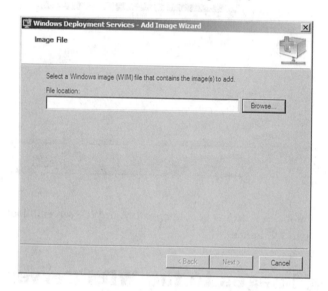

3. Click the Browse button. The Select Windows Image (WIM) File window opens. Select the image file (look in the Sources folder on both the Windows Vista and Windows Server 2008 installation media), boot.wim. Then click Open.

4. You are returned to the wizard page and the path for the boot image is entered in the File Location box. Click Next to continue.

5. On the next wizard page, supply an image name for the image (see Figure 5.7). You can also supply a description for the image. Then click Next.

6. A summary page appears, listing the image to be added. Click Next. The image is added to the WDS configuration.

7. Click Finish to close the wizard.

The boot image is listed in the Details pane when you select the Boot Image node. You can use the wizard to add other boot images as needed.

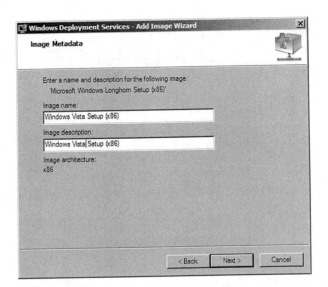

FIGURE 5.7
Enter an image
name for the
boot image.

> You can install a maximum of 13 boot images because of limitations on the boot image menu that will be provided to remote clients.

By the Way

Adding install images follows almost exactly the same process as adding the boot images. There is only one additional step for adding the install image (which is install.wim for Windows Vista and Windows Server 2008).

Start the Add Image Wizard by right-clicking the Install Images node and selecting Add Install Image. The first wizard page gives you an option of creating a image group. Image groups are used to group install images. For example, you might create a group named Windows Clients and store all the install images for your client computers, such as an image for Windows Vista and an image for Windows XP. The default image group is ImageGroup1.

After specifying the image group, the process of adding an install image is exactly the same as that for adding the boot image. You browse for the file install.wim, provide a name and description for the image, and then add it to the WDS configuration.

You can view the images by expanding the Install Images node and then choosing one of the image groups that you have selected. Figure 5.8 shows an install image for Windows Vista in a Vista image group (which is in the Install Images node).

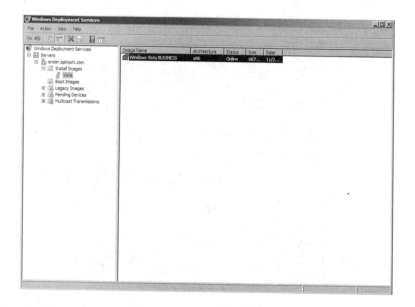

Configuring WDS for Remote Installations

You need to configure some of the properties related to your WDS installation before you can begin to remotely install client or server operating systems on network clients. To open the Properties dialog box for your WDS server, right-click the server node (the node with the actual server name) and then select Properties. The server's Properties dialog box appears (see Figure 5.9).

The Properties dialog box has eight tabs:

▶ **General**—This tab is informational. It provides the computer name, remote installation folder path, and the server mode.

▶ **PXE Response Settings**—This tab enables you to specify whether or not the server responds to clients. You can specify that clients must be known (in the Active Directory) or you can allow the server to respond to both known and unknown clients. The PXE response time can also be set on this tab. It should be zero when you are using only one WDS server on the network.

1. 7710

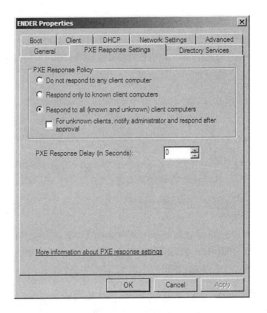

FIGURE 5.9
Open the WDS
server's
Properties dia-
log box.

You can prestage client computer accounts in the Active Directory. This makes the
computer a known client. Create the client computer account in the Active
Directory Users and Computers snap-in. Make sure that you specify that the computer account is a managed computer account. You must also specify the Globally
Unique Identifier (GUID) for the machine: It is found on a label either outside or
inside the computer case. Prestaging computer accounts mean that you can configure the PXE response settings so that the WDS server responds only to known
computers.

**Did you
Know?**

▶ **Directory Services**—This tab enables you to set the format for the computer
naming supplied by the WDS server. The default naming convention uses the
username with sequential numbering to create the computer name. This tab
also enables you to specify where in the domain schema the client computer
account should be created, such as in the same domain as the WDS server, the
same domain as the user, or the same OU as the user.

▶ **Boot**—This tab enables you to set the default boot program (which is by
default pxeboot.com). It also enables you to specify the default boot image to
be used by different processor types: x86, ia64, and x64.

▶ **Client**—This tab allows you to enable unattended installation (for clients running x86, ia64, and x64). The unattend.xml file is an XML answer file that basically provides the username, password, and other information required to install Windows remotely with WDS.

By the Way

To install Windows Server 2008 and Windows Vista remotely with an unattend.xml file, you need to create the XML file in a text editor. The file is then stored on the WDS server in the \WDSClientUnattend folder. For Windows XP clients (and Windows Server 2003), you need to use the sysprep tool (on the Windows Server 2003 installation media) to create the answer file, which has the .inf file suffix.

▶ **DHCP**—This tab provides two check boxes: Do Not List on Port 67 and Configure DHCP Option 60 to 'PXEClient'. If you are running DHCP on the same server as WDS, you should check both boxes.

▶ **Network Settings**—This tab enables you to specify the IP addresses assigned to WDS clients (a range is specified by default). You can select the Obtain IP Address from DHCP option to have WDS clients receive their IP addressing from the DHCP server. This tab is also used to specify the UDP port range (used for WDS connections between clients and the WDS server). You can also set the speed of your network by using the options provided in the Network Profile area of the tab (see Figure 5.10).

By the Way

UDP is the User Datagram Protocol. It is a connectionless transport protocol (meaning it does not require a persistent connection) in the TCP/IP protocol stack. It is used in the case of WDS to provide a connection between the WDS client and the WDS server.

▶ **Advanced**—This tab enables you to specify the domain controller and global catalog to be used by WDS. It also enables you to authorize the WDS server in DHCP (which you should do).

In terms of getting your WDS server up and running, you should allow your DHCP server to provide the IP addresses to clients (on the Network Settings tab) and allow PXE to respond to both known and unknown WDS clients (on the PXE Response Settings tab).

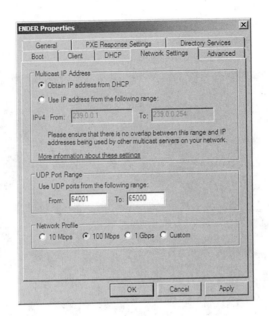

FIGURE 5.10
Set IP related settings and UDP ports on the Network Settings tab.

If DHCP is running on the same server as WDS, make sure to check both the options on the DHCP tab. All other settings on the various tabs on the Properties dialog box (unless you want to tackle unattended installations) can stay at the default settings.

There is one other thing that you must keep in mind related to server settings and WDS. You need to allow the WDS server and the WDS clients to communicate on the network. So, you have to configure the Windows Firewall (see Hour 21, "Working with the Windows Firewall and IPSec") to allow incoming connections.

Remotely Installing a Client Operating System

After you have configured the WDS server and placed boot and install images on the server, you are ready to use WDS to remotely install a client operating system on a computer. Follow these steps:

1. Start the client computer; it does a network boot from the PXE-enabled network interface. The client should be assigned an IP address by the DHCP server on the network (in some cases you may have to press F12 to enable the network boot).

2. If the network boot is successful, the WDS client begins to load the boot image from the WDS server (see Figure 5.11).

FIGURE 5.11
The WDS downloads the image from the WDS server.

3. The Install Windows window opens, denoting that it is being supplied by the Windows Deployment Services. Set the locale (such as United States) and then the keyboard type (such as U.S.). Then click Next.

4. When you click Next, the Connect box opens. It requires a username and password for a user account within the domain. Supply the username in the format *domain\user*, where *domain* is the name of the domain. Enter the password and then click OK.

5. On the next screen you or the user installing the OS selects the operating system that should be installed (see Figure 5.12). Select the client OS and then click Next.

6. On the next screen, you are asked to select the disk where Windows should be installed. Select the disk (and unallocated space) and then click Next.

7. The Windows installation begins. Complete the installation for Windows (such as Vista or Windows Server 2008) as you would for a local installation (see Figure 5.13).

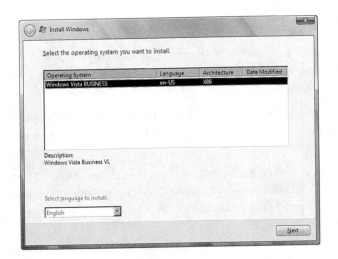

FIGURE 5.12
Select the client OS to be installed on the computer.

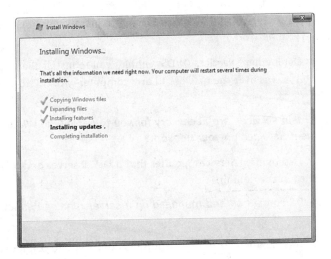

FIGURE 5.13
Complete the installation as you would for a standalone OS installation.

After the Windows installation is complete you need to add the computer to the domain (if you didn't prestage the computer to the Active Directory. As soon as the computer is a domain member, users can access domain resources by logging on to the computer using their domain username.

Obviously, WDS can make installing operating systems on network clients a much less time-intensive endeavor. With boot and install images for a number of desktop client operating systems stored on the WDS server, you can quickly get a new computer up and running with any number of operating systems.

Summary

Windows Deployment Services (WDS) enables you to remotely install client operating systems such as Windows Vista and Windows XP. WDS can also be used to deploy server operating systems such as Windows Server 2008.

The WDS snap-in is used to manage WDS. Boot and install images can be added to the WDS server through the WDS snap-in. This snap-in also enables you to configure the WDS server.

After the WDS server has been configured, network clients with a PXE-enabled network interface can boot to the WDS server. The OS installation then takes place as if the installation were being conducted locally from a CD or DVD drive.

Q&A

Q. *What Windows Server 2008 service is used to install client operating systems over the network?*

A. Windows Deployment Services (WDS) enables you to install client and server operating systems over the network to any computer with a PXE-enabled network interface.

Q. *What domain services are necessary for you to deploy the Windows Deployment Services on your network?*

A. Windows Deployment Services requires that a DHCP server and a DNS server be installed in the domain.

Q. *How is WDS configured and managed on a server running Windows Server 2008?*

A. The Windows Deployment Services snap-in enables you to configure the WDS server and add boot and install images to the server.

HOUR 6

Managing Hard Drives and Volumes

What You'll Learn in This Hour:

- ▶ Managing Disk Drives Using Windows Server 2008
- ▶ Using the Disk Management Snap-in
- ▶ Creating a Simple Volume on a Basic Disk
- ▶ Converting a Basic Drive to a Dynamic Drive
- ▶ Creating a Spanned Volume on a Dynamic Disk
- ▶ Extending a Volume
- ▶ Understanding RAID
- ▶ Implementing RAID 1
- ▶ Implementing RAID 5
- ▶ Viewing Drive Properties
- ▶ Planning Your Server Backups
- ▶ The Windows Server 2008 Backup Utility
- ▶ Backing Up Files with Windows Server Backup
- ▶ Restoring Files
- ▶ Creating a Scheduled Backup

Managing Disk Drives Using Windows Server 2008

An important aspect of configuring a server is setting up the hard drive or drives on the server so that the computer can successfully fulfill its role on the network. For example, a file server on the network needs appropriate storage capacity to provide data storage and access to users on the network. As the number of users on the network and the data on the server grow, it might be necessary to configure unused space on the drive or to add additional drives to the server.

Windows Server 2008 provides you with the Disk Management snap-in, which is used to configure and manage your drives. You can format drives and create drive volumes. You can also configure more advanced drive features such as Redundant Array of Independent Disks (RAID) arrays by using the Disk Manager. RAID arrays can be used to add redundancy to network data storage, helping protect valuable network information and server configurations. Before you take a look at the Disk Management snap-in, a little background information related to how Windows Server 2008 manages drives from different vendors and how Microsoft approaches drive configurations is provided.

By the Way

Although server disk management is one aspect of protecting important network data, how data is shared and the level of access given to users are other important parts of your overall network resources plan. Working with network shares and permissions related to shared data discussed in Hour 12, "Working with Network Shares and the Distributed File System." Share permissions and NTFS permissions are discussed in Hour 13, "Protecting Data with Permission and Encryption." Hour 13 also looks at the new BitLocker Drive Encryption feature and how it relates to protecting data on your servers.

Windows Server 2008 Virtual Disk Service

As with all computer hardware, each component is available from different manufacturers. Hard drives and drive controllers are no different. Managing drives on different servers often has necessitated using a number of different utilities, with each utility specific to a particular drive array and its manufacturer.

In an attempt to provide a consistent approach to drive management, a new service has been added to Windows Server 2008 called the Virtual Disk Service (VDS). VDS is a set of application programming interfaces (APIs) that enable you to manage the configuration of different manufacturers' hard disks while using the same Windows tools (the Windows Server 2008 Disk Management snap-in and the command-line DiskPart—DiskPart is discussed later in the hour).

The burden of making disks manageable using the Windows disk tools is really on the manufacturer of the drives that you use in your servers. Each manufacturer must supply APIs to Microsoft to make the Virtual Disk Service a reality. There might be a time lag before all vendors' drive configurations can be managed directly from Windows Server 2008.

Basic Drive Versus Dynamic Drives

Computers running Windows (even servers running Windows NT) have long embraced the MS-DOS model of disk configuration in which drives were partitioned and the various partitions were then formatted. Not until advances provided with the release of Windows 2000 Server were network administrators provided with an alternative way to divide, combine, and configure the storage capacity of hard drives.

Windows Server 2008 embraces two types of disk storage strategies (which originated with 2000 Server): basic storage and dynamic storage. These storage strategies are also available in Windows Server 2008.

You can use only one storage type (basic or dynamic) on a physical disk.

Basic storage is the traditional standard for how hard drives are formatted and configured, and it is based on the way drives were configured with MS-DOS. A *basic disk* is a physical disk that contains a partition (Windows Server 2008 refers to a partition as a *simple volume*). A *partition* is a logical portion of a hard drive that is actually read by the computer's operating system as a separate drive. Basic storage is the default for Windows Server 2008. Basic disks can be divided into a maximum of four partitions.

Dynamic storage allows for the creation of dynamic disks. A *dynamic disk* consists of one partition that can be divided into any number of volumes. A *volume* is a portion of an entire drive or parts of several drives that are assigned a single drive letter. Dynamic disks can be sized and resized without requiring a restart of Windows Server 2008.

You can shrink and extend dynamic disks as needed. Technically, you can also shrink and extend basic disks; however, the basic disk is converted to a dynamic disk during the process of shrinking or extending it.

The use of dynamic disks allows for the creation of disk arrays that use RAID implementations. As mentioned earlier, the use of RAID allows for redundancy and fault
tolerance on network drives, which helps to protect network data. Because basic
drives are the default for Windows Server 2008, you must convert a drive or drives to
dynamic. Converting a basic drive to a dynamic drive is discussed later in the hour.

GPT Drives Versus MBR Drives

Windows Server 2008 also provides you with the option of deploying GPT drives on
your Windows 2008 servers. A GPT (GUID Partition Table) disk uses the GUID partition table (obviously) as opposed to the older Master Boot Record (MBR) partition
table.

> GUID is an implementation of the Universally Unique Identifier (UUID) standard,
> which replaces the Master Boot Record (MBR) partitioning scheme on hard drives.
> Using GUID, drives can have up to 128 primary partitions and can also support
> volume sizes in excess of 2TB. The MBR standard provides for only four primary
> partitions and volumes cannot exceed 2TB. So, bottom line, GPT is an excellent
> option for very large disks that will be used for data storage and access. Be
> advised that GPT drives are not backward compatible with previous versions of
> the Windows server operating system.

GPT disks can enable you to create more partitions on a drive (up to 128) and also
create very large drive volumes (greater than 2TB). When you initialize a new drive
in the Disk Management snap-in you have the option of initializing the drive as an
MBR or GPT disk (see Figure 6.1).

FIGURE 6.1
You can initial-
ize new disks
as MBR or GPT.

Initialize Disk	☒

You must initialize a disk before Logical Disk Manager can access it.

Select disks:

☑ Disk 0
☑ Disk 1

Use the following partition style for the selected disks:

◉ MBR (Master Boot Record)
○ GPT (GUID Partition Table)

Note: The GPT partition style is not recognized by all previous versions of
Windows. It is recommended for disks larger than 2TB, or disks used on
Itanium-based computers.

[OK]   [Cancel]

You can also convert raw MBR drives or empty MBR drives to GPT drives (right-click an MBR drive in the Disk Management window) and vice versa: Raw or empty GPT drives can be converted to the MBR format. Keep in mind that bootable drives containing system files cannot be initialized as GPT drives.

Using the Disk Management Snap-In

Disk management is handled by the Disk Management snap-in (although disk management can also be tackled from the command prompt as discussed later in the hour). The Disk Management snap-in can be opened in the Computer Management console or via the Server Manager. To open the Disk Management snap-in (in the Server Manager), click the Start button, point at Administrative Tools, and then click Server Manager. Server Manager opens. To open the Disk Management snap-in, expand the Storage node (in the node tree) and then select the Disk Management node. The disks on your computer (and their current configurations) appear in the Details pane (see Figure 6.2).

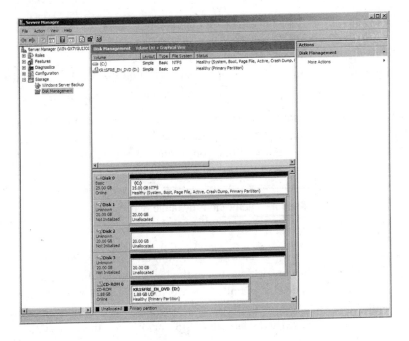

FIGURE 6.2
The Disk Management snap-in provides access to the drives on the server.

The Disk Management snap-in provides you with a great deal of information on each of the physical drives installed on your computer. The top portion of the Details pane (the middle of the Disk Management window) by default lists volumes or partitions that have been assigned a drive letter (including CD-ROMs). Additional information, such as the file system used on the partition or volume, the capacity and free space, and whether the volume or partition is part of a fault tolerance array (RAID), is also provided.

The bottom portion of the Details pane lists each physical drive, including any CD-ROM drives (this would include any CD-writeable or DVD drives on the system). This lower area of the Details pane is the easiest place to access commands related to drive management (by default the bottom pane is in the Graphical View). You can bring drives in the list online, initialize drives as MBR or GPT, change drives from basic to dynamic, and you can create and format partitions or volumes (depending on whether the disk is basic or dynamic).

Did you Know?

> Physical drives are numbered starting with 0. A server configured with three hard drives would list drives 0, 1, and 2 in the Disk Management Details pane. Partitions begin with the number 1 and then number sequentially—2, 3, and so on.

Creating a Simple Volume on a Basic Disk

You can create partitions and logical drives on basic disks that are formatted with NTFS or FAT32. Partitions can be created on any unused space on the disk.

You won't see the word *partition* anywhere on the disk shortcut menu (when you right-click a disk). Microsoft uses the term *simple volume* to refer to a partition on a basic disk. So, to create a new partition, you create a simple volume.

By the Way

> You can also create a simple volume on a dynamic disk.
> PARTITION

Before you can create a simple volume (a partition) on a disk you must make sure that the disk is online (right-click the disk in the lower pane of the snap-in and select Online). You also need to initialize the disk (as either MBR or GPT). Right-click the disk and select Initialize. Select the disk or disks you want to initialize in the Initialize Disk dialog box. Then select either MBR or GPT and then click OK.

After you initialize a disk (either as a MBR or GPT), the disk is a basic disk and can now be partitioned. Follow these steps to create a partition:

1. Right-click the unallocated space of a basic disk (the space is marked unallocated), and select New Simple Volume from the shortcut menu. The New

Simple Volume Wizard appears. Click Next to move past the wizard's introductory screen.

2. The next screen asks you to select the size for the volume, as shown in Figure 6.3. Use the Simple Volume Size in MB box to set the size of the partition. By default, the entire space available on the partition is listed. Click Next.

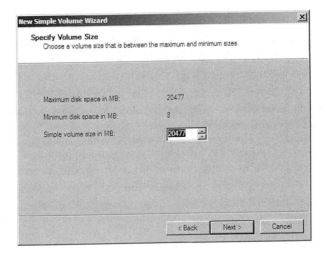

FIGURE 6.3
Designate the amount of free space available on the drive that should be used in the new volume.

4. The next screen enables you to select the drive letter or assign a path for the new volume. Select a drive letter from the drop-down box and then select Next.

5. The next screen enables you to select the file system that you want to use to format the volume (see Figure 6.4). This screen also enables you to set the allocation unit size for the volume and assign a volume name to the new volume.

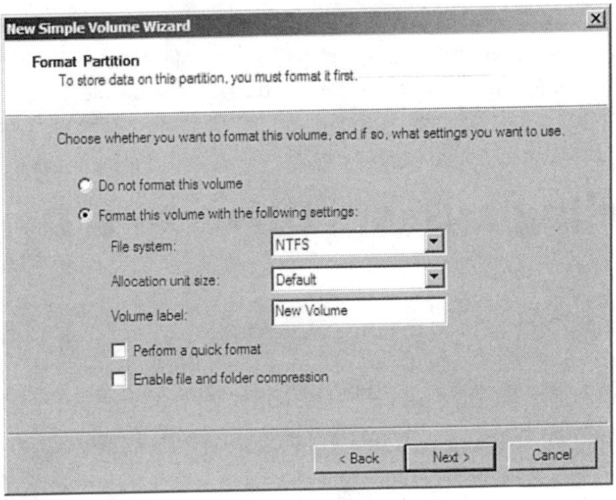

FIGURE 6.4
Select the file system for the volume.

You can format drives on your Windows 2008 servers as FAT32 or NTFS. Microsoft recommends NTFS as the best choice for your server drives. This makes sense because NTFS partitions can be as large as nearly 16 exabytes (a FAT32 partition has a maximum of 2 terabytes), NTFS volumes allow file compression, and NTFS permissions provide additional security to resources on the network.

Select the file system using the wizard's File System drop-down box. Use the Allocation Unit Size drop-down box to select the allocation unit size you want to use on the drive. The allocation unit size selected determines the cluster size used on the partition (which holds the sectors, the basic units of disk space). Using an allocation unit size of 4096MB creates a cluster size no greater than 4KB, which is the limit for NTFS compressions. In most cases, the default allocation unit size will suffice for your partition.

6. After selecting the file system and allocation unit size (optional) and providing a volume name for the partition (also optional), click the Next button. The last wizard screen appears, providing a summary of the options you chose for the new volume. When you click Finish, the new partition is created (as a primary partition) and formatted.

New volumes are color-coded blue in the graphical display. Your unallocated drive space will appear in black. You can create simple volumes or extend a volume using disk space available on other physical disks installed on the system.

Basic disks are somewhat limited in what you can do with them in the Windows Server 2008 environment (such as RAID implementations). Let's take a look at how you convert a basic drive to a dynamic drive.

To delete a volume, right-click the volume and the select Delete Volume. Remember that any data on the volume will be lost if you delete it.

Converting a Basic Drive to a Dynamic Drive

Basic disks can be converted to dynamic disks quickly in the Disk Management snap-in. You will also find, when you attempt to extend a basic disk, that the process also upgrades the disk to a dynamic disk. If you want to build any fault tolerance into your disk arrays using RAID, you will definitely want to convert basic drives to dynamic drives.

To convert a basic disk to a dynamic disk, right-click the disk in the Details pane (on the disk's designation box, such as Disk 1 or Disk 2). Then select Convert to Dynamic Disk from the shortcut menu that appears. The Convert to Dynamic Disk dialog box opens, as shown in Figure 6.5.

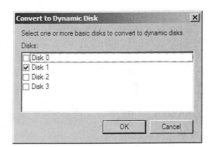

FIGURE 6.5
Designate the drives that you want to convert from basic to dynamic.

All the physical drives on your server are listed in the Convert to Dynamic Disk dialog box. You may select any and all drives (that are currently online) using this dialog box to mark them for conversion. After making your selection, click OK. Quite quickly you will notice that the drive designation changes from Basic to Dynamic.

Converting basic drives to dynamic drives is an imperative in cases where you want to build fault tolerance into a drive array. You should keep in mind some things related to converting drives:

▶ You cannot convert removable media such as USB, Jaz, ZIP, and other disk types considered "nonfixed" drives from basic to dynamic.

▶ If you upgrade a basic disk that is part of a volume that spans several different physical drives, you must convert all the disks in the volume from basic to dynamic.

▶ If you convert a disk that contains another operating system (on a server that offers a dual-boot environment) from basic to dynamic, the other operating system will no longer function or boot. This includes Microsoft Windows NT Server and Linux distributions.

▶ You can upgrade a basic disk containing the boot and system partitions to a dynamic disk. However, you cannot reverse the conversion from dynamic to basic as you can on drives that do not contain boot and system information.

If you plan on implementing Windows Server 2008, it makes sense to take advantage of dynamic disks. Dynamic disks provide many more configuration possibilities when compared to basic disks. The next section discusses the different types of volumes that can be created on a dynamic disk.

Creating a Spanned Volume on a Dynamic Disk

After you have converted a basic disk to a dynamic disk, you have more options in terms of the types of volumes that you create using that disk and the fact that you can expand a volume on a dynamic disk (and include dynamic disks in RAID implementations, which is discussed later in the hour).

As with basic disks, you can create simple volumes on dynamic disks. Dynamic disks also allow you to create the following:

- **Spanned volume**—A non–fault tolerant simple volume that spans more than one physical disk.

- **Striped volume**—A non–fault tolerant volume on which data is striped across multiple disks, speeding up the write and read processes to and from the volume. At least two drives are needed to create a striped volume. A striped volume is also known as RAID 0.

- **Mirrored volume**—A fault tolerant volume on one drive is mirrored (duplicated) on a volume on another drive. This is RAID 1, which is discussed later in the hour. When the drives are on separate drive controllers, you are actually implementing disk duplexing.

- **RAID-5 volume**—A fault tolerant volume that spans multiple drives. Data is striped across the multiple drives with parity information written to the drives, allowing for the regeneration of the whole data set if one of the drives fails. A minimum of three drives is required for this type of volume. RAID 5 is discussed later in the hour.

Did you Know?

> If you need to run legacy network operating systems or want to run other versions of Windows Server on a single server, you might want to take advantage of virtualization. This enables you to run these systems in virtual machines, which allows you to not worry about the type of disk (basic or dynamic) as you deploy your virtual machines.

So, let's say that you want to create a large storage volume that spans several disks. You can use the New Spanned Volume Wizard to specify the dynamic disks (and the appropriate free space on the disks) that will be included in the spanned volume. Follow these steps:

1. In the Disk Management Details area, right-click a dynamic disk that contains unallocated disk space.

2. Select New Spanned Volume from the shortcut menu.

3. When the New Spanned Volume Wizard appears, click Next to bypass the opening wizard screen.

4. On the next screen, use the Select the Amount of Space in MB spinner box to specify the amount of free space on the currently selected drive that you want to use for the spanned volume (see Figure 6.6).

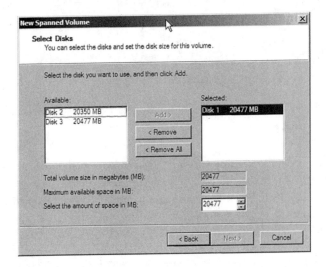

FIGURE 6.6
Specify the amount of disk space to be used for the spanned volume.

5. To add other drives to the spanned volume, select the drive in the Available box and then click Add. Add other available drives as needed.

6. Select each added drive and use the Select the Amount of Space in MB spinner box to specify the amount of space on the drive that will be used in the spanned volume. Then click Next to continue.

7. On next screen specify the drive letter for the new volume (or select the default drive letter provided). Then click Next.

8. On this wizard screen (see Figure 6.7), select the file system for the new volume. You can use FAT32 or NTFS (NTFS is the default). You can also specify a volume name. After choosing the file format, click Next to continue the process.

FIGURE 6.7
Specify the format and volume name for the new spanned volume.

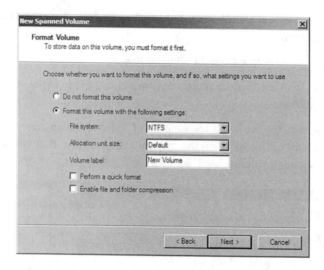

9. A summary screen appears detailing the selections that you made for the new volume; click Finish.

The new volume (spanned) is now formatted, meaning each of the drives that you selected for inclusion in the spanned volume is formatted. The new spanned volume appears in the Details pane of the Disk Management snap-in. Spanned volumes are color-coded purple.

To delete a volume, right-click the volume and select Delete Volume. Remember that any data on the volume is lost if you delete it.

Extending a Volume

Dynamic volumes can be extended easily. And as was the case when creating volumes, a volume can be extended using free space on the same physical drive or space available on other physical drives on the server. To extend a volume, follow these steps:

1. Right-click the volume that you want to extend, and then select Extend Volume. The Extend Volume Wizard appears. Click Next to continue.

2. A wizard screen appears (see Figure 6.8). Here you can select more free space on the physical drive to extend the volume, or you can select additional physical drives that contain free space. After selecting additional drives and specifying the space to be used, click Next.

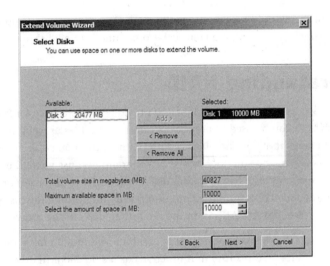

FIGURE 6.8
You can extend
an existing
volume.

3. A summary screen appears. Click Finish to end the process.

When a volume extends across more than one disk, the failure of any of the disks makes the volume unusable.

After you have created volumes on your server, you have the option of shrinking these volumes as needed. Shrinking a volume enables you to take advantage of unused space on a volume for some other purpose (such as another new volume).

To shrink a simple or spanned volume, right-click the volume in the Disk Management snap-in and then select Shrink Volume. In the Shrink dialog box that appears (see Figure 6.9), specify the amount by which you want to shrink the volume (using the Enter the Amount of Space to Shrink in MB spinner box) and then click Shrink.

FIGURE 6.9
You can shrink
an existing
volume.

The results of shrinking the volume appear in the Disk Management snap-in. The amount by which you shrink the volume becomes unallocated disk space.

Understanding RAID

RAID is a collection of strategies designed to provide fault tolerance for files stored on hard drives (it can be used to protect boot and system files as well). In general, using RAID means that you are placing data on more than one disk. If a disk in the RAID set goes down, you still have access to your data because you either have a complete copy of that data (on the other disk in the RAID 1 mirror set) or can read the data on the failed disk from the data and parity information (discussed later in this hour when we look at RAID 5) on the remaining disks in the array.

In the simplest terms, RAID enables you to combine volumes on more than one drive into a volume set (or array) that functions as a single logical drive.

There are at least 13 different levels of RAID and most of these RAID implementations require drive controllers that support hardware RAID configurations. As already mentioned, Windows Server 2008 allows you to implement software implementations of RAID. Windows Server supports software versions of RAID 0, 1, and 5. Table 6.1 provides definitions of these three software RAID possibilities.

By the Way

√

> RAID can be either hardware or software supported. A number of RAID controllers are available for network servers. We discuss the software RAID levels embraced by Windows Server 2008. RAID configurations can even be expanded beyond a single server. Windows Server 2008 also supports server clustering. This enables you to tie a number of servers into a cluster, producing extremely powerful processing and a high storage capacity environment.

TABLE 6.1   Windows 2008 Server Software RAID Levels

Level	Name	Description
0	Striping without parity	Data is written across the disks in the array. RAID 0 is not a fault-tolerance method; it's actually used to speed disk access.
1	Mirroring	Two drives (such as partitions or volumes) are mirrored so that each disk in the array is an exact copy of the other disk.
5	Disk striping with distributed parity	Data is written across a stripe set of multiple disks, with the parity information distributed across the disk array.

Let's take a look at implementing the software RAID levels provided by Windows Server 2008 and how they allow you to build fault tolerance into your server implementations.

Implementing RAID 1

RAID 1 requires two disks and is often referred to as *mirroring* (if these disks are on different drive controllers, it is called *duplexing*). Mirror sets can be very useful for protecting the boot and system volume of your server. You can mirror this volume using unallocated space on another dynamic disk. Then, if the primary boot drive on the server goes down, you can reconfigure the boot.ini file so that the server boots from the mirror.

The volumes used in the mirror must have an equal amount of free space, or there must be more space on the volume that will be used to create the mirror (meaning that you need another drive on the server that has an equal amount of free space or more free space than the volume that you will mirror).

To create a mirror set, follow these steps:

1. In the Disk Management Details area, right-click the dynamic volume that you want to mirror. Select Add Mirror from the shortcut menu. If the option is unavailable, there is no unallocated drive that can be selected as a target for the mirror.

2. The Add Mirror dialog box appears (see Figure 6.10). Select the drive that will supply the mirror volume.

FIGURE 6.10
Select the drive that will supply the mirror volume.

The mirror volume is created and formatted, and the data on the original drive is mirrored onto it. Depending on the size of the original drive and the number of files on the drive, it may take a while for the two drives to synchronize (see Figure 6.11).

FIGURE 6.11
The drives in
the mirror set
will synchronize.

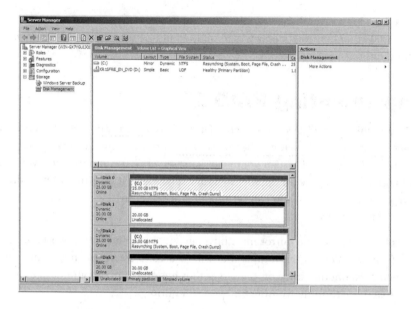

The two drives in the mirror set share the same drive letter and always contain the same files; data is synchronized between the original volume and the mirror partner. Mirror sets are designated in the Disk Management utility by a dark red color.

Breaking a Mirror Set

You can break a mirror if it doesn't fit into your overall fault-tolerance scheme. Follow these steps:

1. Right-click either volume in the mirror set and select Remove Mirror.

2. You are asked to specify which of the volumes in the mirror you want to remove. Select the volume that served as the mirror (not your original disk, or your server might not boot). Then click Remove Mirror.

3. You are asked to verify the process; click Yes.

The specified disk is removed from the mirror set. The drive is specified as unallocated space and can be used for some other purpose.

Implementing RAID 5

RAID 5, disk striping with parity, provides you with faster access time than a single-disk volume and also enables you to rebuild the stripe set if one of the disks in the set goes down. RAID 5 is an excellent choice for file servers when you want to improve access time but also want to build some fault tolerance into the system.

RAID 5 requires at least 3 disks and can be deployed on up to 32 disks. Disks in the stripe set must have either an equal amount or a greater amount of disk space compared to the drive that you select when you initiate the creation of the stripe set. To create a RAID 5 stripe set follow these steps:

1. In the Disk Management Details pane, right-click any dynamic disk that contains unallocated disk space. The amount of unused disk space on this disk dictates the amount of space on the other drives that are in the stripe set. Select New RAID-5 Volume from the shortcut menu. The New RAID-5 Volume Wizard appears.

2. Click Next to bypass the wizard's introductory screen.

3. On the next screen, specify the amount of space that you will use on the selected disk (the disk on which you right-clicked to begin the process) by clicking the Select the Amount of Space in MB spinner box as needed (see Figure 6.12).

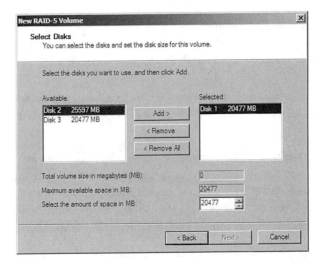

FIGURE 6.12
Set the amount of space that will be used on the disk for the Raid-5 stripe set.

4. Use the Available box to select and then add (by clicking Add) the other drives that will be part of the RAID-5 implementation (you need to have three drives in the set).

5. After adding the drives for the set, click Next.

6. On the next screen specify the drive letter for the RAID-5 set (or go with the default). Then click Next.

7. On the next screen, specify the Volume Label for the new drive (NTFS is the only option for the file system for a stripe set). You can also enable file and folder compression if you wish (see Figure 6.13). Then click Next.

FIGURE 6.13
Specify the volume name for the stripe set.

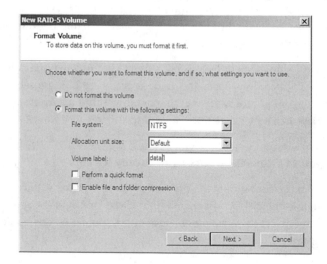

8. The final wizard screen provides a summary of the volume type you created and other information related to the volume such as the disks used and the drive letter specified. Click Finish to complete the process.

The RAID set is then created and appears in the Disk Management snap-in. Figure 6.14 shows a RAID-5 stripe set (RAID-5 sets are color-coded light-blue) using disks 1, 2, and 3.

If one of the drives fails in the stripe set, you can regenerate the whole RAID 5 array. All you have to do is replace the bad drive and then use the Regenerate command in the Disk Management snap-in to get your stripe set up and running again (right-click any of the stripe set volumes to access the Regenerate command). If you decide not to use the stripe set, you can delete it as you would any volume.

ⁿ REGENERATE

Did you Know?

The Event Viewer can help to track problems with RAID sets. Sometimes RAID 5 arrays fail because of bad disk controllers. Look for events in the system log that might provide hints on whether a drive or a controller associated with the RAID set is having problems. The Event Viewer is discussed in Hour 24, "Monitoring Server Performance and Network Connections."

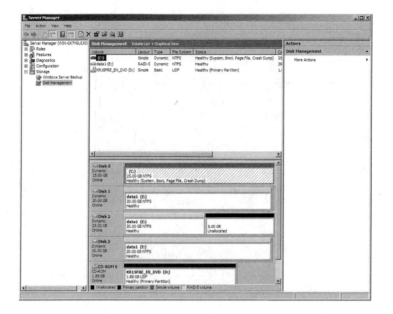

FIGURE 6.14
A RAID 5 stripe set.

Viewing Drive Properties

You can access the detailed properties of any of the volumes on your server in the Disk Management window, in the Computer window (where the volumes are represented as drives with drive letters), or through Windows Explorer.

Open any of these tools (Disk Management, Computer, or Windows Explorer) and right-click a particular drive letter. Select Properties from the shortcut menu.

The Properties dialog box provides information such as the file system used on the volume, the free and used space, and the capacity of the volume (see Figure 6.15).

The Properties dialog box also contains a number of tabs that give you access to drive tools, hardware information, disk quota settings (discussed in Hour 12), and local security options.

Drive-sharing parameters are also found on the Properties dialog box (the Sharing tab), as is the Shadow Copy feature. Both of these features are discussed in Hour 12.

Did you Know?

Let's take a look at the Tools tab and the options it provides. Figure 6.16 shows the Tools tab.

FIGURE 6.15
The Properties
dialog box pro-
vides specific
information on
a selected
volume.

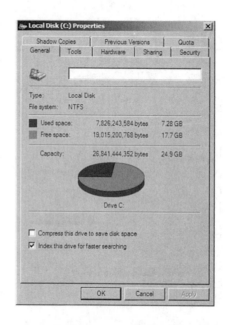

FIGURE 6.16
The Tools tab
provides access
to drive utilities.

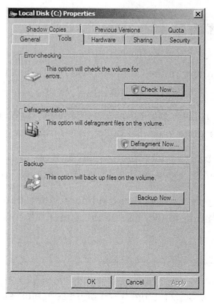

One of the options on the Tools tab of the Properties dialog box is Error-Checking, a utility that checks the volume for any errors. To start the process, click the Check Now button.

The Check Disk dialog box opens, providing two check box options:

▶ Automatically Fix File System Errors

▶ Scan and Attempt Recovery of Bad Sectors

You can select either option (or both) and then click Start. When the scan of the volume is complete, the Disk Check Complete dialog box appears. Click OK to close it.

The Tools tab also provides access to the Disk Defragmenter and the Backup utility. The following section discusses backups.

Planning Your Server Backups

The best way to protect data on the network and important configuration files is to perform scheduled backups on mission-critical servers (or any server for that matter). Installing a backup device on your domain controller or a file server not only enables you to back up the Registry on a particular server, but it also does not add to network traffic by moving the backup files over the network medium.

Backup devices are available from a number of manufacturers, as is specialized backup software. Later in this hour, we take a look at backing up files using the new Windows Server 2008 Backup utility.

A large number of backup devices using different media types are available—everything from DAT tape to 8mm tape to CD-RW jukeboxes. No matter what type of device you choose, you must make sure that the device is listed on the Windows Server 2008 compatibility list, available at www.microsoft.com. Be advised that Windows Server Backup does not support tape drives and you will need to use a third-party backup solution ot take advantage of tape backup devices.

By the Way

Although the media and backup software that you use for your backups should be sufficient for your needs, another important aspect of backing up data is to have a backup plan. Your backup plan must revolve around the data that must be backed up and how often you decide to back up that particular information.

Before determining your backup plan, some basic issues related to backups should be discussed, including the different types of backups that can be made. First, Windows uses file markers (or archive attributes) to specify whether a file has been backed up.

When you create a new file, one of the file's attributes is that the file has not been backed up since changes were made to it last (the changes here are its creation).

When you back up the file, the "never been backed up" tag is removed. In effect, this marks the file as having been backed up. Then when you make new changes to the file, the file is again marked as having not been backed up since recent changes were made. Markers are important because you can use them to your advantage during the backup process.

The fact that files are tagged based on their backup status enables you to use three different types of backups:

▶ **Normal**—A *normal backup* backs up all the files and folders you select (no matter how the files are currently marked). The files' attributes are changed to denote that they have been backed up. Windows Server 2008 Backup also provides a daily backup that operates like a normal backup: It backs up all the files, no matter what the archive attribute says.

▶ **Differential**—A *differential backup* backs up files that have been marked as having changed since their last backup. However, the differential backup does not change the marker attribute indicating that the file has been backed up. It leaves the marker alone, so the file will still read as if it has not been backed up.

▶ **Incremental**—An *incremental backup* backs up only the files that have been changed since the last backup (using the marker attribute on the files to identify those that have been modified). The incremental backup changes the archive marker to identify that the file has been backed up.

So, a possible strategy for a backup plan would be to do a normal backup the first time you run a backup on the server. You can then run an incremental backup on a daily basis to back up any changes made to the files. This speeds up the daily backup process because you are backing up only files that have been modified since the previous backup. Differential backups can be run once a week to back up all the data that changed since the last differential backup (giving you a week's worth of changes).

Using the backup plan discussed, if the server goes down on Tuesday, you have to restore only the differential backup that you ran on Friday and the incremental backup that you ran on Monday evening. This should restore all the files to the state they were in before the crash.

Be advised that the new Windows Server 2008 Backup utility does not support differential and incremental backups. It only provides for a full backup (the same as a normal backup defined above) shadow copies of shared folders. If you want to have a more fine-grained backup strategy for your servers, you will need to take advantage of a third party backup software solution.

> You should also have a backup plan for keeping a copy of backup tapes or other media offsite. This enables you to restore the company data even if a major disaster such as a fire hits the business.

The Windows Server 2008 Backup Utility

The Backup utility provided in previous versions of the Windows Server software has always been considered more a tool of last resort rather than a robustly featured backup and restore utility. Windows Server 2008 provides a new utility, Windows Server Backup, which provides a number of improvements over the Backup utility available in previous versions of Windows Server. Touting faster backups and the ability to back up applications via the Volume Shadow Copy Service, other Server Backup improvements include the following:

- ▶ **Windows Server Backup snap-in**—The new backup utility runs in a Microsoft Management Console (and Server Manager) and so shares a common interface with many of the Windows Server tools and features.

- ▶ **Server Backup Scheduling Wizard**—A new Scheduling Wizard makes it easier for you to create scheduled backups including daily backups.

- ▶ **Remote backups**—Because the Backup feature runs in a snap-in, you can connect to other servers in the Server Manager window and back up these servers remotely.

- ▶ **DVD media support**—You can back up your server or servers to DVDs, which provide a fairly high-capacity and portable backup medium.

The Windows Server Backup feature is not installed as part of your default Windows Server 2008 installation. You must add the backup feature to your server as follows:

1. In the Initial Configuration Tasks window or in the Server Manager, click Add Features (Add Features in the Server Manager). The Add Features Wizard opens.

2. To install both the Server Backup utility and the command-line backup tool, select the Windows Server Backup Features check box (see Figure 6.17).

FIGURE 6.17
The Tools tab
provides access
to drive utilities.

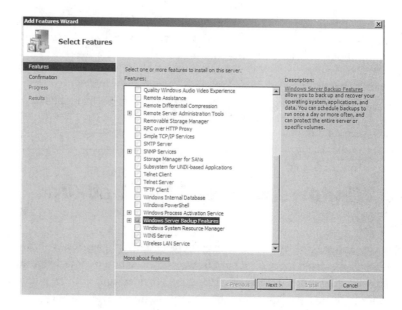

3. Click Next. The Summary screen for the Wizard appears.

4. Click Install. When the installation is complete, click Close to close the Wizard.

After you have the Windows Server Backup feature installed, you can take advantage of it to back up folders and files on your server. Let's look at backing up files and then at the restore process.

Backing Up Files with Windows Server Backup

The Backup snap-in can be accessed in the MMC or the Server Manager. Typically, you will want to use the Backup Schedule Wizard to create a schedule for your backups. We look at the Backup Schedule Wizard later in the hour. To get a first look at the Windows Server Backup snap-in, let's take a look at doing a one-time backup.

To start the Windows Server Backup snap-in in the MMC and backup files, follow these steps:

1. Click the Start menu, point at Administrative Tools, and then click Windows Server Backup. The Windows Server Backup snap-in opens in the MMC (see Figure 6.18).

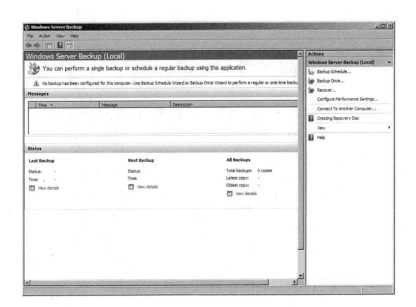

FIGURE 6.18
The Windows
Server Backup
snap-in.

To access the Windows Server Backup snap-in in the Server Manager, expand the
Storage node and then select the Windows Server Backup icon.

Did you Know?

2. In the Actions pane (on the right side of the Windows Server Backup snap-in)
click Backup Once. The Backup Once Wizard opens.

3. Click Next to bypass the wizard's initial screen.

4. On the next screen (see Figure 6.19), you select the backup configuration. You
can select Full Server (the recommended default) or you can back up specific
drives. Let's take a look at how you do a custom backup (specifying the drive).
Click Custom and then click Next.

6. The next screen enables you to specify the destination for the backup. You can
back up to drives on the system such as the CD/DVD-ROM drive, a local hard
drive, or you can specify a network share for the backup. Specify the destination drive (or network share) and then click Next.

5. On the next screen (see Figure 6.20), you can specify the drive or drives you
want to back up. Select the drive or drives and then click Next.

FIGURE 6.19
You can do a full or custom backup.

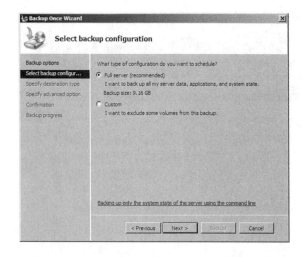

FIGURE 6.20
Specify the drive or drives to back up.

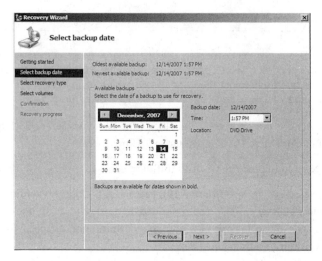

By the Way

On the Select Backup Items screen, the Enable System Recovery option is enabled by default. This means that the volumes containing the system file are backed up automatically as part of the backup. If you do not want to include the system volumes, clear the Enable System Recovery check box and then select the drives to be backed up as needed.

7. On the next screen, you need to specify advanced options that relate to the Volume Shadow Copy Service (VSS). If you are using another backup product on the server to back up applications, you should select the VSS Copy Backup (Recommended) option. This type of backup does not clear the files' archive

attributes and retains the application backup logs. If you are using only Windows Server Backup, select the VSS full backup option. Then select Next.

8. The Confirmation screen opens. This recounts the drive (or drives) to be backed up, the destination for the backup, and the advanced settings for the backup (VSS copy or VSS full). Click Backup to back up the drive or drives.

9. The Backup utility creates a volume shadow copy of the drive. You are then asked to insert a labeled DVD (or CD) if you are using removable media. Then click OK. The backup medium will be formatted if necessary and the drive (or drives) will be backed up. If you are backing up a large volume or doing a full system backup, you are prompted to supply multiple DVDs (or CDs) to complete the process.

10. When the process is complete, click Close.

A drive window may open showing the backup file on the current removable media. You can close this window. The information related to the backup appears in the Status area of the Windows Server Backup snap-in. This includes the status and the time and date of the backup.

Restoring Files

Because regular backups are really the only complete way to protect valuable information, you should also become familiar with the flip side of backing up data, which is restoring data. If a server fails or a user with specific file permissions inadvertently destroys important data, your backup can quickly restore the information to the network.

The restore process enables you to take advantage of the backup files that you have stored on various backup media such as DVDs or on a network share. You specify the backup file that should be restored and the location to which it should be restored.To restore files to your server follow these steps:

1. In the Windows Server Backup snap-in, select Recover in the Actions pane. The Recovery Wizard opens.

2. On the first screen, specify whether you want to recover the data from the local computer or another computer (on the network). If you backed up to media on the local computer such as DVDs, select This Server (which is the default option). Then click Next.

3. On the next screen, specify the date, time, and location (the location of the backup file) for the recovery (see Figure 6.21). Then click Next.

FIGURE 6.21
Specify the
date, time, and
location of the
backup file for
the recovery.

4. You can recover specific files and folders or an entire volume if you backed up to a network share or available local drive. If you used removable media for your backup, you are limited to recovering an entire volume. Let's assume that we are restoring from a DVD. Select the Volumes option button and then click Next.

By the Way

Individual files and folders cannot be recovered from removable media such as DVDs. You can, however, recover an entire volume from removable media.

5. On the next screen, you specify the volume that you want to restore by selecting it in the appropriate check box. Then use the drop-down Destination Volume menu (see Figure 6.22) to select the destination for the restored volume. Then click Next to continue.

6. A message appears informing you that all data on the destination volume will be lost. Click Yes to continue. Then click Recover. You are asked to supply removable media as needed (if you used removable media such as DVDs). Click OK to continue.

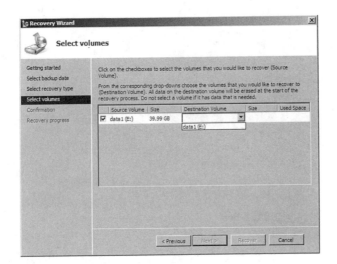

FIGURE 6.22
Specify the destination for the restored volume.

Creating a Scheduled Backup

Because regular backups are an essential part of a fault tolerance strategy for your network servers, it makes sense to create schedules for your server backups. The Windows Server Backup snap-in enables you to create a backup schedule. To create a backup schedule, follow these steps:

1. In the Windows Server Backup snap-in, select Backup Schedule in the Actions pane. Click Next to bypass the Backup Schedule Wizard's initial screen.

2. On the next screen, specify whether you want to do a full or custom backup (if you select custom, you need to specify the volumes on the next screen). Let's assume that you want to schedule a full backup for your server. Click Full Server (Recommended) if necessary (this is the default option). Then click Next.

3. On the next screen (see Figure 6.23), specify the time for the backup (if once daily). You can also specify More than once a day and specify the time for each of these backups.

4. On the next screen specify the destination disk for the scheduled backup. You can click Show All Available Disks to browse for the destination. After specifying the destination, click Next.

FIGURE 6.23
Specify the time
(or times) for
the scheduled
backup.

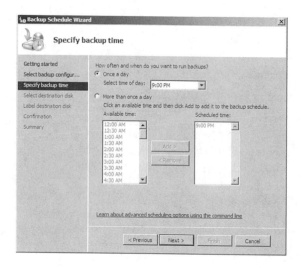

If you are using a fixed drive on the server for backup, the drive is formatted for backups only. The drive is not visible in Windows Explorer when you browse the drives on the server. When the information dialog box opens alerting you to the fact that the drive will be formatted for backups (and all data on the drive will be lost) make sure that you have specified the correct drive before selecting Yes.

5. The Confirmation screen appears. Look over the summary information provided and then click Finish.

Scheduled backups appear in the Details pane of the Windows Server Backup snap-in. You can view the settings for a scheduled backup by selecting View details (for that specific backup).

You can also modify or stop a scheduled backup. Click the Backup Schedule command in the Actions pane. Click Modify Backup (or Stop Backup if you just want to stop the backup from running) and then click Next. If you are modifying the backup, you are walked through the same steps that were used to create the backup schedule and you can change the various settings as needed.

Summary

In this hour, you learned how to manage server drives and create volumes. Windows Server 2008 provides two tools for configuring and managing your server drives: the Disk Management snap-in (available in both the MMC and the Server Manager) and DiskPart, a command-line utility. Windows Server 2008 supports two drive types: basic and dynamic. A basic disk can contain volumes that embrace the legacy partitioning and logical drive scheme that originated with MS-DOS. Dynamic drives can be divided into simple and other volume types, including RAID implementations such as mirror sets and RAID 5 arrays. All drives are basic when you first install the server software; however, you can convert your basic drives to dynamic drives at any time.

The Disk Management snap-in, which is found in the Windows Management console or the Server Manager, can be used to create partitions, format basic disks, and create volumes and RAID arrays on dynamic disks. A RAID 1 array is also known as a mirror set. RAID 5 requires three separate drives with the same amount of disk space to create a disk stripe set.

RAID, or Redundant Array of Independent Disks, enables you to build redundancy and fault tolerance into your servers. RAID 1 is a mirror set, in which two drives mirror each other, supplying a complete copy of a particular drive. When the files change on one drive in the mirror set, they are also changed in the other mirror drive.

RAID 5 enables you to stripe data across three or more drives. This not only speeds up write and access time to the drive set, but because parity data is collected on the array, the data on a stripe set drive that fails can be rebuilt from the information held on the other drives.

Another way to build fault tolerance into your network is to regularly back up your server drives. Windows Server 2008 provides a new Backup utility, Windows Server Backup, that can be used to back up and restore volumes, folders, and files. It is important to develop a backup plan that will protect your data in any situation.

Q&A

Q. *What utility is provided by Windows Server 2008 for managing disk drives, partitions, and volumes?*

A. The Disk Manager provides all the tools for formatting, creating, and managing drive volumes and partitions.

Q. *What is the difference between a basic and dynamic drive in the Windows Server 2008 environment?*

A. A basic disk embraces the MS-DOS disk structure; a basic disk can be divided into partitions (simple volumes). Dynamic disks consist of a single partition that can be divided into any number of volumes. Dynamic disks also support Windows Server 2008 RAID implementations.

Q. *What is RAID?*

A. RAID, or Redundant Array of Independent Disks, is a strategy for building fault tolerance into your file servers. RAID enables you to combine one or more volumes on separate drives so that they are accessed by a single drive letter. Windows Server 2008 enables you to configure RAID 0 (a striped set), RAID 1 (a mirror set), and RAID 5 (disk striping with parity).

Q. *What is the most foolproof strategy for protecting data on the network?*

A. Regular backups of network data provides the best method of protecting you from data loss.

PART II

Network Users, Resources, and Special Server Roles

HOUR 7

Working with TCP/IP Network Protocols

What You'll Learn in This Hour:

▶ Understanding Network Protocols and the OSI Model

▶ Understanding TCP/IP

▶ IPv6 Addressing

▶ Configuring IP Settings

▶ Checking IP Configurations and Server Connectivity

This hour looks at the ins and outs of the TCP/IP protocol stack. The IP protocol has become the de facto (really the only) protocol stack for networking because of the need for network connectivity to the Internet. This hour also looks at the basics of IPv4 subnetting and issues related to implementing IPv6 on a network. The discussion also includes the OSI model (the conceptual model for network protocol stacks) and TCP/IP configuration issues on domain servers and domain clients.

Understanding Network Protocols and the OSI Model

From the genesis of computer networking to the high-speed TCP/IP LANs and WANs that we work with today, network protocols have provided the rules for how computers communicate on a network. Most network protocols are typically not single protocols, but a stack of specialized protocols that work together. Some of these member protocols in the stack are responsible for the user interface and network connections necessary to move the data. Other member protocols in a stack actually address the data (to get it to the right destination). Still others provide the mechanism for transporting the data to and from places on the network.

A number of different protocol stacks have come and gone over the years. NetBEUI (which was designed for workgroups) was once a popular network protocol for small Microsoft networks, and networks using Novell's SPX/IPX protocol stack were the rule during Novell's dominance of the networking arena. With the development of the Internet infrastructure over the last 30 years, the TCP/IP protocol stack has become the dominant protocol stack for all sizes of networks from the small office or home workgroup to extremely large corporate domains.

By the Way

> IPX/SPX (which stands for Internetwork Packet Exchange/Sequenced Packet Exchange) is a network protocol stack developed by Novell for use on networks running early versions of the Novell NetWare network operating system (NetWare now uses TCP/IP as its default networking protocol). NWlink is Microsoft's implementation of IPX/SPX, and was used on network clients and servers in situations where a mixed network of Windows and Novell servers both existed on the network.

Understanding a rather complex protocol stack such as TCP/IP can be aided when the real world protocol stack, in this case TCP/IP, is compared to a conceptual model that provides insight into what each protocol layer in the TCP/IP stack is actually responsible for. In the late 1970s, the International Standards Organization (ISO) began to develop a conceptual model for networking called the Open Systems Interconnect Reference Model. This is now commonly abbreviated as the *OSI model*. In 1983, the model became the international standard for network communications, providing a conceptual framework that helps explain how data gets from one place to another on a network.

The OSI model describes network communication as a series of seven layers; each layer is responsible for a different part of the overall process of moving data. This framework of a layered stack, while conceptual, can then be used to understand how actual protocol stacks work when data moves from a sending computer to a receiving computer. So don't think of the model as a series of layers, but rather as a stack of protocols, with each protocol handing off the data to the next protocol in the stack.

Table 7.1 provides a list of the OSI model layers from the top of the stack to the bottom, with a brief description of each layer. The layers are actually numbered from bottom to top and are often referred to by the layer number (in discussions related to the OSI model). Data moves from the sending computer down the OSI model stack. Then, when it is received by the receiving computer as a bit stream, the data moves back up the model until it is in a form that can be understood by the receiving user (such as an email message).

TABLE 7.1 The OSI Layers

Layer Number	Layer	Function
7	Application	Provides the interface and services that support user applications and provides general access to the network.
6	Presentation	The translator of the OSI model. Responsible for the conversion of data into a generic format and the coding of data using various encryption methods.
5	Session	Establishes and maintains the communication link between communicating computers (sending and receiving).
4	Transport	Responsible for end-to-end data transmission, flow control, error checking, and recovery.
3	Network	Provides the logical addressing system that is used to route data from one node to another, meaning that it is responsible for path determination.
2	Data Link	Responsible for framing of data packets and the data movement across the physical link between two nodes.
1	Physical	Manages the process of sending and receiving bits over the physical network media (the wire and other physical devices).

A protocol stack such as TCP/IP can be mapped to the OSI model. This enables you to understand the general purpose of each protocol in the TCP/IP stack. Let's take a look at the TCP/IP stack and then we can tackle some specifics related to configuring TCP/IP on a server and working with IP addressing.

> The TCP/IP protocol suite was actually developed before the OSI model was created. In fact, a model known as the Department of Defense (DOD) model was used in the development of TCP/IP. Despite these facts, the OSI model is still used today to explain how the different protocols in the TCP/IP stack function in the sending and receiving of data on a network.

By the Way

Understanding TCP/IP

The TCP/IP protocol suite is often referred to as the *Internet protocol suite* because it was created during the development of the Internet. As it later became integrated into all UNIX servers, TCP/IP entered wide use with large networks (often referred to as *enterprise networks*). TCP/IP's scalability from small to large networks and the current heavy interest in connecting LANs to the Internet has enabled TCP/IP to evolve into the most widely used network protocol today. TCP/IP is installed by default on your server running Windows Server 2008. TCP/IP is actually required by the Active Directory and the access protocols that are used to access Active Directory information.

Figure 7.1 shows the TCP/IP stack mapped to the OSI model (it doesn't map exactly to the seven layers, but it does provide some insight into what the TCP/IP protocols do). The list that follows describes a number of the protocols in the TCP/IP stack, which pop up in other hours in this book.

FIGURE 7.1
The TCP/IP protocol mapped to the OSI model.

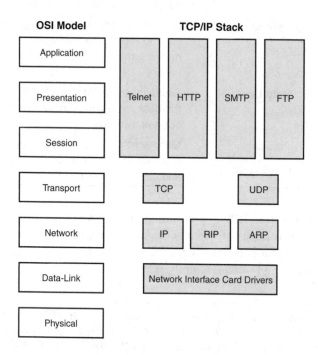

▶ **File Transfer Protocol (FTP)**—FTP provides a method for transferring files between computers.

▶ **Telnet**—With Telnet, users can log on to remote systems across a network.

▶ **Simple Mail Transport Protocol (SMTP)**—SMTP defines the standard for all email sent across the Internet.

▶ **Simple Network Management Protocol (SNMP)**—SNMP makes it possible to collect network information. SNMP uses agents that collect data on network performance. SNMP is discussed in more detail later in the hour.

▶ **Transmission Control Protocol (TCP)**—TCP is the primary transport-layer protocol used within TCP/IP. It provides a reliable, connection-oriented data transportation service in conjunction with IP (defined in the following section). When establishing a connection, TCP uses a port address to determine for which connection a packet is destined. TCP also provides the capability to fragment messages and reassemble packets through sequencing.

▶ **User Datagram Protocol (UDP)**—UDP provides a connectionless transportation service on top of IP.

▶ **Internet Protocol (IP)**—All network addressing and routing in TCP/IP network is handled by IP. IP provides a connectionless datagram service for fast but unreliable communication between network nodes.

▶ **Address Resolution Protocol (ARP)**—ARP is a network-layer protocol that maps hardware addresses to IP addresses for delivery of packets on the local network segment.

▶ **Internet Control Message Protocol (ICMP)**—ICMP is a messaging service and management protocol for IP. ICMP messages are actually carried as IP datagrams. ICMP messages are used for a variety of purposes. The ping command, for example, uses ICMP echo packets.

▶ **Routing Information Protocol (RIP)**—RIP is a distance-vector routing protocol that determines the shortest path between two locations by counting the number of *hops* (basically the number of routers that the packet must traverse) that a packet has to make.

▶ **Open Shortest Path First (OSPF)**—OSPF is a newer link-state routing protocol that is more efficient and needs less overhead than RIP.

IPv4 Addressing

IP addressing comes in two different formats: IPv4 and IPv6, both of which are supported by Windows Server 2008. Let's take a look at IPv4 first. With IPv4, each computer (or device, which is referred to as a *node*) is assigned a 32-bit IP address that resembles the following:

    192.168.24.123

The 32-bit address is divided into four groups of eight bits, called *octets*, with each octet written as a decimal number from 0 to 255, separated from the others by a period (referred to as a *dot*). Part of the IP address defines the network ID of your network (which is assigned to you when you purchase a range of public IP addresses); the remainder of the address provides the host ID of the individual computer. For instance, the 24.123 in the preceding address might identify a specific computer within the TCP/IP network that has the address 192.168. Note that within TCP/IP networking, the term *host* is used to refer to a computer on the network.

Three address classes are used for IP addressing:

▶ Class A is used for very large networks. The default mask is 255.0.0.0. Class A networks range from 1.0.0.0 through 126.0.0.0. Class A networks provide 16,777,214 host addresses. This is because the second, third, and fourth octets are available for host addressing. ARPANET is an example of a Class A network. Class A addresses provide network and host information in the format network.host.host.host.

▶ Class B is used for networks that still need a lot of node addresses, such as a large company or institution. Class B ranges from 128.0.0.0 to 191.0.0.0. The default subnet mask is 255.255.0.0. There are 16,384 Class B network addresses, with each Class B supplying 65,534 host addresses. The third and fourth octets are available for host addressing. Class B addresses provide network and host information in the format network.network.host.host.

▶ Class C is used for small networks. There are 2,097,152 Class C networks. Class C addresses range from 192.0.0.0 to 223.0.0.0. The default subnet mask is 255.255.255.0. Class C networks provide 254 host addresses per network because only the fourth octet is reserved for host addressing. Class C addresses provide the network and host information in the format network.network.network.host.

▶ Two other classes of IP addresses should also be mentioned: Class D and Class E. Class D network addresses are used by multicast groups receiving data from a particular application or server service. An example of a multicast use of Class D addresses is Microsoft NetShow, which can broadcast the same content to a group of users at one time. Class E addresses belong to an experimental class, which is not used for public IP addressing.

IPv4 has been around for nearly 20 years and is actually the fourth version of the IP addressing protocol. IPv4 actually provides a total of 3706.65 million usable IP addresses. Because we will probably run out of IPv4 addresses at some point (there are millions of IPv4 addresses being assigned each year worldwide to end-users and Internet service providers: think about all those new handheld Wi-Fi devices that are coming online), IPv6, which provides a much larger address space than IPv4, is supported by both Windows Server 2008 and Windows Vista. We talk more about IPv6 addressing later in this hour.

By the Way

Understanding what part of the IP address refers to the network and what part refers to the host is a very important aspect of working with IP addresses. And you can't really determine either without seeing the subnet mask that goes with the IP address.

Subnet masks are also represented as four dotted-decimal octets. There is a standard subnet mask for each of the IP address classes. For example, the IP address 10.1.1.1 (a Class A address) would have the standard Class A subnet mask of 255.0.0.0.

255 = ALL one in BINARY

This combination of the IP address and subnet mask enables you to determine what portion of the address is the network address and which portion provides the host address. Because the 255 (all ones in binary) "ands" out the network portion of the address, only the first octet of the address 10.1.1.1 specifies the network address (10.0.0.0). The second, third, and fourth octets provide the host addressing (0.1.1.1). Table 7.2 provides the default subnet masks for Class A, B, and C networks.

TABLE 7.2 Typical Subnet Masks

Subnet Mask	IP Address Class
255.0.0.0	Class A
255.255.0.0	Class B
255.255.255.0	Class C

Understanding IPv4 Subnetting

IPv4 subnetting is as much art as it is math. When you subnet a range of IP addresses, you are dividing the available addresses into logical subunits. Subnetting enables you to place subnets or logical groupings (in terms of IP addresses) of computers on different router interfaces. This enables you to connect disparate groups of users (at different worksites) into one large IP network.

Subnetting is a two-part process. First, you must determine the subnet mask for the network (it is different from the default subnet masks shown in Table 7.3). Then you must compute the range of IP addresses that will be in each subnet. One way to subnet is to refer to subnetting charts. Tables 7.3, 7.4, and 7.5 show Class A, Class B, and Class C subnetting, respectively.

TABLE 7.3   Class A Subnetting

Bits Used	Subnet Mask	# of Subnets	Hosts/ Subnet
2	255.192.0.0	2	4,194,302
3	255.224.0.0	6	2,097,150
4	255.240.0.0	14	1,048,574
5	255.248.0.0	30	524,286
6	255.252.0.0	62	262,142
7	255.254.0.0	126	131,070
8	255.255.0.0	254	65,534

TABLE 7.4   Class B Subnetting

Bits Used	Subnet Mask	# of Subnets	Hosts/ Subnet
2	255.255.192.0	2	16,382
3	255.255.224.0	6	8,190
4	255.255.240.0	14	4,094
5	255.255.248.0	30	2,046
6	255.255.252.0	62	1,022
7	255.255.254.0	126	510
8	255.255.255.0	254	254

TABLE 7.5   Class C Subnetting

Bits Used	Subnet Mask	# of Subnets	Hosts/ Subnet
2	255.255.255.192	2	62
3	255.255.255.224	6	30
4	255.255.255.240	14	14
5	255.255.255.248	30	6
6	255.255.255.252	62	2

Converting Decimal to Binary

Now the question is, what do these charts mean? IP addresses are actually seen by the computers on the network as a bit stream (a collection of ones and zeros). The address 130.1.16.1 would be represented in binary as this:

10000010 00000001 00010000 00000001   *32 BITS*

CLASS B   *130*   *1*   *16*   *1*

Notice that the bits have been divided into four groups of eight, or octets, just as the dotted-decimal version of the address was (130.1.16.1).

This is how you convert dotted-decimal numbers to binary (bits). Each octet has 8 bits. The decimal value of the bits in an octet, from left to right, is as follows:

128 64 32 16 8 4 2 1   *DECIMAL VALUE OF BITS — OCTET*

So, the decimal number 130 in the first octet of this address is determined by 128 + 2. This means that the first bit (the 128 bit) and the seventh bit (the 2 bit) are both turned on (they are represented by ones in the binary format). To convert the decimal to the binary, you mark the bits that are turned on with ones and the rest with zeros. You get 10000010 (which is what you saw previously in the binary format of the IP address).

Now about subnetting: Because the network ID portion of IP addresses is fixed (it is provided by your Internet service provider or another provider of IP address ranges), you actually borrow some bits from the leftmost portion of the host ID of the address to create subnets. (Remember, you can't mess with the network ID portion of the IP address because it is assigned to you.) Let's walk through an example of subnetting.

Imagine that you want to divide the Class B network of 191.1.0.0 (this is the network address you were assigned by your IP address provider) into 30 subnets.

You can't touch the first or second octets because they have been assigned. But you can borrow bits starting from the leftmost portion of the third octet. So, you have to determine how may bits you must borrow from the third octet to create 30 subnets. The number of bits that you borrow determines the new subnet mask for your network (which lets all devices on the network know that the network has been divided into 30 logical subnets). The bits you borrow also help you determine the range of IP addresses that will be in each subnet.

Borrowing Bits

First you borrow the bits; you use the decimal values of the bits in the third octet to do this. You want to come up with 30 subnets. The formula that you use to do this is the sum of lower-order bits (required to get as close to 30 as possible) minus 1 (you must subtract 1 because the 0 network address is used for broadcast messages).

Look at the bit values again (shown next). The lower-order bits are the ones on the right (1, 2, 4, and so on). So, you add $1 + 2 + 4 + 8 + 16$, which equals 31. Then you subtract 1. You get 30. So, you used the 1, 2, 4, 8, and 16 bits; you borrowed 5 bits.

128 64 32 16 8 4 2 1 < lower-order bits

By the Way

> You have to subtract the 1 because you cannot use subnet 0, which is what you derive when you steal only the first lower-order bit (the 1).

The next thing you need to do is determine the subnet mask for the subnetted network. The bits on the left of the decimal values (128, 64, 32, 16, and so on) are referred to as the *higher-order bits*. You now add the first five higher-order bits:

Higher-order bits> 128 64 32 16 8 4 2 1

$128 + 64 + 32 + 16 + 8 = 248$

The default subnet mask for a Class B network is 255.255.0.0.

You borrowed 5 bits from the third octet, so your new subnet mask is 255.255.248.0. Check Table 7.4; when you borrow 5 bits from a Class B network, you get the subnet mask that you derived.

 Computing the number of host addresses available per subnet is very straightforward. The formula you use is 2^X-2, where X is the number of bits left for host addresses after bits have been borrowed for subnetting.

Computing the Host Addresses in a Subnet

You have 30 subnets (remember, that's what you decided to divide the IP address range into at the outset of this problem). Now you can find out how many addresses you will get for each of the 30 subnets. Normally, on a Class B network, two octets are reserved for host addresses. The network address in this case is 191.1.0.0, so originally two full octets (the third and fourth) were available for node addresses. This was 16 bits total (8 bits from each octet). Then you borrowed 5 bits from the third octet, so $16-5 = 11$. You have 11 bits left for node addresses after borrowing 5 bits to create the 30 subnets.

Use the formula 2^X-2. You can see that $2^{11}-2$ is 2,048–2, which equals 2,046 (just as Table 7.4 shows). You get 2,046 addresses per subnet.

Computing Host Ranges

You now have 30 subnets with 2,046 addresses each. Next you need to determine the starting and ending IP addresses for each subnet. This is rather easy, compared to what you've done so far. What was the lowest of the higher-order bits used to create the new subnet mask for the subnetted network? You used 128, 64, 32, 16, and 8. The lowest of the high-order bits is 8, which becomes the increment for your subnet address ranges.

The network address is 191.1.0.0, so the first subnet would start with the address 191.1.8.1 (you can't have a zero in the last position of the address). This subnet would end with 191.1.15.254 (you can't end an address with 255 in the last octet).

Table 7.6 shows the range of addresses for the first 5 subnets (of 30) using the network address of 191.1.0.0.

TABLE 7.6 Address Ranges for First Six Subnets

Subnet	Address Range
1	191.1.8.1 to 191.1.15.254
2	191.1.16.1 to 191.1.23.254
3	191.1.24.1 to 191.1.31.254
4	191.1.32.1 to 191.1.39.254
5	191.1.40.1 to 191.1.47.254

Notice that you can easily come up with the start of each subnet range by adding 8 to the third octet. The ends of range addresses are just one less (in the third octet) than the start of the next subnet. You could easily continue this table to show all 30 subnets.

Class A and C network addresses can be subnetted in a like manner. Just remember that Class A networks provide you three octets of node address space (the second, third, and fourth), whereas a Class C network address supplies only one octet (the fourth).

Another way to do subnetting calculations is to download a subnet calculator on the Web. Several free ones can be found by doing a search for *subnet calculator* in any search engine. You can then tell the calculator how many subnets you want for a specific network address and it gives the subnet mask and the range of addresses for each subnet. It's easy, but it requires that you at least understand what subnetting is so that you know what the calculator is telling you.

Did you Know?

IPv6 Addressing

IP Version 6 (IPv6) was developed under the auspices of the Internet Engineering Task Force (IETF) and was first defined in RFC (Request for Comments) 2460. In terms of functionality, IPv6 is kind of like an extension of IPv4, and the application and transport protocols in the TCP/IP stack don't really need a lot of tweaking to work with IPv6. (FTP, believe it or not, is actually an exception.) IPv6 uses a 128-bit addressing system that provides 40,282,366,920,938,463,463,374,607,431, 768,211,456 addresses. This is certainly a very large number of IP addresses, and it should be a little more difficult to exhaust this pool of addresses when you compare it to the smaller pool of addresses that was provided by IPv4.

You can take a look at the RFCs related to IPv6 (and IPv4) at the IETF Documents website. Go to http://tools.ietf.org/html/. You can also use any web search engine to locate RFCs on the Web.

The IPv6 address is a hexadecimal address that consists of eight 16-bit parts or blocks. Each 16-bit block is delineated by a colon (:). A sample address is

FE80:BA98:7654:3210:FEDC:BA98:7654:3210

In terms of comparing an IPv6 address to how we view an IPv4 address (in terms of what part of the address provides the network ID and what part provides the host ID), IPv6 addresses basically split the available bits in half; the first 64 bits provide the network prefix and the last 64 bits provide the interface ID as shown in Figure 7.2. (IPv6 identifies interfaces rather than hosts.)

FIGURE 7.2
IPv6 addresses divide the bits in an address equally to identify the network prefix and the interface ID.

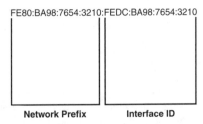

Network Prefix   Interface ID

IPv6 is a more secure addressing protocol than IPv4 in that IPSec (discussed in Hour 21, "Working with the Windows Firewall and IPSec") is built into the protocol rather than an add-on, as it was with IPv4.

The network prefix is really a combination of information. The first 48 bits of the area designated as the network prefix (see Figure 7.2) is the site prefix, which would be the equivalent of the network ID in an IPv4 address. So, in the address

    FE80:BA98:7654:3210:FEDC:BA98:7654:3210

the FE80:BA98:7654, meaning the first three 16-bit parts (for a total of 48 bits), would be the public portion of the IPv6 address in that it identifies your network. The next 16-bit part in the address (the fourth 16-bit part) would then be used to identify the subnet ID; so it is the fourth 16-bit part of the IPv6 address that is used to create subnets for networks.

IPv4 addressing is approached by typically assigning a single IP address to each node on the network (although some servers obviously will have multiple IPv4 addresses for load balancing and special services that require more than one network interface, such as routing or Network Address Translation). IPv6 addressing is approached differently and each interface on a node (a node being a computer or pretty much any type of IP-enabled device) is assigned both a global and a link-local address.

The global or global unicast address is the equivalent of a public IPv4 address and is used to route data to other networks (or *links*, as they are referred to in IPv6 lingo). The link-local address is used by nodes to communicate with other nodes the local network or link.

> IPv6 really assigns three IP addresses to an interface: link-local, global, and loopback. The loopback address for IPv6 is ::1.

By the Way

So, the question then becomes, How are IPv6 addresses assigned to nodes (and their interfaces) on the network? You have three alternatives: the new IPv6 self-addressing strategy, termed *stateless auto-configuration*; a DHCP (DHCPv6) server; or manually assigned, static IPv6 addresses.

Stateless auto-configuration enables an interface to dynamically assign itself an IPv6 link-local address. The address is generated from the interface's MAC hardware address (which is 48 bits; an additional 16 bits are added to make the 64-bit interface ID portion of the IPv6 address). Figure 7.3 shows the auto-configuration link-local address generated by an IPv6-enabled server.

FIGURE 7.3
The IPv6 link-
local address is
auto-generated
by the IP client.

```
Administrator: Command Prompt                                              _ □ ×
Microsoft Windows [Version 6.0.6001]
Copyright (c) 2006 Microsoft Corporation.  All rights reserved.

C:\Users\Administrator>ipconfig/all

Windows IP Configuration

   Host Name . . . . . . . . . . . . . : ender
   Primary Dns Suffix  . . . . . . . . : spinach.com
   Node Type . . . . . . . . . . . . . : Hybrid
   IP Routing Enabled. . . . . . . . . : Yes
   WINS Proxy Enabled. . . . . . . . . : No
   DNS Suffix Search List. . . . . . . : spinach.com
   System Quarantine State . . . . . . : Not Restricted

Ethernet adapter Local Area Connection 2:

   Connection-specific DNS Suffix  . :
   Description . . . . . . . . . . . . : Intel(R) PRO/1000 MT Network Connection #
   2
   Physical Address. . . . . . . . . . : 00-0C-29-2D-57-67
   DHCP Enabled. . . . . . . . . . . . : No
   Autoconfiguration Enabled . . . . . : Yes
   Link-local IPv6 Address . . . . . . : fe80::d127:f078:e9eb:fcc3%13(Preferred)
   IPv4 Address. . . . . . . . . . . . : 10.8.0.1(Preferred)
   Subnet Mask . . . . . . . . . . . . : 255.248.0.0
   Default Gateway . . . . . . . . . . :
   DNS Servers . . . . . . . . . . . . : 10.8.0.1
   NetBIOS over Tcpip. . . . . . . . . : Enabled
```

In terms of DHCP, you can deploy a DHCP server running Windows Server 2008 to provide IPv6 addresses to network clients. DHCP is discussed in Hour 16, "Using the Dynamic Host Configuration Protocol."

As already mentioned, you can also configure a network client with a static IPv6 address. When you specify a static IPv6 address for an interface (configuring TCP/IP settings is discussed in the next section), the auto-configuration is still enabled and so an auto-configured address as well as the static address (you assign) is assigned to the interface.

In terms of subnetting, you already saw that the fourth 16-bit portion of the IPv6 address contains the subnet ID. This provides you with 16 possible bits for your IPv6 subnets (which can then be configured as scopes on subnet DHCP servers). These "subnet prefixes" can actually be advertised by network routers and supplied to IPv6 clients in a specific subnet.

Working with IPv6 addressing is obviously a little more intimidating when compared to working with IPv4 addressing, mainly because IPv6 addresses are larger; after you get used to working in hexadecimal rather than dotted decimal, you will find that IPv6 addressing really is easier to work with and you no longer have to deal with subnet masks.

By the Way

IPv6 does not use broadcasts the way that IPv4 does. This helps cut down on network broadcast traffic on subnets. IPv6 uses multicast addressing and multicasts, negating the need for broadcasts to all nodes.

Configuring IP Settings

IPv4 and IPv6 are installed by default on your server running Windows Server 2008 (the same goes for Windows Vista clients). You reach the IP settings (IPv4 or IPv6) via the Local Area Connection dialog box. You can open this dialog box by right-clicking on a Local Area Connection icon in the Network Connections window (which can be opened via the Server Manager by clicking the View Network Connections link or opened via the Control Panel). The Local Area Connection dialog box lists the various networking protocols and network clients that are installed on the computer (see Figure 7.4). The clients and protocols that are currently enabled are denoted selected check boxes.

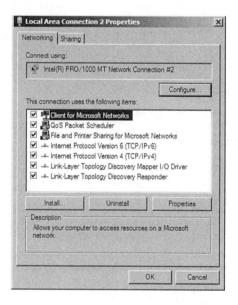

FIGURE 7.4
The installed networking protocols and clients are shown in the Local Area Connection dialog box.

As already mentioned, you can access IPv4 or IPv6 properties from the Local Area Connection dialog box. For example, click the Internet Protocol Version 4 (TCP/IP)v4 item and then click Properties. The Internet Protocol Version 4 (TCP/IP)v4 Properties dialog box opens.

By default, both Vista clients and servers running Windows 2008 Server are configured to obtain their IP addresses automatically. To manually configure static IP settings for a server (domain controllers and other specialized servers such as DNS and DHCP servers should be configured with static IP addresses), click the Use the Following IP Addresses option button (see Figure 7.5).

FIGURE 7.5
Configure a
server with a
static IP
address.

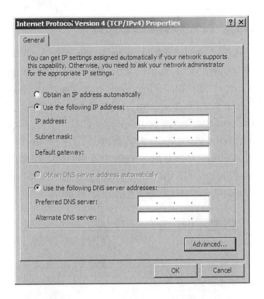

You can enter the IP address, subnet mask, default gateway, and preferred DNS
address for the server. (For IPv6 addressing you need to supply only the IPv6 address
and the default gateway address.) You can also set additional IP settings by clicking
the Advanced button on the Properties dialog box. This opens the Advanced TCP/IP
Settings dialog box. This dialog box includes the following tabs:

▶ **IP Settings**—Enables you to add, edit, or remove IP addresses and default
gateways. (Yes, you can assign multiple IP addresses to a single network
adapter.)

▶ **DNS**—Enables you to add multiple DNS servers to the TCP/IP configuration
and register this computer with the DNS server.

▶ **WINS**—Enables you to specify WINS servers (also known as *NetBIOS name
servers*) to be included in the TCP/IP configuration.

After making changes to the advanced TCP/IP settings, click OK to close the dialog
box. You can also close the Internet Protocol (TCP/IP) Properties dialog box and the
Local Area Connection Properties dialog box.

Checking IP Configurations and Server Connectivity

Windows Server 2008 provides command-line tools that can help you check IP configurations and connectivity. For example, `ipconfig` can be used to both check and renew the IP configuration on a Windows server. The `netstat` command is used to list of the active TCP and UDP connections on your server. The `ping` command is used to check a computer's connection to any device on a network that is configured with an IP address.

Commands such as `ipconfig`, `netstat`, and `ping` are executed at the command prompt. To open a command prompt, select Start and then select Command Prompt. *START → COMMAND PROMPT*

Using `ipconfig`

You can check IP configurations on your Windows Server 2008 from the command line by using the `ipconfig` command. `ipconfig/all` shows the information for all network interfaces on the server and provides more details than `ipconfig`. Figure 7.6 shows the results of the `ipconfig/all` command.

FIGURE 7.6
The ipconfig/all command.

On servers or clients that receive IP addresses dynamically, you can use the `ipconfig` command to release and renew the IP address assignment. Use `ipconfig/release` when you want to release the old address lease. Use `ipconfig/renew` to renew an IP address lease. Dynamic assignment of IP addresses is discussed in Hour 16.

Using `netstat`

`netstat` displays a list of the active TCP and UDP connections on your server (TCP is the Transport Control Protocol and the *TCP* in TCP/IP; UDP is also a connectionless transport protocol). At the command prompt, type **netstat/a** and press Enter. Figure 7.7 shows the results of this command.

FIGURE 7.7
Netstat shows the TCP and UDP connection on the server.

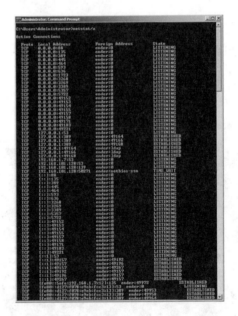

The `netstat` command provides a number of switches. For example, the -s switch displays statistics by protocol in the TCP/IP stack, including TCP, UDP, and IP. The -e switch (which can be combined with the -s switch) displays ethernet statistics, including the number of bytes and packets the computer has sent and received.

Using `ping`

Another useful command is `ping`. It can be used at the command line to send a data packet to any IP address on the network and thereby check connectivity. For example, to see whether your server is connecting to a computer with an IP address 192.5.6.1, you would type **ping 192.5.6**.

If the ping packet reaches the other computer, you get an echo response letting you know that the computer is out there. If it does not reach the computer, you get a request time out, meaning the packet failed to reach the specified destination and did not "bounce" back.

The ping command also provides options that you can specify, such as the number of echo packets to send and the time to wait for a reply. For example, ping -n count is used to specify the number of echo requests that are sent, where count is the number of requests.

Commands such as netstat and ping provide a number of different switches and options. To view the switches for a particular command, type the command, followed by –h (or - ?). A list of the different options is then provided in the command window.

Summary

In this hour, you learned the basics of the TCP/IP protocol and IPv4 and IPv6 addressing. TCP/IP is the most used LAN protocol in the world. An IPv4 address consists of a 32-bit address in the form of a four-octet dotted-decimal number. IPv6 addresses are 128-bit hexadecimal addresses that are divided into eight 16-bit parts. The last 64 bits of the address refer to the client interface and are used to identify the node on the network.

TCP/IP is installed by default on Windows Server 2008 and you can take advantage of both IPv4 and IPv6 addressing via the Local Area Connection Properties dialog box. TCP/IP (v4 or v6) properties such as the IP address, subnet mask, default gateway, and DNS server address are configured in the Internet Protocol (TCP/IP) Properties dialog box (for either v4 or v6).

IP subnetting enables you to subnet your network IP addresses into logical groupings or subnets. IPv4 uses bits from the node address to create subnets. IPv6 provides a specific 16-bit part for subnetting.

The command-line tool `ipconfig` enables you to check a server's IP configuration. Command-line tools such as `netstat` and `ping` enable you to check your active connections and also to check your server's connectivity (respectively) on the network.

Q&A

Q. *What conceptual model helps provide an understanding of how network protocol stacks such as TCP/IP work?*

A. The OSI model, consisting of the application, presentation, session, transport, network, data link, and physical layers, helps describe how data is sent and received on the network by protocol stacks.

Q. *What protocol stack is installed by default when you install Windows Server 2008 on a network server?*

A. TCP/IP (v4 and v6) is the default protocol for Windows Server 2008. It is required for Active Directory implementations and provides for connectivity on heterogeneous networks.

Q. *When TCP/IP is configured on a Windows server (or domain client), what information is required?*

A. You must provide at least the IP address and the subnet mask to configure a TCP/IP client for an IPv4 client, unless that client obtains this information from a DHCP server. For IPv6 clients, the interface ID is generated automatically from the MAC hardware address on the network adapter. IPv6 can also use DHCP as a method to configure IP clients on the network.

Q. *What are two command-line utilities that can be used to check TCP/IP configurations and IP connectivity, respectively?*

A. The `ipconfig` command can be used to check a computer's IP configuration and also renew the client's IP address if it is provided by a DHCP server. `ping` can be used to check the connection between the local computer and any computer on the network, using the destination computer's IP address.

HOUR 8

Understanding and Configuring Active Directory Domain Services

What You'll Learn in This Hour:

▸ Understanding Active Directory Domain Services

▸ Planning the Active Directory Hierarchy

▸ Installing Active Directory Domain Services and Creating the Root Domain

▸ Adding a Regional (Child) Domain

▸ Using the Active Directory Management Tools

▸ Working with Domain User Accounts

▸ Working with Active Directory Objects

To most network professionals who work with Microsoft server platforms, the Active Directory approach to managing users, network devices, and other network resources has become second nature. However, the Active Directory logical structure was only introduced several years ago with the introduction of Windows 2000 Server, which radically changed how an administrator structures a Microsoft network. Such concepts as resource domains, account domains, and the master domain model were replaced by a true hierarchical directory services structure called Active Directory.

Windows Server 2008 also embraces Active Directory as its directory service. Active Directory functionality has been expanded in Windows Server 2008, and the domain hierarchy component of Active Directory is now referred to as *Active Directory Domain Services*. In this hour, we look at the basics of Active Directory Domain Services, its installation, its use, and the Server Manager Active Directory snap-ins.

Understanding Active Directory Domain Services

Active Directory Domain Services (AD DS) is the directory service (a directory service is a database of information that is arranged in a top-down hierarchical manner) for your Windows network; it provides a hierarchical structure for domain management and implementation. The Active Directory provides the namespace for your domains and catalogs users, groups of users, computers, printers, and even security policies in a centralized database that is replicated among domain controllers on the network. Each item, such as a user or a group, is referred to as an *Active Directory object.*

Because Active Directory provides a hierarchical, treelike structure for your domains, sharing resources throughout the domain structure is made easier. And adding new domains to the tree is very straightforward, making the directory service provided by Active Directory highly scaleable.

Planning the Active Directory Hierarchy

Although it doesn't hurt to oversimplify the Active Directory domain hierarchy and characterize it as a branching tree, it is also useful to look at the different levels in the Active Directory hierarchy as administrative containers. This would make the domain the most basic container available. (This is not to ignore the existence of the Organizational Unit, however, which is a very useful Active Directory container; Organizational Units are discussed in Hour 9, "Creating Active Directory Groups, Organizational Units, and Sites.")

The tree, then, (in terms of the Active Directory Domain Services) is a collection of domains. All these domains share the same Global Catalog, which is the central repository for all the objects in a domain (or domain tree). This means that all the domains in the tree can get at the same set of resources, no matter which of the domains in the tree is actually hosting that resource.

When you create a new tree, you are creating a domain that is to serve as the root of the tree. Other domains added to the tree are actually child domains of the root domain (the initial domain that you create is the root—creating the root is discussed in the next section). Figure 8.1 shows a tree root domain called spinach.com. Notice that a number of child domains (such as popeye.spinach.com and wimpy.spinach.com) exist as "subdomains" of the tree root (spinach.com).

Child domains in the tree are in the same namespace as the root domain (the root supplying the root name). The child domains actually take on the root domain name as part of their complete name. This naming convention is also seen in DNS, and child domains in a DNS tree are named in a similar fashion (using the root name as part of the complete name). For more about DNS (which you might want to read before designing your Active Directory tree structure), see Hour 15, "Understanding the Domain Name Service."

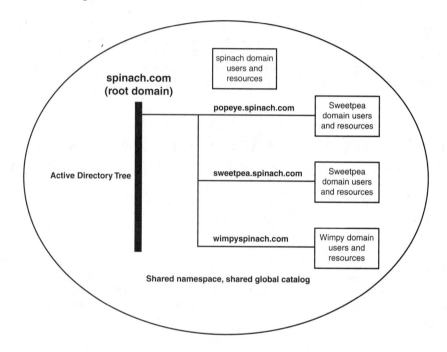

FIGURE 8.1
A Windows Server 2008 Active Directory domain tree.

Although the tree provides an extremely large administrative and security container (you can place a large number of child domains in a tree), there is actually a larger container called a forest. A *forest* is a collection of trees. For example, spinach.com, a tree, could be in a forest with carrot.com, another tree.

Although these trees are managed separately and operate in their own namespaces, they can belong to the same forest; this allows the different domains in these separate trees to share the same Global Catalog. This means that trees in the same forest can share resources (and can locate resources by virtue of sharing the same Global Catalog).

An important aspect of sharing the Global Catalog by domains in the same tree is the replication of this database of Active Directory objects. Global Catalog replication is discussed in Hour 9, in the section "Active Directory Replication and Sites."

By the Way

When you create your first Windows Server 2008 domain, you are creating both a new forest and a new tree. The next section discusses installing Active Directory Domain Services on a Windows Server 2008 installation and creating these administrative and security containers.

> A single Windows Server 2008 domain can serve thousands of users and provide many resources to those users (particularly when a number of specialized servers are used to provide these services). Only very large corporations require a root domain that has child domains in the Active Directory tree. Only the largest of organizations or corporations would require a forest of multiple trees.

Installing Active Directory Domain Services and Creating the Root Domain

Active Directory Domain Services is a server role. You can start the Add Role Wizard from the Initial Configuration Tasks window or the Server Manager.

By the Way

> To install Active Directory Domain Services, you need to have access to at least one server on your network that provides the Domain Name Service (DNS). This can actually be the server on which you are installing Active Directory Domain Services or another server on the network. Bottom line: The Active Directory hierarchy and the DNS namespace are tightly wound together. See Hour 15 for more information on installing and configuring DNS.

Let's assume that you are starting from scratch in terms of establishing your Active Directory hierarchy. This means that you first need to establish a new forest. Then you need a domain controller for the root domain (basically the root of the first tree in your new forest).

The result is a two-step process. First you add the Active Directory Domain Services role and then you specify the current server as a domain controller for the root domain.

To install Active Directory Domain Services, follow these steps:

   1. Open the Add Roles Wizard (click the appropriate icon) in either the Initial Configuration Tasks window or the Server Manager (with the Roles node selected).

2. The first wizard screen suggests that before installing a server role you should assign a strong password to the administrator account, configure static IP addressing (if required by the role), and install the latest Windows 2008 security updates. After you have confirmed that these tasks have been completed, click Next to continue.

3. On the next screen, select the Active Directory Domain Services role (select the appropriate check box as shown in Figure 8.2). Then click Next.

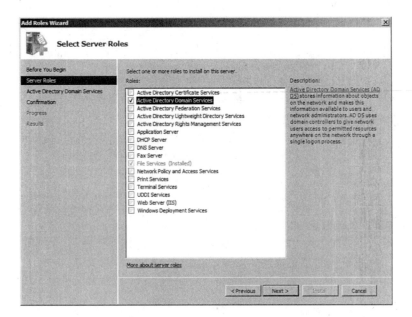

FIGURE 8.2
Select the Active Directory Domain Services.

4. The next screen provides a list of things to note as you proceed with the installation. For example, it suggests that you have at least two domain controllers for each domain (to provide redundancy for logging in users), and that Active Directory requires DNS and you will be prompted to install DNS on the server if you do not have a DNS server on the network. After reading through the notes (additional help links related to AD DS are also provided), click Next.

If you don't have a DNS server available on the network when you attempt to install the Active Directory Domain Services role, it will be added to the server when you promote the server to a domain controller.

By the Way

5. The Install window appears, listing the server roles you will install. In the case of Active Directory Domain Services, it also notes that you will need to use the Active Directory Domain Services Installation Wizard to promote the server to a domain controller. Click Install to continue.

6. The next screen tracks the progress of the Active Directory Domain Services role. When the installation is complete, the Installation Results screen appears. On this screen, click Close This Wizard and Launch the Active Directory Domain Services Installation Wizard (dcpromo.exe).

By the Way

> You can start the Active Directory Domain Services Installation Wizard on any server you want to promote to a domain controller by running `dcpromo.exe` in the Windows Run dialog box (Start, Run).

The Add Roles Wizard closes and the Active Directory Domain Services Installation Wizard opens. This wizard enables you to specify the new forest name and promote the server to a domain controller. Follow these steps:

1. Click Next to bypass the opening wizard screen.

2. On the next screen, click Create a New Domain in a New Forest (see Figure 8.3). Then click Next.

FIGURE 8.3
Specify that a new forest and new domain be created.

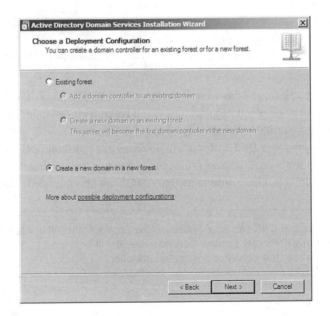

3. On the next screen, type the fully qualified domain name (FQDN) for the forest root domain. This would be the FQDN as defined by your DNS namespace hierarchy. Click Next to continue.

4. The wizard checks to see whether the forest name is already in use and also checks the NetBIOS equivalent name (for the FQDN).

5. The next wizard screen provides a drop-down list that enables you to set the functional level for your forest. The domain functional level is discussed in greater detail in Hour 9; however, the bottom line related to the functional level is that it determines what version of Windows Server (2000, 2003, 2008) you can run on your servers and the additional features that are provided by the functional level.

   The Windows 2000 functional level enables you to have domain controllers in the forest that run Windows 2000 Server, Windows Server 2003, or Windows Server 2008. However, as you raise the functional level (say from Windows 2000 to Windows 2003 or to Windows 2008) you can only use domain controllers with the appropriate version of the Windows NOS installed, but you get more unique and advanced features the newer the NOS.

   Select the appropriate functional level for your forest and then click Next.

If you select Windows Server 2008 as your functional level, you can run domain controllers only when using Windows Server 2008. If you select Windows Server 2003 you can run domain controllers using 2003 and 2008.

By the Way

---

6. The next screen provides a list of additional options for the server, including DNS server, Global Catalog, and Read-Only Domain Controller (RODC). The additional options suggested for installation are based on your network and server configuration (such as an already existing DNS server). Select or deselect options as needed and then click Next.

The first domain controller in the forest must be a global catalog server and also cannot be a read-only domain controller.

By the Way

---

7. The next screen asks you to specify the location for the database folder, the log file, and the SYSVOL folder. Select a location for these files and folders, using the appropriate text boxes (see Figure 8.4), and then click Next.

FIGURE 8.4
Specify the location for the database folder, log file, and SYSVOL folder.

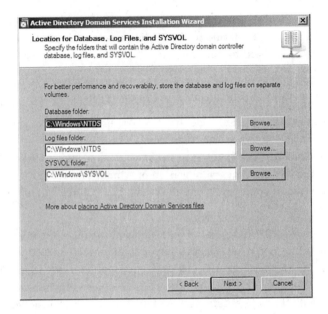

Did you Know?

> You should configure your network server with multiple volumes. At least two volumes are required if you want to back up database, log, and SYSVOL files using the Windows Backup feature. The backup files are held on the volume that does not serve as the volume where you installed the database folder, log file, and SYSVOL folder when installing Active Directory. Working with server drives and volumes is discussed in Hour 6, "Managing Hard Drives and Volumes."

8. On the next wizard page, you must set the Directory Services Restore Mode Administrator password. This password is used to start the Active Directory in the Directory Service Restore Mode. As with all passwords, you should use a strong password, which takes advantage of numbers, alphanumeric characters and different case levels. Enter the password and then enter it a second time to confirm the password, and then click Next.

9. The summary screen then appears, listing your selections and settings. If you need to change any of these settings, click Back. To continue, click Next.

10. The Active Directory Domain Services will be configured according to your settings and selections. When the wizard has completed the configuration, the exit screen appears. Click Finish. You need to restart the server to complete the installation and configuration of Active Directory. Click Restart Now.

After you've installed Active Directory Domain Services, established the forest (and root domain), and brought the first domain controller online, you are ready to begin expanding the logical hierarchy for your network. This process includes the addition of child domains (if needed), the deployment of additional domain controllers, and the population of the Active Directory with users and devices. Let's take a look at adding a child domain and then take a walkthrough of the various Active Directory tools you will typically use.

Adding a Regional (Child) Domain

After the root domain has been created, any number of child domains can be added to the domain tree. Windows Server 2008 puts a slightly different spin on the notion of the child domain (in comparison to Windows 2000 Server and Windows Server 2003). Because a single domain can accommodate a very large corporation, it's really not necessary to create a tree of domains that mimics the company's corporate structure. So, despite what the engineers or the marketing people say, they don't need to have their own domains. The domain hierarchy provides groups that can be used to handle access issues for related groups of users (such as the engineers or marketing people).

Child domains or *regional domains* (Microsoft now prefers the latter term) are best used in situations where regional offices should be outfitted with their own domain controllers that "control" a regional domain. The domain structure for the organization would have a root domain (the tree) and these regional domains would be regional domains (subdomains, if you will) that branch off the main root domain.

Each regional domain controller would be a replication partner with the first domain controller that you brought online when you created the root domain (meaning your domain controller for the root domain). Each regional domain would reside in a site that would define the geographic location of the domain and allow you to determine the intersite replication that takes place between the various sites in the domain hierarchy (we talk more about sites in Hour 9.

To create the regional (child) domain and bring the first domain controller online in that new domain, you use the Add Roles Wizard to install the Active Directory Domain Services (as we did when we created the forest and root domain and brought the first domain controller online in the root domain).

The process of creating the child domain enables you to also configure a domain controller for the new domain and bring a DNS server online (by adding the DNS role to the new domain controller) for the new regional domain.

To create the new regional (child) domain and bring the first domain controller online in that domain, you need to use a Windows server in that domain that already has Windows Server 2008 installed. The steps to create the domain and bring the domain controller online are very similar to the steps for creating the root domain (as discussed in the previous section).

Follow these steps:

1. Open the Add Roles Wizard (click the appropriate icon) in either the Initial Configuration Tasks window or the Server Manager (with the Roles node selected).

2. Click Next to bypass the initial Wizard screen.

3. On the next screen, select the Active Directory Domain Services role. Then click Next.

4. The next screen provides a list of things to note as you proceed with the installation (as discussed in the previous section). Click Install to add the AD DS role.

5. On the final Add Roles Wizard screen, click Close this wizard and launch the Active Directory Domain Services Installation Wizard (dcpromo.exe) as shown in Figure 8.5.

FIGURE 8.5
Specify the location for the database folder, log file, and SYSVOL folder.

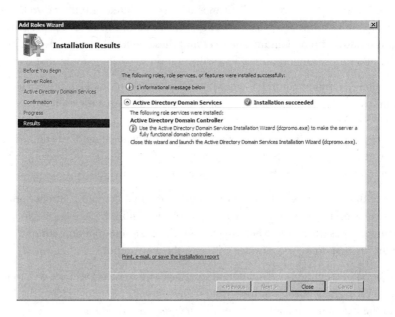

> Adding an additional domain controller for an existing domain is handled with the `dcpromo.exe` utility.

6. On the Active Directory Domain Services Installation Wizard's welcome screen click Next.

7. On the next page (the Deployment Configuration page) click Existing Forest and then click Create a New Domain in an Existing Forest (see Figure 8.6). Then click Next to continue.

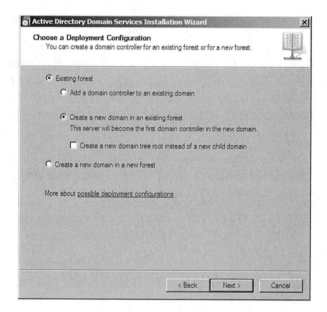

FIGURE 8.6
Select the options that enable you to create a new domain in an existing forest.

8. On the next page (the Network Credentials page), enter the name of the existing domain that will contain the new domain you are creating. For example, if you are creating a regional domain that will be nested in the forest (the root domain), type the name of the forest.

9. Because you have to provide administrative credentials to continue the process, meaning credentials that provide you with the administrative right to add the new child domain to the forest (which includes the original administrative account and password used to create the forest), click either the My Current Logged On Credentials or the Alternate Credentials option. Remember that your current credentials would need to have the rights to add the domain to the forest. If you click Alternate Credentials, you then click Set. Provide the password for the Administrator account (that has administrative rights in the forest; see Figure 8.7.) Click OK and then click Next to continue.

FIGURE 8.7
Provide the
password
for the
Administrator
account that
has administra-
tive rights in the
forest.

10. On the next wizard screen type the FQDN for the domain that will serve as the parent domain for the new child domain you are creating. If you are creating a nested regional domain, the name you enter is your root domain. Also enter the single-label DNS name of the child domain, meaning do not provide the DNS suffix or prefix (which would be the same as the NetBIOS name for the new domain if the label DNS name doesn't exceed 15 characters). Then click Next.

11. On the next screen, the new domain's NetBIOS name is listed (as generated by the wizard based on the single-label DNS name you entered in the previous step). You can edit it if you choose. Click Next.

12. The next screen asks you to select a site for the new domain. The sites you have created for your forest are listed on this screen (see Figure 8.8). Select a site and then click Next.

FIGURE 8.8
Select the site
for the new
domain.

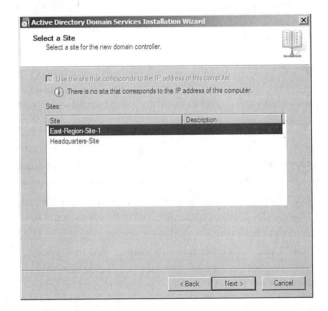

Did you Know?

It may make sense to create your site hierarchy before you begin to deploy your regional domain controllers (and create the regional domains). The sites are important in that they provide the links that allow replication between the domain controllers in each site. You can even pause at step 11 and create your sites and then continue with step 12. Or you can create the sites later if you prefer. For more about sites, see Hour 9.

13. On the next screen, select the domain controller options you want to add to this server installation. These are DNS Server and Global Catalog. If a DNS server is already available in the domain or you have already installed DNS on this server, the option is not selectable. It definitely makes sense to select the Global Catalog option for the domain controller if this will be the only domain controller in the regional (child) domain. Click Next.

14. On the next screen a list of domain controllers in the forest is listed. You can allow the wizard to choose a replication partner for the domain controller you are creating or you can choose a replication partner from the list. Then click Next.

15. On the next screen, select the location for the database folder, log file folder, and SYSVOL folder (you can go with the defaults); then click Next to continue.

16. On the next wizard page, you must set the Directory Services Restore Mode Administrator password. Then click Next.

17. A summary screen provides all the selections that you have made during the process. Click Next.

18. The wizard configures the Active Directory Domain Services and your new domain controller. When the process is complete, click Finish. The system then needs to be rebooted.

When the server reboots, The Initial Configuration Tasks window appears; it now lists the new role, Active Directory Domain Services, and any other roles such as DNS that you added during the domain and domain controller configuration.

Once you have the root domain and regional domain in place, you can view your domain hierarchy. Figure 8.9 shows a domain root (spinach.com) and a regional (child) domain (popeye.spinach.com) in the Active Directory Domains and Trusts snap-in (discussed later in this hour).

FIGURE 8.9
The domain tree
can be viewed
in the Active
Directory
Domains and
Trusts snap-in.

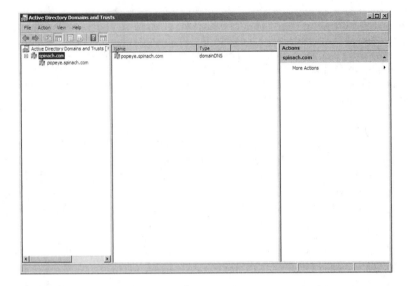

Using the Active Directory Management Tools

After Active Directory is installed on a domain controller (along with DNS and DHCP, if necessary), you will find that the Server Manager is now populated with the Active Directory Domain Services snap-in, which provides easy access to events associated with the Active Directory, system services currently running, role services (which can easily be added), and advanced AD DS tools. Figure 8.10 shows the Server Manager with the Active Directory Domain Services node selected.

In terms of Active Directory Management tools, you access Active Directory Users and Computers and Active Directory Sites and Services by expanding the Active Directory Domain Services node in the Server Manager node pane (and then selecting the specific tool such as Active Directory Users and Computers).

Another important tool, Active Directory Domains and Trusts, can be started from the Server Manager Window when Active Directory Domain Services is selected in the node list. Just click the AD Domains and Trusts link in the Advanced Tools list. The remainder of this hour focuses on the Active Directory Users and Computers snap-in (as does the beginning of Hour 9). Active Directory Domains and Trusts and Active Directory Sites and Services are discussed in Hour 9.

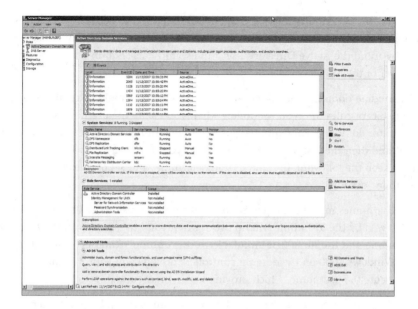

FIGURE 8.10
The Server Manager provides the administrative work space for working with the Active Directory and launching its associated tools.

You can also launch these AD DS tools as MMC snap-ins; select Start, point at Administrative Tools, and then select the appropriate Active Directory tool (such as Active Directory Users and Computers on the Administrative Tools menu that appears.

Did you Know?

Working with Domain User Accounts

Microsoft operating systems, particularly network operating systems, can make user accounts a little confusing, particularly for the novice administrator. Two different types of user accounts exist: local accounts and domain accounts. Two different account types are necessary because two different security systems pervade computers running Microsoft operating systems and network operating systems such as Windows Server 2008: local security and domain-level security.

A *local account* is used to gain access to the local machine and its resources. Having a local account means that the user can be validated to the local security database on the server (or desktop computer running Windows XP Professional or Windows Vista Business) and gain access to local resources. Local accounts are more of an issue on computers in workgroups or on member servers within your domain. Creating local accounts is discussed in Hour 3, "Configuring Windows Server 2008 Basic Settings."

A *domain account* enables a user to log on to a domain and access the resources available on that domain. You add domain users to the Windows Server 2008 network by using the Active Directory Users and Computers snap-in (in the Server Manager or the MMC).

Before adding domain users to the Active Directory, you should determine the set of parameters or rules that you will follow when you create the usernames for your domain (or domains). For example, you might determine that you will use the first initial and then the last name of employees at your company to create each username. Keep the following in mind as you determine your set of rules for naming your users' accounts:

▶ Usernames must be unique. So, the convention of using the first initial followed by the last name will not work when you have users with the same last name and the same first initial. Networks running Windows Server 2008 or Windows 2000 on the domain controllers provide you with 256 characters to create the username, which provides more than enough possibilities.

▶ User logon names can be a combination of numeric and alphanumeric characters. You can use names and even floor locations, such as marysmithfloor2, to help define unique and descriptive usernames.

▶ You cannot end a username with a period or use the reserved characters *, /, ¦, :, ;, =, <, and >.

By the Way

Windows Server 2008 (and Windows Server 2003) domain usernames are also referred to as *user principal names*. These names consist of two parts: the user's name and the user principal name suffix. You create the username; the suffix consists of the @ sign followed by the domain where the user resides.

Adding Users to the Domain

When you create a new user account in the Active Directory Users and Computers snap-in, a security identifier (SID) is created for the account. Windows actually uses the SID to identify the account (in internal processes) instead of the username. The SID is unique for every user account and includes information on the user's group memberships and security settings. When a user logs on to the network from a client computer, the username and password are used to validate or authenticate the user to the domain.

You add user accounts to the domain with the Active Director Users and Computers snap-in. To add a user to your domain, follow these steps:

1. Open the Active Directory Users and Computers snap-in in the Server Manager (expand the AD DS node) or via the Start menu, click Start, Administrative Tools, and then Active Directory Users and Computers.

2. Under the Active Directory Users and Computers snap-in, expand the domain node in the Node pane. Then select the Users folder in the tree. A list of the default groups and users in your domain appears in the Details pane.

3. To create a new user, click the Create a New User in the Current Container button on the Active Directory toolbar (or see the following). The New Object–User dialog box opens (see Figure 8.11).

If you are using the Users and Computers snap-in in the Server Manager window, you won't have the Active Directory toolbar at the top of the window as you will when you run the Users and Computers snap-in in the MMC. To add a new user in the Server Manager window, click the More Actions link in the Actions pane, point at New, and then select User.

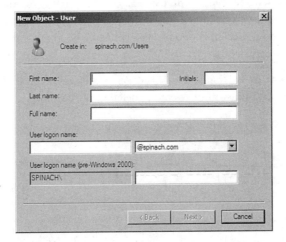

FIGURE 8.11
The New Object–User dialog box is used to create the new user account.

4. Enter a first name, initials, and a last name for the user (this is actually the name that will appear in the Active Directory).

5. In the User Logon Name box, type the username that the user will use to log on to the domain.

When you create the domain user account, note that a pre–Windows 2000 version of the user account is also created for the user, truncating the username that you have created at 20 characters.

6. When you have entered the appropriate information (see steps 4 and 5), click Next to continue.

7. On the next screen (see Figure 8.12), you are asked to provide a password for the user (and confirm it) and to set properties related to the user's password. The password possibilities are as follows:

   ▶ **User Must Change Password at Next Logon**—If you want to let the users have control over the password that they assigned themselves, check this check box. You can then enter something generic, such as **password**, as the user's password. At the first logon, the user is required to change the default password.

   ▶ **User Cannot Change Password**—If you want to assign passwords to your users and not allow them to change passwords, click this check box.

   ▶ **Password Never Expires**—This makes the password selected by you or the user a lifelong password; it has no expiration time limit. When you do not use this option, passwords are good for a month (31 days), by default.

   ▶ **Account Is Disabled**—This check box enables you to disable the current account without actually deleting the account.

FIGURE 8.12
Enter a password for the user and set password properties.

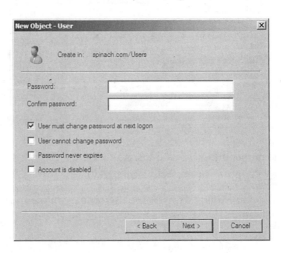

8. After supplying the password and setting password options, click Next. A summary screen for the new user account appears. Click Finish.

Windows Server 2008 embraces the same strengthened password protection for user accounts introduced in Windows Server 2003. Users are not able to change a user password to a blank password (no password at all). Any user attempting to log on to the domain with a blank password is not given access to resources in the domain and can only log on to the local computer.

Did you Know?

The new user account appears in the Details pane of the Active Directory Users and Computers snap-in. You can add additional user accounts as needed.

Setting User Account Properties

After you create a user account, you can access a number of properties related to the account. These properties range from when the user can log on to the domain to the user's business information, such as phone number and address.

To access a user account's properties, right-click a user account in the Active Directory Users and Computers snap-in, and select Properties from the shortcut menu. The Properties dialog box for that user account opens (see Figure 8.13).

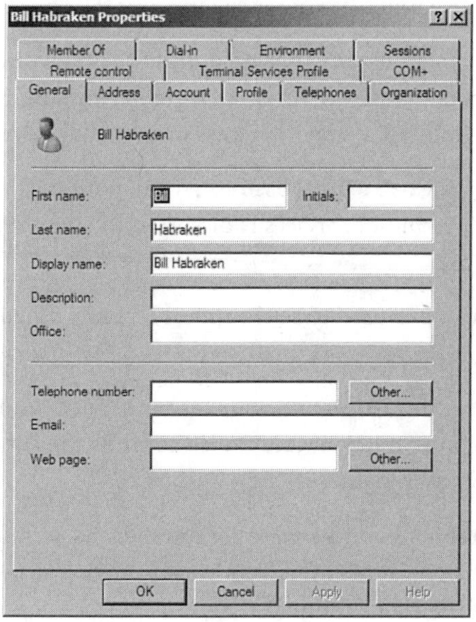

FIGURE 8.13
User properties are set in the account's Properties dialog box.

The various user properties are set in the tabs of the dialog box. The user Properties dialog box includes the following tabs:

- ▶ **General**—Enables you to edit the user's display name. You can also enter optional information, such as the user's office (location) telephone number, email address, and web page URL. This information is available to other users on the network when they search the Active Directory.

- ▶ **Address**—Provides the option of entering address information related to the user.

- ▶ **Account**—Enables you to edit the username or the password options set for the account. This tab also provides access to logon hour and computer logon settings. You can also use this tab to set an expiration date for a user account.

- ▶ **Profile**—Enables you to specify the location of a user's profile and any logon scripts that should run when the user logs on to the network. You can also set the path for a user's home folder (typically on a file server). Setting a home folder is discussed later in this hour.

- ▶ **Telephones**—Gives you the option of entering telephone numbers related to the user, such as home number, pager number, mobile phone number, and fax number.

- ▶ **Member Of**—Used to view (and add or remove) the group memberships for the user. Domain groups are discussed in Hour 9.

- ▶ **Dial-In**—Used to enable the user account to take advantage of remote access dial-in or network access via virtual private networking. Dial-in remote access is discussed in Hour 17, "Remote Access and Virtual Private Networking."

- ▶ **Terminal Services Profile**—Used to set the path for the user's Terminal Services profile. Terminal Services is discussed in Hour 19, "Implementing Terminal Services."

- ▶ **Sessions**—This tab is used to set Terminal Services timeout and reconnect options.

- ▶ **Environment**—Also associated with Terminal Services. It is used to start a certain program upon logon, and it also controls the client devices that are connected upon user login.

- ▶ **Remote Control**—Used to enable (or disable) the Terminal Services remote control feature that allows an administrator to view a user's client session or take control of the client computer.

- ▶ **Organization**—Enables you to enter the user's title and department and company-related information, such as the user's direct reports.

▶ **COM+**—Used to specify the COM+ partition to which the user belongs. COM+ partitions are used to assign applications provided by an application server to users, groups, or Organizational Units.

As noted in this list, a number of these tabs are discussed in more detail in later hours of this book. Before we end our discussion of user account options, let's take a look at setting the logon hours for users and the computers that they can log on to and access domain resources.

Setting Logon Hours and Computers

The is used to set the logon hours for a user and the computers on which that user can log on to the domain. To set the logon hours for the user, follow these steps:

1. Right-click the user's account in the Active Directory Users and Computers Details pane on the Properties dialog box (if necessary).

2. On the Account tab, select the Logon Hours button for the user appears (see Figure 8.14).

FIGURE 8.14

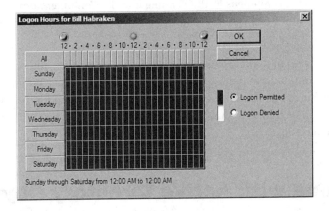

You can control when a user can log on to the network.

3. All hours are allowed by default (all hours are in blue). To disallow certain hours (such as Saturdays) for logon, click and drag to select the time range. Then click the Logon Denied option button. The timeframe that you selected turns white. This timeframe is no longer allowed for user logon. When you have finished specifying the timeframes for logon (and logon denial), click the OK button. You are returned to the Account tab of the Properties dialog box.

4. You can also specify the computers that a user can use to log on to the network. On the Account tab, select the Log On To button. The Logon Workstations dialog box opens (see Figure 8.15).

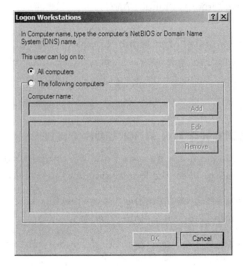

5. Select the The Following Computers option button. To add a computer to the list, type the computer's NetBIOS name into the Computer name box (the NetBIOS name is the first 15 characters of a computer's name and does not include the domain name suffix).

6. After typing in the computer name, click the Add button. You can add a number of computers to the list (computers can also be removed from the list with the Remove button). After entering the computers for the user, click OK. You are returned to the Account tab of the Properties dialog box. Click OK to close the dialog box.

Working with Active Directory Objects

Thus far, we have discussed only one type of Active Directory object: the user account object. However, in this discussion of user accounts, we have looked at some of the basic possibilities for manipulating other Active Directory objects, such as computer accounts and domain printers.

The ways in which you manipulate objects in the Active Directory is fairly uniform across the various object types in the Active Directory schema. We look at additional

Active Directory objects in Hour 9 and Hour 14, "Working with Network Printing" (which includes a discussion of how to publish a printer to the Active Directory).

A feature worth noting is that the Windows Server 2008 Active Directory Users and Computers snap-in now enables you to select multiple objects in the Details pane. This enables you to manipulate a number of user accounts at once or nest multiple user groups in a particular Organizational Unit.

For example, you might want to quickly disable a number of domain user accounts because of some type of security issue. In the Active Directory Users and Computers snap-in, you would expand the Domain node in the snap-in tree and then select the Users node. A list of your users would appear in the Details pane. You then would select the first with a click of the mouse and then hold down the Ctrl key when selecting other users. After selecting the users, you would right-click (see Figure 8.16). Notice that you can select Disable from the shortcut menu (as well as Delete).

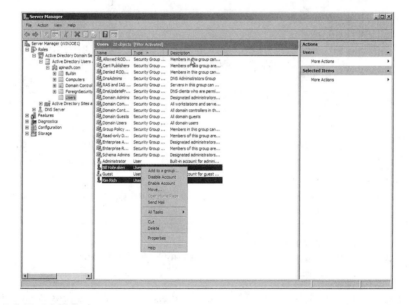

FIGURE 8.16
You can select multiple objects in the Active Directory.

Selecting multiple users is extremely useful when you want to add users to a particular group or groups. Users can be identified, selected, and then added to the group or groups en masse.

Searching for Objects in the Active Directory

The Active Directory Users and Computers snap-in makes it easy for you to find objects in the Active Directory. The Find feature provides a number of built-in queries for searching for particular objects (such as users who have passwords that never expire), and it also enables you to set up search queries and then save them for later use.

To use the Find feature, select a particular node in the snap-in tree (such as Users) and then select the Action menu; then select Find appears (see Figure 8.17).

FIGURE 8.17
The Find feature enables you to select the object and location for a search.

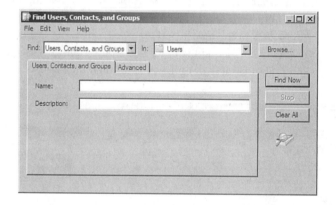

Use the Find drop-down list to specify the object type you want to find, such as Users, Contacts, and Groups; Computers; or Printers. After specifying the object type, use the In drop-down box to specify the container for the search, such as a particular Active Directory node or another location such as an Organizational Unit.

Did you Know?

> You can change the container for the search by clicking the Browse button and selecting a node, folder, or other container from the list provided.

After specifying the object and the location for the search, you can provide additional search parameters, such as a particular username or name of a printer. You then click Find Now to complete the search.

Creating Your Own Queries

Although the Find feature provides a fast way to locate particular user accounts or other Active Directory objects, you might want to create specific queries that locate certain objects. You can then save these queries and reuse them when needed. The Saved Query folder is not available when you run the Active Directory Users and

Computers snap-in via the Server Manager. Open the Active Directory Users and Computers snap-in in the Microsoft Management Console (MMC): click Start, Administrative Tools, and then Active Directory Users and Computers. Then follow these steps:

1. Select the Saved Query folder in the Active Directory tree. Then select the Action menu, point at New, and select Query. The New Query dialog box opens (see Figure 8.18).

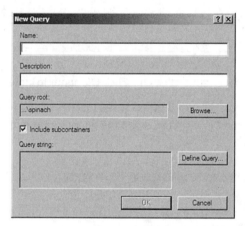

FIGURE 8.18
Search queries can be created and saved.

2. Type a name and a description (optional) for the new query. Then click the Define Query button. The Find Common Queries dialog box opens. Tabs are provided for Users, Computers, and Groups. Use any of these tabs to specify the parameters for the query.

3. Define the variables for your query (on the Users, Computers, or Groups tabs), using the Name and Description drop-down boxes. These enable you to specify that the query find names or descriptions that start (or end) with a particular character string.

4. Check boxes are also included on the Users, Computers, and Groups tabs. For example, on the Users tab, two check boxes are provided that enable you to search for disabled accounts or accounts that have nonexpiring passwords. A drop-down box is also provided that enables you to search based on the last time the user logged on (see Figure 8.19).

FIGURE 8.19
Set the criteria
for the query.

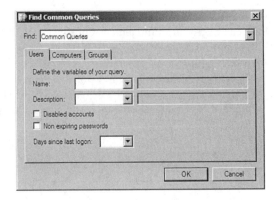

After setting the criteria, click OK. Click OK again to close the dialog box.

5. The new query is displayed in the Saved Queries folder. To see the results of
the query in the Details pane, select the query in the snap-in tree (see
Figure 8.20).

FIGURE 8.20
Query results
are displayed in
the Details
pane.

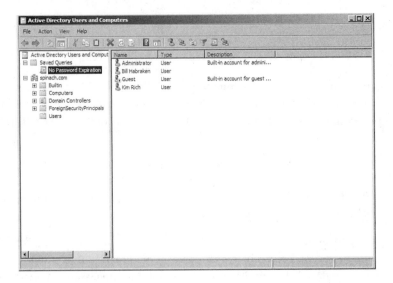

Saving various queries enables you to quickly filter information in the Active
Directory. After you click the query in the tree, results are immediately displayed in
the Details pane.

Summary

Active Directory Domain Services (AD DS) is the directory service for the Windows Server 2008 networking environment. It provides the hierarchical structure for the domain and the objects within the domain. The domain is the basic administrative container for a Microsoft network. Domains that share the same Global Catalog are in the same domain tree. A forest is a collection of domain trees.

To create a domain controller for a domain, you need to install Active Directory on the server. The first domain created for your organization is the root domain of your domain tree (it also is the root of a forest).

Child domains reside inside the domain tree container (they could also be considered branches on the domain tree). Root and child domains in the same tree can share services and resources because they are configured with transitive trusts, by default. This means that these trusts flow up through the tree and child domains on the network, allowing users in any domain on the tree to access resources anywhere in the tree (including the root and child directories.

Active Directory Domain Services can be managed on a domain controller via the Server Manager. Three important management snap-ins related to the Active Directory are Active Directory Users and Computers, Active Directory Domains and Trusts, and Active Directory Sites and Services. The Active Directory Users and Computers snap-in is used to manage your user accounts, Active Directory groups, and Organizational Units.

Q&A

Q. *What term is used to refer to the first domain created in a new Active Directory tree?*

A. The first domain created in a tree is referred to as the *root domain*. Child domains created in the tree share the same namespace as the root domain.

Q. *How is a server running Windows Server 2008 configured as a domain controller, such as the domain controller for the root domain or a child domain?*

A. Installing the Active Directory on a server running Windows Server 2008 provides you with the option of creating a root domain for a domain tree or of creating child domains in an existing tree. Installing Active Directory on the server makes the server a domain controller.

Q. *What are some of the tools used to manage Active Directory objects in a Windows Server 2008 domain?*

A. When the Active Directory is installed on a server (making it a domain controller), a set of Active Directory snap-ins is provided. The Active Directory Users and Computers snap-in is used to manage Active Directory objects such as user accounts, computers, and groups. The Active Directory Domains and Trusts snap-in enables you to manage the trusts that are defined between domains. The Active Directory Sites and Services snap-in provides for the management of domain sites and subnets.

Q. *How are domain user accounts created and managed?*

A. The Active Directory Users and Computers snap-in provides the tools necessary for creating user accounts and managing account properties. Properties for user accounts include settings related to logon hours, the computers to which a user can log on, and the settings related to the user's password.

HOUR 9

Creating Active Directory Groups, Organizational Units, and Sites

---

What You'll Learn in This Hour:

▶ Understanding Active Directory Groups

▶ Using Default Groups

▶ Creating Groups

▶ Adding Users and Groups to a Group

▶ Raising Domain Functional Levels

▶ Using Organizational Units

▶ Using Active Directory Sites

▶ Active Directory Replication and Sites

▶ Understanding Delegation

This hour examines two Active Directory objects: groups and Organizational Units. It also discusses the use of Active Directory sites and issues related to Active Directory replication and the Global Catalog.

Understanding Active Directory Groups

The Active Directory Users and Computers snap-in is used to manage Active Directory objects such as users, computers, and groups. A *group* is a collection of active directory objects (which can include nested groups—more about these later in the hour). The primary purpose of a group is to enable you to group users and define permissions based on group membership. This is a much easier strategy for determining the access levels that users have to domain resources when compared to the alternative of assigning permissions on a per-user basis.

A number of default Active Directory groups are available for the administrator to use. You can create new groups by using the Active Directory Users and Computers snap-in. Before we look at the default Active Directory groups provided, we should expand our definition of Windows Server 2008 groups. There are actually two different group types: security and distribution.

A *security group* is a group that defines permissions related to resources and objects in the domain. Members of a security group (such as users) are assigned a security token when they log on to the domain, which provides them with the necessary permissions to files, printers, and other resources.

The second type of Windows Server 2008 group is the *distribution group*. A distribution group is really nothing more than a list of users, such as a grouping of contacts to which you would send an email. Distribution groups cannot be used to assign permissions to the users in the group. Microsoft Exchange Server is an example of a platform that uses distribution groups.

Security groups are discussed in this hour and they're used throughout the book as permissions are assigned related to various Windows Server 2008 services. Before you look at using or creating groups, however, you need to understand how security groups operate at the different levels in the Active Directory hierarchy (especially when you are working with enterprise networks that contain a number of domains).

Windows Server 2008 Group Scopes

A security group always has a particular scope. The group *scope* refers to the level at which the group operates within the Microsoft network (and within the Active Directory Domain Services hierarchy). It also refers to the types of objects that actually can be contained in the object. Remember that you are potentially working with a network that can consist of not only a single domain, but that also could span a domain tree or even a forest. The three group scopes are universal, global, and domain local.

▶ **Universal group**—A group that spans multiple domains and can have users (or groups) from any of these domains as members. Permissions assigned to a universal group can allow group members to access resources across domain boundaries. Universal groups are designed to contain objects that remain fairly static (such as global groups, which are discussed in a moment). These groups are best used in multidomain networks, where you want to group sets of users and other objects at a higher level in the Active Directory container.

By default, Windows Server 2008 domain controllers operate in the Windows 2000 functional mode if you do not change the default functional level option when you install Active Directory Domain Services on the server and make the server a domain controller (using `dcpromo.exe`). You can change this default option to either the Windows Server 2003 or Windows Server 2008 levels to take advantage of advanced domainwide Active Directory features such as universal groups. If you use the 2008 functional level, all domain controllers in the domain must run Windows Server 2008) Functional levels are discussed in more detail later in the hour.

▶ **Global group**—A group used to organize users in one domain. Membership to the global group is limited to the domain where the global group is created. However, a global group can access resources in any domain in the Active Directory tree.

▶ **Domain local group**—A group created at the domain level and used to provide users with permissions to local resources (within the domain). So, the domain local group members have permissions only to resources that are in the domain where the domain local group was created. However, group membership in a domain local group is not restricted to the domain that actually contains the domain local group. The domain local group can have members from any domain in the tree.

Do not confuse domain local groups with the local groups that you can create on computers running Windows Vista and Windows Server 2008 to provide rights to local resources on a particular computer.

Whether you actually use all these different types of groups depends on the size of your network. If your network consists of only one domain, you would typically use global groups to organize your users into security subsets, with each group assigned a particular level of permissions to resources within the domain.

Universal groups usually come into play only if your network is of greater scope, meaning that your Windows Server 2008 network is big enough to embrace multiple domains. For example, your company might be made up of several divisions, with each division its own domain.

Domain local groups are most often used to assign users permissions to specific resources within a domain (where the group has been created). The fact that other group scopes can be nested (discussed in the next section) within domain local groups means that you can use the domain local group to specify the permissions for domain resources and then add users to groups from the domain tree (or forest) as required.

Nesting Groups and Group Membership

You can actually create a group hierarchy by nesting groups inside other groups. *Nesting* simply means placing a group inside another group. For example, you can add a global group (which provides a way to organize a group of users in a particular domain) to a domain local group. The global group provides the list of users, and the domain local group actually provides the permission level that will be assigned to members of the domain local group; in this case, that includes the global group you've nested.

The nesting of groups is controlled by the group membership rules for each group scope. In the Windows 2000 functional level (or the 2003 and 2008 functional level), the group scopes allow the following memberships:

- ▶ **Universal**—Members can include users, global groups from any domain, and other universal groups.

- ▶ **Global**—Members can include users and global groups from the same domain.

- ▶ **Domain local**—Members can include users, global groups from any domain, domain local groups from the same domain, and universal groups.

> In the Windows 2000 Server functional level, global groups can contain only users from the same domain, and domain local groups can contain only user accounts and global groups from any domain. In this functional level mode, universal groups don't exist.

Using Default Groups

Default, or predefined, groups are found in the Active Directory (meaning, on a Server 2008 domain controller). These groups have been assigned user rights so that members of a particular default group can perform specific actions in the domain. Not only are these groups created automatically when you set up your domain controller, but some of them add members automatically.

In the Server Manager, expand the Roles node and then expand the Active
Directory Domain Services node to access the Active Directory Users and
Computers snap-in. To open the Active Directory Users and Computers snap-in in
the MMC select Start, Administrative Tools, and then Active Directory Users and
Computers.

To view these groups, open the Active Directory Users and Computers snap-in (in the
MMC or in the Server Manager). Expand the Active Directory Users and Computers
node (snap-in) and then select the Users folder. The number of default groups is
based on the functional level you have set for the forest (and the domain controller).
Assuming that you are using the Windows Server 2008 functional level (as shown in
Figure 9.1), a number of groups are provided by default.

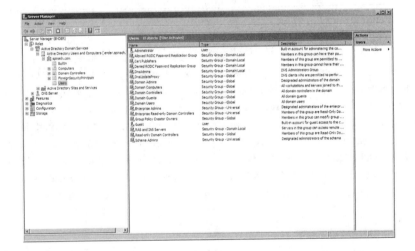

FIGURE 9.1
The default
groups in the
Users folder.

These groups include domain local, global, and universal group types. Four important groups are defined in the list that follows:

▶ **Domain Users**—This is a broad-based global group that, by default, contains
all user accounts in the domain. The Administrator account is a member, and
any new users you create also are added to the group automatically. This
group is automatically added to the Users domain local group on your server.

▶ **Domain Admins**—This global group provides its members with the capabili-
ty to perform administrative tasks on the domain and any computer within it.
It is automatically added to the Administrators domain local group. The
Administrator account is automatically made a member of the Domain
Admins group.

▶ **Enterprise Admins**—This universal group is for users who have the capability to administer the entire network (this means all the domains in the network). However, for the members of this group to actually have the management capabilities they need, you must manually add this group to each of the Administrators domain local groups (that means for all the domains in the network). By default, the Administrator account is added to the Enterprise Admins group.

▶ **Schema Admins**—This universal group is for administrators who have rights related to the changing of the Active Directory schema (which defines the objects in the Active Directory). By default the domain controller Administrator account is a member of the Schema Admins group. Schema Admins are able to alter the schema database and prep the forest so that the Active Directory can support additional schema objects such as those required by a communications server, such as Microsoft's Office Communication Server 2007 or Microsoft Exchange.

Although four default groups are discussed here, you will find that a number of other security groups, such as the Group Policy Creator Owners (Group Policy is discussed in Hour 11, "Deploying Group Policy and Network Access Protection"), are available by default. You will have other predefined groups on your server, depending on the services that have been installed. For example, if your domain controller is also a DNS (Domain Name Service) server, there will be a predefined DnsAdmins group. This group serves as the administrative group for the Domain Name Service (DNS is discussed in Hour 15, "Understanding the Domain Name Service").

Built-in Groups

Windows Server 2008 also provides a number of built-in domain local groups. For the most part, these groups provide users with the permissions needed to perform certain tasks on your domain controllers and in the Active Directory. The default Users group contains all the users in your domain. Domain local groups typically relate to specific tasks on the network such as Backup Operators, Performance Monitor Users, and Remote Desktop Users. All the built-in groups are security groups.

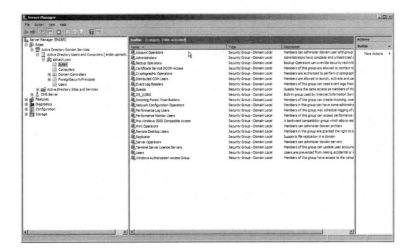

FIGURE 9.2
The built-in domain local groups.

Figure 9.2 shows the default groups available in the Builtin folder. Some of the often-used built-in domain local groups are as follows:

▶ **Account Operators**—This group provides its members with the capability to create, modify, and delete user accounts and groups, which means that it gives its users access to the Active Directory. However, members do not have the capability to change properties or membership related to the Operators groups or the Administrators group.

▶ **Server Operators**—Members of this group can create shares on a server and back up and restore files on the domain controller.

▶ **Print Operators**—This group is for users who need to set up and manage printers that are available on the network on your domain controllers.

▶ **Backup Operators**—Members of this group can back up and restore files within the domain, including on your domain controllers.

▶ **Administrators**—This group is for users who need to perform all the administrative tasks required on your domain controllers. Members are provided with the capabilities of all the Operator groups. Your Administrator account is automatically added to this group, as are the Domain Admins and Enterprise Admins global groups.

▶ **Users**—This group is used to control the access of all your users to resources. It contains the Domain Users global group by default (which, if you remember, contains all your users by default).

Although you aren't required to use these groups, be advised that they have already been assigned permissions that relate to getting certain jobs done in the domain. Adding a user to the Print Operators group, for example, immediately gives that user the capability to set up printers in the domain. Using the group's predefined permissions saves you from having to assign these same permissions to individual users or creating a group of your own and assigning the permissions to the group.

Creating Groups

Domain-level groups are created in Active Directory, using the Active Directory Users and Computers snap-in. After groups are created, you can add users or other groups to them.

Open the Active Directory Users and Computers snap-in (select Start, point at Administrative Tools, and then select Active Directory Users and Computers or open the snap-in in the Server Manager). To view the default domain user groups, expand the domain node and then select the Users container. The default groups (and users) appear in the Details pane.

To create a new group, follow these steps:

1. Right-click below the current groups in the Details pane. On the shortcut menu point at New and then select Group. The New Object – Group dialog box appears (see Figure 9.3).

FIGURE 9.3
The New Object – Group dialog box.

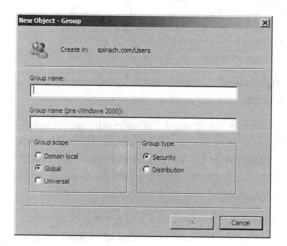

> When you run a snap-in such as the Active Directory Users and Computers snap-in in the Server Manager, all the actions (commands) related to the current snap-in can be accessed via the Actions pane on the right.

2. Type a name for the new group. This name is duplicated (or shortened) and placed in the pre–Windows 2000 name box automatically.

3. Choose the scope for the new group by clicking the appropriate option button: Domain Local, Global, or Universal.

4. Choose the group type (security or distribution) by clicking the appropriate option button (you are likely to be working exclusively with security group types when you are creating groups related to rights or abilities in the domain).

5. When you have finished setting the parameters for the new group, click OK to close the dialog box and complete the creation of the new group.

The new group appears in the Users container (you can see it in the Details pane). You can create groups in other containers. For example, you might want to create a group that is in an Organizational Unit container. Organizational Units are discussed later in the hour.

You can just as easily delete groups. Deleting is actually easier. Right-click a group in the Details pane and select Delete from the shortcut menu. Click OK to go ahead with the deletion. When you delete the group, users who were members of the group are not deleted, but those users lose any privileges that they were afforded to resources as a result of their membership in that particular group.

Adding Users and Groups to a Group

Users and groups can be added to the groups that you create (membership depends on the scope of the group, as discussed earlier in the hour). To add users (or other groups) to a group, follow these steps:

1. Double-click the group in the Details pane to open the group's Properties dialog box. On the group's Properties dialog box, select the Members tab (see Figure 9.4).

FIGURE 9.4
Users are
added to the
Members tab.

2. Click the Add button on the Members tab. The Select Users, Contacts, Computer, or Groups dialog box opens. To specify a user or group to add to the group, type the name of the user or group in the Enter the Object Names to Select box (you can type the first few letters of the user or group and then use the Check Names button to place the object in the box).

If you add multiple users or groups to the dialog box, separate each object name with a semicolon.

3. When you have completed adding users or groups, click OK. The users or groups are added to the Members tab list. If you decide to remove any of the users or groups from the Members list, select the user or group and then click the Remove button. When you have finished working in the group's Properties dialog box, click OK to return to the Active Directory Users and Computer snap-in.

An alternative to adding the users to the group in the group's Properties dialog box is to select the users in the Details pane (select the first with a click and then Ctrl+click to select additional users). Right-click any of the selected users and select Add to a Group on the shortcut menu. The Select Group dialog box opens. Enter the name of the group (or the first couple of letters in the group's name) and then select Check Names. When you have specified the group, click OK. All the selected users are added to the group.

Raising Domain Functional Levels

Windows 2000 Server introduced the concept of domain functional levels. A domain could operate in either *mixed mode* (running Windows NT and Windows 2000 servers) or *native mode* (Windows 2000 servers only). The domain functional levels for Windows Server 2003 included a new (higher) functional level for domains that only deployed domain controllers running Windows Server 2003 (the Windows Server 2003 functional level).

In the Windows Server 2008 environment are three possible functional levels: Windows 2000, Windows Server 2003, and Windows Server 2008. The Windows 2000 functional level enables you to run domain controllers that use Windows 2000 Server, Windows Server 2003, and Windows Server 2008. The Windows 2003 functional level allows only servers running Windows Server 2003 and Windows Server 2008. The Windows Server 2008 functional level allows only domain controllers that are running Windows Server 2008.

The functional level that you select also affects the type of groups that are supported. For example, the Windows 2000 functional level provides an environment that supports universal groups in the Active Directory.

In the Windows Server 2003 functional level mode, you can fully nest groups and you can also rename domain controllers. This functional level also enables you to continue to use servers running Windows Server 2003 in the domain along with servers that are running Windows Server 2008.

The Windows Server 2008 function level provides new groups related to new features provided by the 2008 network platform. For example, because Windows Server 2008 allows you to deploy read-only domain controllers, groups have been added to the User folder that can be used to either allow or deny the replication of group member passwords to read-only domain controllers on the network. There is even a new universal security group for read-only domain controllers named Enterprise Read-Only Domain Controllers.

By the Way

The Windows Server 2003 and Windows Server 2008 functional levels include the capability to change security groups from one domain to another.

Forest functional levels can be raised and the options available to you in terms of raising the functional level depend on the functional level that you set when you installed Active Directory Domain Services and brought the domain controller online. For example, if you selected the Windows 2000 functional level when you created your forest, you can raise the functional level to either Windows Server 2003 or Windows Server 2008. If you selected Windows Server 2003 as your functional level, you can raise it to Windows Server 2008.

Be advised that raising the domain or forest functional level is a one-way process. After you raise the functional level, you cannot change it and go back. Raising the root domain functional level of any tree in a forest also raises the functional level of all the child domains in the tree.

Remember that the functional level determines what version (or versions) of the Windows Server operating system you can run in the domain on domain controllers. It also determines the default groups and types of groups that you can take advantage of.

To raise the domain functional level, follow these steps:

1. In the Active Directory Users and Computers snap-in (click Start, Administrative Tools, and then Active Directory Users and Computers, or access the snap-in in the Server Manager node tree), right-click Active Directory Users and Computers. Point at All Tasks on the shortcut menu that appears and then Raise Domain Functional Level. The Raise domain functional level dialog box opens (see Figure 9.5).

FIGURE 9.5
Raising the domain functional level.

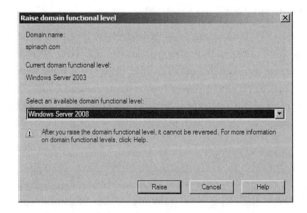

2. Click the Select an Available Domain Functional Level drop-down list. Select either Windows Server 2003 or Windows Server 2008 (if you were at the

Windows 2000 functional level). If you were already at the Windows Server 2003 functional level, select Windows Server 2008. Then click the Raise button.

3. A message box appears letting you know that you cannot reverse this action. Click OK to complete the process.

4. A message appears letting you know that the functional level was raised. The new functional level is replicated to the domain controllers in your domain. Click OK. You can close the Active Directory Users and Computers snap-in if you want.

Using Organizational Units

Hour 8, "Understanding and Configuring Active Directory Domain Service," covered the logical hierarchy provided by Active Directory Domain Services when working in networking environments that embrace multiple domains in trees or forests. You can actually add additional compartmentalization to your Windows Server 2008 domains using Organizational Units. An *Organizational Unit* (OU) is an Active Directory object that serves as a domain container. This container can be used to hold users, groups, computers, and other OUs.

OUs basically provide a container environment that enables you to refine the logical grouping of Active Directory objects (such as users or groups) within the domain. You can apply Group Policy settings to OUs, enabling you to refine policies and security settings at a level below the domain level. OUs provide you with a domain container that can be used to mimic the hierarchical structure of your business. For example, within the domain, you could create an OU for each company department, such as Accounting, Receiving, and so on. Policies and security settings could then be applied on the OU level. This also provides you with a way to logically group employees (at a higher level than with actual groups).

Creating OUs is very straightforward:

1. In the Active Directory Users and Computers snap-in with the Active Directory Users and Computers node expanded. Right-click on your domain node (the icon named for your domain). Then point at New on the shortcut menu and select Organizational Unit. The New Object – Organizational Unit dialog box opens (see Figure 9.6).

2. Supply a name for the OU and then click OK. The new OU appears in the snap-in tree.

FIGURE 9.6
Create an
Organizational
Unit.

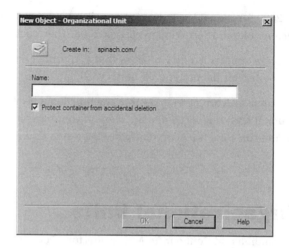

You can also create OUs inside other OUs. Right-click the OU in the Active Directory Users and Computers tree, point at New on the shortcut menu, and then select Organizational Unit. Create the new OU as you would a new OU that lives at the domain level (such as one created in the steps in this section).

3. To add users, groups, or other Active Directory objects to the OU, drag the items from their current location (such as the Users node). Remember that you can select and drag multiple items from one location to another (use Ctrl+click for objects that are not adjacent). A mouse click and then Shift+click allows you to select a series of adjacent objects.

4. You also control the properties associated with an OU. OU properties include information such as the OU's location, description, and group policies that have been set for the OU. To open the Properties dialog box for an OU, right-click the OU and then click Properties. The Properties dialog box opens (see Figure 9.7).

The OU's Properties dialog box includes three tabs:

▶ **General**—Used to enter a description and location for the OU.

▶ **Managed By**—Enables you to select a user account (or accounts) to serve as manager for the OU.

▶ **COM+**—Enables you to specify the COM+ partition that is a member of the COM+ partition set. COM+ partitions are used to synchronize information between the Active Directory and an application server.

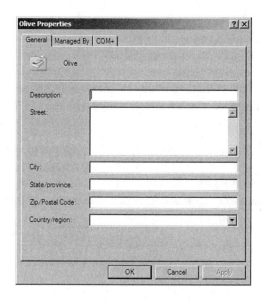

FIGURE 9.7
The OU's
Properties dia-
log box.

When you have completed setting the properties for the OU, click OK. You are returned to the Active Directory Users and Computers snap-in.

> You can also view additional tabs on the OU Properties dialog box. Select the View menu and then Advanced Features. Three additional tabs, Object, Security and Attribute Editor, are provided. The Security tab can be used to step through the permissions for the OU. Use the Security permissions only if you want to set specific permissions for another user or group.

By the Way

Using Active Directory Sites

Much of the discussion related to the Active Directory Domain Services thus far (in this hour and Hour 8) has revolved around the Active Directory's logical hierarchy (domains, OUs, and so on). Sites, on the other hand, are physical entities (having an actual physical location) and help to determine your network's physical topology.

When creating regional (child) domains in your root domain, each regional domain is placed in a site. Each site operates at least one domain controller for the regional domain (which branches off the root domain or forest in the Active Directory hierarchy). This allows for intersite replication between the various domain controllers in the tree.

Sites, which are Active Directory schema objects (and so contained in the Active Directory), also typically represent IP subnets that are connected by LAN or WAN connections (meaning reliable, high-speed connections). So, in a nutshell, an *Active Directory site* is typically a physical location on the network that represents a schema container for a regional domain, and the site is also typically one or more IP subnets. IP subnetting is covered in Hour 7, "Working with the TCP/IP Network Protocol."

Because you will have a map (meaning an actual diagram) of your domain hierarchy before you bring your regional domains online, it actually makes sense to begin setting up your network's site structure immediately after creating the forest for the domain. When you create regional domains, you must specify the site in which the domain will reside during the domain creation process.

> Creating the sites before adding the regional domains allows you to place each regional (child) domain in the appropriate site up front. You won't have to go back and change the site assignments after the fact.

Using sites as a way to structure both the regional domain locations and your IP subnets not only helps to keep local IP traffic on the subnet but it also allows you to determine how intersite replication will take place, which conserves bandwidth on the LAN or WAN connections between the different sites. Because it makes sense to have a domain controller within a site so that users on that subnet can log on using a local (to the site) domain controller, using regional domains with unique physical sites enables you to get the most out of your network bandwidth (particularly since you control the replication of the Active Directory database between the domain controllers in these sites).

> Hour 8, also discusses the use of sites in conjunction with regional domains, in the section "Adding a Regional (Child) Domain."

Creating a Site

Sites are created using the Active Directory Sites and Services snap-in. You can access the Active Directory Sites and Services snap-in in the MMC (select Start, Administrative Tools, Active Directory Sites and Services) or in the Server Manager node tree. To create a new site, follow these steps:

1. Right-click the Sites folder and then select New Site. The New Object – Site dialog box opens (see Figure 9.8).

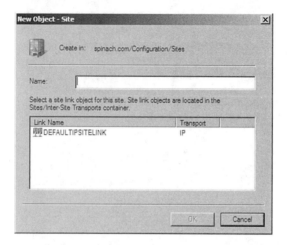

FIGURE 9.8
The New Object – Site dialog box.

2. Type a name for the new site. You must also select a site link object for this site. By default, there is only the DEFAULTIPSITELINK object. This object type is stored in the Active Directory (and is part of the schema). After you supply the site name and select the site link object, click OK.

3. A message box appears, letting you know that the new site has been created. A list of tasks that need to be performed related to the site, such as linking the site to other sites and adding a subnet or subnets to the new subnet container, is also provided. Click OK to close the information box.

By default, you are provided with a site named the Default-First-Site-Name. You can rename this site and use it as one of your sites. Right-click the site icon and select Rename. Then you can type a new name for the site.

By the Way

Configuring a Site

To configure a site, you must associate a subnet (or subnets) to the site and connect the site to other sites, using an Active Directory connection (this takes care of replication between the sites). To associate a subnet to the site, follow these steps:

1. Right-click the Subnets folder in the snap-in tree and select New Subnet. The New Object – Subnet dialog box appears (see Figure 9.9).

FIGURE 9.9
Associate a
subnet with
a site.

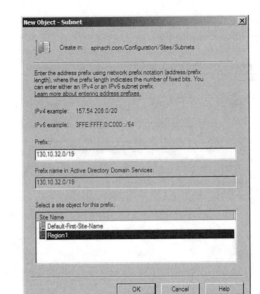

2. In the prefix box, enter the network ID (or address) for the subnet followed by
    the prefix. The prefix is the number of bits used to create the subnet, plus the
    network ID bits. The prefix can be converted to the subnet mask used for the
    subnet. The information entered in the prefix box can be in the IPV4 notation
    or the IPv6 notation (depending on whether the site uses IPv4 or IPv6). Figure
    9.9 shows a Class B subnet 130.10.32.0/19 with a 19-bit prefix, which would
    convert to the subnet mask 255.255.224.0.

 By the
Way

| IPv4 subnetting and working with IP addresses, subnet masks, and IPv6 notation are discussed in Hour 7. |

3. In the Select a Site Object for This Prefix box, select the site that is to be associ-
    ated with this subnet. Click OK. The new subnet appears in the Subnets folder,
    as shown in Figure 9.10.

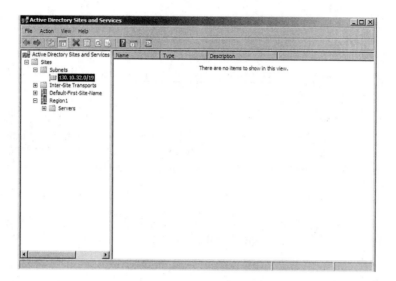

FIGURE 9.10
New subnets and sites appear in the Active Directory Sites and Services snap-in tree.

For replication to occur between the sites in your network, you must create a site link between the sites. The steps that follow walk you through the creation of a site link.

1. Click the Inter-Site Transports folder in the Active Directory Sites and Services tree. To create an IP link, right-click the IP folder in the snap-in Details pane and click New Site Link. The New Object – Site Link dialog box opens (see Figure 9.11).

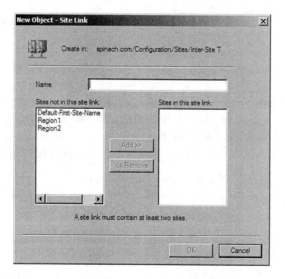

FIGURE 9.11
The New Object – Site Link dialog box.

2. Enter a name for the site link. Then add two or more sites to the site in this site link box on the left of the dialog box (select the site and then click Add). When you have entered the information required, click OK. The new site link is stored in the IP folder (or the SMTP folder, if you created the new site link in that protocol container).

By the Way

> You can also create site links using the SMTP protocol. However, this requires that you have an Enterprise Certificate Authority server available and that SMTP has been installed on all domain controllers that use the link. Typically your site links are of the IP variety.

3. You can also add sites to an existing site link. Right-click the site link icon and select Properties. Make sure that the General tab is selected.

4. Select the site names listed and then add them to the site link as needed, using the Add button. Click OK when you have finished adding sites to the site link.

Active Directory Replication and Sites

Replication is the process that allows domain controllers to keep Active Directory data consistent throughout the network. The Active Directory uses remote procedure calls to replicate data between domain controllers over IP (another reason why TCP/IP is the default transport protocol installed when you install Windows Server 2008 on a computer).

In terms of replication between sites, you can control intersite replication by the site links that you create. You can also specify the schedule for replication between sites that are linked by a site link.

To edit the properties for a site link, follow these steps:

1. Right-click a site link in the IP or SMTP folders in the Active Directory Sites and Services snap-in. Select Properties from the shortcut menu. Select the General tab on the Properties dialog box, if necessary (see Figure 9.12).

2. To change the replication interval, use the Replicate Every spin box to set the minutes between replication events. To actually change the schedule for replication, click the Change Schedule button.

3. The schedule for the link opens (see Figure 9.13). By default, replication is available every day of the week. To remove certain days and time periods

from the schedule, use the mouse to select the day and time frame, and then select the Replication Not Available option button. Repeat as necessary. Then click OK to close the Schedule box.

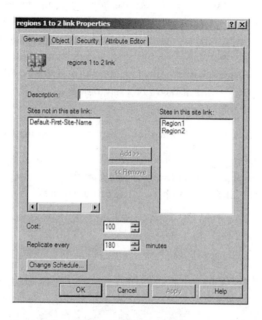

FIGURE 9.12
The Properties dialog box for a site link.

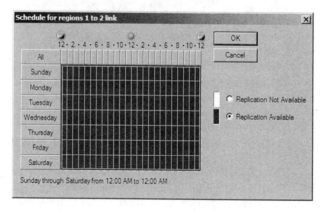

FIGURE 9.13
You can set a precise schedule for intersite replication.

4. When you have finished working with the link's Properties dialog box, click OK to close the dialog box.

You can modify links as needed. You may want to fine-tune replication over time after you have had an opportunity to monitor your network traffic between sites during your schedule replications.

Understanding Delegation

Every action discussed so far related to the Active Directory requires that a user be a member of the Domain Admins or Enterprise Admins group. Otherwise, a user must be delegated the appropriate authority to make changes to the Active Directory, such as adding OUs or sites. So, what is delegation? It is the assignment of administrative responsibility to a user or group (it can also be assigned to a computer). Delegation can be handled using group memberships or Group Policy settings. The Delegation of Control Wizard also can be used to delegate the control of Active Directory objects such as OUs or sites.

To delegate the control of an organizational unit or site, follow these steps:

1. To start the Delegation of Control Wizard for an Active Directory OU or site, right-click the object and select Delegate Control. The Delegation of Control Wizard opens. Click Next to bypass the initial wizard screen.

2. On the next wizard screen, you are asked to select users or groups that will be delegated control for the object. Click the Add button. The Select Users, Computers, or Groups dialog box opens (see Figure 9.14).

FIGURE 9.14
Select the users that will be delegated control of the object.

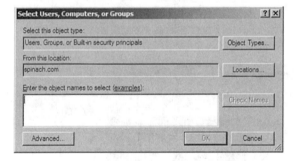

3. Specify the object names in the Enter the Object Names to Select box (you can type key letters in an object name and then click Check Names to see a list of objects that begin with those characters).

4. After specifying the users or groups for delegation, click OK. Then click Next. The next wizard screen asks you to specify the tasks to be delegated (see Figure 9.15).

5. You can delegate common tasks, such as the capability to manage Group Policy links, or you can create custom tasks to delegate. Custom tasks enable you to manage objects in the container and specify control based on object permissions. Select Manage Group Policy links or Create a custom task to delegate. Then click Next. If you selected Manage Group Policy links, the wizard takes you to the final screen, where you can click Finish.

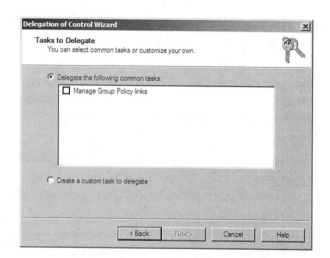

FIGURE 9.15
Group Policy
links or custom
tasks can be
delegated.

6. If you choose to create a custom task to delegate, the next screen provides you with the capability to delegate control of all the objects in the current object folder (such as an OU or site) or to specify objects from a list (such as only account objects or computer objects). After making your selection, click Next.

7. A permissions list is provided on the next screen, which enables you to specify the permissions that you want to delegate for the object. Select the permissions using the appropriate check boxes, and then click Next.

8. The wizard provides a summary screen; click Finish.

The task or tasks related to the object are now delegated to the user, users, or group listed when the delegation was created. Delegation can be used in situations where you have regional domains and sites and you want to allow some local control of group policies or other tasks related to an Active Directory object such as a site.

Summary

Active Directory groups come in two types: security and distribution. Security groups are used to determine the access levels that users (members of the group) have to resources on the network.

Domain group scopes consist of universal, global, and domain local. Universal groups are available only if the domain functional level has been raised to the Windows 2000, Windows Server 2003, or Windows Server 2008 functional level. Groups can be nested within groups. For example, you can nest global and universal groups in domain local groups.

You create groups by using the Active Directory Users and Computer snap-in. You can add users to the group in the Member tab of the group's Properties dialog box.

Domain functional levels are raised in the Active Directory Domains and Trusts snap-in. By default, the functional level is set to Windows 2000 (when you create the domain). You can raise the level to either Windows Server 2003 or the Windows Server 2008 functional level. After you raise the functional level, however, you cannot reverse the process.

An Organizational Unit (OU) provides a security container that can be used to hold users, groups, computers, and other OUs. OUs can be used to define logical groupings of users or other objects in the Active Directory, specify security settings, and assign policies to the OU.

Active Directory sites define the IP topology of your Windows Server 2008 network. A site can consist of a subnet or subnets. You create sites and associated subnets with the Active Directory Sites and Services snap-in. To link sites, use site links, which determine the replication paths on your network.

Delegation is used to assign an object such as a user or group a certain level of control over an object, such as a Active Directory OU or site. Delegation can be set in the Delegation of Control Wizard.

Q&A

Q. *What type of Active Directory objects can be contained in a group?*

A. A group can contain users, computers, contacts, and other nested groups.

Q. *What type of group is not available in a domain that is running at the mixed-mode functional level?*

A. Universal groups are not available in a mixed-mode domain. The functional level must be raised to Windows 2003 or Windows 2008 to make these groups available.

Q. *What types of Active Directory objects can be contained in an Organizational Unit?*

A. Organizational Units can hold users, groups, computers, contacts, and other OUs. The Organizational Unit provides you with a container directly below the domain level that enables you to refine the logical hierarchy of how your users and other resources are arranged in the Active Directory.

Q. *What are Active Directory sites?*

A. Active Directory sites are physical locations on the network's physical topology. Each regional domain that you create is assigned to a site. Sites typically represent one or more IP subnets that are connected by IP routers. Because sites are separated from each other by a router, the domain controllers on each site periodically replicate the Active Directory to update the Global Catalog on each site segment.

HOUR 10

Adding Client Computers and Member Servers to the Domain

What You'll Learn in This Hour:

- ▶ Adding Client Computers to the Domain
- ▶ Using Active Directory to Add Computers to the Domain
- ▶ Adding and Configuring Vista Clients
- ▶ Adding and Configuring XP Clients
- ▶ Adding Windows 2000 Client Computers
- ▶ Viewing Client Computer Network Settings
- ▶ Adding Member Servers to the Domain
- ▶ Creating a Workgroup

In this hour, you learn about adding client computers to your Windows Server 2008 domain or workgroup. We also discuss adding member servers to the domain.

Adding Client Computers to the Domain

Windows Server 2008 supports a variety of client computer operating systems, including Windows 2000 Professional, Windows XP Professional, and Windows Vista. So in terms of desktop operating system options, Windows Server 2008 provides the same possibilities as those that were provided by Windows Server 2003 (even including Windows desktop legacy versions such as Windows NT and 9X).

However, because Windows Server 2008 and Windows Vista were really parts of a single Microsoft development project, a number of advanced features related to event monitoring, local print job rendering, network access protection, and even IPv6 deployment are best realized when Windows Vista is run on the desktop. And although you may be thinking that Terminal Services can still allow you to get a little more mileage out of legacy desktop operating systems, even some advanced Terminal Services features, such as Terminal Services web access, are limited to clients running Windows Vista (SP1 or better) and Windows XP (SP3 or better).

By the Way

> Not only does Windows Server 2008 provide a "typical" network environment for a variety of desktop operating systems, it also makes it possible to connect to Windows Server 2008 running Terminal Server, which can actually enhance the remote connection for legacy operating systems. However, Windows Server 2008 has been built with the assumption that desktop computers will take advantage of Windows Vista and so some advanced features, including new Terminal Services features, are not compatible with computers running legacy operating systems. For more about the Terminal Server possibilities, see Hour 19, "Implementing Terminal Services."

In an ideal situation (although an ideal situation probably does not exist in the networking world), running only one or two types of the possible client operating systems such as Windows Vista (and perhaps Windows XP) allows you to standardize the user desktop as much as possible. This keeps you from having to configure (and troubleshoot) many different client platforms.

Another aspect of standardizing client computers is standardizing their hardware configurations. If you have the luxury (the budget, in most cases) of configuring your client computers with a consistent hardware configuration, it will be easier to select and configure a particular client operating system.

A network client must be configured so that a user (or users) can log on to the domain. However, the computer must also be configured with the appropriate network protocol (in most cases TCP/IP) so that it can "talk" to the domain controller that grants a user access to the domain and the other servers on the network that provide services such as file and print services. Hour 7, "Working with the TCP/IP Network Protocol," provides an overview of configuring TCP/IP (v4 and v6) on computers running Windows Server 2008. This hour discusses the basic aspects of configuring network clients with TCP/IP.

Setting up and configuring client computers is a somewhat consistent task when you are working with Microsoft operating systems such as Windows Vista and Windows XP. And if you do plan on running some legacy operating systems such as Windows 2000, you will find that the network configuration only differs slightly (when compared to Vista or XP). Because computers are added to the Active Directory from the server, the minor differences between desktop operating systems doesn't even play a role.

Windows 2000, Windows XP, and Windows Vista clients must be added to the domain (as opposed to a legacy Windows operating system such as Windows 9X), which means these operating systems provide a secure user environment because the domain administrator determines the computers that are added to the domain and the level of access these computers have to network resources. Let's take a look at how a computer can be added to the domain using the Active Directory for Users and Computers snap-in.

Deploying Windows Vista clients and additional servers running Windows Server 2008 can be an arduous task in terms of installing these operating systems one at a time on client computers or servers. Windows Server 2008 can help automate this task with Windows Deployment Services, which is discussed in Hour 5, "Implementing Windows Deployment Services."

By the Way

Using Active Directory to Add Computers to the Domain

As you already know from the discussion in Hour 8, "Understanding and Configuring Active Directory Domain Services," a user needs a domain user account to log on to a domain. The user's client computer must also be added to the domain. You can add the computer to the domain by using the Active Directory Users and Computers snap-in, which can be run in the MMC or in the Server Manager.

To add a computer to the domain with the Active Directory Users and Computers snap-in follow these steps:

1. Open the Active Directory Users and Computers snap-in on your Windows Server 2008 domain controller by selecting Start, Administrative Tools, Active Directory Users and Computers (or expand the Roles, Active Directory Domain Services and Active Directory Users and Computers nodes in the Server Manager).

2. Expand your domain node to view the Builtin, Computers, and other domain folders.

3. In the snap-in tree, select the Computers folder (see Figure 10.1).

1. 切短

FIGURE 10.1
Select the
Computers
folder.

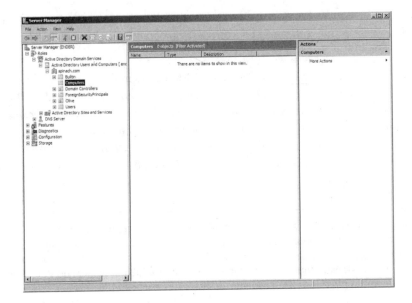

4. To add a new computer to the domain, right-click the Details pane, point at
   New, and then select Computer. The New Object–Computer dialog box opens.

Did you Know?

If you have multiple domains in the domain tree, expand the domain node to
which you intend to add the computer before selecting the computers node. You
want to make sure that you place the new computer in the appropriate domain
container.

---

3. In the Computer Name box, type the name of the computer that you are
   adding to the domain (see Figure 10.2). Because DNS is the default name-
   resolution mechanism for the Windows Server 2008 environment, the
   computer name can be up to 63 characters. (The Fully Qualified Domain
   Name of the computer can be up to 255 characters, including all the suffixes.)
   In some cases, you might also want to truncate the name to a NetBIOS length
   (15 characters) if you have NetBIOS clients (those using WINS for name resolution) on the network. This NetBIOS name is typed in the Computer Name
   (Pre–Windows 2000) box.

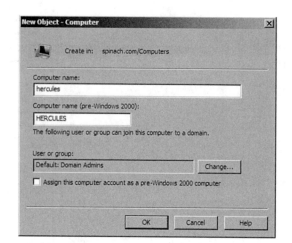

FIGURE 10.2
Enter the name of the computer being added to the domain.

4. You can also change the group membership required to join the computer to the domain. Select the Change button. Then use the Select User or Group dialog box to specify the groups (or specific user) who can join the computer to the domain.

5. The dialog box includes a check box that enables you to specify the new computer account as a pre–Windows 2000 computer (assign this account as a pre–Windows 2000 computer). Check this box if applicable.

6. After making your selections and providing the computer name, click OK to close the dialog box and return to the Active Directory Users and Computers snap-in.

The added computer appears in the Details pane (when the Computers folder is selected) of the Active Directory Users and Computers snap-in. Figure 10.3 shows the Active Directory Users and Computers snap-in containing computers added to the domain.

FIGURE 10.3
Computers
added to the
domain appear
in the Active
Directory.

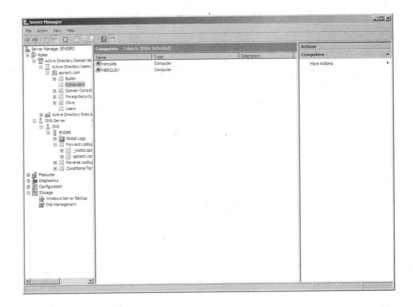

Managing a Computer Account

After you have created the account, the Active Directory Users and Computers snap-in provides you with the capability to manage the computer. For example, you can disable the computer account if you think there is a security issue or some other issue related to the computer. Right-click the computer name in the Details pane and select Disable Account. The computer can no longer log on to the domain.

You can also move the account from one domain to another; right-click the computer account and then select Move. The Move dialog box opens. You can use it to expand the node for a particular domain that appears in the domain tree. When you're finished, click OK to relocate the computer account to that domain.

Did you Know? ✓

> If you want to delete a computer account, right-click the account in the Details pane and select Delete from the shortcut menu. Click Yes when prompted to delete the object.

You can also manage the client computer by opening its Computer Management snap-in from the Active Directory Users and Computers snap-in (this is true for Windows Vista, Windows XP, and Windows 2000 clients and Windows 2003 and Windows 2008 member servers). You can then add or remove local user accounts and even manage volumes and disks on the client computer.

Before you can access a remote computer via the Users and Computers snap-in, you must allow the remote administration application through the client computers firewall. The Windows Server 2008 firewall is described in detail in Hour 21, "Working with the Windows Firewall and IPSec," so let's look at how to "turn on" remote administration on a Windows Vista client.

Follow these steps:

1. Select Start, and then Control Panel. The Control Panel opens.

2. In the Control Panel, click Allow a Program Through Windows Firewall (under the Security group). The Windows Firewall Settings dialog box opens.

3. In the exceptions list, click the Remote Administration check box (see Figure 10.4) .

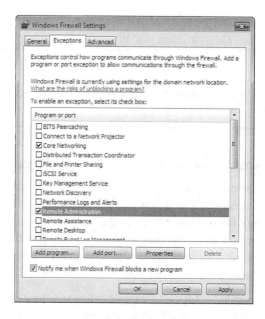

FIGURE 10.4
Add Remote Administration to the firewall's exceptions.

4. Click OK. The Windows Firewall Settings dialog box closes and you are returned to the Control Panel.

After you have enabled remote administration on a client or server computer through the Windows Firewall, right-click the computer account (on your domain controller) in the Active Directory Users and Computers snap-in and select Manage from the shortcut menu. The Computer Management snap-in for that computer opens (see Figure 10.5). You can then manage the computer as needed.

FIGURE 10.5
You can remote-
ly manage a
computer via
the Active
Directory Users
and Computers
snap-in.

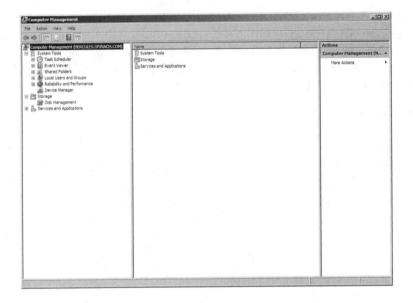

By the Way

> For more information about using the Computer Management snap-in, see Hour 6,
> "Managing Hard Drives and Volumes."

Viewing Computer Account Properties

You can also view the properties for the computer associated with the Active
Directory computer account (both clients and member servers). You can view the
operating system that the computer is running (including service packs installed)
and set other features related to the computer, such as whether the computer should
be trusted for delegation (delegation is discussed in Hour 9, "Creating Active
Directory Groups, Organizational Units, and Sites").

To open the Properties dialog box for a computer listed in the Active Directory, right-
click the account and select Properties. The Properties dialog box for the computer
opens. This dialog box contains seven tabs:

▶ **General**—This tab provides the computer name, the DNS name, and the role
of the computer.

▶ **Operating System**—This tab (see Figure 10.6) shows the operating system
running on the computer and the service packs that have been installed.

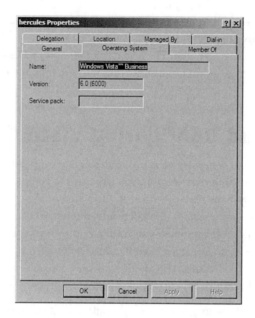

FIGURE 10.6
You can view
and set the
properties of a
client computer
or member
server in the
domain.

▶ **Location**—This enables you to specify the building or the floor where the computer is located.

▶ **Delegation**—On this tab, you can specify whether the computer should be trusted for delegation.

▶ **Managed By**—This tab is used to specify which user or group has the management rights to the computer.

▶ **Dial-In**—You can specify whether the computer can be used to dial in and remotely connect to remote access servers in your domain. Remote access and dial-in accounts are discussed in Hour 18, "Implementing Network Routing."

▶ **Member Of**—This tab shows the group to which the computer belongs. The default is Domain Computers. This tab also shows the domain container where the computer resides.

When you have finished viewing (or changing) the properties for a computer account, click OK to close the dialog box. You are returned to the Active Directory Computer and Users snap-in.

You can also access additional tabs related to a computer account's Properties dialog box by selecting the Advanced Features command under the View menu. After you enable Advanced Features (a check mark appears next to the command on the View menu), you also have access to the Object tab, which provides the canonical name of the object, and the Security tab. The Security tab enables you to set the different permission levels for users and groups in relation to the management of the computer account.

Adding and Configuring Vista Clients

Although you can add computer accounts to the Active Directory using the Active Directory Users and Computers snap-in, you still have to configure client computers running operating systems such as Windows Vista so that the computer logs on to the domain when a user provides a logon name and password. You may also have to configure network protocols when you configure the client computer, depending on whether you are using DHCP or fixed IP addresses or even other network protocols beyond the TCP/IP default (configuring network protocols on client computers is discussed later in this hour).

Although the Active Directory Users and Computers snap-in provides an environment in which you can quickly add a number of computer accounts, you can also add the computer account for a Windows Vista computer directly from the client workstation (as long as you have the appropriate administrative rights).

To configure a Windows Vista client as a domain member from the client computer, follow these steps:

1. Select Start. Then right-click Computer and select Properties. The System window opens.

2. Click the Change settings link. The System Properties dialog box opens (see Figure 10.7).

3. You have the option of changing the domain (or workgroup) affiliation for the computer via a wizard by clicking the Network ID button or by clicking the Change button.

   If you click the Network ID button, a wizard walks you through the steps of identifying the domain or workgroup to which you wish to add the computer and the username and password required to add the computer.

   Although the wizard is useful, it is easier to click Change. The Computer Name/Domain Changes dialog box opens (see Figure 10.8).

FIGURE 10.7
The System Properties dialog box shows the computer name and current network ID.

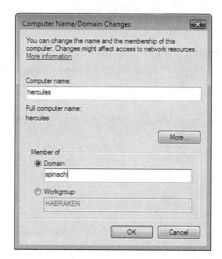

FIGURE 10.8
Specify the domain name in the Domain box.

4. Select the Domain option button and then type the domain name in the Domain text box. Then click OK.

5. The Windows Security dialog box opens. Supply the username and password that has the permission rights to add the computer to the domain. Then click OK.

6. A message box appears with a message welcoming the computer to the specified domain. Click OK to close the message box.

7. A restart is required for the domain change to go into effect. Close the System Properties box and agree to restart the computer.

The computer is added to the list of domain computers found in the Computers folder in the Active Directory Users and Computers snap-in. You may have to refresh the snap-in to view the added computer or computers (right-click in the Details pane and select Refresh from the shortcut menu).

Adding and Configuring XP Clients

Windows XP can also serve as a client OS on a Windows domain. To configure an XP domain client (a computer running Windows XP Professional; XP Home does not support domain membership) from the client computer, follow these steps:

1. Select Start. Then right-click My Computer and select Properties. The System Properties box for the XP computer appears. Select the Computer Name tab on the Properties dialog box.

2. To make the computer a member of the domain, select the Change button on the Computer Name tab. The Computer Name Changes dialog box appears (see Figure 10.9).

FIGURE 10.9
Specify the domain in the Computer Name Changes dialog box.

3. Click the Member of Domain option button and then type the name of the domain in the Name box. Click OK. A Computer Name Changes dialog box appears (yes, this is a second dialog box with the same name, as shown in Figure 10.10), asking you for a username and a password. The user must have administrative privileges to add the computer to the domain. This privilege is afforded to any user account that is a member of the Domain Administrator group.

FIGURE 10.10
Provide a user account with permission to join the domain.

4. Enter the username and password, and then click OK. It might take a moment, but a dialog box opens welcoming you to the domain. The computer is now configured to log on to the domain. A computer account is added to the Active Directory automatically because you provided an account with administrative privileges for joining the computer to the domain. The computer needs to reboot to complete the process.

Another option exists for adding XP Professional computers to the domain and adding a domain user account to the computer: using the Network Identification Wizard. This wizard is accessed on the Computer Name tab of the Systems Properties dialog box. Click the Network ID button to start the wizard; it walks you through the steps of adding the computer to the domain and then adding a domain user account. In my opinion, however, the wizard makes a very short process (the process already discussed in this section) longer than necessary.

By the Way

Adding Windows 2000 Client Computers

You can also configure Windows 2000 Professional computers as domain clients on the client computer. The process is very similar to adding an XP client to a domain. You can access the Network Identification tab via the Properties dialog box. Follow these steps:

1. On the computer desktop, right-click the My Computer icon and then select Properties. The Properties dialog box opens. Select the Network Identification tab.

2. On the Network Identification tab, select the Properties button. The Identification Changes dialog box appears.

3. Click the Member of Domain option button and then enter the name of the domain of which the computer will be a member. Then click OK. The computer must be rebooted for the process to be completed. As with Windows XP, a computer account is added to the Active Directory automatically.

Viewing Client Computer Network Settings

By default, Windows Vista and Windows XP clients are configured for the TCP/IP protocol. These clients are configured to use DHCP to receive their IP addressing and other TCP/IP protocol settings (also by default).

Windows Vista is enabled for both IPv4 and IPv6. And because we are living in a TCP/IP world when it comes to networking, the only network settings that you may need to edit are related to the TCP/IP protocol. For example, you may want to configure a client computer with a fixed IP address or specify the default DNS server for your clients (although this can be configured as part of the parameters received from the DHCP server).

Although TCP/IP is the default (and de facto) network protocol for networking, you may find yourself in a situation where you need to run multiple network protocols on a client computer. You may need to add a network client or service that allows the client computer to connect to a specialized third-party server. Typically these third-party products provide a CD (or a downloadable set of files) with the appropriate client or service and you can add these additional clients, protocols, or services via the Local Area Connection Properties dialog box.

A basic fact related to network protocols is that multiple network protocols can be bound to a single network adapter (connection). This means that if you do have the need to run another network protocol (other than the default TCP/IP), you can configure the protocol on the computer's network connection.

You may also want to disable File and Printer Sharing for Microsoft Networks (if it has been enabled). Allowing users to share files and printers at will, using this non–password-protected scheme, can lead to possible security problems.

All the various flavors of Windows clients such as Windows Vista, Windows XP, and Windows 2000 handle the network connection configuration in a similar fashion. Network clients, protocols, and services are installed and configured in a Properties dialog box for the local area network connection.

For example, to open the Windows Vista Local Area Connection Properties dialog box, you would follow these steps:

1. Select Start, and then right-click Network. Select Properties from the shortcut menu that appears. The Network and Sharing Center opens (see Figure 10.11).

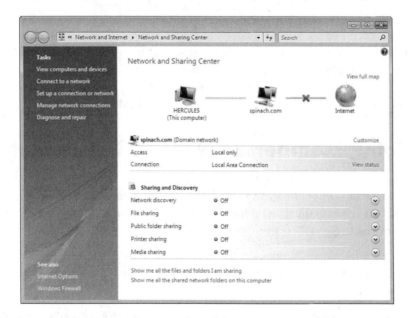

FIGURE 10.11
The Windows Vista Network and Sharing Center.

2. In the Tasks pane of the Network and Sharing Center, click the Manage Network Connections task. The Network Connection window opens.

3. To open the Local Area Connection Properties dialog box, right-click a Local Area Connection and then select Properties on the shortcut menu.

Figure 10.12 shows the Windows Vista Local Area Connection Properties dialog box.

FIGURE 10.12
The Windows
Vista Local Area
Connection
Properties dia-
log box.

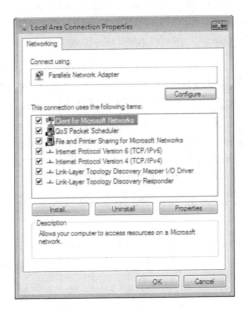

You can open the properties of any of the items listed in the Local Area Connection Properties dialog box and configure them. You can also disable features (deselect a check box) and install other features as needed. We looked at issues related to TCP/IP settings for both servers and clients in a Windows domain in Hour 7.

Adding Member Servers to the Domain

Adding member servers to a domain is very similar to adding desktop clients. You can add the server from the Active Directory Users and Computers snap-in or you can add the server to the domain from the server itself. To add a Windows Server 2008 member server, follow these steps:

1. Open the Systems window for the member server (select Start, right-click Computer, and then select Properties from the shortcut menu). The System window opens.

2. In the Tasks pane (on the left of the window), click the Advanced system settings task. The System Properties dialog box opens. Select the Computer Name tab of the dialog box (see Figure 10.13).

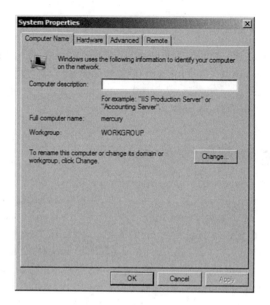

FIGURE 10.13
The Computer Name tab of the System Properties dialog box.

3. Click the Change button and the Computer Name/Domain Changes dialog box will open.

4. Click the Domain option button and enter the name of the domain that the member server is to join. Then click OK. The Windows Security dialog box opens (see Figure 10.14).

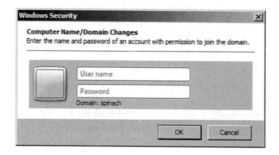

FIGURE 10.14
A username and password with rights to add the server to the domain is required.

5. Provide the username and password of an account that has the permissions to add the server to the domain. Then click OK.

6. A message box opens, welcoming the computer to the domain; click OK. You are required to restart the server (a message box opens telling you to restart; click OK).

After the server has restarted it will be a member server in the domain. Adding the Windows member server to the domain in this way automatically adds the server's computer account to the Active Directory. Member servers that have been added to the domain appear in the Computers node of the Active Directory Users and Computers snap-in (as opposed to domain controllers, which are listed in the Domain Controllers node of a particular domain).

Creating a Workgroup

In terms of Microsoft networking, the alternative to the domain is the workgroup. The workgroup is a collection of computers (in many cases, a peer-to-peer network that does not include a server) that share resources such as files and a printer. The workgroup certainly isn't a true alternative to the domain. When you have a very limited number of clients, you can use the workgroup model for networking the computers. However, adding a computer running Windows Server 2008 to this type of small network might be an expense that is difficult to justify.

When you install Windows Server 2008 on a computer, it is (by default) assigned to a workgroup called WORKGROUP. So, creating a workgroup and adding the server to the workgroup is really just a matter of configuring the clients and the server with the appropriate workgroup name.

The steps provided for adding a computer to a domain also apply (in part) to adding a peer computer or a server to a workgroup. Again, the process varies slightly among the Windows operating systems but is somewhat consistent. For example, to add a Windows Vista computer or a Windows Server 2008 computer (which is similar to adding a computer running Windows XP or Windows 2000) to a workgroup, open the computer's Systems Properties dialog box and then select the Computer Name tab (this is the Network Identification tab on a Windows 2000 computer).

On the Computer Name tab, click the Change button. In the dialog box that appears, select the Workgroup option button (if necessary) and then type the name of the workgroup. Then click OK. The computer is welcomed to the workgroup that you specified.

Computers in workgroups (including servers) can share files, printers, and other resources. A computer running Windows Server 2008 can provide a workgroup a number of specialized services, such as an Internet connection, remote access/VPN, and basic firewall protection.

Client operating systems such as Windows Vista and Windows XP provide a network wizard. This wizard can be used to create and configure the small network work-group. After a peer workgroup has been created, clients and servers can be added to the workgroup as needed.

Summary

The Active Directory Users and Computers snap-in can be used to add Windows Vista, XP, or 2000 client computer accounts to the domain. Client computers run-ning Windows Vista, XP, and 2000 can also be added to the Active Directory from the client workstation. You do so in the Systems Properties dialog box. A username and password with administrative rights are required to add the client computer account to the domain.

You must configure client computers with the appropriate TCP/IP settings so that they can "talk" with other computers in the domain. In cases where you are using specialized servers or third-party products, clients can run multiple network proto-cols, if required.

Windows Server 2008 member servers are added to the domain in the Computer Name tab on the computer's Systems Properties dialog box. Workgroups provide a peer-to-peer environment for sharing files and other resources such as printers. Client computers can easily be added to a workgroup (in the same manner that they are added to a domain).

Q&A

Q. *How can client computer accounts be added to the Active Directory?*

A. Client computer accounts can be added through the Active Directory Users and Computers snap-in. You can also create client computer accounts via the client computer by joining it to the domain via the System Properties dialog box. This requires a user account that has administrative privileges, such as members of the Domain Administrator or Enterprise Administrator groups.

Q. *What firewall setting is required to manage client computers such as Vista clients and Windows 2008 member servers?*

A. The Windows Firewall must allow remote administration for a computer to be managed remotely.

Q. *Can servers running Windows Server 2008 provide services to clients when they are not part of a domain?*

A. Servers running Windows Server 2008 can be configured to participate in a workgroup. The server can provide some services to the workgroup peers but does not provide the security and management tools provided to domain controllers.

HOUR 11

Deploying Group Policy and Network Access Protection

What You'll Learn in This Hour:

- ▶ Understanding Group Policy
- ▶ The Group Policy Feature
- ▶ Working in the Group Policy Management Snap-In
- ▶ Creating Group Policies
- ▶ Editing Group Policies
- ▶ Enabling the Auditing Policy
- ▶ Understanding Policy Inheritance
- ▶ Viewing GPO Details in the GPO Management Snap-In
- ▶ Understanding Network Access Protection
- ▶ Adding the Network Policy Server Service
- ▶ Configuring the Windows Security Health Validator
- ▶ Adding Remediation Servers
- ▶ Enable the Network Access Protection Service on Clients

A method of controlling the user environment provided to your network clients is the deployment of group policies. This hour takes a look at how to use Group Policy to control the user environment and enable features such as user logon auditing. It also looks at Group Policy in terms of the bigger picture of controlling domain policies related to security settings and their inheritance by downstream objects (such as Organizational Units [OUs]).

There's also a new Windows feature, the Network Policy Server service, which enables you to require that network clients meet certain "health requirements" (such as the Windows Firewall being enabled and the antivirus software signatures being up to date) for full network access. The Network Policy Server service is part of the Network Policy and Access Services role.

Understanding Group Policy

Group Policy provides a framework for controlling the user or computer environment in any Windows server container, including domains, sites, and Organizational Units. Security policies can also exist at the local computer level and are very much like a local set of group policies. However, Group Policy at the domain level is tightly wound with the Active Directory Domain Services (AD DS), which is where you manage the various domain containers (such domains, sites, and OUs).

Group Policy objects actually dictate the rules or settings that determine how Group Policy affects users and computers in the target container (or on the local computer). For example, a Group Policy object (GPO) can determine the applications available to users in a particular domain or OU (creating OUs is discussed in Hour 9, "Creating Active Directory Groups, Organizational Units, and Sites"). To affect a container such as a domain or site with a particular GPO, the GPO is linked to the container.

GPOs can contain two types of settings: computer configuration settings and user configuration settings. Group Policy is managed with two different tools: the Group Policy Management snap-in, which was first introduced with the release of Windows Server 2003, and the Group Policy Object Editor. Both these tools are examined in this hour.

The Group Policy Feature

When you add the Active Directory Domain Services to a server and "promote" that server to a domain controller, the Active Directory Domain Services Installation Wizard checks to see whether the Group Policy feature is already installed on the server (you would have had to install it in the Add Features Wizard). If Group Policy is not installed, it is included in the Active Directory Domain Services installation (see Figure 11.1).

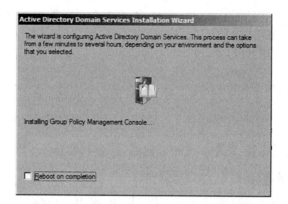

FIGURE 11.1
Group Policy is
added when you
install the AD
DS role.

After the server has been "promoted" to a domain controller, you are ready to work with the Active Directory (as discussed in Hours 8, 9, and 10) and you are ready to begin the process of using Group Policy to manage the domain's security.

Because Group Policy Management is installed as a feature (rather than a role or service), it should be listed with all the other features that have been installed on the server. You can view installed features in the Server Manager (click the Server Manager icon on the Quick Launch toolbar).

To view installed features, click the Features node in the Server Manager node tree. The installed features are listed in the Details pane (see Figure 11.2).

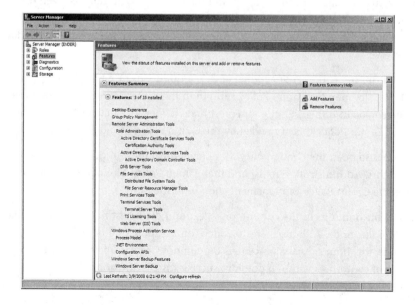

FIGURE 11.2
View installed
features in the
Server Manager.

If you wish to work with Group Policy from another computer such as a domain member server, you need to install Group Policy Management on that server. Open the Add Features Wizard via the Initial Configuration Tasks window or the Server Manager (click Add Features in both cases). You can then select Group Policy Management in the Features list and add it to the server, using the wizard's feature installation process.

Working in the Group Policy Management Snap-In

The Group Policy Management snap-in makes it easy for you to view the Group Policies linked to objects in the Active Directory tree. It also provides two wizards that help determine how a GPO actually affects the users or computers in a particular domain container: the Group Policy Modeling tool and the Group Policy Results tool.

The Group Policy Modeling tool enables you to determine how a set of GPOs will affect a particular object in the Active Directory tree such as a user or computer. The Group Policy Results tool enables you to take a look at the resultant set of policies, meaning how both direct and inherited policies actually affect an object in the Active Directory.

So, the Group Policy Management snap-in provides all the information related to the various containers in the domain and the Group GPOs that have been assigned to these containers. When you actually create or edit a Group Policy, you use the Group Policy Object Editor, which has been available since the release of Windows 2000 Server.

You can run the Group Policy Management snap-in via the Server Manager or in the MMC. To open the Group Policy snap-in in the Server Manager, expand the Features node and then select your Forest node to view the Active Directory containers and Group Policy tools provided by the Group Policy Management snap-in.

You can also open the Group Policy Management snap-in in the Windows MMC. Select Start, Administrative Tools, and then Group Policy Management. Figure 11.3 shows the Group Policy Management snap-in in the MMC.

To view the domains in the current forest, expand the Forest node and then expand the Domains node. Although Group Policy can be applied to both sites and domains, this hour's discussion centers on domain Group Policies and the Group Policies of containers within a domain, such as an Organizational Unit.

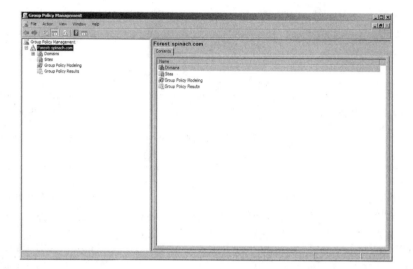

FIGURE 11.3
The Group
Policy
Management
snap-in.

The Group Policy Management snap-in is actually quite flexible in terms of getting the most out of existing GPOs. You can import GPOs from other forests and you can copy any GPO available in the current forest. This means that you have plenty of existing GPOs that you can copy and then "dissect" to determine how they will affect objects in the domain. Although creating Group Policies is discussed in the next section, you may want to begin your exploration of Group Policies by editing copies of existing GPOs.

Did you Know?

Creating Group Policies

You will find in the Group Policy Management snap-in that certain Group Policy objects exist by default. For example, on a domain controller, the snap-in shows that a default domain policy and default domain controllers policy exist. These policies can be edited and can include settings that enable you to control Registry-based settings, security options, and software installation and maintenance options. The next section looks at editing GPOs. For example, to activate certain types of auditing on a domain controller, you must edit certain GPOs related to auditing events.

Before editing existing GPOs, it makes sense to create a new GPO and link it to a particular Active Directory container object. This also enables you to edit the settings for the GPO. For practice, you might want to create a new OU, using the Active Directory Computers and Users snap-in, and then link a new GPO to it (using the Group Policy Management snap-in, as discussed in a moment). You can then edit the settings for the new GPO. You can later delete the OU and its GPO without affecting any of the default Group Policies in force for your domain (creating OUs is discussed in Hour 9).

Did you Know?

> The Group Policy Management snap-in also makes it easy to back up and restore individual GPOs. Right-click a GPO in the Details pane (when the Group Policy Objects node is selected) and select Back Up. You are asked to provide a location and description for the GPO backup. You then click Back Up. You can also restore backups of a GPO; right-click the policy and select Restore from Backup.

Two different options exist for creating new GPOs in the Group Policy Management snap-in. You can create a new GPO and simultaneously link it to an Active Directory object such as a domain or an OU. Or, you can create a new GPO in the Group Policy Objects folder and then link it to a container. The latter method provides you with the ability to "play" with the settings of the GPO before you actually link it to a particular Active Directory object.

Let's look at creating the new GPO and link, and then look at creating a GPO in the Group Policy Objects folder.

To create a new GPO and a link simultaneously, follow these steps:

1. Open the Group Policy Management Console (Start, Administrative Tools, Group Policy Management).

2. Expand the various nodes in the snap-in tree until you see the container object that you want to link the new Group Policy to.

3. Right-click the object (such as an OU) and select Create a GPO in This Domain and Link It Here. The New GPO dialog box appears (see Figure 11.4).

4. Enter a name for the GPO. You can also use the Source Starter GPO drop-down box to base the new GPO on a starter GPO (see Did You Know that follows). Then click OK.

FIGURE 11.4
Supply a name for the new GPO.

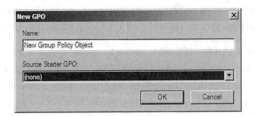

Starter GPOs can be created (just as any GPO can be created) in the Group Policy Object Editor (discussed later in this hour). You can use any of the policy settings from the various administrative templates to create the starter GPO. You can then base new GPOs on a starter GPO (kind of like using frozen pizza dough for a pizza rather than making the crust from scratch). You can still customize your new GPO, but the fact that the GPO is based on a premade starter GPO means that common settings that you want in your GPOs are already available in the starter GPO. To create starter GPOs you must first create the Starter GPOs folder; click on the Starter GPOs node in the Group Policy Management snap-in. Then click Create Starter GPOs Folder in the Details pane. You can then create starter GPOs by right-clicking the Starter GPOs node and then selecting New. The Group Policy Object Editor opens and you can configure the settings for the starter GPO.

Did you Know?

The new GPO appears in the Details pane of the Group Policy Management snap-in, along with any other GPOs linked to the object that you selected when you created the new (and linked) GPO. Figure 11.5 shows a new GPO that has been linked to an OU named olive.

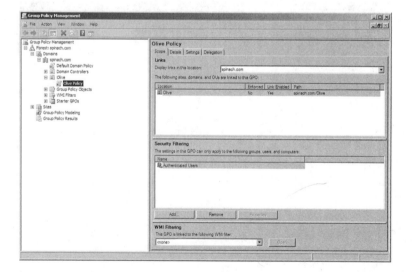

FIGURE 11.5
GPO linked to an OU.

If you want to create a new GPO without linking it, right-click the Group Policy Objects folder in the Group Policy Management snap-in. Select New from the shortcut menu that appears. The New GPO dialog box opens. Supply a name for the GPO and then click OK. The GPO appears in the list of policies found in the Group Policy Object folder.

WITHOUT LINKING

All the GPOs in the forest appear in the Group Policy Objects folder. Policies linked to a specific object, such as a domain, also appear under that object in the Group Policy Management tree.

Editing Group Policies

Creating a new GPO (and linking it) is actually only half of the work that you have to do to create a functional GPO. You have to edit the new GPO and configure its settings before it provides you with any functionality.

To edit a GPO, right-click on the GPO in the Group Policy Management node tree. Select Edit from the shortcut menu. The Group Policy Object Editor opens with the GPO to be edited loaded in the snap-in (see Figure 11.6).

FIGURE 11.6
GPOs are edited in the Group Policy Object Editor.

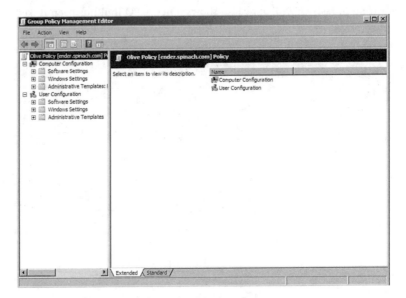

GPOs contain two main sections (or settings, as mentioned earlier): Computer Configuration and User Configuration. Settings that you place in the Computer Configuration section affect all users logging on to computers to which the GPO has been linked.

The User Configuration section affects all users, no matter the computer to which they log on (all users in the container to which the GPO has been applied). User configuration policies go into effect when users log on.

Each section of the GPO (Computer Configuration and User Configuration) contains three different setting types: Software, Windows, and Administrative Templates. These setting types are used as follows:

▶ **Software Settings**—By default, the Software Installation policy is contained in Software Settings (for both the Computer Configuration and User Configuration settings), as shown in Figure 11.7. You add applications to the Software Installation policy that you want to be available to the computers or users to which the GPO applies. You add applications to the Software Settings policy by right-clicking Software Settings and adding the appropriate Windows installer packages to the configuration.

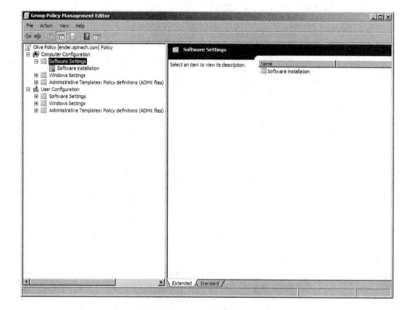

FIGURE 11.7
Software settings can be configured in the Computer Configuration and User Configuration areas of a GPO.

Windows installer packages (.msi files) are typically provided by software vendors for the applications that you want to deploy.

Did you Know?

▶ **Windows Settings**—Windows Settings (for both the Computer Configuration and User Configuration settings) contains the security settings that you select and also holds any scripts that you choose to run. Scripts are beyond the scope of this hour's discussion; the focus here is on security settings. Many of the important security settings are actually located in Windows Settings under the Computer Configuration node. These include account policies (which include Password and Account policies as shown in Figure 11.8), and local policies that include the audit policy and user right assignments. The next section examines how to enable the Audit policy.

> In the User Configuration area, Windows Settings also includes policies not found in the Computer Configuration area, such as maintenance settings related to Internet Explorer.

FIGURE 11.8
Settings for security policies and local policies are located in the Windows Settings node of the Computer Configuration node.

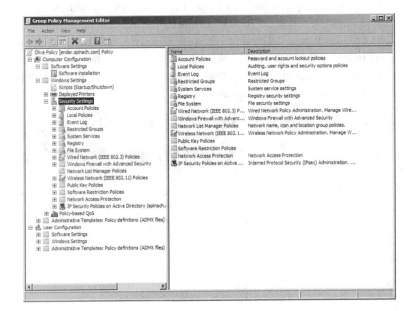

▶ **Administrative Templates: Policy Definitions (ADMX files)—**
Administrative templates are found in both the computer and user configurations. These templates enable you to control the settings for Windows components such as the Task Scheduler, Windows Messenger, and Windows Update. Settings related to the Control Panel can also be controlled with Administrative Templates, as can settings related to Network Connections and System Settings. How to configure Administrative Templates is discussed later in this hour. Figure 11.9 shows the Administrative Templates found under the Computer Configuration node.

> Windows Server 2008 provides a new administrative templates file format: ADMX. This file format is an XML-based file format that incorporates multilanguage support, making it easier to work with Group Policy in multilingual administrative environments. Microsoft has also embraced the XML file format across its operating systems and even applications to make them more interoperable with the open source XML file standard.

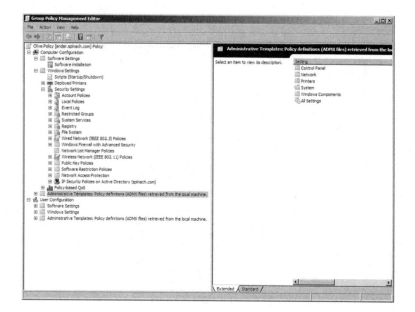

FIGURE 11.9
Administrative templates enable you to control Windows components and system and network settings.

How you design and implement your Group Policy strategy depends on whether you decide to approach policies from the Computer Configuration or User Configuration settings. A particular GPO does not have to contain settings for both sections.

By the Way

To make a long story short, editing a GPO is really a matter of locating individual policies and administrative templates that you want to use, and then enabling and configuring them. For example, let's say that you want some help in adding new workstations to the domain (this typically requires membership in a group that has administrative privileges). You can actually specify certain users who could help you add the new workstations by enabling and configuring the Add Workstations to Domain policy, which is found in the Local Policies node under the User Rights Assignment node (as shown in Figure 11.10).

FIGURE 11.10
You can config-
ure policies
related to user
rights, such
as adding
computers.

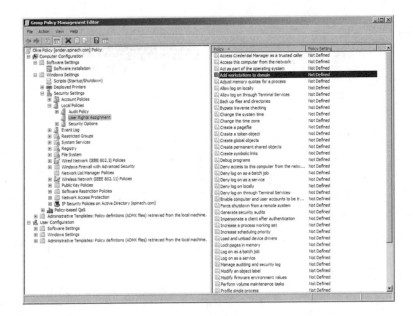

Policies that have not been enabled or configured are labeled Not Defined in the
Details pane. To enable and configure a particular policy, follow these steps:

1. In the Details pane, double-click the policy that you want to enable and configure (in this case, the Add Workstation to Domain policy). The Properties
   dialog box for the policy opens.

2. In the case of the Add Workstations to Domain policy, click the Define These
   Policy Settings check box and use the Add User or Group button to add users
   or groups to the policy. These users and groups now have the capability to add
   workstations to the domain (see Figure 11.11).

3. After you configure the policy (in some cases, you must actually click an
   Enable check box, but this varies from policy to policy), click the OK button.

The policy is now enabled and so affects the computers (or users) in the container
(such as the domain) to which the GPO containing the enabled policy is linked.
Obviously, to fully configure a GPO, you need to enable and configure a number of
the policies that reside in the GPO.

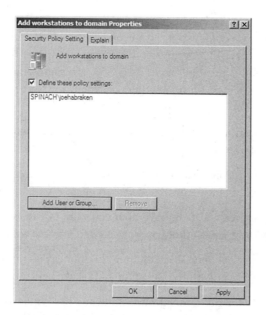

FIGURE 11.11
Individual policies must be configured for them to take effect.

Obviously, a lot of the individual policies and administrative templates found in a GPO can relate to servers on the network and also to computers and users running client operating systems such as Windows XP and Windows 2000 Professional. Typically, you are trying to control client environments on the network (more so than you are your servers, which are already controlled by password protection and access restraints), so as you peruse the basics of a GPO, you should be thinking in terms of how you can fashion the overall environment that users will experience as they work in the domain.

By the Way

Enabling the Auditing Policy

For an individual policy to take effect in a GPO, you must enable and configure that policy (as discussed at the end of the last section). The policies that you enable in a GPO and how you apply that GPO to a domain or other Active Directory container depend on your overall plan for controlling the network environment for your users and computers. Some networks require very tight control using Group Policy, whereas others do not require the same intensity (and amount of work for the network administrator) in relation to the Group Policy configuration.

Whether or not you totally buy into the controls provided by Group Policy, a useful ability for any network administrator is the ability to audit events on your domain controllers, such as successful or unsuccessful logons. So, it makes sense to take a look at how you enable the audit policy in a GPO. (This also enables you to walk through the process of configuring another policy in a GPO—the more you enable and configure, the more it makes sense.)

Let's say that you want to enable certain aspects of the Audit policy at the domain level. You would follow these steps:

1. Open the Group Policy Management snap-in (Start, Administrative Tools, Group Policy Management).

2. In the snap-in tree, locate the GPO that you want to edit (such as the default domain policy or a GPO that you've created to practice with).

3. Right-click the GPO and select Edit from the shortcut menu. The Group Policy Object Editor opens, with the GPO that you selected open in the snap-in.

4. Expand the Computer Configuration node and the Windows Settings node. Expand the Security Settings node and then the Local Policies node. The various local policies should appear in the Details pane, as shown in Figure 11.12.

FIGURE 11.12
Local security settings include policies for auditing object access and account logon events.

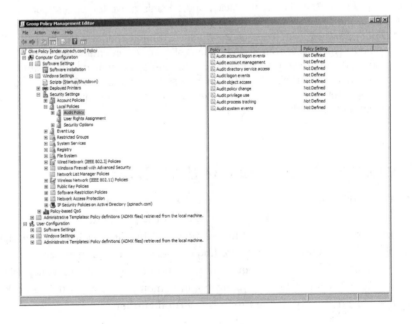

5. To enable and configure an audit policy such as the Audit Account Logon events policy, double-click the policy in the Details pane. The Properties dialog box for the policy opens.

6. In the case of the Audit Account Logon Events policy (see Figure 11.12), click the Define These Policy Settings check box. To audit both successful and failed logon attempts, select both the Success and Failure check boxes.

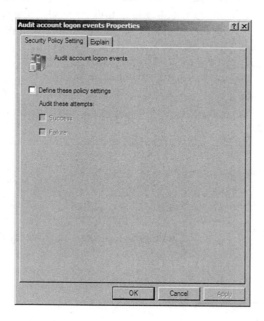

7. To close the Properties dialog box, click OK.

Now account logon events (such as a failed logon) will be logged in the security log of the Event Viewer. You can enable and configure other Audit policies as needed.

Understanding Policy Inheritance

An important aspect of understanding and using Group Policy is having a good grasp of policy inheritance. Enabled Group Policies flow down through the Active Directory tree from top to bottom. This means that domain-level Group Policies are inherited by OUs (and other Active Directory objects, such as domain controllers) that reside within the domain. A particular computer in an OU could then inherit GPO settings from the domain and the OU in which it resides. That computer might also have local policies that have been configured.

Although inheritance flows down through the Active Directory tree, the sequence in which Group Policy is actually processed by a computer is exactly the opposite. By default, the local GPO is applied first, followed by site GPOs, and then domain GPOs, and finally OU GPOs.

To view GPOs linked to an object such as an OU or a computer, select the object in the Group Policy Management tree. In the Details pane, click the Group Policy Inheritance tab (see Figure 11.14). Figure 11.14 shows the GPO inheritance for an OU named Olive. The Olive Policy is a policy created and linked specifically for the Olive OU. Notice that the OU also inherits the default domain policy.

Did you Know?

To view just the GPOs that are directly linked to an object, select the Linked Group Policy Objects tab.

FIGURE 11.14
The Group Policy Inheritance tab shows both directly linked and inherited GPOs for the object.

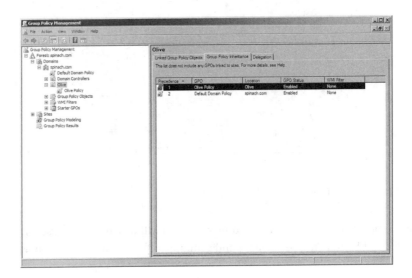

You can control which GPOs are inherited by a particular object. You can also have GPOs from higher in the Active Directory tree actually override local policies. Let's take a look at blocking inheritance and then enforcing a GPO to override local policies.

Watch Out!

The Delegation tab of an Active Directory object's Group Policy link enables you to change the permissions related to linking GPOs to that particular object. By default, the Administrators, Domain Admins, and Enterprise Admins groups have the Link GPO permission for Active Directory objects such as sites, domains, and OUs.

Blocking Inheritance

You block the inheritance of policies from GPOs assigned farther up the Active Directory tree by using the Group Policy Management snap-in. For example, you can block a domain GPO from affecting local policies or from affecting policies that you specifically assigned (linked) to an OU that you have populated with users and computers (in the Active Directory).

In the Group Policy Management snap-in, locate the container for which you want to block inheritance of the Group Policy provided by upstream Active Directory containers. For example, if you want to block domain policies from affecting an OU, right-click the OU in the Group Policy Management tree. A shortcut menu appears. Select Block Inheritance on the shortcut menu.

When you view the Group Policy Inheritance for the object, you will find that upstream GPOs have been removed from the Group Policy Inheritance tab. If you want to "unblock" the inheritance at any time, right-click the object (such as an OU) and select Block Inheritance to remove the check mark.

Enforcing a Group Policy Object

In some cases, you might want a particular GPO link to override any local Group Policy settings on an object. For example, you might want the domain Group Policy to override any settings made locally on a server (in the local Group Policy). You can do this by enforcing the GPO link for the Domain Group Policy.

In the Group Policy Management tree, right-click the GPO that you want to enforce. Select Enforced on the shortcut menu. If you want to no longer enforce a GPO, right-click the policy and select Enforced to remove the check mark.

Viewing GPO Details in the GPO Management Snap-In

Before ending this discussion of Group Policy, we should look at some of the other capabilities that the Group Policy Management snap-in provides. You can quickly view the scope (the objects that are linked to the GPO) and the details of the GPO (such as who owns the GPO, when it was created, and its current status). You can also view the enabled settings for the GPO and view the current delegation of the GPO.

To view all the GPOs in the current forest, expand the Group Policy Objects node. Select any of the GPOs listed to view the policy details.

The information provided in the Details pane of the Group Policy Management snap-in for a selected GPO is divided into four tabs:

▶ **Scope**—This tab shows the sites, domains, and OUs that are linked to the GPO. This tab also shows the group users and computers to which the GPO is applied.

▶ **Details**—This tab tells you the domain in which the GPO resides, the owner of the GPO, and when the GPO was created. It also supplies the date when the policy was last modified. The GPO Status drop-down list on the tab enables you to enable or disable the GPO, or disable only computer or user settings in the GPO.

▶ **Settings**—This tab (see Figure 11.15) shows you the different policies that have been enabled in Computer Configurations and User Configurations. Select a heading such as Security Settings and expand it to see the actual policies that have been set. To view all the enabled settings, click Show All at the top right of the tab. This tab provides a listing of only enabled settings, whereas the Group Policy Object Editor (discussed earlier in the hour) shows you all the polices available in the GPO.

▶ **Delegation**—This tab shows the allowed permissions for the GPO. You can add or remove groups from this tab as required.

FIGURE 11.15
The Settings tab allows you to view the policies enabled in the GPO.

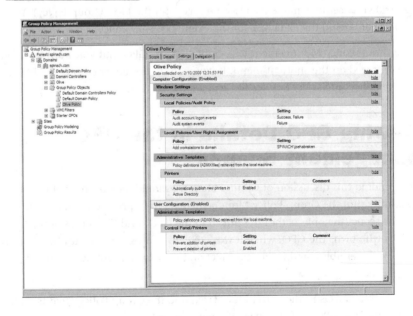

> A final note on Group Policy: Group Policy is designed to provide consistency and security on the network. You should definitely create a number of GPOs and develop a clear understanding of how individual policies and administrative templates affect the user and computer configurations. It would be very wise to set up a small test network and deploy Group Policy so that you can see how the different GPOs at different levels in the Active Directory tree actually interact. Group Policy is not something that should be used without a very clear understanding of how it really works.

Understanding Network Access Protection

Group Policy provides you with a both fine-grained and yet extensible strategy for deploying policies on the network that control both computer and user behavior in the domain. And although you might think that Group Policy provides you with enough administrative control over domain users and computers, there is a new addition to the Windows Server 2008 network operating system that extends your bag of tricks in terms of securing the network: the Network Policy and Access Services.

In terms of network access protection (NAP), we will concentrate (at least in this hour) on the Network Policy Server (which is one component of the Network Policy and Access Services and is Microsoft's implementation of a RADIUS server) and how you configure it as a NAP health policy server. The network access protection provided by a NAP health policy server enables you to create "health" policies related to network clients in the domain and then enforce these policies. This may mean that network clients that are not using automatic updates to keep Windows Vista up to date (and more secure, because many updates are related to security issues), or have had their Windows configuration changed from a designated standard configuration (by a network user who doesn't comply with your "written" network policies), can be provided restricted network access until the client computer has been configured in accordance with the network access protection policies. The NAP health policy server can also help users get computers that do not comply with health policies up to date.

By the Way

> The Network Policy and Access Services role is kind of a grab bag of services and features related to remote access, routing, and network policy. This hour looks at how to use network policy to help secure the network and keep network clients up to date (in terms of their OS software). Hour 17, "Remote Access and Virtual Private Networking," looks at how to configure a server running Windows Server 2008 for remote access by using a Network Policy server (Microsoft's implementation of a RADIUS server), and how virtual private network networking is configured on a domain server. Hour 18, "Implementing Network Routing," discusses how a server with the Network Policy and Access Services role can function as an IP router on a small network. So, you can see that the Network Policy and Access Services role has a number of different functions that relate to network access, protection, and data routing.

Every network administrator wants to keep network client configurations up to date and maintain desktop operating system deployments with a standard configuration. For example, you want all desktop clients to have the Windows Firewall enabled or you want to make sure that every desktop client has the latest antivirus signatures installed. Now, the NAP health policy server provides a method to actually enforce desktop operating system configuration requirements in the domain and help keep desktop operating systems such as Microsoft Vista and Windows XP (Service Pack 3) secure by making sure that the latest OS updates have been installed.

Let's take a look at how to add the Network Policy Server (as part of the Network Policy and Access Services) to a server running Windows Server 2008. You can then see how to configure the Network Policy Server as a NAP health policy server.

Adding the Network Policy Server Service

The Network Policy and Access Services role is installed via the Add Roles Wizard. You can start the wizard from either the Server Manager or the Initial Configuration Tasks window.

1. From the Server Manager (with the Roles node selected) or the Initial Configuration Tasks window, select Add Roles. The Add Roles Wizard opens. Click Next to bypass the initial wizard page.

2. On the next wizard page, select the Network Policy and Access Services check box (see Figure 11.16) and then click Next.

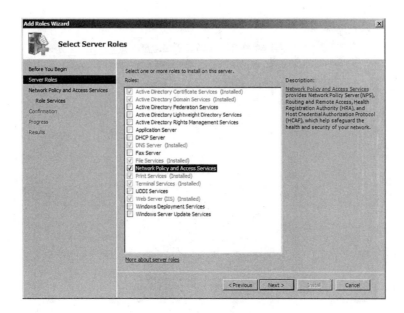

FIGURE 11.16
Add the
Network Policy
and Access
Services role.

3. On the next page, you are provided an overview of the Network Policy and Access Services and additional links for more information about these services. After exploring the information, click Next.

4. On the next wizard page (the Select Role Services page), select the Network Policy Server check box. Then click Next.

5. The Confirmation page appears, detailing the role and role services (Network Policy Server) that you are about to add to the server's configuration. Click Install.

When the installation of the role is complete, the Results page appears. Click Close to close the wizard. The Network Policy and Access Services role is added to the server. If you expand the Roles node in the Server Manager, you can select the Network Policy and Access Services role (see Figure 11.17).

You can then view any events that have been logged related to Network Policy and Access Services. You can also view the role's services that are running and the services that have been installed for the role. You will also find that the Network Policy Server command (for opening the Network Policy Server snap-in) has been added to the Administrative Tools menu on the Start menu.

FIGURE 11.17
Select the
Network Policy
and Access
Services role.

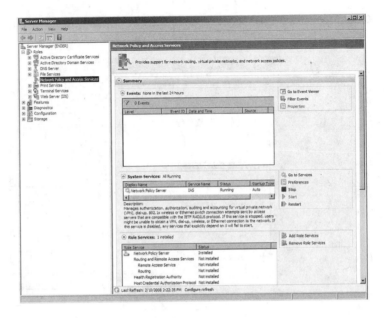

You can administer the Network Policy Server from the Server Manager or in the MMC, using the Network Policy Server snap-in. In terms of setting health requirements for network clients, you need to configure the Network Policy Server with health validators. (A *validator* is basically the health policy that needs to be verified by the server when it examines the "health" of a particular network client.)

By default, the Network Policy Server provides a Windows Security Health Validator. Let's take a look at how to configure this provided health validator.

> The Network Policy Server can also provide network protection when you work with remote access and virtual private networking. Check out Hour 17 for more about the various roles of the Network Policy Server.

Configuring the Windows Security Health Validator

As already mentioned, the Network Policy Server provides (by default) the Windows Security Health Validator. This health validator is designed to check the health of network clients running Windows Vista and Windows XP (Service Pack 3). On these network client operating systems, the counterpart to the Windows Security Health

Validator or WSHV (which contains the validation rules) is the Windows Security Health Agent (WSHA). The WSHA is used by the WSHV as a sort of declaration of health by the client operating system, and the Network Policy server can compare the WSHV to the WSHA to make sure that the computer is compliant with the configured network policies.

When the client computer is not compliant, you want the problem fixed. This is where remediation comes in. You can configure remediation server groups, which are the servers that contain the update files or other software that the client computer needs to access to become compliant with the Network Policy Server's WSHV.

To configure the WSHV in the Network Policy Server snap-in, follow these steps:

1. Open the Network Policy Server snap-in in either the Server Manager (expand the Roles, Network Policy and Access Services and NPS nodes) or the MMC (Start, Administrative Tools, Network Policy Server).

2. In the snap-in, select the Network Access Protection node in the node tree (see Figure 11.18).

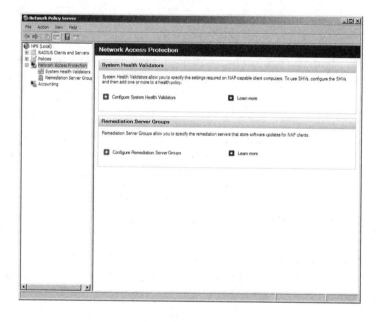

FIGURE 11.18
Open the Network Policy Server snap-in.

3. In the Details pane, click the Configure System Health Validators link. The Windows Security Health Validator (WSHV) is listed in the Details pane.

4. To open the WSHV and configure it, double-click Windows Security Health Validator. The Windows Security Health Validator Properties dialog box opens.

To configure the WSHV, click the Configure button. The Windows Security Health Validator dialog box opens (see Figure 11.19).

FIGURE 11.19
The WSHV dialog box.

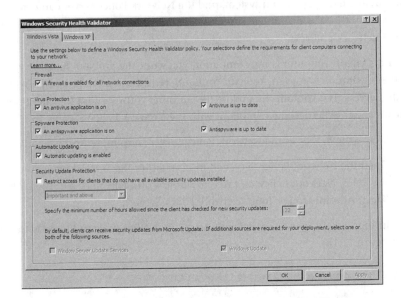

5. The WSHV dialog box has two tabs: one for Windows Vista and one for Windows XP. The two tabs are identical except the Windows XP tab does not require that spyware protection be installed on Windows XP clients. Let's walk through the settings on the Windows Vista tab:

   ▶ **Firewall**—The Windows client must run either the Windows Firewall or a third-party firewall that is compatible with the Windows Security Center. The firewall must be enabled on all network connections on the client.

   ▶ **Virus Protection**—The Windows client must be configured with antivirus software.

   ▶ **Spyware Protection** (not required for Windows XP)—Antispyware software (such as Windows Defender) must be installed and running on the client computer.

▶ **Automatic Updating**—Automatic updating must be enabled on the
  client computer.

▶ **Security Update Protection**—The client must be running the
  Windows Update Agent and also must be registered with a server running the Windows Server Update Service.

The Windows Server Update Service is a service that is provided by Microsoft and
can be downloaded from http://www.microsoft.com/downloads/
details.aspx?FamilyId=F87B4C5E-4161-48AF-9FF8 A96993C688DF&displaylang=
en#Overview. This service can be used along with the Windows Update Agent
(on client computers) to make sure that the client OS has all available security
updates installed.

By the Way

Select (or deselect) the configuration parameters for the WSHV as needed (on
both the Vista and XP tabs if you have a mixed client-base on the network).

6. Click OK to return to the Windows Security Health Validator Properties dialog
   box, and then click OK to close the Properties dialog box.

Now that the WSHV has been configured, you still need to add remediation servers
to the Network Policy Server and also enable the Network Access Protection Service
on your network clients. Let's look at adding a remediation server and then
enabling network access protection on network clients.

Adding Remediation Servers

Remediation servers are the servers to which the network client connects when it
needs to remediate a violation of an access policy such as those provided by the
WSHV. The purpose of the remediation server is to help the client take care of the
problem. So, if the problem is that the client does not have the latest antivirus signatures installed, the remediation server should supply the most up-to-date
antivirus signatures.

To add a remediation server (or servers) to the Network Policy Server configuration,
expand the Network Access Protection node (in the Network Policy Server snap-in).
Then right-click on the Remediation Server Groups node and select New from the shortcut menu. The New Remediation Server Group dialog box opens (see Figure 11.20).

FIGURE 11.20
Create a new
remediation
server group.

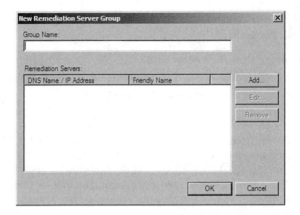

Type a name for the server group. Then click Add to add a server to the group. The
Add New Server dialog box opens (see Figure 11.21).

FIGURE 11.21
Add servers to
the remediation
group.

You can add a server (or servers) to the new remediation group by friendly name, IP
address, or DNS name. After entering the name (or IP address) to identify the server,
click OK. The server is added to the group. You can add other servers to the group as
needed and create more remediation groups as needed. Click OK to close the New
Remediation Server Group dialog box when you have finished creating groups and
adding servers. The new group or groups appear in the Details pane when you select
the Remediation Server Groups node in the node tree. (You can edit a group by
double-clicking the group.)

Remember that the purpose of the remediation server is to help the client remedy
the policy violation. The server needs to be configured with the appropriate fix (an

example would be a share that provides needed files) to get the client back onto the network with full functionality.

> Some remediation related to the WSHV is handled automatically. For example, if the Windows Firewall is required by the WSHV and it is turned off on the client, the client OS is instructed to enable the firewall.

By the Way

Enable the Network Access Protection Service on Clients

For this whole Network Policy Server scenario to function, you need to enable the Network Access Protection service on clients. This is accomplished in the client's Control Panel. Let's look at how you would enable Network Access Protection on a Windows Vista client.

> A user needs to be a member of the Domain Admins group to enable the Network Access Protection service on a domain client. You can also use Group Policy to enable the service.

By the Way

Open the Control Panel (Start, Control Panel) and then click the System and Maintenance group. Scroll down and select Administrative Tools. In the Administrative Tools window, double-click the Services shortcut.

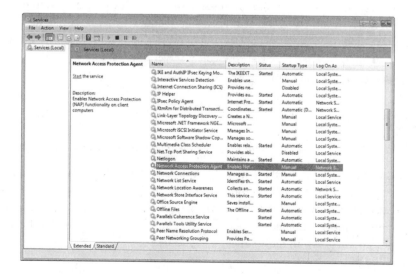

FIGURE 11.22
Locate the Network Access Protection Agent in the Services list.

In the Services list (see Figure 11.22), double-click the Network Access Protection Agent. The Network Access Protection Agent Properties dialog box opens. Click the Startup Type drop-down list and change the setting from Manual to Automatic. Then click OK (you can close the various Control Panel windows that were opened).

The next time the client computer is started, the operating system settings will be subject to health validators configured on the Network Policy Server. Client computers in violation of the health validators such as the WSHV will need remediation to gain full network access.

Summary

In this hour, you learned how to navigate the Group Policy Management snap-in You also learned how to view the GPOs for an Active Directory forest and how to view the properties and settings of an individual GPO.

This hour also discussed the creation of new GPOs, the linking of GPOS to Active Directory containers, and the editing of GPO policies in the Group Policy Object Editor. You also learned how to enable and configure individual policies and administrative templates with the GPO Editor.

In addition, you learned how to add the Network Policy Server service when installing the Network Policy and Access Services role. The Network Access Protection server serves as a NAP health policy server and enables you to control client network access with health policies.

The Network Policy Server (which supplies network access protection) is managed in the Network Policy Server snap-in. In this snap-in, you can configure health policy validators such as the Windows Security Health Validator. After the validator has been configured (providing the policies that network clients must meet), you can add remediation servers to the Network Policy Server that help network clients remediate violations of the policies required by a validator.

Q&A

Q. *What does the use of Group Policy provide you as a network administrator?*

A. Group Policy provides a method of controlling user and computer configuration settings for Active Directory containers such as sites, domains, and OUs. GPOs are linked to a particular container, and then individual policies and administrative templates are enabled to control the environment for the users or computers within that particular container.

Q. *What tools are involved in managing and deploying Group Policy?*

A. GPOs and their settings, links, and other information such as permissions can be viewed in the Group Policy Management snap-in.

Q. *How do you deal with Group Policy inheritance issues?*

A. GPOs are inherited down through the Active Directory tree by default. You can block the inheritance of settings from upline GPOs (for a particular container such as an OU or a local computer) by selecting Block Inheritance for that particular object. If you want to enforce a higher-level GPO so that it overrides directly linked GPOs, you can use the Enforce command on the inherited (or upline) GPO.

Q. *How can you make sure that network clients have the most recent Windows updates installed and have other important security features such as the Windows Firewall enabled before they can gain full network access?*

A. You can configure a Network Policy Server (a service available in the Network Policy and Access Services role). The Network Policy Server can be configured to compare desktop client settings with health validators to determine the level of network access afforded to the client.

HOUR 12

Working with Network Shares and the Distributed File System

What You'll Learn in This Hour

- ▶ Configuring a File Server
- ▶ File Server Disk Quotas
- ▶ Using the Share and Storage Management Snap-In
- ▶ Creating News Shares with the Share and Storage Management Snap-In
- ▶ Managing the File Server
- ▶ Publishing a Share to the Active Directory
- ▶ Using the Volume Shadow Copy Service
- ▶ Understanding the Distributed File System
- ▶ Installing and Configuring the Distributed File System
- ▶ Adding DFS Folders
- ▶ DFS Folder Replication

Two of the most compelling reasons for networking computers are to share data files and to share printers. Early computer networks and the network operating systems that they used were designed around these needs.

This hour takes a look at strategies for sharing files on a server running Windows Server 2008. This exploration of Windows Server 2008 file server possibilities includes a look at the new Share and Storage snap-in and other file services tools.

Configuring a File Server

A file server provides a repository for files that the users on your network must access. Not only do file servers provide data access to users, but they also often serve as a place where users can save files in either a home directory or a directory that other users can also access. You can configure a domain controller or a domain member server as a file server.

Whether you need a dedicated file server on the network depends on the amount of data that must be accessed and the number of users accessing this data. On a larger network, a dedicated file server that takes advantage of a RAID 5 configuration would provide fast and dependable access for your users. (RAID 5 and configuring server drives are discussed in Hour 6, "Managing Hard Drives and Volumes.")

Before configuring a server as a file server, configure the drives and volumes that will be used to hold the shared folders. Use the NTFS file format on your file server. This enables you to take advantage of NTFS permissions and also monitor NTFS volumes, using the new Windows Server 2008 File Server Resource Manager.

You can assign the file services role to your server running Windows Server 2008 via the Initial Configuration Tasks window or the Server Manager. The Add Roles Wizard walks you through the addition of the file services role to the server's configuration as discussed in the following steps:

1. Open the Add Roles Wizard (click the appropriate add roles link) in either the Initial Configuration Tasks window or the Server Manager (with the Roles node selected).

2. The first wizard screen suggests that before installing a server role you assign a strong password to the administrator account, configure static IP addressing (if required by the role), and install the latest Windows 2008 security updates. After you have confirmed that these tasks have been completed, click Next to continue.

To bypass the initial Add Roles Wizard's initial page when you use the wizard in the future (for adding additional roles), click the Skip This Page by Default check box when installing a new role.

3. On the Select Server Roles page, select the File Services check box (see Figure 12.1). Then click Next.

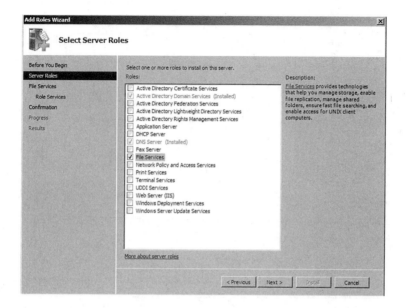

FIGURE 12.1
Select the File
Services role.

4. The next screen provides a brief introduction to the Windows Server 2008 file services and also provides links to an overview of File Services and Share and Storage Management. Explore the links if you choose and then click Next.

5. On the next screen you are provided with a list of the various file server services that can be installed as you install the File Services role (see Figure 12.2). These services include

▶ **Distributed File System (DFS)**—DFS provides hierarchical tree structure that enables users to access resources anywhere in the domain. The actual location of the resource, such as a volume or a folder, is transparent to the users. DFS is discussed in more detail later in the hour.

▶ **File Server Resource Manager**—This tool enables you to set disk and volume quotas and also generate storage reports.

▶ **Services for Network File System (NFS)**—This service enables UNIX-based clients to access files on your network server.

Select the services you want to add to the File Services role installation (for sake of discussion add the File Server Resource Manager). Then click Next.

FIGURE 12.2
Services such as DFS and NFS can be installed as part of the File Services role.

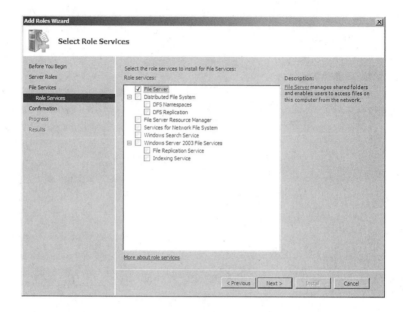

6. The next screen allows you to select the NTFS volumes you want to monitor in the Server Resource Manager (see Figure 12.3). Select the volume or volumes (using the appropriate check boxes).

FIGURE 12.3
Select the volume or volumes that are to be monitored.

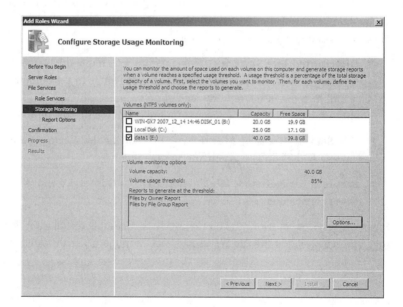

7. You can configure the threshold and the type of reports that are generated when the volume reaches a particular threshold (percentage use) by clicking the Options button (when a volume is selected). In the Volume Monitoring Options dialog box, set the volume usage threshold and the reports to be generated, which include Large Files Report, Most Recently Accessed Files, Files By Owner Report (selected by default), and Files by File Group Report (selected by default). Then click OK.

8. After selecting the volumes to monitor and setting the options for each volume, click Next to continue.

9. The next screen is the Report Options page. Use the Browse button to specify where volume reports are to be saved when they are generated.

Did you Know?

You can configure the report options to email volume reports to a particular email. This makes it easy for you to quickly deal with file servers that have reached their configured threshold. The server, in effect, alerts you to the fact that the threshold has been reached by emailing the various reports you have selected directly to an email address. All you have to do is supply the email address (or addresses) and the SMTP server on the Report Options page.

10. The Confirmation page appears with a summary of the roles and role services that will be installed (in this case the File Services role). Click Install.

When the installation is complete, the Installation Results page appears. Click Close. The File Services role appears in the roles listed in the Initial Configuration Tasks window and in the Server Manager window (when the Roles node is expanded).

When you select the File Services role in the Server Manager (click the Server Manager icon in the Quick Launch toolbar), you can view events related to File Services. You can also start and stop services related to the File Services role and add other services to the role as needed (see Figure 12.4).

When you expand the File Services node you can access the Share and Storage Management node, which provides access to the File Server Resource Manager. Expanding the File Server Resource Manager provides access to the Quota Management snap-in, which is covered in the next section.

FIGURE 12.4
View events and services related to File Services in the Server Manager.

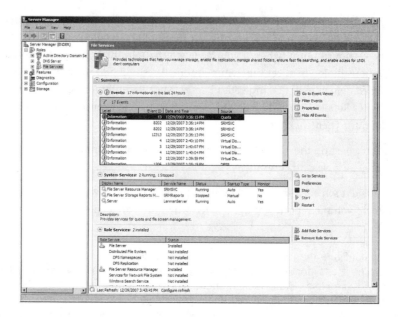

File Server Disk Quotas

The Quota Management snap-in enables you to create quotas that limit the space allowed for a volume or folder. These quotas can be also be applied to subfolders on a particular volume (or a particular folder).

Windows Server 2008 enables you to control and track shared volume usage on a per-volume and per-user basis. Notifications can also be built into the quota settings, alerting you or folder owners when a particular threshold has been reached.

Did you Know?

> Windows Server 2008 also provides a command-line tool, `fsutil`, for working with disk volumes. Its capabilities include manipulating disk quotas. For example, `fsutil quota` is used to create and edit user disk quotas.

You definitely will want to spend some planning time to determine an appropriate disk space for your users before enabling disk quotas. Quotas can be created that are specific to a volume or folder, and you can also create auto-apply quotas that also apply to any subfolders in a volume or folder to which you assign the auto-apply quota.

Two types of quotas are available to you: hard quotas and soft quotas. Hard quotas dictate a size limit that users cannot exceed. A soft quota allows users to exceed the limit and is used to monitor volume (or folder) use by your users.

> Soft quotas can send alert emails, generate reports, or log an event in the Event Viewer (hard quotas can also be created that log events and send alerts). Using the Event Viewer and viewing events in the log files such as the system log are discussed in Hour 24, "Monitoring Server Performance and Network Connections."

By the Way

Disk quotas can be created with the Quota Management snap-in (in the Server Manager or the MMC, it is a subnode of the File Server Resource Manager). Templates are provided (using various threshold settings) that can be used to create both your "regular" quotas and you auto-apply quotas.

To create a quota for a volume or folder, follow these steps:

1. Expand the File Server Resource Manager node in the Server Manager (first, expand the Roles, File Services, and Share and Storage Management nodes) or in the File Server Resource Manager snap-in in the MMC (Start, Administrative Tools, and then File Server Resource Manager).

2. Expand the Quota Management node and then select the Quotas node. Any existing quotas appear in the Quotas detail pane (see Figure 12.5).

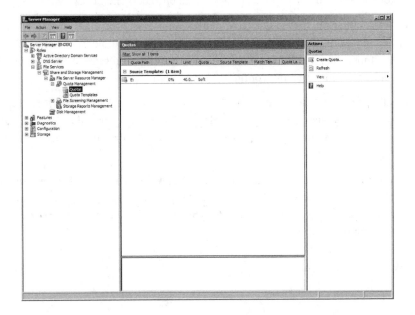

FIGURE 12.5
The Quotas node contains any quotas created for the server.

3. To create a new quota, click the Create Quota link in the Actions pane. The Create Quota dialog box opens (see Figure 12.6).

FIGURE 12.6
The Create
Quota dialog
box is used to
create a quota
for a volume or
folder.

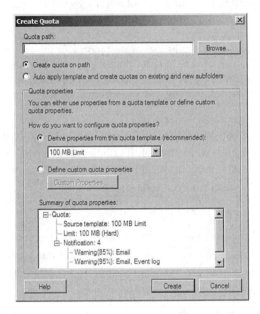

4. Click the Browse button in the Create Quota dialog box and use the Browse for Folder dialog box to select the volume or folder. Then click OK.

5. Select either the Create Quota on Path option (the default) or the Auto Apply Template and Create Quotas on Existing and New Subfolders option. The latter applies the quota to any existing or new folders that are in the volume or folder for which you are configuring the quota.

6. Click the Derive Properties from This Quota template (Recommended) drop-down list to select a limit or a monitor property for a particular limit. Choices include 100MB limit (the default), 200MB Limit Reports to User, and 250MB Extended Limit.

   You can also set custom limits if you do not want to use one of the quota templates. Click the Define Custom Quota Properties option button and then select the Custom Properties button. The Quota Properties dialog box opens (see Figure 12.7).

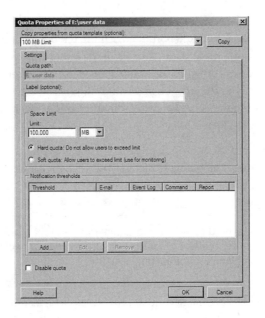

FIGURE 12.7
Use the Quota
Properties dia-
log box to cre-
ate a custom
quota.

7. Set a space limit for the quota (you can copy the limit from a template or set it in the Limit box). You can also enter an optional label for the quota.

8. Select either the Hard Quota or Soft Quota option button and then click the Add button if you want to create notification thresholds for the quota. The Add Threshold dialog box opens (see Figure 12.8).

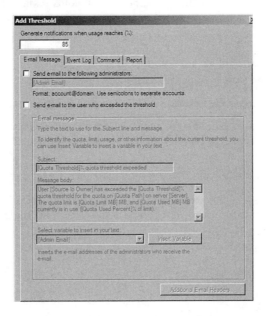

FIGURE 12.8
Configure the
threshold notifi-
cations for the
quota.

9. Set the usage percentage for the threshold and then select the Email Message, Event Log, Command, or Report tab. Each tab enables you to configure the type of notification that takes place when the quota threshold is reached. For example, you can configure the notification as an email sent to an administrator or directly to the user. Or you can configure the Event Log option to send an event to the Event Log when the threshold is reached. Reports can be configured in the Report tab.

After configuring the threshold properties, click OK. You are returned to the Quota Properties dialog box. Click OK. You will be returned to the Create Quota dialog box.

By the Way

> A quota can be configured to generate a number of different types of reports. Multiple reports can be configured for a single quota and can include Duplicate Files, Files By Owner, and Most Recently Accessed Files.

10. Click Create to create the new quota. If you selected custom properties for the quota, the Save Custom Properties as a Template dialog box opens. To save the quota properties as a template, enter a template name and then click OK. If you do not want to save the custom properties as a template, click the Save the Custom Quota Without Creating a Template option button and then click OK. *SAVE as a TEMPLATE or SAVE QUATA w/not TEMPLATE*

The new quota appears in the Details pane of the Quotas node. When a quota is selected, you can view the quota's details in the bottom pane of the Details area of the snap-in.

You can edit quotas; right-click on a quota and select Edit Quota Properties from the shortcut menu. The Quota Properties dialog box opens.

Did you Know?

> To view all the quotas that affect a single volume or folder, right-click any quota related to that volume and select View Quotas Affecting Folder. The quotas are filtered for that folder (or volume).

You can also delete quotas. Right-click a selected quota (or quotas) and select Delete Quotas from the shortcut menu. You will be asked to confirm the deletion. Click OK to delete the quota or quotas.

Using the Share and Storage Management Snap-In

Windows Server 2008 provides a new snap-in, the Share and Storage Management snap-in, that makes it easy for you to manage network shares. The Share and Storage Management snap-in also allows you to manage storage disks on a server. For example, you can extend a volume, format a volume, or delete a volume directly from the snap-in (working with disks and volumes is discussed in Hour 6.

Shares can be created (or provisioned as it is defined in the Windows 2008 environment) in the Provision a Shared Folder Wizard. A *share* is simply a drive or folder that you share for user access.

You can open the Share and Storage Management snap-in in the Server Manager (expand the Roles and File Services nodes) or in the MMC (Start, Administrative Tools, Share and Storage Management).

The Share and Storage Management snap-in provides two tabs: Shares and Volumes. Figure 12.9 shows the snap-in (in the Server Manager) with the Shares tab selected.

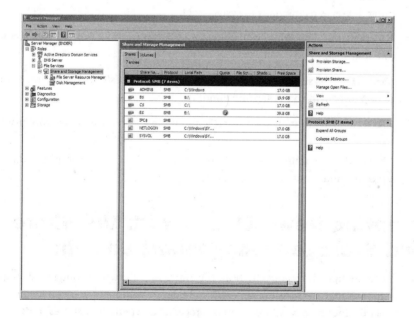

FIGURE 12.9
Shares and volumes can be viewed in the Share and Storage Management snap-in.

By default the shares are listed by protocol and you can use the details buttons on the Shares tab to list the shares by other parameters such as local path, quota, or whether or not shadow copy has been applied to the share (shadow copy is discussed later in this hour).

When you open the Share and Storage Management snap-in (and the Shares tab is selected), you can see any existing shares on the server. This includes any shares you may have created using other tools (such as the Computer folder, which is discussed in the next section) and also shows the administrative shares.

Depending on the roles that you have configured for a server running Windows Server 2008, a number of administrative shares are created automatically. These administrative shares serve as special resources related to specific server features. You do not access these special shares as a user would access a share providing files; instead, these administrative shares are accessed by server processes and services.

Whereas some of these administrative shares are configured as hidden shares, others are not. It is important that these special shares not be deleted, moved, or renamed—doing so affects the server's functionality. Some of these special administrative shares are listed here:

- **ADMIN$**—This hidden share is used during remote administration of a computer. It serves as the path to system root.

- **NETLOGON**—This share is installed on domain controllers and helps facilitate user logon.

- **SYSVOL**—This share serves as a domain controller resource and is important to domain client computer functionality.

- **PRINT$**—This share is used when you remotely administer a network printer.

Remember that these administrative shares are necessary for server functionality. They typically should not be tampered with.

Creating News Shares with the Share and Storage Management Snap-In

You can create new shares directly from the Share and Storage Management snap-in. The new share can consist of an existing folder or volume or you can create a new folder during the new share creation process. You create new shares in the Share and Storage Management snap-in, using the Provision a Shared Folder Wizard. To create a new share using the wizard, follow these steps:

1. In the Actions pane of the Share and Storage Management snap-in click the Provision Share link. The Provision a Shared Folder Wizard opens (see Figure 12.10).

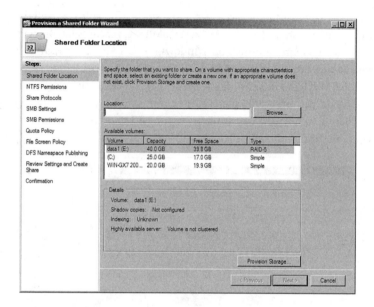

FIGURE 12.10
The Provision a
Shared Folder
Wizard.

2. The wizard lists the available volumes on the server. To browse for an existing folder (or to create a new folder) for the new share, click the Browse button. The Browse for Folder dialog box opens.

> If you have unused disk space on a disk (or disks) and want to create a new volume for a shared folder, you can click the Provision Storage button in the Provision a Shared Folder Wizard window. This opens the Provision Storage Wizard, which walks you through the process a creating a new volume on the server. You are then returned to the Shared Folder Wizard window and can continue the process of creating the new network share.

3. Expand the volume and select the folder that will be used for the new share. If you need to create a new folder, click the Make New Folder button. After selecting the folder for the share, click OK. The folder path appears in the Location box. Click Next.

4. The next wizard page enables you to set the NTFS permissions for the new share. NTFS permissions can also be edited after the share has been created.

Share permissions are discussed in detail in Hour 13, "Protecting Data with Permissions and Encryption." So, for now, do not edit the permissions. Click Next to continue.

5. On the next wizard page, you specify the share protocols that will be used to access the new share (see Figure 12.11). SMB (Server Message Block) is the protocol used to share resources on Windows-based systems (by granting permissions to individual users and groups). This is selected by default. If you also installed Services for Network File System (NFS) when you installed the File Services on the server (discussed earlier in this hour), you can also configure the share to allow UNIX-based users to use NFS to access the share. After specifying the share protocols, click Next to continue.

FIGURE 12.11
Specify the
share protocols.

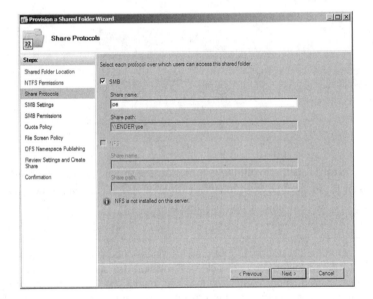

6. On the next wizard page, specify an optional description for the share. You can also change advanced settings such as the user limit (maximum allowed is the default) and whether files can be cached for offline access. Click the Advanced button. In the Advanced dialog box, set the user limit on the User Limits tab and the offline settings on the Caching tab. Then click OK to close the Advanced dialog box. Click Next to go to the next wizard page.

7. On the next wizard page (see Figure 12.12), you set the SMB permissions for the folder (we are assuming that NFS is not also being used to access the share). Share (SMB) permissions are discussed in detail in the next hour. So, for now, it makes sense to give all users read-only access to the share and give

administrators full control. Click the Administrators Have Full Control; All Other Users and Groups Have Only Read Access option button (all access can be edited after that share is created). Then click Next to continue.

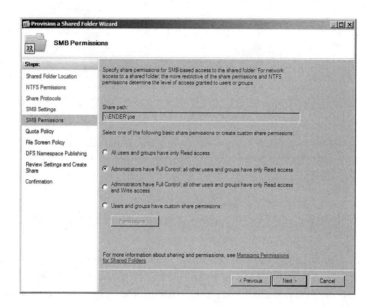

FIGURE 12.12
Specify the share permissions.

8. On the next wizard page, you can apply a quota to the share and derive the quota from one of the quota templates (this screen is very similar to the Quota dialog box shown earlier in the hour in Figure 12.6). Click the Apply Quota option button and then select a quota template from the drop-down list. If you want to create an auto-apply quota, also click the Auto Apply Template option button. Then click Next.

9. On the next wizard page, you can specify a file screen policy for the share. File screen policies enable you to block certain file types from being stored in the share. For example, you can block audio and video files or executable files. Click the Apply File Screen check box and then use the Derive Properties from This File Screen Template drop-down list to select a screen template (see Figure 12.13).

You can edit existing file screen policy templates or create your own screen templates. You can access these templates by using the File Server Resource Manager (Start, Administrative Tools, and then File Server Resource Manager). Expand the File Server Resource node to access the File Screening Management node. You can then work with file screens and file screen templates.

Did you Know?

FIGURE 12.13
Specify a file
screen policy for
the new share.

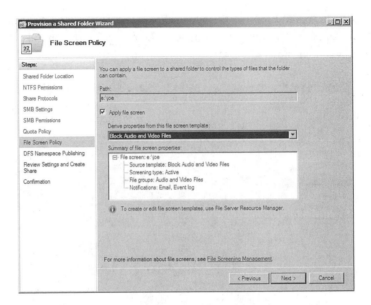

10. After specifying the file screen settings, click Next to continue. The next screen enables you to publish the new share to the distributed file system (DFS). To publish to DFS, you must have the Distribute File System installed on the server. DFS is discussed in detail later in the hour, so for now, click Next to continue.

11. The Settings Summary page opens. Review the settings for the new share and then click Create. When the confirmation screen appears, click Close.

The new share appears in the Details pane of the Share and Storage Management snap-in (when the Shares tab is selected). You can access the properties for a share (right-click the share), which include both the share and NTFS permissions for the share. You can also stop sharing a share by selecting the share and then clicking Stop Sharing in the Actions pane.

Managing the File Server

After you have configured shares on the server, you can manage all the parameters related to shares by using the Share and Storage Management snap-in and the File Server Resource Manager. The Share and Storage Management snap-in enables you to configure new shares and volumes via the Provision Share Wizard and the Provision Storage Wizard respectively.

You can manage quotas, file screening, and storage reports via the File Server Resource Manager. Quotas, file screening, and reports each have a node and set of tools for creating and managing each aspect of managing shares.

The easiest way to access all these tools in a single window is to use the Server Manager. When the Share and Storage Management node and the File Server Resource Manager node are expanded in the Server Manager, you can access all the tools and wizards discussed in previous sections of this hour. Figure 12.14 shows these nodes expanded in the Server Manager.

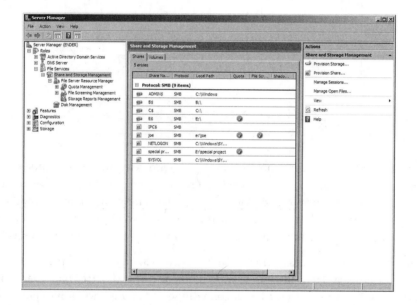

FIGURE 12.14
The Server Manager and the various file services nodes.

The Server Manager also provides you with access to events related to your file services and enables you to view services that have been installed related to file services. Later in this hour, we will use the Add Role Services Wizard to add the Distributed File System to the file services already installed in this hour.

As you manage your file server, you may want to view current sessions and also view folders and files that are currently open (by user). The Share and Storage Management node enables you to open both current sessions and files.

For example, if you want to view the current sessions (meaning the current connections to shares on your server), you can click the Manage Sessions link in the Actions pane (when the Share and Storage Management node is selected). Figure 12.15 shows the Manage Sessions window with a session listed.

FIGURE 12.15
You view current
sessions relat-
ed to the
shares on your
server.

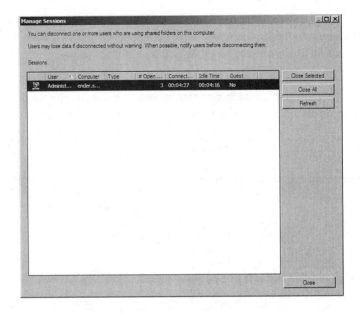

Obviously, a file server being accessed by a number of users will have a large number of sessions listed. You can actually select sessions and close them or close all the
sessions on a server. If you need to take a server down for maintenance or configuration changes, you need to notify users that the server will be taken down. You can
then close any sessions that have inadvertently been left active by network users.

You can also list open files by user via the Share and Storage Management node.
Click the Manage Open Files link in the Action pane. The Manage Open Files window opens. This window is used to disconnect users from a particular file connection
if needed.

An aspect of share management not discussed until the next hour is the use of share
and NTFS permissions to control share and file access. The Share and Storage
Management node also provides access to the properties of each of your server's
shares and so you can change the various permissions related to each share.

Publishing a Share to the Active Directory

You can publish a share (or shares) to the Active Directory. Publishing a share to the
Active Directory makes the share an Active Directory object. This means that users
can search for the share as they would any other object included in the Active

Directory catalog. Publishing the share also allows it to be replicated to other
domain servers in the domain as part of the Global Catalog.

> You must be a member of the Domain Administrators or the Enterprise
> Administrators groups to publish a share to the Active Directory.

To publish a share to the Active Directory, open the Active Directory Users and
Computer snap-in (either in the Server Manager or MMC). Then follow these steps:

1. Expand the Active Directory Users and Computers node. Select the node container for your domain.

2. Right-click in the Details pane and point at New. Then select Shared Folder.
   The New Object — Shared Folder dialog box opens (see Figure 12.16).

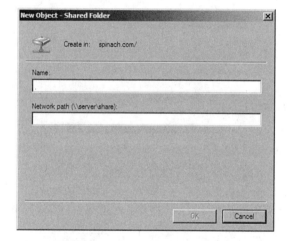

FIGURE 12.16
You can publish a share to the Active Directory.

3. Specify the share name and the network path for the share. Then click OK.
   You are returned to the Active Directory Users and Computers snap-in.

The new shared folder object appears in the Active Directory catalog. You can move
the object, explore the object, or delete the object directly from the Active Directory
Users and Computers snap-in as needed.

Using the Volume Shadow Copy Service

The Volume Shadow Copy Service provided by Windows Server 2008 creates different point-in-time versions of files in a volume. It is also part of the backup infrastructure provided by Windows Server 2008, and it enables users to recover a particular version of a file from the file server. This feature enables users to recover overwritten or inadvertently deleted shared files.

You can quickly enable Volume Shadow copy on a file server and the Computer Management snap-in provides the easiest access to the Shadow Copy Service for your server's shares. To open the Computer Management snap-in, select Start, Administrative Tools, and then select Computer Management.

Right-click the Shared Folder node in the snap-in tree, point at All Tasks, and then select configure Shadow Copies. The Shadow Copies dialog box opens (see Figure 12.17).

FIGURE 12.17
Enable the
Shadow Copy
Service.

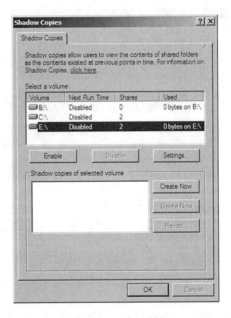

In the dialog box, select the volume you want to enable for Shadow Copy. Then click the Enable button. The Enable Shadow Copies dialog box opens, asking whether you want to enable shadow copies. Click Yes.

To change the settings for Shadow Copy, such as the schedule and the amount of space allotted for shadow copies on the file server, select the Settings button. The Settings dialog box opens. To set the maximum size available for shadow copies, use the Use Limit spinner box. The default is 4095MB (you need a minimum of 300MB free space to create a shadow copy). Be advised that there is <u>an upper limit of 64</u> <u>shadow copies per volume</u>. This means that you should create a schedule that retains an appropriately long enough history of the files without reaching the upper limit.

To set the schedule for the Shadow Copy server, select the Schedule button. The Schedule dialog box opens (see Figure 12.18).

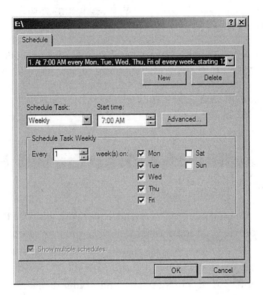

FIGURE 12.18
Use the Schedule dialog box to set the timing of the shadow copies.

The default schedules shadow copy files twice a day (during the work week, Monday through Friday) at 7 a.m. and 12 p.m. If you want to increase the number of scheduled shadow copies (Microsoft recommends that you do not increase the number beyond one shadow copy per hour), select New and then create a new scheduled shadow copy event. (It is best to select Weekly, specify the days in the week, and then specify a certain time, which is how the sample schedule has been configured.)

When you have finished setting the schedule, click the OK button. Then click OK again to close the Settings dialog box. You are returned to the Shadow Copies dialog box.

If you want to create Shadow copies of the selected volume immediately, select the Create Now button. A date and time listing appears in the Shadow Copies of Selected Volume box. Click OK to close the dialog box and return to the Computer Management snap-in.

For client computers to access and take advantage of file server shares enabled for Volume Shadow Copy, the client computer must be running the client software for

Shadow Copies of Shared Folders. The Windows Vista client comes with the client installed. If you are running Windows XP or Windows 2000 clients, you need to install the Volume Shadow client.

The Shadow Copy client can be downloaded from the Microsoft TechNet. On the client computer, open Internet Explorer and go to http://technet.microsoft.com/en-us/windowsserver/bb405951.aspx. Follow the instructions to download and install the client for the version of Windows that you are using on the client computer.

> You can also make the Shadow Copy client available in a network share and allow users to install the client to desktop computers as needed. With Windows XP and Windows Vista clients also providing Remote Desktop, you can connect to clients and install the Shadow Copy client yourself.

Understanding the Distributed File System

Another possibility for sharing resources on the network is to use the *Distributed File System* (DFS). DFS provides a hierarchical tree structure that enables users to access resources anywhere in the domain. The actual location of the resource, such as a volume or a folder, is transparent to the users. This allows resources to be spread across file servers and also supports the creation of identical shared folders that supply the same resources to the users and also provide fault tolerance for the resource or resources themselves.

The best thing about DFS is that users do not need to know the name of the server that is providing the shared resources (as a user does when trying to map a drive to a shared resource). Network administrators also benefit from the use of DFS because, if a file server fails, the DFS tree can be made to point to a redundant set of the shares on another server. This action is transparent to the users, who still can access the share or shares as if they were still available at the original location.

DFS enables you to use the shares that you have created and the various share and NTFS permissions that you have set for shares and files. DFS is really just supplying an overall structure for how users see and access the shares.

Installing and Configuring the Distributed File System

To take advantage of DFS, you must install the Distributed File System service as part of the File Services role for your server running Windows Server 2008. As part of the installation of the DFS service, you also install DFS Namespaces and DFS replication.

The Distributed File System (and its associated services) can be installed when you run the Add Server Role Wizard to install the File Services role (as discussed earlier in the hour). However, if you don't install the DFS service initially, it is very easy to add to the File Services role, using the Add Role Services Wizard.

To open the Add Role Services Wizard from the Server Manager, select the File Services node in the node tree. Then select the Add Role Services link in the details pane. The Add Role Services Wizard appears (see Figure 12.19).

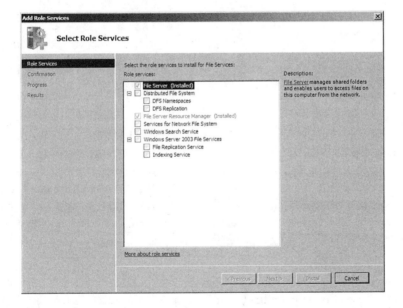

FIGURE 12.19
Add the Distributed File System to the File Services role.

Select Distributed File System in the Role Services list and then click Next. On the next page, the DFS root must be identified. The DFS root supplies the main DFS container. Then child links can be added to the DFS root that point at other shares on the network. Users will see the DFS hierarchical tree when they want to map a network drive or access network shares.

Type a name for the DFS root. For example, I will call my root "public," as shown in Figure 12.20.

FIGURE 12.20
Specify the DFS root.

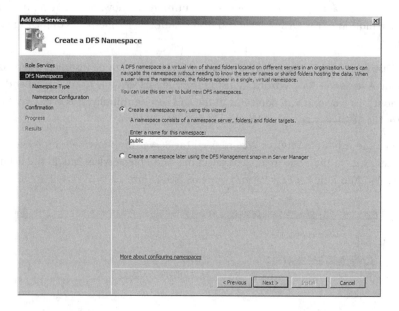

After specifying the DFS root name, you can click Next to continue. On the next wizard page you have the option of creating a domain-based DFS namespace or a standalone namespace. Because a domain-based namespace is stored on namespace servers and in the Active Directory, it makes sense to take advantage of a domain-based DFS root. Figure 12.21 shows that this setting is selected by default, as is the Windows Server 2008 mode, which enables you to easily add to the DFS tree and also take advantage of access-based enumeration (meaning user access based on permissions).

The namespace for a DFS root that is domain-based includes the Active Directory domain name as a prefix for the DFS root (refer to Figure 12.21). After specifying the type of DFS root, click Next.

On the next page, you need to associate the share (folder) that is to be at the root of the DFS hierarchy. You can then add branches to the DFS root (and the associated share), using the Distributed File System snap-in (which is discussed in a moment). Click the Add button on the Configure Namespace page. The Add Folder to Namespace dialog box appears. Use the Browse button to locate the shared folder that is to be associated with the DFS root. You can create a new shared folder during the process if you have not already created the share.

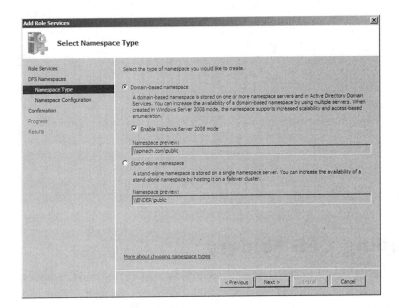

FIGURE 12.21
Take advantage of a domain-based DFS root.

You can click Next after specifying the folder. The Confirmation page appears and you are ready to install the DFS services and also establish the DFS root and namespace. Click Install.

After the installation is complete, you can close the Installation Results page. After DFS has been installed on the server, you can manage the DFS tree in the DFS Management snap-in (in the MMC). To start the DFS Management snap-in, select Start, Administrative Tools and then DFS Management.

You can view the namespace created for the root of your DFS tree by selecting the Namespaces node in the snap-in node tree. Figure 12.22 shows the DFS Management snap-in.

FIGURE 12.22
The DFS
Management
snap-in.

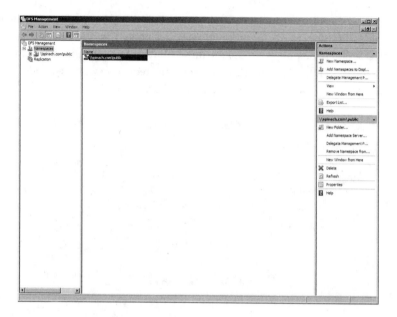

Adding DFS Folders

After the DFS root has been created, additions to the DFS tree and the namespace can be added. You can add DFS folders to the tree that provide hierarchical containers. These containers can be used to provide a structure to your DFS tree and also can be the "host" for shared folders on the server or any server on the network. These shared folders can be located anywhere on the network, meaning that shares from multiple servers in the domain can easily be added to the DFS tree.

To add a folder from the DFS Management snap-in, follow these steps:

1. Expand the namespaces node and then select the root of your DFS namespace (in the node tree, or select the namespace level where you will add the folder).

2. Click New Folder in the Actions pane (of the DFS Management snap-in). The New Folder dialog box opens (see Figure 12.23).

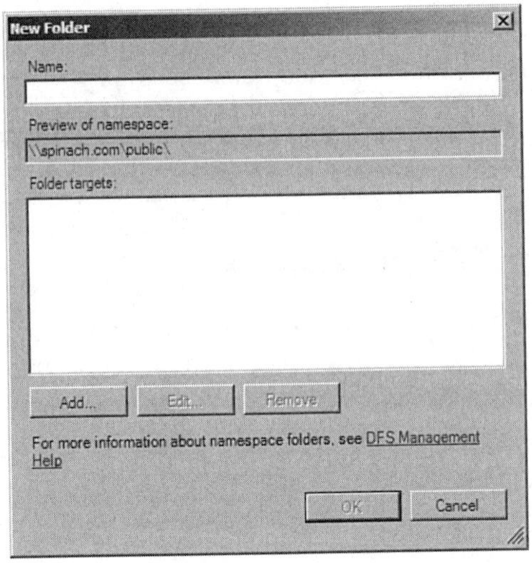

FIGURE 12.23
Add folders to
the DFS root
that point to
shares on the
network.

3. Enter the name for the new folder. A preview of this DFS folder will be added to the root namespace.

4. To associate this folder with a share on the server (or on the network), click the Add button. The Add Folder Target dialog box opens.

5. Provide the UNC address of the share, using the //server name/share format to specify the target for the DFS folder. If you plan on replicating the folder (between two or more file servers), you need to specify multiple targets for the DFS folder. After specifying the folder targets, click OK.

6. You are returned to the New Folder dialog box and the folder target (which you entered in step 5) appears in the Folder targets box. Click OK to create the new folder.

The new folder now appears in the DFS tree. When you select the folder in the DFS tree, two tabs are provided for the folder: Folder Targets and Replication. The Folder Targets tab shows all the targets for the DFS folder. As already mentioned, you need to have more than one target share for the folder if you want to take advantage of replication. DFS replication builds fault tolerance into your DFS tree. Configuring replication is discussed in the next section.

You can add DFS file servers to the DFS tree. In the DFS Management snap-in, select your DFS root and then click Add Namespace Server. You can then browse the network to enter the name of a network namespace server. Adding servers to the DFS Management snap-in makes it easier to locate DFS namespace folders and manage your DFS structure.

DFS Folder Replication

After you have created a DFS folder with multiple target folders (on domain controllers or domain member servers), you can configure replication for that folder. Make sure that you have DFS installed on the servers that will serve as the replication partners (meaning the servers that hold the shares that are pointed to by the DFS folder).

You can then configure replication by using the Replicate Folder Wizard. Follow these steps:

1. Expand the namespaces node and then expand the root of your DFS namespace. Select the folder that you want to replicate.

2. Select the folder's Replication tab and then click the Replicate Folder Wizard link at the top of the tab. The Replication Folder Wizard opens.

3. On the first wizard page, the replication group name and the replicated folder are listed. These are based on the DFS folder name (and the root namespace) selected in step 1. Click Next to continue.

4. The next screen lists the folder targets (shares) that are eligible for replication (this is all the share targets on domain servers running DFS). You should see all the targets you specified when you created the DFS folder. Click Next.

5. On the next wizard page, you specify the DFS server that will be the primary member for the replication group. This is the server that contains the data (in the share) that you want replicated to other shares (on the other servers involved in the replication). Use the Primary Member drop-down list (see Figure 12.24). Then click Next to continue.

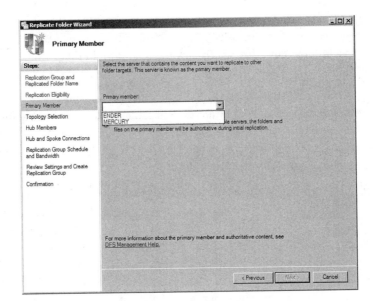

FIGURE 12.24
Select the replication primary member.

6. The next wizard page requests that you select a topology for your replication group. You can select one of the following (some options are not available if you do not have three or more servers in the replication group):

  ▶ **Hub and Spoke**—Spoke members connect to one or two hubs. Data would originate on the hub (or hubs) and be replicated out to the spoke members (requires at least three servers).

  ▶ **Full Mesh**—All the members of the replication group replicate with each other. This is fine for a small-to-medium-size DFS structure (10 or fewer servers). Remember that replication requires network bandwidth and so larger DFS implementations may work more efficiently in a hub and spoke configuration.

  ▶ **No Topology**—The wizard proceeds without creating a topology. You can then configure a custom topology in the DFS Management snap-in via the Replication node.

Select a topology (for sake of discussion, let's assume that you select Full Mesh). Then click Next to continue.

7. On the next wizard page, you must select the bandwidth to be used for replication. The default setting is Full. You can select the bandwidth in the Bandwidth drop-down list, which provides a bandwidth range from 256Mbps to 16Kbps.

   This wizard page also enables you to determine the schedule for replication. The default is Replicate Continuously. You can click Replicate during the specified days and time and then use the Edit button to configure the replication schedule (in the Edit Schedule dialog box). When you have set the bandwidth and schedule for replication, click Next.

8. The next wizard page provides a summary of the settings for your new replication group. Click Create.

The replication group is then created. A Confirmation page opens, letting you know whether there were any errors during the creation process. Click Close. A Replication Delay message appears, which lets you know that replication will not start until the server members of the replication group pick up the replication configuration.

After you configure your DFS structure and add shares to DFS folders, users on the network can access these shares by browsing the network (just as they would to access shares not included in the DFS tree). Adding replication to the DFS structure means that users can access files on the network even if a replication group member is not available.

Summary

In this hour, you learned how to configure and manage a file server.

Files are made available to users in a share. You can create shares on a file server with the Share and Storage Management snap-in (or the Computer folder).

File servers can be managed in the Share and Storage Management snap-in. You can view the current shares on the server and also view user sessions and a list of open files. You can create and manage share and volume quotas, file screen, and storage reports on a file server by using the File Server Resource Manager.

To make shares accessible throughout the domain and domain tree, you publish a share (or shares) to the Active Directory Domain Services. This makes the share information part of the Global Catalog.

The Volume Shadow Copy Service creates point-in-time versions of files in a network share. Users can then recover previous versions of a file. Network clients must be configured with the Shadow Copy client. Windows Vista is configured with the client but other Windows desktop client versions such as XP and 2000 require that you download and install the client.

The Distributed File System provides a hierarchical, logical structure for arranging network shares. A DFS root provides the base container for the DFS tree, and other shares on the network are added to the DFS tree as DFS folders. DFS folders that point to multiple shares on the network (originating on servers running DFS) can be configured for replication, which replicates share contents with a replication group.

Q&A

Q. *What is the fastest way to bring a file server online in the domain?*

A. Using the Add Roles Wizard, you can quickly add the File Services role to a member server or domain controller. The File Services role includes tools such as the File Resource Manager (which enables you to configure quotas and reports) and also additional services such as DFS and NFS (for UNIX-based clients).

Q. *What are two methods for adding shares to a file server?*

A. You can use the Share and Storage Management snap-in to provision new shares on a server. You can also add shares using the Computer folder on any server.

Q. *How can you create a hidden share on a server?*

A. Create the share and follow the share name with the $ (dollar sign) symbol. Only users who specify the exact name of the share can gain access to it.

Q. *What can you do to make it easier for users on the network to locate a share?*

A. Publishing a share to the Active Directory places the share in the Global Catalog as an Active Directory object. This makes it easier for users to locate the share on the network.

Q. *What does the Distributed File System offer in terms of providing shares to users on the network?*

A. The Distributed File System provides a hierarchical tree structure that makes it easy for users to access resources no matter where the files are stored on the network. The DFS root provides the root of the DFS tree and allows users to view shares on the network as if they were stored in one location rather than on multiple file servers on the network. DFS also provides DFS folder replication that helps build fault tolerance into your file services structure.

HOUR 13

Understanding Share and NTFS Permissions

What You'll Learn in This Hour:

▶ Understanding Share Permissions
▶ Assigning Share Permissions
▶ Understanding NTFS Permissions
▶ Assigning NTFS Permissions
▶ Taking Ownership of an NTFS File
▶ Mixing Share and NTFS Permissions
▶ Using Data Encryption
▶ Using BitLocker Encryption

In Hour 12, "Working with Network Shares and the Distributed File System," you saw how to configure a file server and share drives and folders on the network. This hour looks at how you secure network shares. First, we examine share permissions. Then we cover the additional security from using NTFS permissions on your file server volumes. We also take a look at some of the options for encrypting files and drives on your server.

Understanding Share Permissions

When you use the Provision a Share Wizard to share a volume or folder on the network, the default share permission assigned to the newly created share is Read Only for all users and groups. A share permission is the access level that you give to a particular user or group of users in relation to a particular share on your file server (or other server on the network). Setting the share permission for a folder or volume also sets the share permission level for the files and folders contained in the share.

By the
Way

Although Read Only was the default permission for a share created with the Provision a Share Wizard, the wizard supplied you with other options in terms of the level of access for administrators and users during the share-creation process. See Hour 12 for more information about creating a new share with the wizard.

When you have added the File Services role to a server, the "one-stop" tool for working with shares and volumes is the Share and Storage Management snap-in. You can run this snap-in in the Server Manager or in the MMC (Start, Administrative Tools, Share and Storage Management).

When you select the Share and Storage Management node (again in the Server Manager or the MMC), a list of all the shares on the server is provided in the Details pane. You can access a particular share in the Details pane and then view the share permissions for that share.

To view the permissions for a share, follow these steps:

1. With the Share and Storage Management node selected, right-click a share in the Details pane and then select Properties.

2. Click the Permissions tab on the Properties dialog box (see Figure 13.1).

FIGURE 13.1
The Permissions tab provides access to the share's share and NTFS permissions.

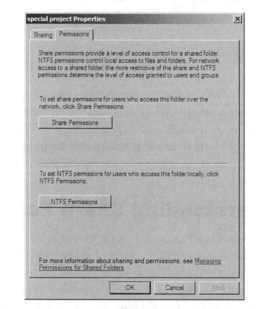

3. To view the share permissions, click the Share Permissions button. The Permissions dialog box opens. This dialog box shows users and groups that have been assigned permissions. To view the specific permissions for a user or group (related to that share), select the user or group in the Group or User Names box (see Figure 13.2).

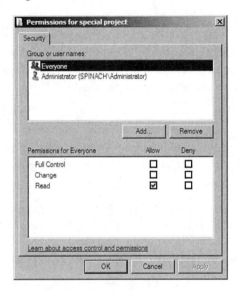

FIGURE 13.2
Select a user or a group to view the share permissions.

Share permissions can be set at three different levels: Full Control, Change, and Read. A description of each share permission level follows:

▶ **Full Control**—This permission level enables the user to modify file permissions and perform all the tasks permitted by the Change and Read permission levels. This access level gives a user the same access that an administrator would have to the share, meaning that a user with full control could change the share permissions on the folder.

▶ **Change**—This permission level enables the user to create folders in the share and add new files. Users can change data in the files and add new data to the files contained in the shared folder.

▶ **Read**—This permission level enables the user to display folders and files in the share, open the files in the share (in read-only mode), and run program files that are contained in the share.

You have the option of either allowing each permission level (using the Allow check box) or denying a particular permission (using the Deny check box). Typically, you assign a permission level, such as a change to a user or group, by selecting the Allow check box to the right of the permission (in this case, Read).

The Deny setting is used to fine-tune permission levels. Typically, you will want to assign share access levels by domain groups. (It makes sense to create groups for users and then assign share permissions to the groups.) The Deny permission always overrides any granted permissions for the object.

You might run into a case, however, in which most of the users in a group need a higher permission level, such as the Full Control permission for a share. But you might not want to assign that level of access to a few other users in the group (perhaps they could destroy important files in the share).

Here's what you do: You assign the Full Control permission to the group in the Allow check box. You then add the users from the group who do not need this level of access, and you change their Full Control permission from Allow to Deny. Denying the permission level at the user level overrides the higher level of permission that you provided to the group.

In some cases, you might want to assign a group or user the No Access permission level. This permission level allows a connection to the shared folder (the folder can be seen on the network), but access to the folder and its contents are denied. To assign No Access, clear all the Allow check boxes for a particular group or user.

This permission level is useful when fine-tuning individual user access in a group that has been assigned an access permission level. For example, you might want the Accounting group to see the database, with the exception of the support people in the group, such as administrative assistants. You can allow the group access but use the No Access permission for those users you don't want to see this highly sensitive data.

You should now see that you need to plan the level of permissions that you will supply to your domain groups (and individual users, if necessary) for the shares on the network. You should analyze what users will be doing with the files in each share and plan access levels accordingly.

> You can also view (and edit) the Share permissions for a share via the Computer folder. Locate the share using the Computer folder; right-click the folder and select Properties. Select the Security tab to view the share's current permissions.

Assigning Share Permissions

Share permissions are assigned in the Share Permissions dialog box, when you have selected Share Permissions on the Permission tab of the share's Properties dialog box (look back at Figure 13.2). You can add groups or users to the Group or User Names list in the dialog box and then assign the appropriate permission level.

To add a group or a user to the Share Permissions dialog box, follow these steps:

1. Select the Add button. The Select Users, Computers, or Groups dialog box appears (see Figure 13.3).

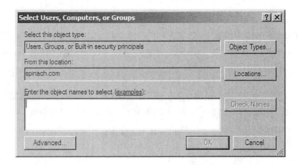

FIGURE 13.3
Use the Select Users, Computers, or Groups dialog box to specify groups or users to be added.

2. By default, the domain in which the server resides appears as the location in the dialog box. If you want to change the location (the domain or the local computer) where the group or user resides, click the Location button. A domain tree enables you to select the domain to serve as the location. Click OK to return to the Users, Computers, or Groups dialog box.

3. The group or user (or groups and users) that you will add to the Share Permission list is entered in the Enter the Object Names to Select box. Type the name of the first group or user. You can add multiple names to the box by separating the entries with a semicolon.

4. After adding the group names or usernames to the box, you can check the accuracy of your entries by clicking the Check Names button. If anyone of your entries is not found, the Name Not Found dialog box opens (see Figure 13.4).

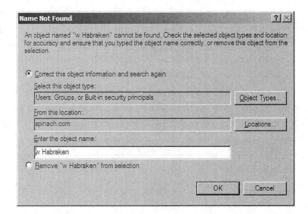

FIGURE 13.4
The Name Not Found dialog box enables you to correct entries not found in the selected domain.

5. (Optional) You can change the entry (if you typed it incorrectly) or change the location to look for the entry. If you decide not to include the entry (for inclusion in the permission list), select the Remove option button. Then click OK. You are returned to the Select Users, Computers, or Groups dialog box.

6. To add the groups or users to the permission list, click the OK button. You are returned to the Share Permissions tab.

To assign permissions to the group or user that you have added to the permission list, select the group or user. By default, the newly added group or user already is assigned the Read permission.

Select the permission level by using the appropriate Allow check box that you want to provide for the group or user. Repeat this for other added groups or users as necessary. When you have completed assigning share permissions, click the OK button. This closes the Properties dialog box for the share.

When you assign permissions to groups and users, remember that the permissions are cumulative. A particular user picks up permissions from both the groups that the user belongs to and any permissions applied specifically to the user.

Likewise, remember that a Deny always overrides all other permissions. If a user is a member of two groups and a share is configured to allow Full Control to one group and deny Full Control to the other, the user is denied access to the share.

Understanding NTFS Permissions

The NT File System, or NTFS, is a file system developed for the Windows NT environment (the NT stands for *New Technology*). It is now considered the standard file system for servers running Windows network operating systems such as Windows Server 2008. Folders and files on NTFS volumes can also be assigned NTFS permissions. This differs from share permissions, which can be applied only to drives and folders. NTFS permissions can secure a folder or file on the local computer (these permissions actually affect local users on the computer) and also can secure the object in respect to users who access the folder or file over the network.

By the Way

Each file and folder on an NTFS volume has an Access Control List. This list is used to determine the access level of a user or a group to the file or folder. The Access Control List entry for a group or a user is based on the NTFS permissions set for that group or user (in relation to the file or the folder).

Standard NTFS permissions exist for both folders and files. The NTFS folder permissions are listed in Table 13.1.

TABLE 13.1 NTFS Folder Permissions

Folder Permission	Access Level
Full Control	Enables the user or group to change permissions; delete the folder, subfolders, and files; take ownership of the folder; and permit all other permission levels (Read, Write, List Folder Contents, and so on)
Modify	Enables the user or group to modify the folder, such as delete subfolders and files and permissions related to all other lower-level permissions (Read and Execute, List Folder Contents, Write, and Read)
Read and Execute	Enables the user or group to navigate the folder contents (subfolders and files) and execute contained executables and actions related to the List Folder Contents, Read, and Write permissions
List Folder Contents	Enables the user or group to view the contents of the folder, such as subfolders and files in the folders
Write	Enables the user or group to create new contents in the folder, such as subfolders and files; change the folder attributes; and view the folder ownership and permissions information for the folder
Read	Enables the user or group to view the files and subfolders in the folder and to view other information related to the folder, such as ownership, permissions, and file attributes

Setting NTFS permissions for a folder requires two major steps. First, you add groups or users for which you want to create permissions. Then you assign the user or group the permissions. Remember that, by default, the Everyone group is assigned Full Control to any resource on a NTFS volume (whether it has been shared or not).

NTFS file permissions enable you to control access down to the file level (NTFS file permissions actually override NTFS folder permissions, which we discuss in a moment). Table 13.2 provides a list of standard NTFS file permissions.

TABLE 13.2   NTFS File Permissions

File Permission	Access Level
Full Control	Enables the user or group to change permissions, take ownership of the file, and exercise all other actions permitted by the other file permission levels
Modify	Enables the user or group to modify and delete the file, and provide permissions related to all other lower-level permissions (Read and Execute, and Write)
Read and Execute	Enables the user or group to navigate the folder contents (subfolders and files), execute contained executables, and list folder contents and Read and Write permissions
Write	Enables the user or group to create new contents in the folder, such as subfolders and files; change the folder attributes; and view the folder ownership and permissions information for the folder
Read	Enables the user or group to view the files and subfolders in the folder and to view other information related to the folder, such as ownership, permissions, and file attributes

As with share permissions, you set NTFS permissions by selecting either Allow or Deny next to a particular permission. Figure 13.5 shows the different NTFS permissions for a file and the accompanying Allow or Deny check boxes.

FIGURE 13.5
NTFS permissions for a file are set in the Allow and Deny check boxes.

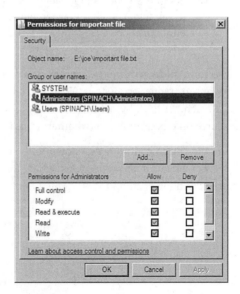

NTFS permissions might seem to be as straightforward as share permissions, but they are more complex because they can be assigned to files; therefore, a file can have different NTFS permissions than its parent folder. NTFS permissions can also become confusing because they can be assigned to both groups and users. Thus, a user might have NTFS permissions for a folder or a file that have been individually assigned, as well as NTFS permissions that have been assigned to a group that the user belongs to. These are important points to keep in mind when working with NTFS permissions:

▶ NTFS permissions are cumulative. A user's final NTFS permission is a combination of the NTFS permissions assigned to groups of which the user is a member and NTFS permissions assigned directly to the user.

> The combination of NTFS permissions that apply to a user (or a group) based solely on group membership is referred to as *effective permissions*. How to view a user's or group's effective permissions for a folder is discussed later in the hour.

By the Way

▶ NTFS file permissions override NTFS folder permissions. Even if a user has the NTFS permission of Full Control for a folder, that user can read a file in that folder only if the NTFS file permission for the user has been set to Read.

▶ If you use the Deny check box, you deny a user or group access to the folder or file. Using Deny effectively overrides any other cumulative NTFS permissions that a user might have for a folder or file.

▶ Permissions are inherited from parent folders. This means that subfolders and files contained in a parent folder inherit the permissions that you set for the parent folder. However, you can choose to not allow permissions to be inherited from the parent if you want to set different permissions for the child subdirectory or file. (Turning off inheritance is covered during the discussion of setting NTFS permissions later in the hour).

Copying or moving files from one location to another can also be problematic when you are dealing with NTFS permissions. The final permissions depend on whether you are copying or moving, and whether you are copying or moving within or between NTFS partitions or volumes.

▶ When you copy a file within an NTFS volume (from folder to folder, it is treated as a new file and takes on the permissions of the parent folder), make sure that anyone who will copy a file on the volume has Write permissions for the destination folder. The user copying the file to the folder becomes the owner of the new folder.

▶ If you move a file from one folder to another on an NTFS volume, the file retains the original permissions assigned to that file (again, the user moving the file must have Write permissions for the destination folder, and Modify permission is necessary on the file that is being moved).

▶ When you move a file from one NTFS volume to another, the file takes on the permissions of the destination folder (again, Write permissions are necessary for the destination folder, and Modify permissions are necessary for the file being moved). The user moving the file becomes the owner of the file.

As you can see, you need to plan how you will use NTFS permissions to secure the various folders and files that you share on the network. Keeping track of your users' cumulative permissions can enable you to foresee problems that involve a user accessing a folder or file to a greater degree than you had intended as you assigned permissions. Using groups (instead of users) to assign NTFS permissions is likely to make the entire process a little less confusing.

By the Way

> If you are still running FAT32-formatted disks, you can convert them to NTFS (allowing you to take advantage of NTFS permissions). This process does not affect the files or folders currently on the volume. At the command prompt, type `convert c:/fs:ntfs`, where c is the drive letter assigned to the volume. Press Enter. The volume is converted to NTFS.

Assigning NTFS Permissions

NTFS permissions can be assigned to shares via the Share and Storage Management snap-in. When assigning NTFS permissions to a file, you need to use the Computer folder to access the file's Properties dialog box. Let's look at assigning NTFS folder permissions and then setting NTFS file permissions.

By the Way

> Volumes can also be assigned NTFS permissions. This means that volume's NTFS permissions can be propagated to the folders and the files on that volume (there is an advanced setting to set the inheritance for the permissions).

Assigning and Viewing NTFS Folder Permissions

You can assign NTFS permissions to folders on NTFS volumes. Files in the folder inherit their NTFS permissions from the folder. Because folders are synonymous (in most cases) with shares on the network (there would be little reason to add permissions to a folder that was not shared), the best tool for quickly accessing a folder's NTFS permissions (meaning a share's permissions) is the Share and Storage Management snap-in. To view and edit the NTFS permissions for a folder share, follow these steps:

1. Open the Share and Storage Management snap-in in the MMC (Start, Administrative Tools, Share and Storage Management) or expand the File Services node in the Server Manager to access the Share and Storage Management node. Shares (folders and volumes shared) are listed in the Details pane of the snap-in (see Figure 13.6).

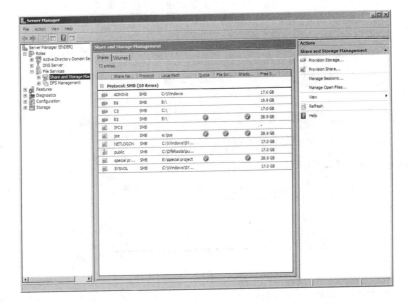

FIGURE 13.6
Share NTFS permissions can be accessed in the Share and Storage Management snap-in.

2. Right-click a share in the Details pane and then select Properties. The Properties dialog box for the share opens.

3. Click the Permissions tab on the Properties dialog box and then click the NTFS Permissions button. The Permissions dialog box opens, showing the NTFS permissions for the share (see Figure 13.7).

3. To add a group or user (or groups and users) to the Group or Usernames list, click the Add button. The Select Users, Computers, or Groups dialog box opens (see Figure 13.8).

FIGURE 13.7
NTFS permissions are assigned in the share's Permissions dialog box.

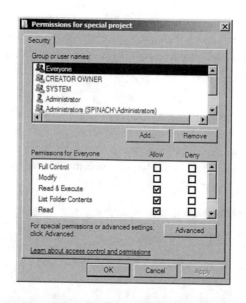

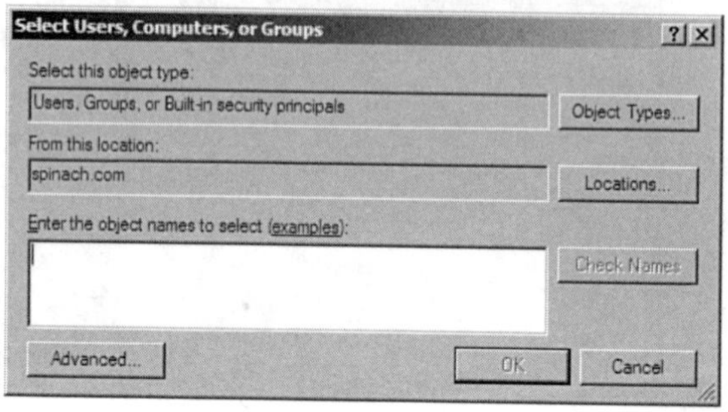

FIGURE 13.8
Add users or groups to the Permissions dialog box, using the Select Users, Computers, or Groups dialog box.

4. Use the Location box to specify the local computer or domain that you want to access for the group or user to be added to the list.

5. Enter the group name or username (multiple entries can be made by separating each entry with a semicolon) in the Enter the Object Names to Select box.

6. To check the validity of your entries, click the Check Names button.

7. After the names have been checked, click OK. You are returned to the Security tab.

8. Select a group or user that you have added to the list, and set the permissions for the folder by using the Allow (or Deny) check boxes for the NTFS folder permissions listed. By default, the group or user that you add to the list is given the Read and Execute, List Folder Contents, and Read permissions. Set the permissions for each group or user that you added to the list.

Remember that assigning NTFS permissions to a folder secures the folder both locally and as a share on the network. Make sure that you give local users the appropriate access to the folder if you are using NTFS permissions.

Negating NTFS Permission Inheritance

In some cases, you may not want a subfolder or file to inherit the NTFS permissions that have been set for the parent folder (or volume). On the Security tab of a file's (or folder's) Properties dialog box (look back at Figure 13.7), click the Advanced button. The Advanced Security Settings dialog box for the file or subfolder opens.

Select the Permissions tab of the dialog box. This tab shows the current permissions for the file or folder by user and group. To edit the permissions and to have access to the inheritable permissions option, click Edit. A second Permissions tab opens (it's the same as the Permissions tab on the Advanced Security Settings dialog box) with the settings active and available for editing (see Figure 13.9).

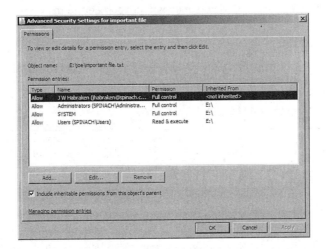

FIGURE 13.9
You can enable or disable permission inheritance.

By default, inheritable permissions for the file or folder are included, meaning permissions propagate from the parent down to the actual file or folder. To turn off propagation of permissions from parent containers to the current object, click the Include Inheritable Permissions from This Object's Parent check box to clear it. The file or subfolder now no longer inherits permissions that have been set for a parent container.

Viewing Effective Permissions

Because NTFS permissions to an object by a user are affected by the user's group memberships, it can become confusing when you are trying to sort out what actual permissions a user has in relation to a particular network resource such as a share or a specific file in a share.

It really does make sense to base permission levels for users on group memberships and so when you set up the various user groups in the Active Directory Domain Services, you should keep in mind that the group is going to be a security container and membership in a group will affect the access that the group's users have to network resources.

You can view the effective permissions for a file or folder. The effective permissions are the permissions that are afforded a user or group based entirely on group membership (remember that groups can be nested inside other groups in the Active Directory). You access the effective permissions for a user or group via the Advanced Security Settings dialog box.

> The fact that permissions to network resources are so tightly connected to group membership in the Active Directory means that you need to think carefully through the creation of your various groups and the needs of the users who will be in those groups before you begin to assign permissions. Having your group structure well defined before deploying your file servers and the associated permissions for the resources provided by the file servers makes your file access troubleshooting chores a lot less nightmarish in the future. Check out Hour 9, "Creating Active Directory Groups, Organizational Units, and Sites," for more about groups and other ways to organize objects in the Active Directory tree.

Click the Effective Permissions dialog box on the Advanced Security Settings dialog box. To specify a particular user or group, click the Select button and the Select User, Computer, Group dialog box opens.

Type the name of the user or group (or enough of the user or group name to use the Check Names button) and then click OK to return to the Effective Permissions tab of the Advanced Security Settings dialog box. The effective permissions for the user or group are displayed (see Figure 13.10).

Viewing effective permissions can help you sort out the bottom-line access that a user or group has to a particular shared file or folder. This information can be very useful when fine-tuning resource access on the network.

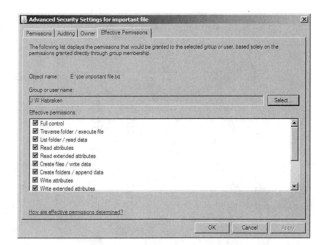

FIGURE 13.10
View the effective permissions for a user or group.

Taking Ownership of an NTFS File

By default, the creator of a folder or a file on NTFS volumes is the owner of that object. This enables that user to set the permissions related to that file or folder (or to delete the file and folder). Ownership of an NTFS file or folder is similar to having the Full Control permission.

Administrators (by virtue of the Administrators group) can take ownership of any file or folder (no matter what permissions have been assigned for that file or folder). Administrators can also grant ownership of files or folders to a group or user. In effect, this means that ownership of files or folders can be transferred from a group or user to another group or user.

Ownership can be given to a user or group if the Full Control standard permission is supplied to that user or group. Ownership can also be given to the user or group in the Take Ownership special permission (see Figure 13.11).

FIGURE 13.11
Use the Take
Ownership spe-
cial permission
to give owner-
ship of a file or
folder.

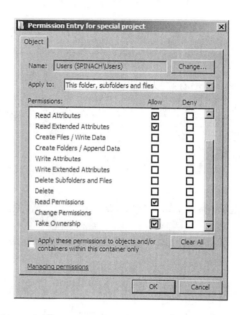

Mixing Share and NTFS Permissions

Having two different sets of permissions—share and NTFS—to protect folders and files can lead to some confusion because these permissions interact to determine a user or group's access to a particular object. Basically, the share permissions enable you to interact with the share (the folder), and the NTFS permissions determine what you can do with the files in that share (when both types of permissions have been used).

Because both NTFS permissions and share permissions can be assigned to a folder, the resulting access level that a user or group has is the most restrictive permission provided by the combined settings. For example, if the user's group membership gives Read permissions based on NTFS permissions, but another group membership provides Full Control based on share permissions, the user has only Read permissions. The most restrictive permission provides the final access level.

When planning how you want to supply access to shares on the network, determine how you will use group membership to determine an individual user's access to a particular folder or file. A good rule of thumb is to assign only the minimum level of access that a user needs to get the job done in relation to a particular folder or file.

You might also want to use share permissions to control folder access, but then use NTFS permissions to drill down your security settings to the file level. However you determine to use these different permission possibilities, make sure that you create a written plan that provides guidelines for how permissions are assigned to the groups and users present on your network.

Using Data Encryption

Another way to protect file server data is to use encryption. Windows Server 2008 actually provides two different methods for encrypting data. You can use the Encrypting File System (EFS) or BitLocker Drive Encryption. Let's take a look at t he Encrypting File System first, and then we can return to a discussion of the BitLocker Drive Encryption (which is a new feature of Windows Server 2008).

The Encrypting File System enables you to encrypt data on NTFS volumes using a system of public and private keys. The encryption/decryption process is transparent as files are accessed by network users. EFS can be used to encrypt the contents of individual folders (shares) and even individual files.

Follow these steps to encrypt a file or folder (contents):

1. Open the Computer window (Start, Computer) and then locate the file or folder you want to encrypt.

2. Right-click the file or folder that you want to encrypt, and then select Properties from the shortcut menu.

3. On the General tab of the file or folder's Properties dialog box, select the Advanced button. The Advanced Attributes dialog box opens (see Figure 13.12).

FIGURE 13.12
You can encrypt a file or folder.

4. To encrypt the file or folder, select the Encrypt Contents to Secure Data check box. Then click OK to return to the Properties dialog box.

Obviously, encrypting a folder enables you to encrypt all the files in the folder. This means that you can quickly encrypt data files instead of encrypting the files in a folder one at a time.

Using BitLocker Encryption

Windows BitLocker drive encryption is a new encryption feature that was created during the development cycle that produced Windows Vista and Windows Server 2008. BitLocker encrypts all the data on the volume. It can be used to encrypt all the data on the volume that contains the Windows operating system, including paging files, applications, and data used by applications. Data volumes (volumes other than the Windows volume) can also be protected with BitLocker encryption.

BitLocker does have hardware requirements. To make full use of all BitLocker features, a computer system that has a compatible Trusted Platform Module (TPM) microchip (TPM 1.2) and BIOS (meaning a very recent server system in which you have requested the TPM chip) is required. The TPM chip is where the encryption and decryption keys for BitLocker are stored. (You can do a workaround if you do not have a server with a TPM; see the note at the end of this section.)

The TPM chip on a server is a microcontroller that stores keys, passwords, and digital certificates. A number of computer manufacturers sell systems with the TMP chip. The TPM standard is part of the hardware specifications developed by the Trusted Computing Group, which is a nonprofit consortium that develops open standards for hardware-enabled trusting computing and security technologies. For more about the TPM standard and the Trusted Computing Group, see https://www.trustedcomputinggroup.org/faq/TPMFAQ.

 BitLocker also requires that there be two volumes (partitions) on the drive that contains the Windows Server 2008 operating system. You must create the volumes before you install Windows Server 2008, and both volumes must be formatted with the NTFS file system. One volume will be for the Windows operating system and BitLocker will encrypt this volume (protecting the OS files and other information such as password files). The second volume (which can be smaller than the Windows OS volume) will serve as the active volume (so that the system boots) and will not be encrypted by BitLocker. The second volume or system volume must be at least 1.5GB (remember, this will be the active partition).

You can use BitLocker if you do not have a system with a TPM chip. Your system needs to be able to boot to a USB drive, however (from BIOS). The BitLocker key is stored on the USB drive. The Local Group Policy is configured so that you need a TPM, but you can edit the local policy. Run `gpedit.msc` (Start, Run) and then expand the Local Computer Policy, Computer Configuration, Administrative Templates, and Windows Components nodes. Then select the BitLocker Drive Encryption node. In the Details pane, double-click Control Panel Setup: Enable Advanced Startup Options. On the Control Pane Setup: Enable Advanced Startup Options Properties dialog box, click Enabled (near the top of the dialog box). The Allow BitLocker Without a Compatible TPM check box should also be checked. Close the dialog box and the editor window.

Creating Volumes Before Installing Windows Server 2008

Here is a very important point: You must create these volumes (or partitions if you like) before you install Windows Server 2008 on the server. The easiest way to create these volumes is to boot the system to the Windows Server 2008 installation DVD.

When the Install Windows dialog box opens, click Next. On the next screen, click Repair Your Computer (in the lower left of the Install Windows dialog box; do not click Install Now). The System Recovery Options dialog box opens (ignore it). Click Next and the System Recovery Options dialog box opens a second time (see Figure 13.13).

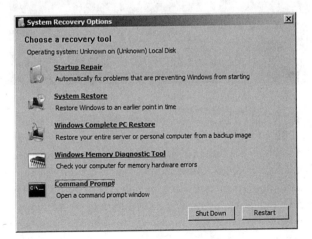

FIGURE 13.13
Select the Command Prompt.

On the System Recovery Options dialog box, click the Command Prompt icon. A command prompt window opens.

Use diskpart (type **diskpart** and press Enter) to create the two volumes, using the following commands:

▶ select disk 0—This command selects the first hard drive on the system.

▶ create partition primary—This creates a new partition; to create a partition of a particular size use create partition primary size=5000 (where 5000 creates a 5GB volume).

▶ assign letter=—This command is used to assign a drive letter.

▶ active—Makes the created partition the active volume (you need to make the smaller of the two partitions the active partition).

Figure 13.14 shows the series of diskpart commands used to create two partitions. H is 5GB and is the active partition. C is the larger of the two partitions and will be used as the target for the Windows installation.

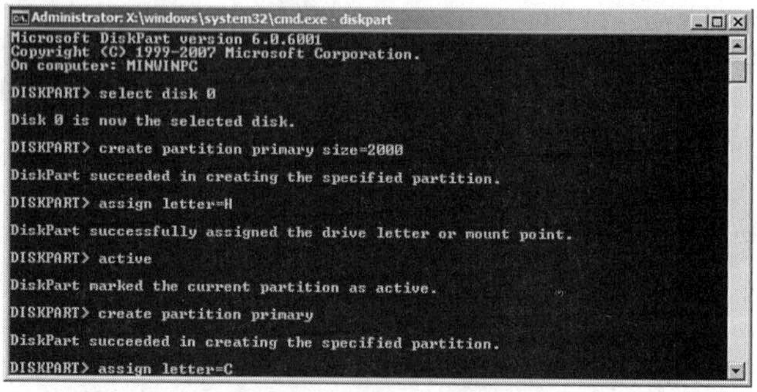

FIGURE 13.14
Use diskpart
to create two
volumes.

```
Administrator: X:\windows\system32\cmd.exe - diskpart
Microsoft DiskPart version 6.0.6001
Copyright (C) 1999-2007 Microsoft Corporation.
On computer: MINWINPC

DISKPART> select disk 0

Disk 0 is now the selected disk.

DISKPART> create partition primary size=2000

DiskPart succeeded in creating the specified partition.

DISKPART> assign letter=H

DiskPart successfully assigned the drive letter or mount point.

DISKPART> active

DiskPart marked the current partition as active.

DISKPART> create partition primary

DiskPart succeeded in creating the specified partition.

DISKPART> assign letter=C
```

After using diskpart to create the two volumes, exit diskpart (type **exit** and then press Enter) and then format the drives, using the format syntax, format c:/y/q/fs:ntfs (where c is the drive letter of the partition). Now you can "bounce" back to the Windows Server 2008 installation. Type **exit** and then press Enter to exit the command prompt window. Then click the Close button at the top right of the System Restore Options window. This returns you to the Windows Server 2008 installation box and you can continue with the installation of the server OS (to the C: drive you created).

Adding the BitLocker Feature

BitLocker is an optional feature and so is not installed by default. You have to add it to your Windows Server 2008 installation. Follow these steps:

1. In the Initial Configuration Window or the Server Manager (with the Features node selected), click Add Features. The Add Features Wizard opens.

2. Select the BitLocker Drive Encryption feature (see Figure 13.15), and then click Next.

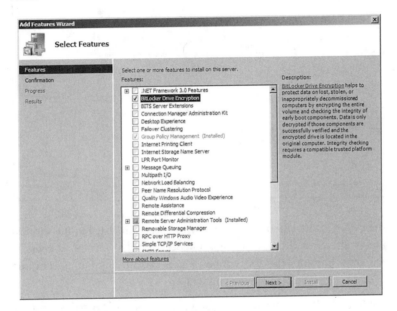

FIGURE 13.15
Add the BitLocker feature.

3. On the next wizard page, click Install.

4. After the installation, click Close. You are then prompted that the system must be restarted. Click Yes to restart the system.

After BitLocker is installed as a feature (and the system rebooted), a BitLocker Drive Encryption icon is added to the Windows Control Panel. You use this icon to enable BitLocker on your system.

Enabling the BitLocker Feature

After you have BitLocker installed on the system, you can enable this encryption security feature. Open the Control Panel (Start, Control Panel). Then follow these steps:

1. Double-click BitLocker Drive Encryption in the Control Panel. The BitLocker Drive Encryption window opens (see Figure 13.16).

FIGURE 13.16
Open the
BitLocker Drive
Encryption win-
dow.

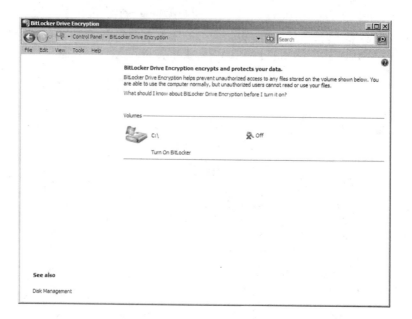

2. The volumes that will be encrypted by BitLocker are listed in the window. To enable BitLocker, click the Turn On BitLocker link. A warning appears, letting you know that Bitlocker encryption reduces disk throughput; to continue click Continue with BitLocker Drive Encryption.

3. The BitLocker Drive Encryption dialog box opens. You have three options (select one):

   ▶ Use BitLocker Without Additional Keys—No startup key is created.

   ▶ Require PIN at Every Startup—You will need to enter the PIN each time you boot the system.

   ▶ Require Startup USB Key at Every Startup—Use this option if you do not have a compatible TPM on the system.

   Select an option (for sake of discussion select the third option).

4. The next screen will differ depending on the option you selected. In the case of the Require Startup USB key (the third option), you are asked to insert a removable USB memory device.

5. After the USB drive is inserted (see Figure 13.17), click Save.

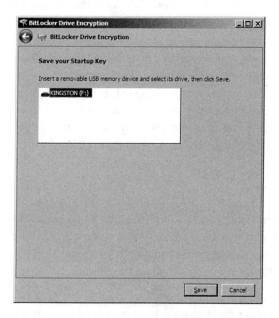

FIGURE 13.17
The startup key
can be saved to
a USB drive.

6. On the next screen, you are asked to save the recovery password on a USB drive or in a folder, or to print the password. It makes sense at the very least to save the password in a location (or two) and definitely print out the password. Click Next after saving and printing the recovery password.

You cannot save the recovery password to a drive that you will be encrypting with BitLocker. You need to save it to another volume on the server or save it to a USB drive. The volume that you created as the small active partition in the previous section could always be used because the password is only a small text file (1KB). Create a new folder on the volume and then save the password to the folder.

By the Way

---

7. The next screen (by default) runs the Bitlocker system check. This makes sure that your keys work before your volume is encrypted. Definitely run the check if you are using BitLocker on a system without a TPM because this check determines whether the system can boot to the USB drive that holds the startup key. Click Continue and then click Restart Now.

8. Windows reboots to the TMP (or USB drive holding the startup key). Windows also encrypts your drive volumes. You are returned to the Windows desktop and the Encryption in Progress status bar appears.

After the volume is encrypted you need to reboot the system. The system uses the TPM or your USB drive to boot the system. Your server's Windows software volume and any data on this volume is now encrypted. This provides a great deal of protection from hackers who may attempt to steal passwords or compromise your network by hacking into the server. Remember to keep your recovery password in a safe place if you have a problem booting a server that you have configured for BitLocker.

Summary

Share permissions enable you to control access to volume and folder shares on a file server. Share permissions can be set for groups and users. NTFS permissions can be assigned to volumes, folders, or files on an NTFS volume. NTFS permissions secure a folder or file on the local computer and on the network.

When share and NTFS permissions are used together, the most restrictive setting provided by the combined permissions is in force. A good best practice is to assign users only the minimum level of access that they need for a particular folder or file on the network.

NTFS volumes also provide folder and file encryption, using the Encrypting File System. This encryption strategy uses public and private keys to secure files and folders on your file servers and the network.

Windows BitLocker drive encryption is an encryption feature that encrypts all the data on a volume. It can be used to encrypt volumes that contain the Windows operating system, including applications and data used by applications. BitLocker can also be used to encrypt entire data volumes.

Q&A

Q. *How can share permissions be used to secure a share in the domain?*

A. Share permissions for a share, such as a shared folder, can be assigned to both groups and users. Assigning different levels of access to a share, which typically means greatly limiting full control of the share, enables you to protect the data in a share from being overwritten or deleted.

Q. *How are share permissions assigned to groups and users?*

A. The Share Permissions tab of the share's Properties dialog box enables you to add users and groups and then assign them different permission levels for the share.

Q. *How do NTFS permissions differ from share permissions?*

A. NTFS permissions can be applied only to folders and files on a NTFS volume. NTFS permissions can be applied at the file level, differing from share permissions, which can be applied only at the share or folder levels (not the file level).

Q. *What security feature provided by NTFS volumes can be used to secure files both on the server and as they move across the network wire when they are accessed by users?*

A. You encrypt files on NTFS volumes by using the Encrypting File System. This encryption system protects files transparently as they are accessed by domain users.

Q. *What file encryption system can be used to encrypt the volume that contains the Windows operating system files?*

A. BitLocker drive encryption can be used to encrypt the Windows operating system volume, including paging files and applications.

HOUR 14

Working with Network Printing

What You'll Learn in This Hour:

- ▶ Networking Printing and Windows Server 2008
- ▶ Installing a Local Printer
- ▶ Installing Direct-Connect Network Printers
- ▶ Sharing a Printer
- ▶ Adding the Print Services Role to a Server
- ▶ Managing Printers and Print Servers
- ▶ Managing Print Jobs
- ▶ Using Printer Filters
- ▶ Working with Printer Permissions
- ▶ Auditing Printer Access

Another essential service that a network provides to users is the capability to print. Sharing printers was one of the "historical" reasons that personal computers were first networked. This hour looks at the Windows Server 2008 print services, including the configuration of a print server. It also looks at managing the print environment in the domain.

Networking Printing and Windows Server 2008

Windows Server 2008 makes managing printers and print servers very straightforward. It provides two tools for managing print issues: the Server Manager and the Print Management snap-in. The Server Manager enables you to install the Print Services role on a server and to quickly view print-related events when the Print Services role is selected.

After the Print Services role is installed, you also have access to the Print Management snap-in (in the Server Manager or MMC). This snap-in enables you to install, view, and manage printers and print servers on the network.

Before any discussion of setting up a print server and the print-related tools, you need to know some of the terminology used for working with domain print services. A *shared printer* is simply a printer that accepts print jobs from more than one computer. Printers on the network actually fall into two different categories, depending on where the printer is located in relation to your network server: local printer or remote printer.

A *local printer* is a printer that is directly attached to a server. The printer is only local, however, in relation to the server (to which it is connected). This server assumes the role of print server for the printer. A *remote printer* is a printer attached to a computer other than your server. You can configure a server running Windows Server 2008 to act as the print server for a printer that is attached to another computer on the network.

A third type of printer is used on networks: the *direct-connect printer*. This printer is outfitted with an internal or external direct connection hardware device (which acts as both a local print server and a network interface card for the printer). A direct-connect printer is connected to the network hub or other connectivity device by a twisted-pair cable (or the same networking media that you use to connect the computers on your network). Establishing a print server on the network is really just a matter of connecting your printers (whether locally, remotely, or directly) to the network so that the appropriate printer can be "identified" during the process of configuring a server for print services. Let's take a look at installing printers and then explore the steps for adding the Print Services role to a server running Windows Server 2008.

Although you can share printers on the network that are connected to computers other than dedicated print servers, remember that the local computer hosting the printer experiences performance hits when queuing up print jobs and sending them to the printer. This is why dedicated print servers are used to handle the large number of print requests that are typically dealt with on a Windows domain.

Installing a Local Printer

Setting up a local printer is really just a matter of directly attaching the printer to the Windows Server 2008 computer with a USB cable. Because Windows Server 2008 embraces Plug and Play, most printers (unless you are dealing with a fairly old legacy printer) are recognized automatically and installed by the network operating system.

To add a plug-and-play printer to a server, connect the printer to the server. A message box appears in the system tray letting you know that the system is installing the device driver software.

Click the message box to view the status of the printer's driver installation. When the installation is complete, the Driver Installation Box provides a summary of the device (printer) installation and the status of the device (such as Ready to use, as shown in Figure 14.1).

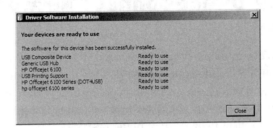

FIGURE 14.1
USB printers are installed automatically by Windows Server 2008.

After the printer is installed, you can view it in the Printers window. Select Start and then Control Panel. Double-click the Printers icon to open the Printers window (see Figure 14.2).

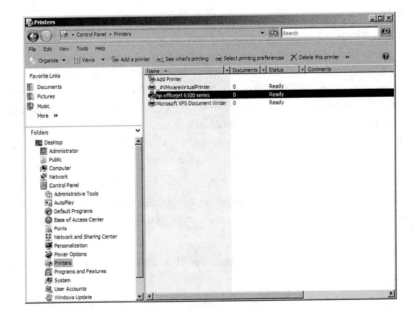

FIGURE 14.2
You can view installed printers in the Control Panel's Printers window.

The newly installed printer appears in the list of printers in the window's right pane. If this is the first printer installed on the server, it is marked as the default printer for the computer.

When you are installing a non–plug-and-play printer, use the Add Printer Wizard (you can access it via the Control Panel's Printers icon). This enables you to add a legacy printer connected to the computer by a method other than a USB cable.

Installing Direct-Connect Network Printers

An alternative to attaching the printer directly to the server is attaching the printer directly to the network. To attach the printer directly to the network, the printer needs a network card that also provides the spooling and processing power to handle incoming print jobs (directly connected printers also typically have a lot more memory installed in them to avoid print buffer overflow).

A number of manufacturers (such as Intel and Hewlett-Packard) make both internal and external print server devices that can be installed in (or on) a printer. These devices then connect directly to the network over the same network media (such as twisted-pair cable connected to a hub or switch) that other devices and computers on the network use.

Because TCP/IP is the default network protocol for Windows Server 2008, printers using direct-connect devices can be configured with an IP address (using the configuration software that ships with the device or the printer) or can receive an IP address from the domain's DHCP server. When a DHCP server is used on the network, the DHCP server assigns an IP address as soon as the direct-connect printer is attached to the network and brought online. You can find this IP address using the DHCP snap-in; all you have to do is examine the new leases that have been supplied to devices on the network. (For more about DHCP, see Hour 16, "Using the Dynamic Host Configuration Protocol").

After you have established the IP address for the printer, you can connect the server to the printer by creating an IP port on the server. You do so by using the Add Printer Wizard; follow these steps:

1. Select Start, Control Panel, and then double-click Printers. The Printer window opens.

2. Double-click Add Printer. The Add Printer Wizard opens (see Figure 14.3).

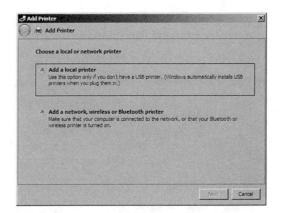

FIGURE 14.3
Add a network printer to the server.

3. Select the Add a <u>Network, Wireless or Bluetooth Printer option.</u> The Add Printer Wizard searches for available printers on the network.

4. If the printer that you want is on the list, click the printer and then click Next. The printer is identified and added to the server.

5. If the network printer is not listed, click The Printer That I Want Isn't Listed link (this option should be used when you are connecting the printer to a server for the first time). The next wizard page opens, allowing you to find a printer by name or TCP/IP address (see Figure 14.4).

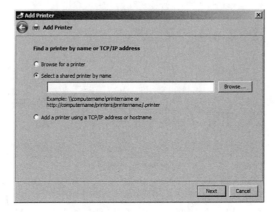

FIGURE 14.4
You can add a printer by share name or TCP/IP address.

6. In cases where a direct-connect printer has not already been connected to a server and the network and shared (you can't use the share name), you need <u>to find the printer by TCP/IP address or hostname.</u> Click the Add a Printer Using a TCP/IP Address or Hostname option button. Then click Next.

7. On the next screen, enter the hostname or the IP address for the printer (see Figure 14.5) . Then click Next and the server detects the printer and TCP/IP port.

FIGURE 14.5
Enter the host-name or the IP address for the printer.

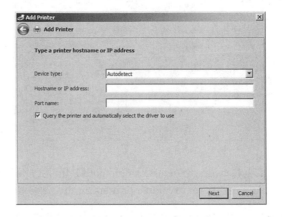

8. After the printer and TCP/IP port are identified, the Add Printer Wizard identifies the print driver to use for the printer. The printer is also set as the default printer for the server (see Figure 14.6). Click Next to continue.

FIGURE 14.6
The Add Printer Wizard identifies the print driver for the network printer.

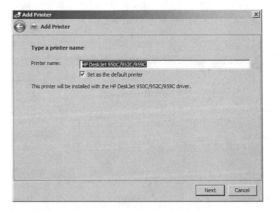

9. The next wizard screen, by default, shares the printer on the network. It also provides a default share name (which you can edit if you wish). Click Next to continue.

If you do not want to share the printer at this point, click the Do Not Share This Printer option button before selecting Next.

10. The last wizard page lets you know that the printer has been successfully added. If you want to print a test page, click the Print a Test Page button. Click Finish when you have completed adding the printer.

The printer is added to the printer list. The benefit of using direct-connect printers on the network is that they can be located anywhere on the network without requiring that a server be deployed to act as a print server in that same location. They also negate the need to overtax a server that might provide other network services because a server is not required to spool or process print jobs directed to the printer.

Sharing a Printer

When you install a local printer as discussed in the previous section (by attaching the USB cable), you still need to share the printer. (When you add a network printer that has not previously been shared, you are given the option of sharing it.) Printers are shared via the printer's Properties dialog box, which can be accessed in your Printers window.

Open the Printers window via the Control Panel (Start, Control Panel, and then double-click Printers). Right-click the printer that you want to share and select Sharing from the shortcut menu. The printer's Properties dialog box opens with the Sharing tab selected.

Click the Share This Printer check box. A share name for the printer is automatically placed in the Share Name box (see Figure 14.7). You can edit the name if you wish.

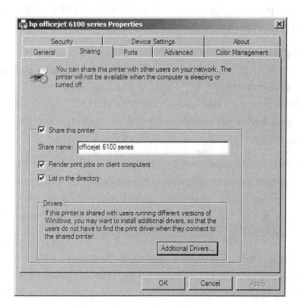

FIGURE 14.7
Share the printer.

By default, print jobs are rendered on client computers (which takes a load off your print server). You should also click the List in Directory check box so that the printer is listed in the Active Directory.

If you need to add additional drivers for the printer (such as for computers using Itanium or X64 processors), click the Additional Drivers button and check the additional drivers you need in the Additional Drivers box.

When you have completed the share configuration for the printer, click OK. The printer icon includes the share symbol in your printer list.

By the Way

> A printer's Properties dialog box (which includes the Sharing tab) has a number of tabs that enable you to control the printing options for the printer. They include the device settings, the ports, and security settings. Printer permissions (set on the Security tab) are discussed later in this hour.

Adding the Print Services Role to a Server

As soon as you have installed a local printer (or a direct-connect printer, as discussed in the previous section) and shared the printer, you have, in effect, created a print server; all you need to do to make the printer available to other computers on the network is to share the printer. However, to effectively manage the print server and its associated printers (and have access to the Print Management snap-in), you must install the Print Services role on the server.

When you install the Print Services role, you are installing three services: Print Server, LPD Services, and the Internet Printing service. The Print Server service adds the Print Services role to the Server Manager and also installs the Print Management snap-in. The Print Server service also enables the File and Printer sharing exception in Windows Firewall with Advanced Security when a printer is shared. So, bottom line, it is a required service in terms of the Print Services role.

The LPD (Line Printer Daemon) Service provides the TCP/IP Print Server (LPDSVC) service (it installs and starts the service). This service allows computers (typically UNIX-based computers) using the Line Printer Remote (LPR) service to print to the shared printers on the server. This service does not require you to configure it and runs automatically after you install the Print Services role.

The Internet Printing service creates a web page for your print server (hosted by Internet Information Service; IIS is discussed in Hour 23, "Using the Internet Information Sercie") that enables users to manage print jobs in a web browser. Users can also use a web browser to print to the print server if their client computer is outfitted with the Internet Printing client.

> Windows Vista clients can also be configured as print servers. This is an option for an office location where you don't want to deploy a server or have only a few users that need to connect to the printer. This is also an option where you have a specialized printer (such as a color printer) that you want to make available to only certain users on the network. In Windows Vista the Print Services feature can be added via the Control Panel (by adding it as a Windows feature).

By the Way

To install the Print Services role, follow these steps:

1. In the Initial Configuration Tasks window or the Server Manager (with the Roles node selected), select Add Roles. The Add Roles Wizard opens. Click Next to bypass the initial wizard page.

2. On the next page (see Figure 14.8). Select the Print Services check box. Then click Next.

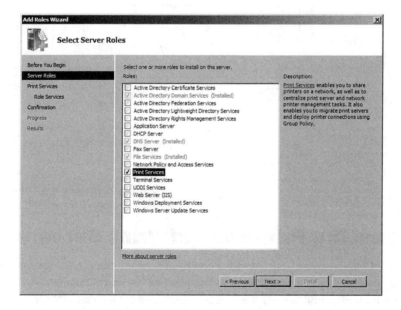

FIGURE 14.8
Select the Print Services role.

3. The next page provides an overview of the Print Services role and provides links to additional information related to Print Services. Click Next.

4. On the next page, the services related to the Print Services role are listed: Print Server, LPD Service, and Internet Printing. The Print Server role is required.

You can also select the LPD Service and Internet Printing if you expect to use these additional services. Click Next.

5. The Confirmation page opens. Click Install. The Print Services role is added to your server.

After the installation has completed, click Close. In the Server Manager (and the Initial Configuration Tasks window), the Print Services role is now listed.

When you expand the Roles node in the Server Manager, you can select the Print Services role. This enables you to quickly view any events related to Print Services and also view the system services associated with the role and the services that were installed when you added the Print Services role (see Figure 14.9).

FIGURE 14.9
In the Server Manager, you can view events, services, and installed servic-es for the Print Services role.

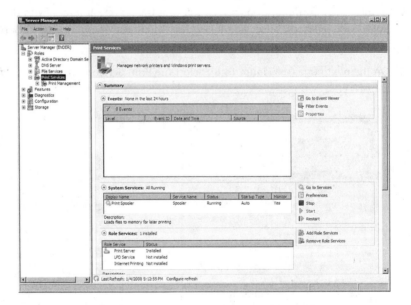

Managing Printers and Print Servers

The Print Management snap-in (which can be accessed in the Server Manager or the MMC) enables you to manage printers and print servers in your domain. You can view print servers and the printers that they provide for the domain. You can even locate (using filters) printers that currently have print jobs and printers that are not ready (meaning paused or offline). Figure 14.10 shows the Print Management snap-in in the Server Manager.

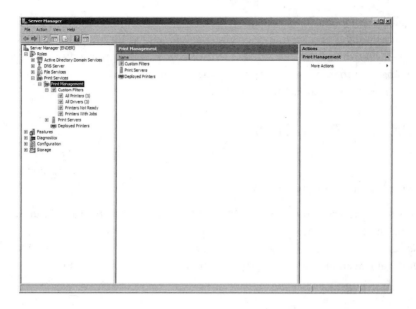

FIGURE 14.10
The Print Management snap-in enables you to view and manage your domain print servers and printers.

The Print Management snap-in allows for centralized management of the printing environment in the domain. For example, you can use it to quickly view the printers that are attached to a particular print server. Expand the Print Management node and then expand the Print Servers node. Expand the node for a print server and then click the Printers node. The printers attached to the print server are listed in the Details pane.

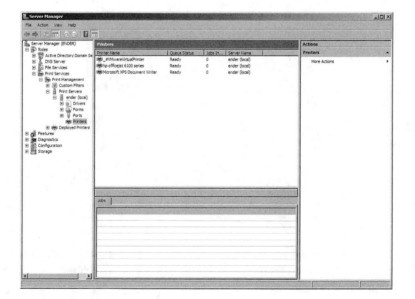

FIGURE 14.11
You can quickly view the printers attached to a print server.

A number of tasks can be accomplished from the Print Management snap-in, including adding printers to a print server, managing device drivers, and deploying printers via Group Policy. Let's take a look at how to add a print server to the Print Management snap-in and then sort out some of the other capabilities that this snap-in provides for managing printers.

Adding a Print Server

You can add additional print servers to the Print Management snap-in. This enables you to manage the printers attached to your local print server and also manage the printers on the remote print servers.

To add a print server to the Print Management snap-in, open the snap-in in the Microsoft Management Console; click Start, Administrative Tools, Print Management. The Add/Remove Servers command is not available in the Print Management snap-in when you run the snap-in in the Server Manager.

Follow these steps:

1. Right-click the Print Management node and select Add/Remove Servers from the shortcut menu. The Add/Remove Servers dialog box opens (see Figure 14.12).

FIGURE 14.12
Add a print server to the Print Management snap-in.

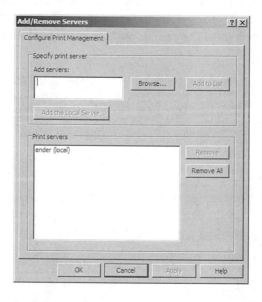

2. You can enter the name of the server or use the Browse button (which provides a list of all print servers in the domain). Click the Browse button. The Select Print Server window opens.

3. Select the print server that you want to add (see Figure 14.13).

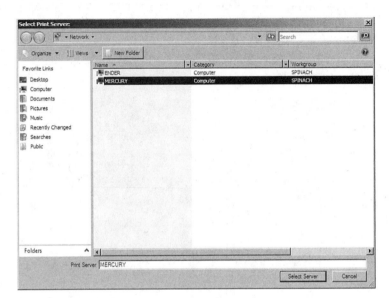

FIGURE 14.13
Select the print
server to be
added.

4. Click the Select button. You are returned to the Add/Remove Servers dialog box. The selected server name appears in the Add Servers box.

5. Click the Add to List button. The server is added to the print servers box (which already has your local print server listed).

6. Click OK.

The print server is added to the Print Servers list in the Print Management snap-in. You can add more print servers as required. You can also use the Add/Remove Servers dialog box to remove print servers if needed.

Adding a Network Printer to a Print Server

You can add printers to your print servers via the Print Management snap-in. This makes it very easy to add direct-connect printers in the domain to a particular print server.

Follow these steps:

1. In the Print Management snap-in, expand the node for a listed print server. Right-click the Printers node and select Add Printer. The Network Printer Installation Wizard appears.

2. It's probably easiest to locate network printers with the IP address or hostname of the direct-connect printer. Select the Add a TCP/IP or Web Services Printer by IP Address or Hostname option button (see Figure 14.14).

FIGURE 14.14
Locate the print-
er by IP address
or hostname.

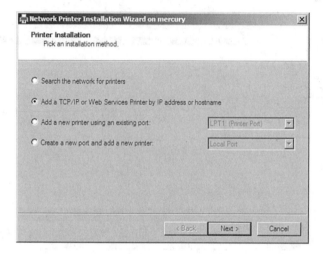

3. Click Next. On the next wizard page, enter the hostname or the IP address for the printer. Then click Next.

4. Windows communicates with the printer and determines the model of the printer and the appropriate device driver. It then advances to the next wizard page, which shows the printer (see Figure 14.15).

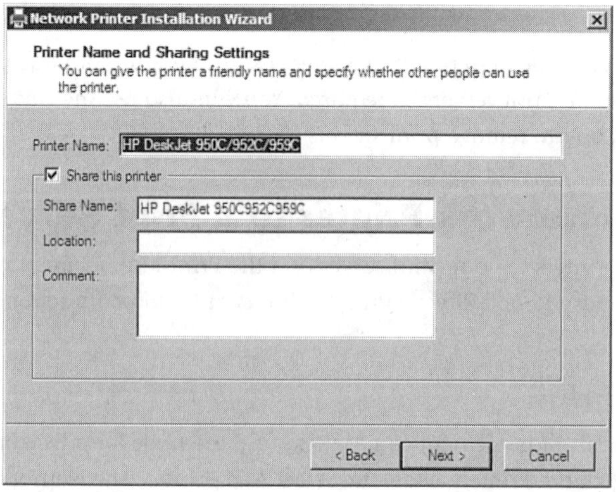

FIGURE 14.15
The printer
model is identi-
fied automati-
cally.

5. The printer is shared by default. Click Next.

6. The next page is informational and lets you know that the printer is ready to be installed. Click Next.

7. The device driver and the printer are installed on the print server.

8. The final wizard page opens. You have the option to print a test page to the printer and add additional printers. To close the wizard, click Close.

The printer is listed in the Details pane (along with any other printers connected to that print server) when you click the Printer node for the print server. To add the printer to the Active Directory, right-click the printer and select List in Directory from the shortcut menu that appears.

To quickly view the Sharing tab of a printer, right-click the printer and select Manage Sharing. The Properties dialog box for the printer opens (see Figure 14.16).

FIGURE 14.16
Quickly access the share settings for a printer.

If necessary, you can also remove printers from a print server. Right-click the printer (in the Details pane) and select Delete. You need to confirm the deletion to remove the printer.

Managing Print Jobs

The Print Management snap-in enables you to manage the printers on your network. You can view and control the print jobs that are currently in the print queue of a particular printer in the domain (or in the domain tree). You can set the printing defaults for a printer and quickly access the Properties dialog box for a printer (which enables you to configure permissions related to the printer—discussed later in this hour).

You can view the current print jobs on a printer with the Details pane of the Print Management snap-in. First, right-click the Printers node for a printer server and select Show Extended View. This opens a Jobs pane in the bottom half of the Details pane.

To view the print jobs currently running on a printer, select the printer in the Details pane. The print jobs are listed in the Jobs pane (see Figure 14.17).

FIGURE 14.17
View the current print jobs on a printer.

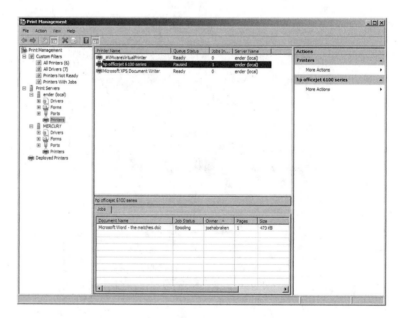

To pause a print job, right-click the print job in the Jobs pane and select Pause. You can also cancel a print job in the list; click Cancel.

You can also open the printer queue from the Details pane. Right-click a printer in the list and select Open Printer Queue. The queue opens, displaying current print jobs and the status of the print jobs.

Select a print job in the printer queue and then click the Document menu. You can pause, resume, restart, and cancel a print job from the Document menu (see Figure 14.18).

If you want to pause all the print jobs (meaning pause the printer) in the queue, click the Printer menu in the printer queue and select Pause Printing. You can also cancel all the print jobs in the queue by selecting Cancel All Documents on the Print menu.

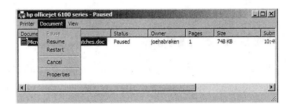

FIGURE 14.18
Manage print jobs on a printer in the printer queue.

You can also open the Properties dialog box for a print job via the Document menu. The Properties dialog box for a print job enables you to control the priority for the print job (on the General tab) and also enables you to set a schedule for the print job (see Figure 14.19).

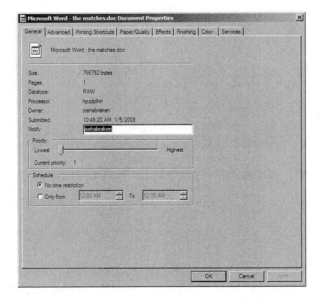

FIGURE 14.19
Open the Properties dialog box for a print job.

Other tabs on the print job's Properties dialog box enable you to access printer settings such as paper, print quality, finishing, and color settings (if the printer is a color printer). The Properties dialog box for a print job can also be accessed directly from the Jobs pane (in the Print Management snap-in) if you don't want to open the printer queue. Right-click a print job and select Properties.

The Print Management snap-in really provides a "one stop" tool for viewing and managing print jobs. Because print servers (and their associated printers) can quickly be added to the Print Management snap-in, you can manage print jobs in the domain from a single print server.

Using Printer Filters

The Print Management snap-in provides custom filters (by default) that enable you to view printers based on defined filter criteria. The default custom filters are

- **All Printers**—Displays all the printers "attached" to the print servers shown in the Print Management snap-in.

- **All Drivers**—Displays all the print drivers that have been installed based on the printers attached to the print servers currently shown.

- **Printers Not Ready**—Displays any printers that have been paused or are offline.

- **Printers with Jobs**—Displays printers that currently have printer jobs.

To use one of the custom filters to view printers that meet the filter's criteria, expand the Custom Filters node and then select a filter (such as Printers Not Ready). The printers meeting the filter's criteria appear in the Details pane (see Figure 14.20).

You can also create your own custom filters. These filters can take advantage of up to six conditional statements to provide a truly custom view of the printers in the domain. To create a custom filter, follow these steps:

1. In the Print Management snap-in, right-click the Custom Filters node and select Add New Printer Filter. The New Printer Filter Wizard appears.

2. Type a name for the new filter. You can also check a box on the name page that shows the number of printers meeting the filter's criteria. Click Next to continue.

3. On the next wizard page, you set the criteria for the filter. Click the drop-down list for the first field. You can select from a number of different fields including Printer Name, Queue Status, Server Name, and Share Name.

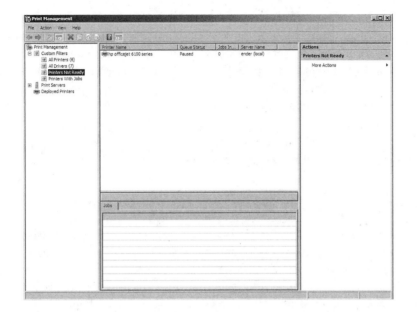

FIGURE 14.20
Use custom fil-
ters to view
printers meeting
defined criteria.

4. After selecting the field, set the condition and the value for the field (see Figure 14.21).

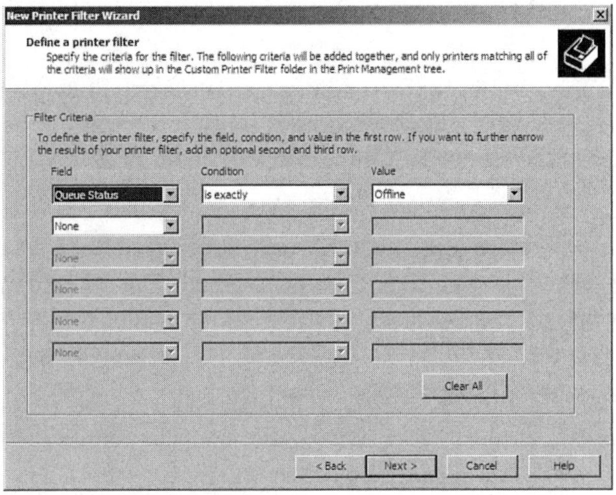

FIGURE 14.21
Set the field,
condition, and
value for the
filter.

5. You can select additional fields and set conditions and values for these fields (as needed). Click Next. The Set Notifications page opens.

6. You can set optional notifications related to the custom filter with email (or by running a script). Select the Send E-mail Notification check box or the Run Script check box (or both) and set the parameters for the notification. For email, you need to enter the recipient email, the sender email, the SMTP server, and the message. For a script, you need to provide the path to the script. After setting the optional notification settings, click Finish.

Select your new custom filter in the Print Management node tree (with Custom Filters expanded). Printers meeting your filter criteria are listed in the Details pane.

Working with Printer Permissions

When a printer is shared on the network, different levels of default permissions are assigned to domain groups. For example, the Everyone group (which includes all users in the domain) is provided with the Print permission. Depending on your inclination toward printers and security, you can remove the default permissions for the Everyone group and instead assign your users their basic access to printers by assigning the default permissions to the Authenticated Users group. This means that a user must be authenticated to the domain before acquiring print permissions.

The Print permission enables users (or members of a group assigned the permission) to print to the printer but does not enable them to manage the print queue (as discussed in the next section).

To view the default permissions for a printer, open the printer's Properties dialog box (right-click the printer in Printer Management snap-in or in the Control Panel's Printers window). Then select the Security tab (see Figure 14.22).

The default groups for printer permissions are Administrators, Server Operators, Everyone, Print Operators, and Creator Owner. Administrators are assigned the Print, Manage Printer, and Manage Documents permissions. The Creator Owner is assigned only the Manage Documents permission, by default. This means that users can manage documents that they create and send to the print server. They are not provided control over other users' print jobs.

The Print Operators group is designed to be used to assign certain special users on the network the ability to manage the printer and its documents. Only responsible users should be included in the membership of the Print Operators group.

Each permission provides a group or user with a different level of access to the printer. The Print permission enables a user to send documents to the printer. That's it—it provides no management permissions to the printer.

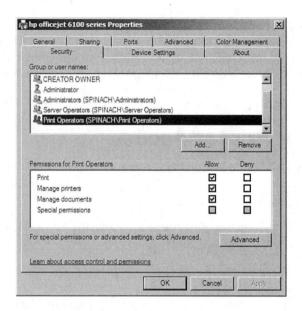

FIGURE 14.22
Printer permissions are set on the Security tab.

The Manage Printers permission provides a user with the capability to completely manage the printer and its drivers. This permission level includes the capability to control job settings for documents, such as pausing, resuming, or canceling print jobs. This permission level also enables the user to cancel documents in the print queue. This permission even provides the capability to delete the printer as a resource on the network.

The Manage Documents permission provides a subset of the Manage Printers permissions–level privileges. A user with Manage Documents permission can control job settings for documents and can pause, resume, or cancel print jobs.

As with share and NTFS permissions, printer permissions can be assigned to users and groups. For a discussion of share and NTFS permissions, see Hour 13, "Using Share and NTFS Permissions." For a discussion of group memberships, see Hour 9, "Creating Active Directory Groups, Organizational Units, and Sites."

By the Way

Printer permissions are used, ideally, to determine who can print to a particular printer on the network (or who can manage the print jobs on that printer). Allowing the Everyone group access to all shared printers on the network can cause print traffic problems, particularly if many users print to the same printer. New groups that contain users who work on certain floors or in the same part of an office can be created so that users are compelled to print to a printer that is in their work area.

You might want to remove the Print permission from the Everyone group and create your own groups for printer access. You can then use the Add button to add Active Directory groups to the printer's Group list. The permissions for that particular group can then be set. In most cases, you want "typical" users to have only the Print permission.

Auditing Printer Access

You can also set up auditing for printer use (and management) via the Security tab of the printer's Properties dialog box. This enables you to track group (or specific user) access to printers.

1. Click the Advanced button on the Security tab. The Advanced Security Settings dialog box opens. Click the Auditing tab.

2. To add a group (or user) to the Auditing Entries list, click the Add button. The Select User, Computer, or Group dialog box opens. Type the name of the group or the user. Then click OK. The Auditing Entry dialog box for the printer opens (see Figure 14.23).

FIGURE 14.23
You can audit group or user access to printers.

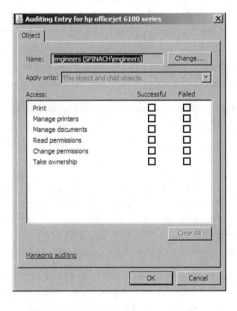

3. You can audit print access or events related to managing the printer or documents. Select either the Successful or Failed check boxes for the access event, and then click OK to close the Auditing Entry dialog box. You are returned to the Auditing tab. Add other users or groups as discussed for auditing, and

then click OK to return to the printer's Properties dialog box. Click OK to close the dialog box.

Printer access events appear in the print server's Event Viewer security log. You can open the Event Viewer by selecting Start, Administrative Tools, Event Viewer.

> **By the Way**
>
> Auditing and other security settings are part of the local computer or the domain's Group Policy settings. Group Policy is discussed in Hour 11, "Deploying Group Policy and Network Access Protection."

Summary

In this hour, you learned how to create a print server for local and direct-connect printers. Shared printers provide print services to users on the network.

To function as a print server in the domain, the Print Services role must be added to the server. After the Print Services role is added, the print server (and printers supplied by the print server) can be managed through the Print Management snap-in. Print servers and printers can be added to the Print Management snap-in, enabling you to monitor and manage all the print services in the domain.

Print jobs can be viewed, paused, and reordered via the Print Management snap-in. Printer filters can be used to create custom views of printers in the domain that meet criteria you configure.

The Security tab of a printer's Properties dialog box provides you with access to the permissions for the printer. You can set permissions for users or groups.

The Security tab also provides the auditing settings for the printer's access. User or group access to the printer can be audited.

Q&A

Q *How is a printer installed on a print server?*

A USB printers need only be connected to the server. You can add remote printers and direct-connect printers to a server running Windows Server 2008 by using the Add Printer Wizard.

Q *What is the benefit of direct-connect printers?*

A This type of printer provides either an internal or external device that spools and processes print jobs at the printer.

Q *What snap-in provides for the management of network printers and print servers?*

A The Print Management snap-in enables you to manage the print servers and printers in the domain. You can view and manage individual print jobs and use custom filters to view printers that meet criteria that you set.

Q *How are different access levels to print jobs and printer management determined?*

A Printer permissions are set on a per-printer basis on each shared printer. Different permission levels include Print, Manage Printers, and Manage Documents.

HOUR 15

Understanding the Domain Name Service

What You'll Learn in This Hour:

▶ DNS Server Overview

▶ Installing the Domain Name Service

▶ Configuring the DNS Server

▶ Managing DNS

▶ Creating Resource Records

▶ Configuring DNS Clients

▶ Configuring a Caching-Only Server

▶ Monitoring and Troubleshooting the DNS Server Service

As network operating systems have moved away from proprietary network protocols and have embraced the open TCP/IP protocol stack, the need for resolving names to IP addresses has arisen. This hour looks at the Domain Name Service (DNS) provided by Windows Server 2008.

DNS Server Overview

The Domain Name Service provides a hierarchical name-resolution strategy for resolving a Fully Qualified Domain Name (FQDN), hostnames, and other service-related names to IP addresses. DNS servers provide this resolution from a "friendly name" to logical address (the IP address) on TCP/IP networks such as the Internet. For example, when you type Microsoft.com into your web browser address window, a DNS server somewhere on the Internet actually resolves the FQDN name (Microsoft.com) to the IP address of the Microsoft website.

So, in terms of TCP/IP networks and the Internet in particular, each organization deploys DNS servers that provide FQDN resolution to IP addresses. In effect, each large company, organization, or service provider manages the name-resolution duties for its own portion of the Internet. In fact, when a company registers a domain name with InterNIC, it must submit the IP addresses of two DNS servers that will handle the name-resolution duties for that domain. You can choose to run your own DNS implementation or outsource it to an ISP or other networking company that provides the service. (For individuals who register a domain name, the DNS server addresses are typically provided by your service provider.)

Servers maintained by InterNIC provide the mechanism for a local DNS server to resolve an FQDN to an IP address on a remote portion of the Internet. Because the InterNIC servers hold a database that provides a listing of all domain DNS servers and their IP addresses, the local DNS merely queries the InterNIC server for the IP address of the DNS server that services a particular domain (using the friendly name). When the local server receives the IP address of the remote DNS server, it can then query it directly for the resolution of the remote FQDN to an IP address.

With each network really responsible for the local mapping of friendly names to IP addresses (meaning the network must deploy its own DNS servers), the DNS database is a distributed database. Each organization maintains its part of the overall DNS database.

By the Way

An alternative to DNS is the hosts file. Hosts files are used as a system to resolve the friendly name to the IP address on TCP/IP networks when DNS is not employed (or was not employed—hosts files served as a precursor to DNS). A hosts file is an ASCII text file that contains two columns of information (and is stored in the %systemroot%\system32\etc\drivers folder). The computer's hostname is listed in the first column; the corresponding IP address is listed in the second column.

With Windows Server 2008 embracing the Active Directory as its directory services platform, DNS, FQDNs, and TCP/IP become an integral part of implementing and administering a Windows network. Because Windows Server 2008 is outfitted with the newer Dynamic DNS server standard (DDNS), the administrative chores related to maintaining the DNS database are greatly reduced (when compared to other DNS servers). The DDNS database is built dynamically by the server and the DNS clients.

The DNS Namespace

To understand how DNS or FQDN names are determined, you need to understand the domain namespace, which is an integral part of how Internet websites are named.

The *domain namespace* is the actual scheme used to name domains that are at different levels in the DNS domain hierarchical tree. The domain namespace also provides for down-level names of individual computers and other devices on a network.

The first thing to define is what a domain is in relation to DNS. Each division on the DNS tree (which takes the form of an inverted tree) is considered a domain.

DNS domains and Microsoft Active Directory domains are not the same thing and should not be confused (even though they are closely related and based upon different logical hierarchies). When you use the DNS naming structure on your network as the Active Directory domain structure, the two naming systems appear to be the same. In fact, when you configure a new domain controller and add the Domain Name Service during the domain controller creation, the forward lookup zone for the DNS server is identical to the Active Directory domain structure (lookup zones are discussed later in this hour).

By the Way

At the base of the DNS tree is the root domain. The Internet's root domain is represented by a period (see Figure 15.1). Below the root domain are the top-level domains. The top-level domains consist of suffixes such as .com and .edu. Some of the top-level domain names available are listed here:

▶ **com**—Used by commercial organizations. For example, http://www.informit.com is the domain name for InformIT, the publishing umbrella group that hosts the Sams Publishing website.

▶ **edu**—Reserved for educational institutions. For example, www.une.edu is the domain of the University of New England.

▶ **org**—Used by noncommercial organizations and institutions. For example, gsusa.org is the domain name of the Girl Scouts of America. This top-level domain is now unrestricted, however, and can be used by anyone.

▶ **gov**—Reserved by the United States for governmental entities. For example, senate.gov is the domain for the U.S. Senate.

▶ **net**—Used typically by companies involved in the Internet infrastructure, such as ISPs; however this top-level domain is now unrestricted.

▶ **Country names**—For example, bs for the Bahamas and ga for Gabon. These are based upon the ISO-registered two-character country codes.

▶ **biz**—A relatively new top-level domain added recently to accommodate businesses.

▶ **info**—A top-level domain that can be used for informational websites; however, it is unrestricted and can be used by anyone looking for a domain name.

Below the top-level domains are the second-level domains; these secondary domains consist of company, institutional, and private domains commonly used to access a site on the Web, such as samspublishing.com (Sams Publishing's domain name) and une.edu (the domain name of the University of New England in Biddeford, Maine). Under the second-level domains are found subdomains. These subdomains are typically used to divide a larger secondary domain into geographical or functional units. For example, if I have a company that uses the secondary domain name of Habraken.com and my business is divided into two distinct divisions (consulting and sales), I could create the two subdomains consulting.Habraken.com and sales.Habraken.com (see Figure 15.1) .

FIGURE 15.1
The domain namespace tree provides the naming conventions for domains and objects that reside in domains, such as hosts.

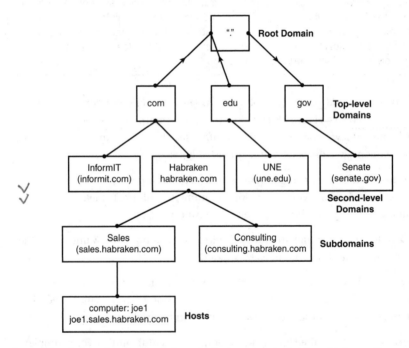

Second-level domains (and subdomains) also contain hosts, which are the computers and other devices that reside within the second-level domain or subdomain namespace. For example, if I have a computer named joe1 and it is in the sales.Habraken.com subdomain, it is referred to as joe1.sales.Habraken.com, using the DNS nomenclature.

How DNS Works

Now that you've seen the DNS naming hierarchy, it's time to delve into how DNS resolves FQDNs to IP addresses, and vice versa. The DNS service consists of two different entities: the resolver and the server. The resolver is software built into a

WinSock application, such as a web browser that queries the server when a host's FQDN needs to be resolved to an IP address. The server component of DNS is handled by the DNS server, which, in our discussion, is a server running Windows Server 2008 and the DDNS service.

When a client computer attempts to resolve a FQDN to an IP address, the resolver checks a local cache (if the resolver is set up to maintain a local cache) to see whether the resolution information for going from FQDN to IP address is available. If the information is in the cache, the process is over when the FQDN is resolved to an IP address by the client computer itself.

All Windows clients and servers maintain a DNS cache, which helps a DNS client quickly resolve a DNS query basically by itself. The cache is typically useful only when trying to resolve a friendly name to an IP address for a resource that is used often. All other queries go to the DNS server. You can view the DNS cache with the command-line utility `ipconfig/displaydns`.

If the information is not available in the cache, the resolver software obtains the IP address of the local DNS server, using the settings found in the client computer's TCP/IP settings. Windows clients and servers on the network are configured with a preferred DNS server either statically or by a DHCP server. (The types of TCP/IP settings that a DHCP server can provide are discussed in Hour 16, "Using the Dynamic Host Configuration Protocol.") Figure 15.2 shows the TCP/IP properties of a Windows Server 2008 member server that specifies a preferred DNS server (and is also configured with a static IP address).

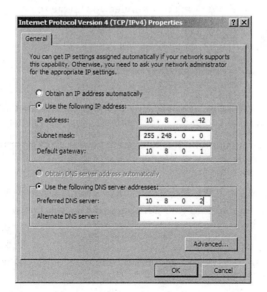

FIGURE 15.2
The preferred DNS server is listed in a client's TCP/IP properties.

The client sends a request to the preferred DNS; if the FQDN to be resolved is for a host computer in the local DNS domain, the DNS server looks up the name in the DNS database and returns the appropriate IP address to the requesting computer. If the name is for a computer that is not in the local domain, the name can be resolved using the cache that is maintained by the local DNS server.

If the information is not cached on the local DNS server, your DNS server contacts the root server for the hostname's top-level domain (these IP addresses are built into the Windows Server 2008 DNS implementation) by querying it with the hostname. The root server uses the hostname to determine the IP address of the authoritative DNS server for the domain to which the particular host belongs. When your DNS server has the IP address of the other domain's DNS server, it can query that server, which then supplies the resolution information for moving from FQDN to IP address. The local DNS server can then pass this information on to the original requesting host.

> So, in a nutshell, DNS can resolve DNS names to IP addresses (and vice versa) because DNS servers host the information needed by a computer running the DNS client when it needs to resolve a FQDN to an IP address. The DNS client on the local computer needs the aid of the DNS server only if it does not have the FQDN and IP address equivalent stored in its cache.

Active Directory Domain Services and DNS

When you add the Active Directory Domain Services role to a server on the network and promote the server to a domain controller, you create the Active Directory structure for the network. The first domain created is at the forest level. You can then create subsequent domains such as regional domains that provide the branches in domain root.

> When you define your own domain namespace keep your second-level domain names simple and use geographic location or company division information for subdomain levels. Also try to limit the number of domain levels if possible. Don't create subdomains just for the sake of creating divisions in the namespace.

DNS is tightly wound with the Active Directory Domain Services (AD DS). In an ideal network implementation, your DNS and AD DS structure will mirror each other. The integration of DNS and AD DS enables you to take advantage of DNS features that directly relate to AD DS, such as AD DS replication. Also be aware that DNS is necessary for the location of domain controllers on the network (by DNS clients) and that the Netlogon service uses DNS for the registration of domain controllers in the DNS domain namespace.

When you install DNS as part of the process of creating a new domain or adding a domain controller to an existing domain, the DNS namespace is derived from the Active Directory namespace. This means that the AD DS domain hierarchy is incorporated in the DNS zone hierarchy.

For example, when you bring AD DS, a domain controller, and DNS online during the Active Directory Directory Services installation (discussed in Hour 8, "Understanding and Configuring Active Directory Domain Services") the forward lookup zones created for DNS directly reflect the Active Directory domain structure (see Figure 15.3).

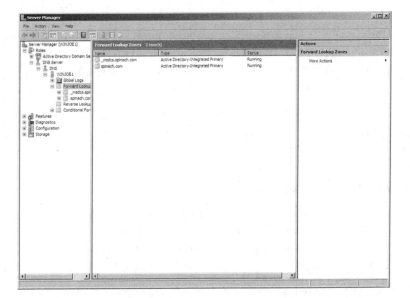

FIGURE 15.3
DNS and AD DS can be tightly integrated in terms of their logical hierarchies.

Lookup zones are examined more closely later in this hour. Let's take a look now at how to install the Domain Name Service on a server that will provide DNS as one of its primary functions on the network (meaning it is not a domain controller).

Installing the Domain Name Service

The Windows Server 2008 implementation of DNS, which was known as the Dynamic Domain Name Service in previous versions of the Windows Server product line (DDNS was originally implemented in the Windows 2000 Server product), provides for dynamic updates, which allows network clients using the DNS service to automatically update their client resource records in the DNS database. Microsoft's DDNS also allows for integration with the Active Directory Domain Services, which means that the DNS database is replicated among all the domain controllers within the domain (domain controllers that also serve as DNS servers). DNS is also integrated with the Windows Server 2008 implementation of DHCP; the DNS server can work with DHCP to synchronize mappings from hostname to IP address for the hosts on your network.

There is more than one way to install DNS on Windows Server 2008. You can install DNS during the installation of Active Directory Domain Services and the configuration of a domain controller for the new domain that you are creating. (This scenario is discussed in Hour 8. You can also install the DNS role on any server running Windows Server 2008 (whether that server is a domain controller or just a member server in your domain).

To add roles (such as DNS) to a server running Windows Server 2008, use the Add Roles Wizard. The Add Roles Wizard can be started from the Initial Configuration Tasks window (which opens when you boot a server running Windows Server 2008) or you can add the DNS role via the Server Manager.

By the Way

> Before installing DNS on a server, you must configure the computer with static IPv4 and IPv6 addresses.

To install DNS with the Add Roles Wizard, follow these steps:

1. Start the Add Roles Wizard; in the Initial Configuration Tasks window, click Add Roles in the Customize This Server section of the window or click Add Roles in the Server Manager Details pane (when the Roles node is selected). Then click Next to bypass the initial wizard screen.

2. The first screen reminds you to configure a strong password for the administrator's account and configure a static IP address for the server. Click Next.

3. A list of server roles appears (see Figure 15.4). Select the DNS Server role and then click Next.

3. On the next screen, you are provided a basic introduction to DNS. Links are also provided for a DNS overview, planning a DNS deployment, and understanding DNS zone replication. Take advantage of the resources this screen provides as needed and then click Next to continue.

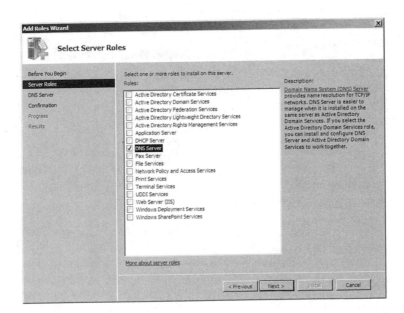

FIGURE 15.4
Select the DNS
server role.

4. The next screen lists the roles, role services, and features that will be installed (related to your selections in step 2). If you select DNS Server, only the Domain Name Server role is installed. Select Install.

5. When the installation is complete, click Close. The Add Roles Wizard closes.

After the Domain Name Service role has been installed on the server, which is now a DNS server, you need to configure the DNS server with lookup zones and also potentially add resource records to the DNS database. Let's take a look at monitoring the DNS server and creating lookup zones.

Configuring the DNS Server

The Domain Name Service that has been installed on the server is managed through the DNS snap-in. You open the DNS snap-in in the Server Manager by expanding the Roles and DNS Server nodes in the Nodes pane.

The Server Manager also provides you with a quick fix in terms of monitoring the DNS service in that it shows events being logged that are related to DNS. The services needed to run the DNS role (the DNS service) are also displayed. Figure 15.5 shows the Server Manager with the DNS role selected.

FIGURE 15.5
Server Manager
shows events
and services
associated with
DNS.

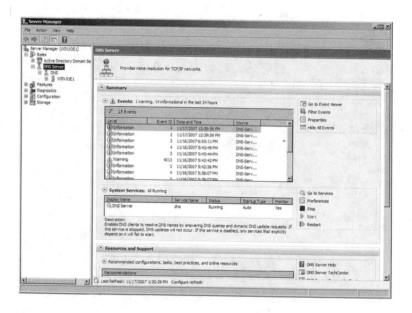

The other alternative for configuring DNS is the DNS snap-in running in the Microsoft Management Console (MMC). You lose the Server Manager view of the events and services related to DNS but you still have access to the lookup zones and other options related to DNS. If you have managed DNS by using servers running Windows Server 2003, you are familiar with the DNS snap-in running in the MMC.

Let's take a look at some of the configuration issues related to DNS, such as the creation of lookup zones, zone replication, and working with resource records. The discussion begins with a look at forward lookup zones.

Creating a Forward Lookup Zone

A *forward lookup zone* allows for forward lookup queries, which enable a host to find the IP address using the hostname of a particular computer or device. (It finds the address because the DNS answers the host computer's query.) For DNS to work on the network, at least one forward lookup zone is required.

To create a new forward lookup zone, follow these steps:

1. With the DNS and Server nodes expanded in the DNS snap-in (in the Server Manager or MMC window), right-click the Forward Lookup Zones folder (in the node tree) and select New Zone. The New Zone Wizard opens. Click Next to bypass the initial wizard screen.

2. On the next screen, you are provided with three options for creating different types of forward lookup zones:

  ∨ ▶ **Primary Zone**—A primary zone is the master copy of the DNS database. The primary zone is administered on the computer server where the zone was created. So, the server would be considered the authoritative DNS server for the zone.

  ▶ **Secondary Zone**—A secondary zone uses a database file that is a read-only replica of an existing zone. The DNS server configured with the standard secondary zone helps the primary DNS server handle the name resolution required for the network.

  ▶ **Stub Zone**—A stub zone contains only the records necessary to specify the authoritative DNS server (or servers) for a particular zone. The stub zone basically points at the servers that manage the primary zone.

If you are bringing the first DNS server onto the network, you need to create the primary zone (which is assumed for this series of steps). Select the Primary Zone option (see Figure 15.7). Click Next to continue.

A check box on this DNS wizard screen also is selected by default to store the zone in the Active Directory. This means that the zone (along with the Active Directory) is replicated to other domain controllers on the network that are also running DNS.

Did you Know?

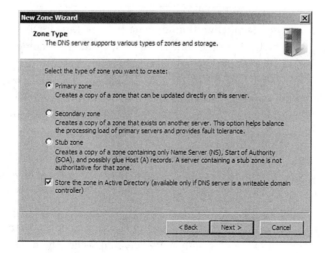

FIGURE 15.6
Create a primary zone for the DNS server.

3. The next screen provides options related to the replication of the DNS data for the new zone.

 ▸ **To All DNS Servers in This Forest**—Using this option, all the DNS servers in the forest share and replicate their DNS databases. This means that all the DNS servers have access to the same zones and records.

 ▸ **To All DNS Servers in This Domain**—Using this option, all the domain DNS servers (DNS servers in the domain named) share their zones and records through replication.

✓ ▸ **To All Domain Controllers in This Domain (for Windows 2000 Compatibility)**—This option is useful if you are running DNS on your domain controllers. The DNS database is stored as part of the Active Directory and is replicated (shared) among the domain controllers/DNS servers. Note that this is the default option and is considered the best practice for DNS deployment. This option is also backward compatible with Windows 2000.

Select the option that you want to use (use the default option for the sake of discussion) and then click Next.

Did you Know?

It is important that DNS servers on the network replicate the DNS database (and the zone records) so that they share the same DNS records. Because each DNS server uses the same replicated database, any of these DNS servers can field a query by a host for a hostname-to-IP-address resolution (or vice versa).

4. The next wizard screen requests a name for the new forward lookup zone (see Figure 15.7). The name of the zone is the same as the DNS domain name for the portion of your network for which this DNS server is authoritative (which can be the same as your AD DS domain name). For example, if your DNS domain for the network is spinach.com, the zone name would be spinach.com. If you are setting up DNS in a child domain (of spinach.com) named popeye, the zone would be popeye.spinach.com. Enter the name and then click Next to continue.

5. The next screen provides options related to dynamic updates of your host computers as they register (and update) their records with the DNS server. The default option button is Allow Only Secure Dynamic Updates (Recommended for Active Directory). This option allows only secure updates. There are two other option buttons: Allow Both Nonsecure and Secure Dynamic Updates and

Do Not Allow Dynamic Updates. The option that allows nonsecure and secure dynamic updates could open some security holes in your network. Selecting the no dynamic updates option means that you will have to manually enter all the records for this zone. Make sure that the default dynamic update option is selected for the new zone and click Next to continue.

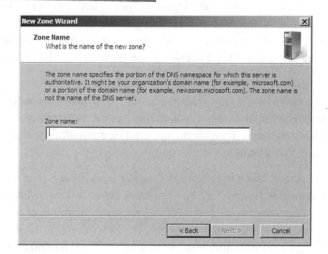

FIGURE 15.7
Enter a name for the new zone.

The dynamic update option (which is the default) provides the greatest security, but it also requires that the DNS servers be running Active Directory, meaning that they will also be serving as domain controllers. It also means that only domain members can create and update their own resource records.

By the Way

6. The summary screen appears for the New Zone Wizard. Click Finish to close the wizard and create the zone.

The new zone is added to your DNS configuration. Resource records are added to the new DNS zone automatically if you chose dynamic updates. If you did not choose dynamic updates, you need to add resource records to the zone, which is discussed later in the hour.

Creating a Reverse Lookup Zone

Forward lookup zones are used to resolve FQDNs to IP addresses. Another zone type, the *reverse lookup zone*, allows for the resolution of IP addresses to hostnames, which is called a *reverse lookup query*. You don't have to configure a reverse lookup zone on your DNS server for it to work (remember at least one forward lookup zone is required), but reverse lookup zones are useful. For example, if you want to enable Internet Information Service to record hostnames as well as IP addresses in its log file, you need to configure your DNS server with a reverse lookup zone.

To create a reverse lookup zone, follow these steps:

1. With the DNS and Server nodes expanded in the DNS snap-in (in the Server Manager or MMC window) and the Reverse Lookup Zones folder selected, right-click the Reverse Lookup Zones folder (in the node tree) and select New Zone. The New Zone Wizard opens. Click Next to bypass the initial wizard screen.

2. The next screen asks you to select the zone type: primary, secondary, or stub. Because this is the first reverse lookup zone on the authoritative DNS server, a primary reverse lookup zone is the appropriate choice (this is also the default). Click Next to continue.

3. The next screen asks you to select the type of replication for the new reverse lookup zone (see Figure 15.8). You can have the zone data replicated to all the DNS servers in the forest, all the DNS servers in the domain, or all the DNS/domain controllers in the domain. The latter choice is the default. It is also the best choice in environments in which DNS is running on your domain controllers. Click Next to continue.

FIGURE 15.8
Select the repli-
cation type for
the reverse
lookup zone.

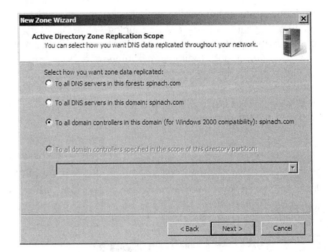

4. On the next screen, select the IP type for the reverse look zone: IPv4 or IPv6 (this example assumes IPv4). Then click next.

5. On the next screen (see Figure 15.9) provide your network ID. This is used to create the name for the reverse lookup zone. The network ID is the portion of

an IP address that does not contain any references to host address. For example, in the Class C IP address 192.168.5.1, only the fourth octet contains host address information. (The default Class C subnet mask of 255.255.255.0 basically tells you which octet is used for host addressing.) This means that the 192.168.5 is the network ID and would be entered as 192.168.5. Enter the network ID and then click Next.

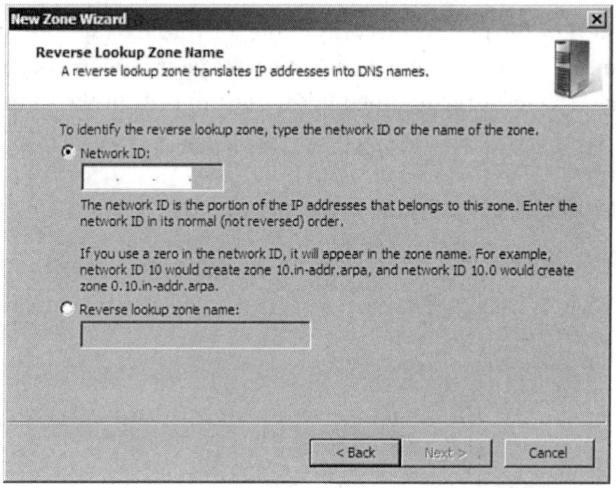

FIGURE 15.9
Enter the network ID to name the reverse lookup zone.

> For more information related to IPv4, IPv6, and IP addressing issues, see Hour 7, "Working with the TCP/IP Network Protocol."

By the Way

6. The next screen asks you to choose the type of dynamic updates used by the new zone: secure dynamic updates, secure and nonsecure updates, or no dynamic updates. It is best to go with the default of secure dynamic updates. Click Next to continue.

7. The New Zone Wizard completion screen appears with a list of the settings for the new zone. Click Finish to create the zone and close the wizard.

The new zone will be listed in the Reverse Lookup Zones folder in the DNS tree on your server. If you enabled Dynamic Updates (the default) on the reverse lookup zone, member computers automatically create a reverse lookup, or PTR, record. You can also add resource (pointer or PTR) records to the zone as needed.

Managing DNS

As already mentioned earlier in the hour, you use the DNS snap-in to both manage DNS and reconfigure it, if necessary. The DNS snap-in enables you to view the records in your DNS zones and add zones to the DNS server. Because records are created dynamically, you can view the records in a particular zone (such as a forward lookup zone) by opening that zone in the DNS snap-in.

For example, to view the resource records in the forward lookup zone, expand the Forward Lookup Zones node and then select one of your forward lookup zones in the snap-in tree. The records contained in the zone appear in the snap-in pane (see Figure 15.10).

FIGURE 15.10
Zone records can be viewed in the Details pane.

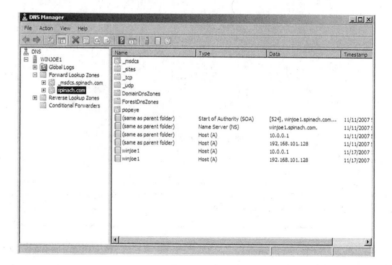

A number of different resource record types are found in the DNS environment. One type of record is a host record, which is designated as an A record in the DNS environment. A records are found in forward lookup zones. The winjoe1 host or A record is shown in the Details pane of Figure 15.10. You should also notice that other resource record types, such as Start of Authority (SOA) and Name Server (NS), appear in the DNS Details pane. A number of different types of DNS resource records exist; a summary of these types is provided in Table 15.1.

TABLE 15.1   DNS Resource Record Types

Record Type	DNS Snap-In Name and Description
SOA	Start of Authority. Identifies the name of the server that is authoritative for data within the domain and that is the first record in the zone database file. It is created automatically when you bring your primary name server online.
NS	Name Server. A record is created for each name server assigned to the zone.
A	Host. This record provides the mapping of hostname to IP address in a forward lookup zone.
PTR	Pointer. This type of record is the converse of an A record and points to a host record. Found in the reverse lookup zone, the PTR record provides for mappings from IP addresses to hostnames.
SRV	Service. This type of record shows which services are running on a particular host computer. For example, SRV records could identify the domain controllers on the network.
MX	Mail Exchanger. This record type identifies the mail servers on the network and details in what order the mail servers should be contacted.
CNAME	Canonical Name or Alias. This type of record is used to create an alias for an existing record. This enables you to point several different names at the same IP address. This is particularly useful for pointing at your web server on the network.
HINFO	Host Information. This record type can be used as a sort of low-rent resource-tracking tool for your DNS server. This record can provide information on the CPU, operating system, and other software/hardware information.
WINS	WINS. This type of record supplies DNS with the capability to use WINS to help resolve a hostname.

A number of these record types—such as the A (host), SOA, and NS records—are created automatically. The other record types can be created manually within the DNS-MGMT snap-in.

Creating Resource Records

Although Dynamic DNS creates many of the resource records for the DNS database, you might want to create some resource records, such as a CNAME or a WINS record, manually. In some cases, you might also need to create host records for the DNS database (for clients that cannot work with DNS to dynamically create an A record).

To create a DNS resource record, follow these steps:

1. Expand a zone node (such as the Forward Lookup Zones node) and then select a zone in the snap-in tree. The records currently in the zone appear in the Details pane.

2. Right-click the zone icon in the snap-in tree. A shortcut menu appears that contains choices such as New Host and New Alias. You can click any of these record types to start the process of creating a new resource record. For example, if you select New Host (A or AAAA) from the shortcut menu, the New Host dialog box appears (see Figure 15.11).

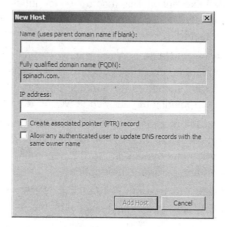

3. To create the new host record, supply the hostname for the computer and then supply the IP address of the computer (or other device, such as a printer). A check box is also included to create a PTR record for the host (the reverse lookup zone record). It makes sense to check this box and create both the host and PTR records simultaneously.

4. After supplying the appropriate information for the new record, click Add Host. The record is added to the selected zone.

You can view all the possible resource records that you can create; right-click a DNS zone in the snap-in tree and then select Other New Records from the shortcut menu. The Resource Record Type dialog box appears. Choose a resource record type from the list and then click the Create Record button to create the new resource record.

Did you Know?

Configuring DNS Clients

We have been looking at DNS so far from the server side, but there are also DNS management duties related to clients on your network. You need to configure TCP/IP clients on the network to use the DNS service.

You should configure any clients on the network (including servers) that are set up with a static IP address to use a particular DNS server on the network to resolve hostnames. You can specify a preferred DNS server and a secondary DNS server for the client.

To configure a client for specific DNS servers, follow these steps:

1. Log on to the client computer or member server as an Administrator and open the Network and Sharing Center (Control Panel, Network and Sharing Center). Then click Manage Network Connections.

2. Right-click a local area connection and then select Properties. This opens the Local Area Connection Properties dialog box.

3. Scroll down through the components list and click Internet Protocol Version 4 (TCP/IPv4) or Internet Protocol Version 6 (TCP/IPv6), depending on what version of the IP protocol you want to configure (see Figure 15.12). Then click the Properties button.

4. The Internet Protocol properties box opens. Select the Use the Following DNS Server Addresses option button. Then enter the preferred DNS server IP address and the alternative DNS server IP address (if one exists).

5. If you need to enter additional DNS server addresses, click the Advanced button and then select the DNS tab on the Advanced TCP/IP Properties box. You can add other DNS servers on this tab. Enter the server addresses in the order that you want the host to query them.

6. Click OK to return to the TCP/IP Properties box. Click OK to close the Local Area Connections dialog box. You can now close the various open windows and return to the desktop.

FIGURE 15.12
Select the version of IP you want to configure.

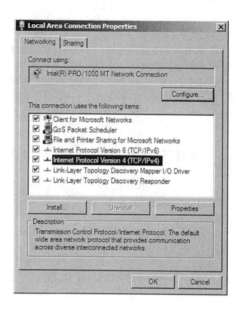

An alternative to manually entering information such as preferred DNS servers is to use DHCP in your domain. It can configure all the TCP/IP properties for your clients dynamically. See Hour 16 for more about DHCP.

Configuring a Caching-Only Server

DNS servers cache information that they receive from queries that they have made to other DNS servers. You can configure a DNS server that operates as a *caching-only server*, meaning that it supplies information to hostname resolution queries based on the data that it has acquired in its cache.

Caching-only servers are very useful because they do not generate network traffic related to zone transfers; they are not authoritative for any zones. Caching-only servers are often used as forwarders that sit outside a firewall and are used by a company's internal DNS server to resolve hostnames to IP addresses that reside outside the internal network, such as on the Internet.

To create a caching-only server, install DNS on a server running Windows Server 2008. When configuring DNS, do not create any zones on the server. A member server on your network is an ideal candidate for a caching-only server. All the FQDN-to-IP address resolution is handled by the server's DNS cache.

Monitoring and Troubleshooting the DNS Server Service

The DNS snap-in not only lists dynamic updates resulting in host records for hosts on the network; the snap-in also provides you with a way to test the DNS server and monitor the results. Two different tests in the form of queries are available: a simple query and a recursive query.

- ▶ **Simple**—A simple query tests the mapping of host-to-IP address, so the simple query performed in the DNS snap-in uses the DNS client on the DNS server to query the name server. This is a test of the DNS server's capability to handle forward lookups by itself.

- ▶ **Recursive**—A recursive query enables you to test the mapping of IP address to hostname, which is a test of the DNS server's reverse lookup capabilities. You must have a reverse lookup zone configured to run the recursive query.

To monitor and run these test queries, follow these steps:

1. Right-click the DNS name server in the DNS snap-in, and then select Properties from the shortcut menu that appears. The Properties dialog box opens for the DNS server.

2. Click the Monitoring tab to select it. Two check boxes are available on the tab (see Figure 15.13): a simple query against this DNS server and a recursive query to other DNS servers.

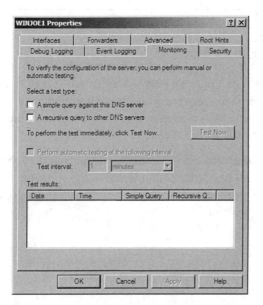

FIGURE 15.13
You can test the DNS server with queries.

3. Click the appropriate check box to set up the test (you can select both check boxes). Then click the Test Now button. The test results appear in the Test Results box of the Monitoring tab.

You can also monitor a DNS server over time with these query tests. Click the Perform Automatic Testing at the Following Interval check box and then set the time Interval in the Test interval box.

If your server fails one of these tests when they are performed periodically (if you set up for automatic testing), the server is marked with an alert icon (a triangle with an exclamation point on it). This lets you know when you view the Server icon in the DNS snap-in that there is a problem with the server.

Viewing DNS Events

You can view events related to your DNS server in the Server Manager window and the Windows Server 2008 Event Viewer. The Server Manager shows events related to the DNS server when you select the DNS Server node in the Node pane of the Server Manager window. Double-click any event to view the details of that event.

You can also use the Event Viewer to view DNS events. In the Server Manager window, click the Go to Event Viewer link on the right side of the Server Manager window.

You can start the Event Viewer from the Start menu: Click Start, Administrative Tools, and then Event Viewer. The Event Viewer opens in the MMC.

The Event Viewer helps you to track a number of event logs related to your server's performance, the network operating system, and the services installed on the server. Windows Server 2008 provides a new look for the Event Viewer, which provides a multi-paned snap-in that makes it easy to view details related to a selected event. For more about the Event Viewer and the type of information it provides in its log files (which operates in its own snap-in), see Hour 24, "Monitoring Server Performance and Network Connections."

To view DNS log events, expand the Event Viewer node in the Server Manager node tree. Then expand the Applications and Services Logs and select the DNS Server icon. The events logged in this file appear in the Details pane (see Figure 15.14).

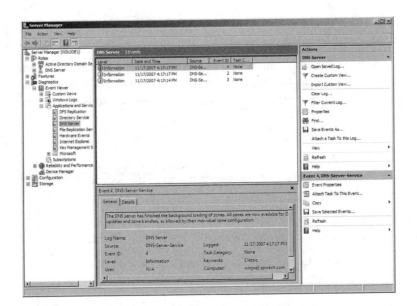

If your DNS service is running smoothly, you will typically see only information events in the log. If you see Warning or Error icons, you might have a DNS problem (see Hour 24 for more about the types of events logged by the Event Viewer).

Using Nslookup

Nslookup is an excellent troubleshooting tool for DNS. Nslookup is a command-line utility, and you can use it to view host records, do query testing of DNS servers, and perform other tasks related to DNS from the command line.

You can use the nslookup command to find information such as the IP address of a particular host on the network. The command takes the syntax nslookup *name1 name2*, where *name1* is the hostname for the host computer that you want to look up and *name2* is the name of the DNS server that you want to query. Running these queries with Nslookup enables you to see whether the DNS server is dynamically recording the host records needed to resolve the queries.

Each time you run the nslookup command as described in the previous paragraph, you are returned to the command prompt. This is called the *Nslookup noninteractive mode*. If you want to run several Nslookup commands in succession, you can enter the Nslookup interactive mode.

Open a command window (Start, Run, type **cmd**, and then click Run). At the command line, type **nslookup** (with no additional parameters) and then press Enter. This command provides the default DNS server information and the IP address of the server. This also places you in Nslookup interactive mode (the command prompt is replaced by the Nslookup > prompt).

When you are in interactive mode, you do not have to type the nslookup command. The command syntax becomes *name1 name2*, where you supply the hostname (*name1*) to be resolved, followed optionally by the DNS server (*name2*) you want to query.

> When you want to exit Nslookup interactive mode, type **exit** at the Nslookup prompt (>) and then press Enter. You are returned to the command prompt.

Nslookup can also be used to verify that a forward lookup zone is configured correctly. Let's look at how to run Nslookup at the command prompt.

To test that a forward lookup zone is configured correctly, use the following steps to simulate a zone transfer:

1. At the command prompt (click Start and then select Command Prompt), type **nslookup** and press Enter. This places you in interactive mode.

2. Type the command **server ip address** (where *ip address* is the IP address of the DNS server that you want to test). Then press Enter.

3. Use the set command to set the query type to any type of record: set query-type=any. Then press Enter.

4. To simulate the zone transfer type, use the command ls -d *domain name*, where *domain name* is the name of the forward lookup zone. Then press Enter.

If the zone is configured to allow zone transfers, you see the results of the "fake" zone transfer in the command prompt window.

Using the queries provided by the DNS snap-in, the Server Manager and Event Viewer DNS logs, and the nslookup command can help you stay on top of your DNS implementation. Even when you know that you have configured the DNS service perfectly, you should periodically use these tools to check your DNS implementation.

Summary

In this hour, you looked at the Domain Name Service. DNS provides a hierarchical name-resolution system for resolving FQDNs (friendly) to IP addresses. Each organization typically deploys its own DNS server that handles the resolution duties of that domain.

The root of the DNS tree is represented by the . (dot). Top-level domains under the root are identified by suffixes such as com, edu, and biz. Computer hostnames consist of the name of the computer followed by the DNS domain name (the child domain preceding the parent domain).

The Windows Server 2008 implementation of DNS is Microsoft's dynamic DNS, also called DDNS in earlier implementations of the Windows Server product. Dynamic DNS enables DNS clients to automatically update their client resource records in the DNS database. Because the database is configured automatically, you spend much less time creating resource records.

The Windows Server 2008 DNS service is installed in the Add Roles Wizard. For the DNS service to operate correctly, you must configure a forward lookup zone on the server. This allows for resolution from hostname to IP address. Reverse lookup zones are used to resolve IP addresses to hostnames. Reverse lookup zones are useful but are not required on your DNS server. DNS is managed in the DNS snap-in, which can be accessed in the Server Manager or the MMC snap-in.

You can use the snap-in to view resource records in your zones, create new zones (and delete zones), and create new resource records. DNS clients are computers that have been configured to refer to a preferred DNS server when they need to resolve a hostname to an IP address (or vice versa). You can specify a preferred DNS server in the client's TCP/IP properties. Or you can configure your DHCP server to provide DHCP clients with the IP address of a preferred DNS server.

Q&A

Q. *What is the purpose of deploying local DNS servers?*

A. A domain DNS server provides for the local mapping of fully qualified domain names to IP addresses. Because the DNS is a distributed database, the local DNS servers can provide record information to remote DNS servers to help resolve remote requests related to fully qualified domain names on your network.

Q. *What types of zones would you want to create on your DNS server so that both queries to resolve hostnames to IP addresses and queries to resolve IP addresses to hostnames are handled successfully?*

A. You would create both a forward lookup zone and a reverse lookup zone on your Windows Server 2008 DNS server.

Q. *What tool enables you to manage your Windows Server 2008 DNS server?*

A. The DNS snap-in enables you to add or remove zones and to view the records in your DNS zones. You can also use the snap-in to create records such as a DNS resource record.

Q. *In terms of DNS, what is a caching-only server?*

A. A caching-only DNS server supplies information related to queries based on the data it contains in its DNS cache. Caching-only servers are often used as DNS forwarders. Because they are not configured with any zones, they do not generate network traffic related to zone transfers.

Using the Dynamic Host Configuration Protocol

What You'll Learn in This Hour:

▶ Understanding DHCP

▶ Installing the DHCP Role

▶ Configuring the DHCP Service with a Scope

▶ Using the DHCP Snap-in

▶ Editing DHCP Server Options

▶ Configuring DHCP Clients

▶ Monitoring DHCP Leases

▶ Loading the DCHP Database Backup

▶ Troubleshooting DHCP

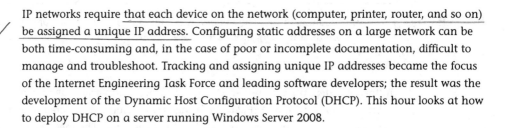

IP networks require that each device on the network (computer, printer, router, and so on) be assigned a unique IP address. Configuring static addresses on a large network can be both time-consuming and, in the case of poor or incomplete documentation, difficult to manage and troubleshoot. Tracking and assigning unique IP addresses became the focus of the Internet Engineering Task Force and leading software developers; the result was the development of the Dynamic Host Configuration Protocol (DHCP). This hour looks at how to deploy DHCP on a server running Windows Server 2008.

Understanding DHCP

The Dynamic Host Configuration Protocol enables you to dynamically assign IP addresses to your network computers and other devices. IP addresses are taken from a pool of addresses and are assigned to computers either permanently or for a fixed lease time.

When you consider that you must configure every client computer on an IP network with such things as an IP address, a subnet mask, a default gateway address, and a DNS server address, you can see that there is an incredible margin for error if this is done manually.

DHCP provides a dynamic environment for assigning IP addresses to computers and devices on the network. It actually simplifies much of the drudgery that would be involved in manually assigning IP addresses.

> DHCP evolved from a protocol called *BOOTP*, short for the *Bootstrap Protocol*, which was used to assign IP addresses to diskless workstations. BOOTP did not assign IP addresses dynamically, however; it pulled IP addresses from a static BOOTP file that was created by the network administrator.

A DHCP server (any Windows Server 2008 configured with the DHCP service) can supply an IP address, subnet mask, default gateway, DNS server address, and WINS server address to a DHCP client. A DHCP client is any computer or device on the network that is configured to acquire its IP address (and other TCP/IP settings) dynamically.

When a DHCP client boots up for the first time, it goes looking for an IP address. The client initializes TCP/IP (a stripped-down version) and broadcasts a DHCPDISCOVER message, which is a request for an IP lease that is sent to all DHCP servers (addressed to 255.255.255.255, meaning all nodes on the network). This broadcast message contains the client's hostname (which, in most cases, is also the client's NetBIOS name) and the client's MAC hardware address.

> The MAC address is the unique hardware address burned into a ROM chip on a device such as a network interface card or a router interface by the device manufacturer.

In the next step, a DCHP server (or servers, if more than one is available) on the subnet responds with a DHCPOFFER message that includes an offered IP address, an accompanying subnet mask, and the length of the lease. The message also contains the IP address of the DHCP server, identifying the server. The DHCPOFFER message is also in the form of a broadcast because, at this point, the client does not have an IP address.

When the client receives the first DHCPOFFER message (it might receive multiple offers, but it goes with the first appropriate offer it receives), it then broadcasts a

DHCPREQUEST message to all DHCP servers on the network, showing that it is accepting an offer. This broadcast message contains the IP address of the DHCP server whose offer the client accepted. Knowing which DHCP server was selected enables the other DHCP servers on the network to retract their offers and save their IP addresses for the next requesting client. (Yes, it does sound a little bit like a used car lot.)

Finally, the DHCP server that supplied the accepted offer broadcasts an acknowledgement message to the client: a DHCPACK message. This message contains a valid IP address lease and other TCP/IP configuration information. The client stores this information in its Windows Registry.

Installing the DHCP Role

You use the Add Roles Wizard to install the DHCP server. Before you install DHCP on a server, you must configure the server with a static IP address.

When you bring your first Windows Server 2008 domain controller online by installing Active Directory Domain Services (AD DS), you are given the option of installing DNS as you bring AD DS online and create the new domain controller. You may want to also install the DHCP role on that server, using the Add Roles Wizard. The instructions that follow would install the DHCP role on either a domain controller (running AD DS) or a standalone DHCP server running Windows Server 2008. The remainder of the hour then looks at useful configuration information that applies to both standalone DHCP servers and domain controllers also providing the DHCP role.

To add DHCP using the Add Roles Wizard, follow these steps:

1. Start the Add Roles Wizard; in the Initial Configuration Tasks window, click Add Roles in the Customize This Server section of the window or click Add Roles in the Server Manager Details pane (when the Roles node is selected). Then click Next to bypass the initial wizard screen.

2. The first screen reminds you to configure a strong password for the administrator's account and configure a static IP address for the server. Click Next.

3. A list of server roles appears (see Figure 16.1). Select DHCP Server and then click Next.

FIGURE 16.1
The wizard pro-
vides a list of
server roles.

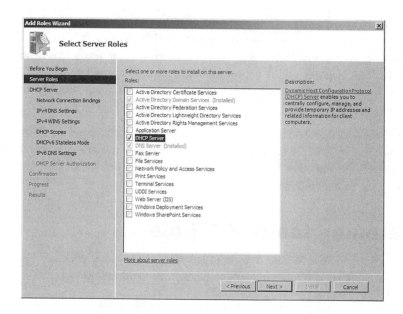

4. The next screen provides an introduction to the DHCP Server role and also provides a list of things to note such as configuring the server with a static IP address and <u>creating a plan for your IP subnets scopes and exclusions</u>. (More about IP addressing is discussed in Hour 7, "Working with the TCP/IP Network Protocol.") Click Next to continue.

5. The next screen detects network connections on the server that have been configured with a static IP address. (The number of connections detected depends on the number of network interfaces on the server.) Select the network connection or connections that the DHCP server is to use for servicing clients (see Figure 16.2) and then click Next to continue.

6. On the next screen, you need to specify the parent domain (that the clients will use for name resolution) and the preferred DNS server IPv4 address (see Figure 16.3). If the server is also configured with AD DS and DNS, this information is entered automatically. Click Next to continue.

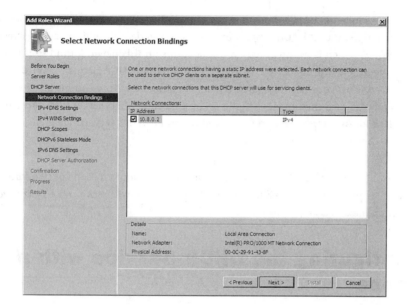

FIGURE 16.2
Select the network connections to be used by the DHCP server.

FIGURE 16.3
Provide the parent domain name and the preferred DNS server IP address.

You can also provide the IP address of an alternate DNS server when you provide the parent domain and preferred DNS server IP address.

7. Some network applications may require a WINS server. (WINS is discussed in detail in Hour 20, "Understanding WINS.") The default setting on this screen is WINS, which is not required for applications on this network (and so is not integrated with the DHCP settings transmitted to DHCP clients). If WINS is needed on your network, click WINS Is Required for Applications on This Network and then provide the IP address of your WINS server (you can enter IP addresses for both a preferred and alternate WINS server). Then click Next to continue.

The next step in configuring the DHCP server is to configure a scope of IP addresses. Because scopes require some background discussion, we will pick up the next wizard step in the next section.

Configuring the DHCP Service with a Scope

The DHCP scope provides the range of IP addresses that the server can hand out to requesting DHCP clients. The DHCP server can't function without a scope. The scope includes a start address (for the range of IP addresses) and an end address. IP address scopes may also include an exclusion range.

You may also want to exclude some of the IP addresses from the scope on computers that require static IP addresses (for example, your DHCP server requires a static IP address). Other devices on the network, such as routers and some printers (those directly connected to the network), also require static IP addresses, so the exclusion range that you specify might include a number of IP addresses. (Remember that this is supposed to be a range of addresses that are excluded, so pick a logical starting and stopping point in the address scope that is available.) Exclusion ranges are discussed later in this hour.

In the previous section, the installation of DHCP using the Add Roles Wizard provided an Add or Edit DHCP Scopes wizard screen (during the DCHP Server installation process). Figure 16.4 shows this screen. We pick up the DHCP installation by adding a new scope.

To continue the DHCP installation and configuration and add a new IP scope, follow these steps:

1. On the Add or Edit DHCP Scopes screen (see Figure 16.4), click Add. The Add Scope dialog box appears.

2. Enter the scope name, starting and ending IP address for the scope, the subnet mask, and the Subnet Type (see Figure 16.5). The subnet type is either Wired (with a lease duration of 6 days) or Wireless (lease duration of 8 hours).

3. You are asked to provide the range of IP addresses that are available in the Scope (see Figure 16.5). Enter the scope range (the beginning and ending IP addresses in the range). Also enter the subnet mask for the network and other parameters as needed (such as the default gateway). Click OK.

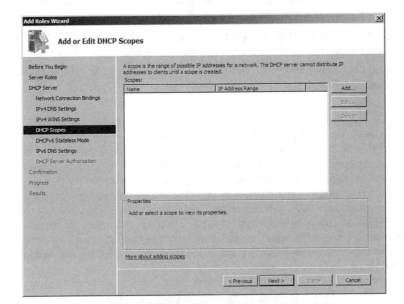

FIGURE 16.4
You must add a scope of IP addresses for the network.

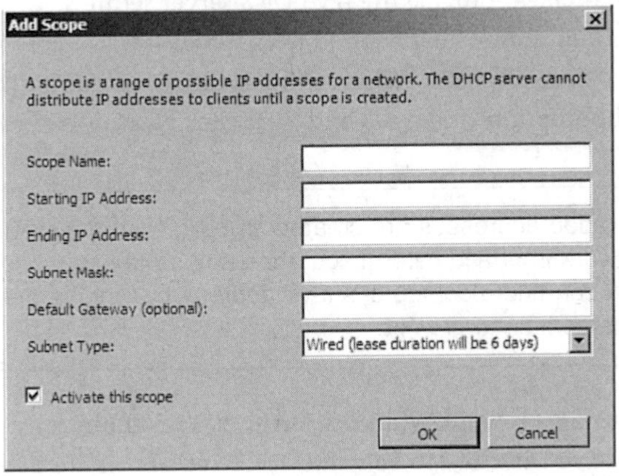

FIGURE 16.5
Provide the parameters for your IP address scope.

> For a scope to be available, the scope must be activated. Note that an Activate This Scope check box is provided in the Add Scope dialog box. You should leave this check box selected in most cases.

4. You can use the Add button to add additional scopes if necessary. When you have completed adding (or editing scopes), click Next to continue.

5. On the next screen, you are provided with the option of configuring the DHCPv6 mode for your network. You can use the stateless mode (which enables IPv6 clients to configure their own IP addresses without using the DHCP server) or you can disable the stateless mode and configure DHCPv6 using the DHCP snap-in. The default is the stateless mode (which automates IPv6 addressing; see the accompanying note). With the default mode selected, click Next.

> In terms of DHCPv6 addressing, the stateless mode provides the easiest route to getting computers and devices using TCP/IPv6 up and running on the network. TCP/IPv6-enabled devices (enabled in the network configuration for that computer or device) can obtain settings such as the DNS server addresses from the DHCPv6 stateless mode settings on the DHCP server. IPv6 addressing of these devices (when using the stateless mode) is a process that does not involve the DHCP server, and addresses are configured automatically based on information such as the IPv6 prefixes that are included in the router advertisements broadcast on your network.

6. On the next screen, provide the IPv6 DNS server settings. This includes the parent domain name, the preferred DNS Server IPv6 address, and optional alternate DNS server IPV6 address (IPV6 is discussed in more detail in Hour 7. Enter the appropriate addresses and then click Next.

> IPv6 stateless mode addresses are created, in part, from the MAC address of a computer's network interface card. If you are using stateless mode for IPv6 addressing, you can find a computer's IPv6 address by running the `ipconfig/all` command at the command prompt.

7. All DHCP servers in your Windows Server 2008 domain must be authorized with the Active Directory to be valid DHCP servers on the network. This screen requires that you provide credentials that authorize this DHCP server in the Active Directory Domain Services (see Figure 16.6). You can use the current

credentials (if you are logged on with an account that has domain rights) or you can use the Use Alternate Credentials option button and then supply an account name and password that provides the appropriate credentials for authorization. (The best set would be the administrator account that you used to create the original forest.) Provide the credentials (if using alternate credentials) and then click Next.

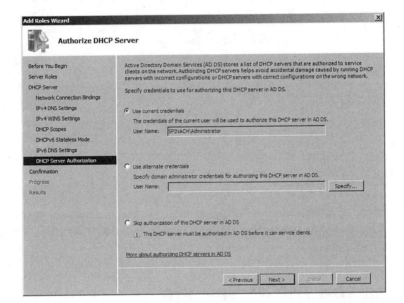

FIGURE 16.6
You must authorize the DHCP server.

A DHCP server must be authorized because this negates the possibility of a rogue DHCP server on the network (for example, someone testing a DHCP server that is unknowingly connected to the network) assigning spurious IP addresses to your DHCP clients (which typically means that you get tons of support calls because everyone is having trouble getting at network resources).

By the Way

8. The next screen provides a summary of the settings for your new DHCP server. Check the settings (you can use Previous to return to earlier screens to edit settings), and then click Install to complete the DHCP installation process).

The Installation Results screen appears, letting you know that the installation succeeded. Click Close. The DHCP Server role is now listed in the Initial Configuration Tasks window for the server (in the Customize This Server area) and also appears as a role in the Server Manager (see Figure 16.7). Events related to the DHCP server appear in the Events window when the DHCP Server node is selected.

FIGURE 16.7
The DHCP
Server is now
listed in the
Server Manager
roles.

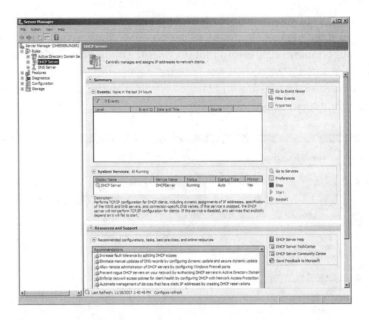

Now that the DHCP role has been added to the server, you can manage the new DHCP server using the DHCP snap-in, which runs in the MMC. Let's take a look at the DHCP snap-in.

Using the DHCP Snap-In

The DHCP snap-in is started via the Start menu: Start, Administrative Tools, DHCP. The DHCP snap-in uses the MMC window layout of nodes in the Node pane (on the left) and the information related to a selected node appearing in the Details pane (the right pane in the window). Figure 16.8 shows the DHCP snap-in window.

The DHCP snap-in enables you to work with your address pools, address leases, reservations, and other server options. Let's a look at some of the things you might want to configure in relation to the initial scope that was created when you installed the DHCP role on the server using the Add Roles Wizard. The topics that follow include a look at creating IP address reservations and DHCP exclusion ranges.

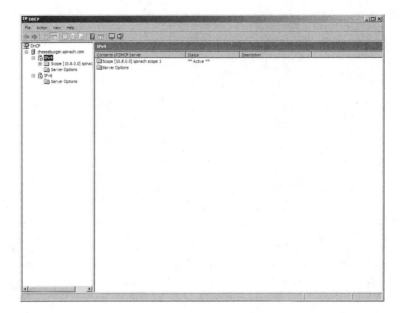

FIGURE 16.8
The DHCP
Server is man-
aged in the
DHCP snap-in.

Creating Reservations and Exclusion Ranges

You might want to have certain devices on the network, such as network printers or other devices, always receive the same IP address, although you still want the address assigned dynamically by the DHCP server. This enables you to still take advantage of DHCP for the assignment of IP addressing information to the computer or device and not have to deal with the configuration of static IP addresses. An address that is reserved in an IP address scope is called a *reservation*.

To create a reservation (or reservations), follow these steps:

1. In the DHCP node pane, expand the IP version node (such as IPv4) and then expand a scope in the Node pane.

2. In the Details pane, right-click the Reservations icon and select New Reservation from the shortcut menu. The New Reservation dialog box appears (see Figure 16.9).

FIGURE 16.9
Enter the reservation settings.

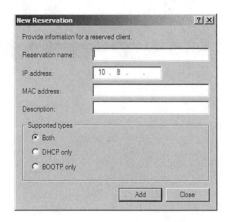

3. In the New Reservation dialog box, provide a name for the reservation, the MAC hardware address of the device for which you want to reserve the IP address, and the actual IP address. You also can select the reservation type, such as DHCP only or BootP only. The default is Both and is the best bet for a setting. Then click Add.

> To find the MAC hardware address for any computer running Windows 2000, XP, or Vista, use the `ipconfig/all` command at the command line. You can also use the nbstat command to find the MAC address of any computer on the network. Type **nbstat -a**, followed by the computer's IP address.

4. You can add additional reservations as needed. When you have completed adding the reservations, click Close (to close the New Reservation dialog box).

Now when you select the Reservations node in the Node pane, the reservations that you have configured for the scope appear in the Details pane. To view the DNS server and DNS domain settings for a particular reservation, select the reservation node in the node tree.

You can also configure an exclusion range for the address pool in a scope. The exclusion range excludes addresses from being assigned to DHCP clients by the DHCP server. The exclusion range is typically made up of IP addresses that you have used as static IP addresses. These are typically assigned to various domain controllers and other servers on the network that require a static IP address.

To create an exclusion range, follow these steps:

1. In the DHCP Node pane, expand the IP version node (such as IPv4) and then expand a scope in the Node pane.

2. In the Node pane, right-click the Address Pool icon and select New Exclusion Range from the shortcut menu. The Add Exclusion dialog box appears (see Figure 16.10).

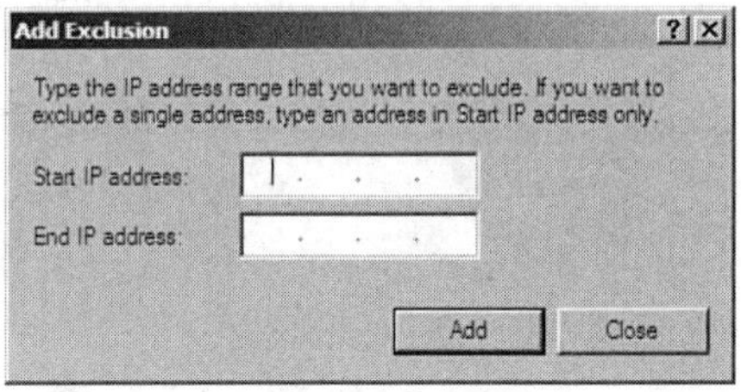

FIGURE 16.10
Create an exclusion range for the scope.

3. Enter the start IP address and the end IP address for the exclusion range. Then click Add. You can add other exclusion ranges as needed. To close the Add Exclusion dialog box, click Close.

The exclusion range appears in the Address Pools Detail pane when the Address Pool icon is selected in the node tree. To delete an exclusion range, right-click the exclusion in the Details pane and select Delete from the shortcut menu.

Understanding DHCP Lease Issues

The duration that you set for your IP address leases can affect your network's efficiency. If you have a number of computers, such as laptops, that are moved around on the network a great deal, shorter lease lengths make it easier for these users to gain access to network resources if they connect on a different subnet (subnets are discussed in Hour 7).

The length of an IP address lease is also related somewhat to network security. Because crackers attempt to purloin valid network addresses, shorter leases enable you to negate the use of a dynamic IP address that has been pirated. However, the shorter the lease times, the more network traffic will be generated as DHCP clients seek to renew their IP addresses (and obtain other IP-related configuration information).

If your network is fairly static in terms of the movement of devices, and if band-width is an issue, longer leases lessen the number of DHCP broadcasts because com-puters do not have to renew their IP leases that frequently. Fewer broadcasts mean that less bandwidth is soaked up by the broadcast traffic.

The default lease duration for scopes on a wired network is 6 days and the default lease duration for a scope on a wireless network is 8 hours (these default settings were selected when you configured DHCP in the Add Roles Wizard). You can set the lease duration for any scope on the General tab of the scope's Properties dial box (see Figure 16.11).

FIGURE 16.11
Set the lease duration for your IP scope.

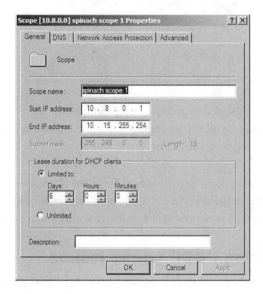

To open the Properties dialog box for a scope, right-click the scope node in the Node pane and then click Properties on the shortcut menu. Make sure that the General tab is selected. In the Lease Duration for DHCP clients area of the General tab, use the spinner boxes to set the lease duration (in days, hours, minutes). If you do not want to limit leases, you can select the Unlimited option button. When you have finished setting the lease duration for the scope, click OK.

By the Way

A DHCP client actually requests to renew its IP address lease halfway through the lease duration period that you set.

Creating a New Scope

As your network expands, you may want to add new scopes to your DHCP server. This provides additional IP addresses for your network clients. The New Scope Wizard makes it easy for you to add a scope to the DHCP server. To create a new scope, follow these steps:

1. In the DHCP snap-in, expand the Server node. Right-click the IPv4 node or the IPv6 node and select New Scope from the shortcut menu. (for discussion's sake, right-click the IPv4 node and select New Scope to follow the steps provided).

2. The New Scope Wizard appears. Click Next to bypass the initial screen. On the Scope Name screen, provide a name and description for the scope. Then click Next.

3. On the IP Address Range screen, specify the start and end addresses of the IP scope. Also apply the subnet mask for the scope (see Figure 16.12). Then click Next.

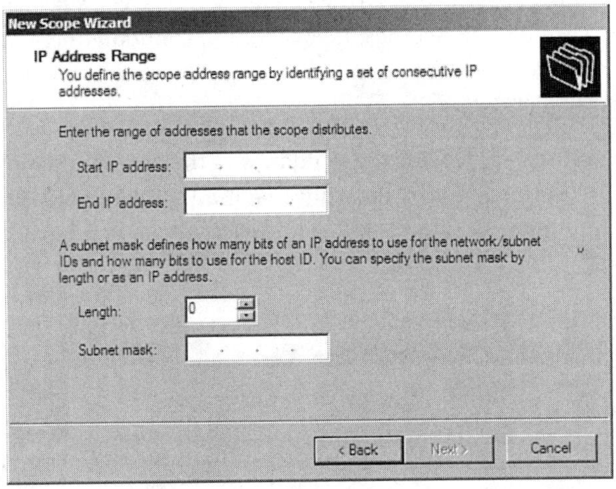

FIGURE 16.12
Provide a range of IP addresses for the scope.

4. On the next screen, enter the start and end IP address for any exclusion ranges you may wish to add. Click Add after adding the address range. You can add other exclusion ranges as needed. Then click Next to continue.

5. On the next screen (see Figure 16.13), set the lease duration for the IP addresses provided in this scope, using the Days, Hours, and Minutes spinner boxes. Then click Next to continue.

FIGURE 16.13
Set the lease
duration for the
new scope.

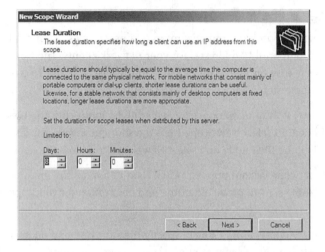

6. On the next screen, you are provided the option of configuring other information that will be provided to DHCP clients by the server, such as gateways,
   DNS server, and WINS settings. If you want to configure these options, make
   sure that the Yes, I Want to Configure These Options Now option button is
   selected. Then click Next.

7. On the next screen, provide the IP address of the default gateway (you can
   also enter the IP address of alternative gateways if available). Enter an IP
   address and then click Add (see Figure 16.14). When you have finished adding
   the gateway IP addresses, click Next.

FIGURE 16.14
Enter the IP
address of the
default gateway.

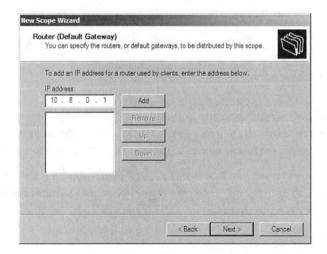

Use the Up and Down buttons on the Router (Default Gateway) screen to order the gateway addresses by how you want the DHCP clients to use the gateways. For example, the first IP address in the list should be for the default gateway and the other IP addresses should be for alternative gateways (in the order that you would want the clients to use them).

8. On the next screen, you are asked to provide the domain name and the IP address of the DNS servers in the domain. This enables you to specify the parent domain and the DNS servers that you want your network clients to use when they need DNS name resolution. Enter the parent domain name and then add the DNS servers, either by using the server name (and then the Resolve button) or by entering the IP address of the DNS server or servers. Then click Next to continue.

9. On the next screen, enter the WINS server IP address or addresses that you want your DHCP clients to use when they need to convert NetBIOS computer names to IP addresses (WINS is discussed in Hour 20. After entering the IP addresses (or addresses), click Next.

10. The next screen asks whether you wish to activate the scope. Remember that a scope is not available to DHCP clients until it has been activated. Make sure that the Yes I Want to Activate This Scope Now option button is selected and then click Next.

11. The final wizard screen appears. Click Finish to create the scope and close the wizard.

If you do not want to activate the scope (perhaps you don't have all the configuration settings for the scope at this time) and make the address range available, you can select No, I Will Activate This Scope Later and continue with the scope creation process. You can active a scope in the DHCP snap-in by right-clicking the Scope node and selecting Activate from the shortcut menu.

The new scope appears in the DHCP snap-in node tree. To view the scope address pool, leases, and reservations, select the Scope node in the tree and then double-click any of the scope's folders, such as Address Pool, Reservations, and so on.

Creating Superscopes

Before we leave the subject of scopes, we should discuss the superscope. When you create a scope on your DHCP server, it is assumed that the IP address range encompasses no more than one logical subnet (the basics of subnetting are discussed in Hour 7).

Now let's play devil's advocate and say that you need to implement more IP addresses than those available in one of the subnets that you have created; you need to create a scope that includes the addresses of more than one subnet. This means that you need to create a *superscope*. A *superscope* is really a container that contains the "normal" scopes that you want treated as a single scope or superscope. The easiest way to create a superscope is to create the scopes that encompass the IP subnets that you want to include in the superscope. You then use the Create Superscope Wizard to specify the scopes that are to be included in the superscope.

To create the superscope, follow these steps:

1. In the DHCP snap-in, expand the DHCP server node in the node tree. Right-click one of the IP version nodes such as the IPv4 node. Select New Superscope. The New Superscope Wizard appears.

2. Click Next to bypass the initial screen. On the next screen, enter the name for the new superscope. Then click Next to continue.

3. On the next screen (see Figure 16.15), select the scopes that are to be included in the superscope (hold down the Ctrl key to select multiple scopes). Then click Next to continue.

FIGURE 16.15
Select the scopes that are to be included in the super-scope.

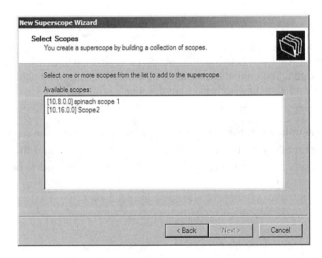

4. The final wizard screen appears, listing the scopes that are included in the superscope. Click Finish. The superscope is created and the wizard closes.

The superscope appears in the node tree. If you expand the Superscope node, you will find that it contains a node for each of the scopes that you added to the superscope. You can expand the individual scope nodes to set the address pool, address leases, and reservations for that particular scope.

> You can also create a new superscope without having created the scopes contained in the superscope. Use the New Scope Wizard to begin the process of creating a new scope. When you enter a range of IP addresses that exceeds one subnet (enter a range that includes at least two subnets), the wizard opens the Create Superscope screen. You can then create the superscope in the wizard. Because scope parameters such as lease, exclusion range, and server settings (gateway and DNS server) have not been set for the scope, you are walked through a process that is very similar to that used for creating a "regular" scope.

By the Way

Editing DHCP Server Options

You can edit data related to the DHCP server options such as the default gateway, DNS server, and WINS server settings. These options are edited (or entered for the first time, if you did not include them when configuring your scope) in the Server Option Properties dialog box.

Click to expand your DHCP server node in the snap-in tree. Then expand one of the IP version nodes such as IPv4. Then right-click the Server Options icon (under that IP version node) and select Configure Options. The Server Options dialog box appears.

Each option listed on the General tab (such as DNS Server or WINS Server) is designated by an option number. For example, the router (the default gateway) is option number 003; the DNS server is 006, and the WINS server is 044.

So, for example, to set the WINS server for DHCP clients receiving this information from the DHCP server, you would click the 044 check box and then enter the IP address of the WINS server, as shown in Figure 16.16. The default DNS server can be configured in the same way (by selecting option number 006). After changing the configuration information, click the OK button to close the dialog box.

FIGURE 16.16
You can edit the server settings for the gateway, such as the WINS server.

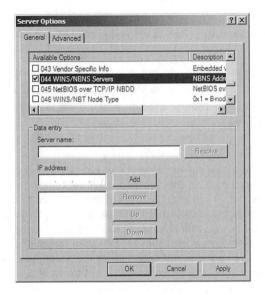

Configuring DHCP Clients

A DHCP client is any computer or device that is configured to receive its IP address dynamically from the DHCP server. All Windows clients and Windows servers that do not require a static IP address can be configured as DHCP clients (actually all of them are configured as DHCP clients by default).

Figure 16.17 shows the Internet Protocol Version 4 (TCP/IPv4) Properties dialog box for a client computer running Windows Vista Business Edition that has been configured as a DCHP client. Note that it is configured to get both its IP address and DNS server address automatically (both of which would be supplied by the DHCP server). All the Windows clients (including Windows Server 2008) use a similar dialog box to configure their IP properties.

FIGURE 16.17
You can easily configure any computer running Windows to be a DHCP client.

Monitoring DHCP Leases

Because the whole point of DHCP is to provide IP leases to DHCP clients, you should monitor the leases that the DHCP server provides. You can view current leases in the DHCP snap-in. Follow these steps:

1. In the DHCP snap-in, click the Expand (+) button to the left of the DHCP server icon. The Scope folder appears.

2. Expand the Scope folder (click the plus symbol next to it). This gives you access to the Address Leases icon.

3. Click the icon. All the current leases appear in the Details pane of the snap-in (see Figure 16.18).

You can also add more servers to the snap-in. This enables you to monitor multiple DHCP servers from the same management console.

In the DHCP snap-in, click the DHCP icon in the tree. Then click the Action menu and select Manage Authorized Servers opens.

To add a server to the snap-in, click the server in the dialog box and then click OK. The computer is added to the DHCP snap-in. This enables you to monitor the server's IP address scope and current leases.

FIGURE 16.18
You can view
the leases that
have been
assigned to
your DHCP
clients.

Loading the DCHP Database Backup

Another aspect of managing DHCP on the network is working with the backup of the DHCP database. By default, the database is automatically backed up every 60 minutes. If you find that clients are having trouble leasing addresses, the DHCP database could be corrupt.

To load the backup copy, do the following:

1. Right-click your DHCP server node (the name of the server, such as cheeseburger.spinach.com) in the tree in the Node pane. On the shortcut menu that appears, select Restore. The Browse for Folder dialog box appears, enabling you to specify the folder that contains the DHCP backup (it typically points to the default backup folder, backup).

2. Click OK. You are notified that the server must be stopped and then restarted for the backup database to be loaded.

3. Click Yes. The backup database is loaded and the server is restarted.

> You can also choose to manually back up the DHCP server's database. Right-click your DHCP server node and then select Backup from the shortcut menu. Select a folder for the backup (the default is backup) and then click OK. A backup will be made of the DHCP database.

By the Way

Troubleshooting DHCP

Two commands that are very useful in troubleshooting DHCP connectivity are ping and ipconfig. Both are executed at the command line. ping enables you to check the connection between a client and a DHCP server, or a DHCP server and a client. For example, to ping a DHCP server with the IP address of 10.8.0.2, you would type **ping 10.8.0.2** in the command window. Figure 16.19 shows a successful ping of this address.

FIGURE 16.19
You can use ping to examine the connection between two computers.

ipconfig is useful on the client side. When executed at the command line, it tells you the IP configuration of the client (ipconfig/all provides more information). If you don't see an IP address and subnet mask (or a default gateway or DNS server) when you run this command, the client is not receiving the information from the DHCP server.

> A problem that crops up with DHCP on routed networks is that the broadcast messages that are used to secure an IP lease for a client are not forwarded by routers from subnet to subnet. This can be remedied by configuring a DHCP Relay Agent, which is configured in the Routing and Remote Access Service. DHCP Relay Agent configuration is explored in Hour 18, "Implementing Network Routing."

By the Way

Summary

This hour looked at the Dynamic Host Configuration Protocol, which is used to dynamically assign IP addresses to DHCP clients on a Windows Server 2008 network. The DHCP server can provide the IP address, subnet mask, default gateway (router), DNS server, and WINS server to the DHCP clients.

You use the Add Roles Wizard to install the DHCP role. DHCP servers are configured with a scope (or scopes), which contains a range of IP addresses that will be leased to the DHCP clients. Some IP addresses can be excluded from a scope; this is called an exclusion range. An important aspect of configuring a scope is determining the duration of the lease for the IP addresses that are to be assigned to clients by the DHCP server. Windows Server 2008 requires that DHCP servers be authorized with the Active Directory Domain Services. DCHP is configured, monitored, and managed in the Microsoft Management Console's DHCP snap-in.

Q&A

Q. *How is the range of IP addresses defined for a Windows Server 2008 DHCP server?*

A. The IP addresses supplied by the DHCP server are held in a scope. A scope that contains more than one subnet of IP addresses is called a superscope. IP addresses in a scope that you do not want to lease can be included in an exclusion range.

Q. *What TCP/IP configuration parameters can be provided to a DHCP client?*

A. The DHCP server can supply a DHCP client an IP address and subnet mask. It also can optionally include the default gateway address, the DNS server address, and the WINS server address to the client.

Q. *How can you configure the DHCP server so that it provides certain devices with the same IP address each time the address is renewed?*

A. You can create a reservation for the device (or create reservations for a number of devices). To create a reservation, you need to know the MAC hardware address of the device. You can use the `ipconfig` or `nbstat` command-line utilities to determine the MAC address for a network device such as a computer or printer.

Q. *To negate rogue DHCP servers from running with a domain, what is required for your DHCP server to function?*

A. The DHCP server must be authorized in the Active Directory before it can function in the domain.

PART III

Advanced Networking

HOUR 17

Remote Access and Virtual Private Networking

What You'll Learn in This Hour:

- ▶ Understanding Microsoft Remote Access
- ▶ Adding the Network Policy and Access Services Role
- ▶ Enabling and Configuring RRAS
- ▶ Configuring Modem Ports
- ▶ Understanding Authentication Protocols
- ▶ Configuring Authentication
- ▶ Configuring Remote Access Clients
- ▶ Understanding Virtual Private Networks
- ▶ Understanding Virtual Private Network Ports
- ▶ Configuring the VPN Client
- ▶ Managing VPN or Dial-In Connections
- ▶ Understanding RADIUS and the Network Policy Server

Microsoft has combined a number of connectivity services and security features into the Network Policy and Access Services role. This role provides a number of remote connectivity possibilities, including dial-in connections and connection via virtual private networking (VPN). This hour looks at the installation and configuration of the Network Policy and Access Services role, and more specifically at remote access via dial-in and VPN connections. It also looks at some of the security measures related to remote access, including Microsoft's implementation of a RADIUS server, the Network Policy Server (NPS). It also looks at specific authentication protocols provided by the Network Policy Server.

Understanding Microsoft Remote Access

The Network Policy and Access Services role provides a number of specific services on a server running Windows Server 2008. These services include the Network Policy Server, Routing and Remote Access, which includes the Remote Access Service (RAS). RAS can be used to configure secure Virtual Private Networking connections and traditional dial-in connections for your remote users.

> The Network Policy Server can also be configured for network access protection (NAP) for your wired network, based on health policies. This means that your network will be secured because the NAP server checks the "health" of client computers based on whether or not they are running the Windows firewall, have the latest antivirus signatures, and have the latest Windows updates. Hour 11, "Deploying Group Policy and Network Access Protection," discusses NAP as related to health policies.

The NPS role also enables you to configure a multihomed server (a server with two or more network cards) as a fully functional router. Configuring a server running Windows Server 2008 as a router is covered in Hour 18, "Implementing Network Routing." A server with multiple network interfaces also allows you to connect a group of computers with private IP addresses to the Internet using the Network Address Translation protocol and one public IP address (meaning the computers can share the Internet connection provided by the server). This NPS feature is examined in Hour 22, "Using Network Address Translation and Certificate Services."

VPN also requires a multihomed computer; meaning a server with two or more network interfaces. So, you must install a second network adapter on a server that is to be used for VPN connections.

A server supplying remote access via NPS supplies a remote host with a connection to the network. It also provides the remote host with access to the same network resources that can be accessed by computers directly connected to the network. A domain controller can function as an RAS server for your domain.

Dial-up access requires the installation of communications hardware such as an analog modem (or modems in a modem pool), an ISDN modem (an ISDN terminal adapter), or some other connectivity device on the computer. The end user also uses a modem to connect to the RAS server via a network such as the Plain Old Telephone System (POTS).

VPN connections are a secure and private way for a remote user connected to the Internet to connect to your private corporate network. In effect, you are creating a private communication line over an otherwise public communication system.

Let's take a look at adding the Network Policy and Access Services role and the services needed for remote access. We can then look at specific issues related to dial-in connections and VPNs, respectively.

Adding the Network Policy and Access Services Role

To add the Network Policy and Access Services role to the server's configuration, use the Add Roles Wizard. Because the Network Policy and Access Services role is actually a group of bundled remote access, routing, and access security services, you should add only the services you need on the server when you install the role. For example, this hour concentrates on remote access and virtual private networking, so we install only a subset of the services provided by the Network Policy and Access Services role.

You can add the Network Policy and Access Services role from the Initial Configuration Tasks window or the Server Manager (the Add Roles link is available in the Server Manager when the Roles node is selected in the node tree). Follow these steps:

1. Select the Add Roles link. The Add Roles Wizard opens. Click Next to bypass the Add Roles Wizard's initial page.

2. On the next wizard page, select the Network Policy and Access Services check box (see Figure 17.1). Then click Next.

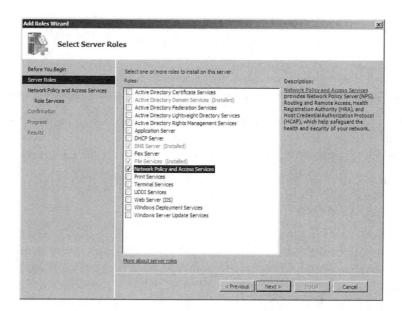

FIGURE 17.1
Add the Network Policy and Access Services role.

3. The next page provides a short overview of the Network Policy and Access Services and also provides links to more information related to this role. Click Next to continue.

4. On the next page, you select the Network Policy and Access Services that you want to install. Check the Network Policy Server and the Remote Access Service check boxes (see Figure 17.2). Then click Next.

FIGURE 17.2
Select the
Network Policy
Server and the
Remote Access
Service.

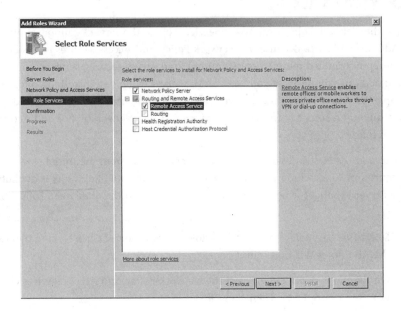

5. The confirmation page for the installation of the Network Policy and Access Services role appears. Click Install.

The Network Policy and Access Services role, including the Network Policy Server and the Remote Access Services, is installed. Click Close to close the wizard window.

In the Server Manager (click the Server Manager icon in the Quick Launch toolbar), expand the Roles node and then click the Network Policy and Access Services node. Any events logged related to the role appear in the Events area of the Details pane.

The status of services related to the role is also shown in the Details pane in the System Services area (see Figure 17.3). The Routing and Remote Access Service is currently "stopped."

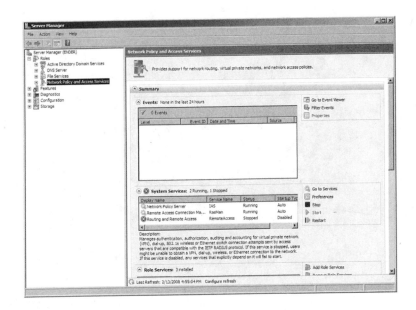

FIGURE 17.3
View events logged and services installed for the Network Policy and Access Services role.

The Routing and Remote Access Service (RRAS) must be started before you can configure remote access. Let's look at starting RRAS and then look at the RRAS configuration possibilities.

Enabling and Configuring RRAS

RRAS is configured in the Routing and Remote Access snap-in. This snap-in can be accessed in the Server Manager (expand the Network Policy and Access Services node), or you can run the RRAS snap-in in the MMC (Start, Administrative Tools, and then Routing and Remote Access).

The first thing you must do is enable RRAS; you can then configure it. Follow these steps:

1. In the RRAS snap-in, right-click the Routing and Remote Access node in the Server Manager or your RRAS server name node in the MMC and then select Configure and Enable Routing and Remote Access from the shortcut menu. The Routing and Remote Access Server Setup Wizard appears.

2. Click Next to bypass the opening wizard page. The next page supplies a list of common configurations for the RRAS service (see Figure 17.4) including dial-up and VPN, VPN (only), VPN and NAT, or a custom configuration. We are concentrating on remote access, so select the Remote Access (Dial-Up or VPN) option button and then click Next.

FIGURE 17.4
Select the RRAS
service that you
want to install.

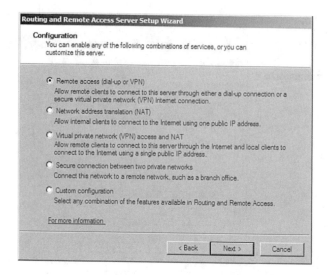

Routing and Remote Access Server Setup Wizard

Configuration
You can enable any of the following combinations of services, or you can
customize this server.

- ● Remote access (dial-up or VPN)
  Allow remote clients to connect to this server through either a dial-up connection or a
  secure virtual private network (VPN) Internet connection.
- ○ Network address translation (NAT)
  Allow internal clients to connect to the Internet using one public IP address.
- ○ Virtual private network (VPN) access and NAT
  Allow remote clients to connect to this server through the Internet and local clients to
  connect to the Internet using a single public IP address.
- ○ Secure connection between two private networks
  Connect this network to a remote network, such as a branch office.
- ○ Custom configuration
  Select any combination of the features available in Routing and Remote Access.

For more information

< Back   Next >   Cancel

4. On the next page (Remote Access), you can select either VPN or Dial-Up or both for your remote access settings. Because we discuss both RAS possibilities, select both check boxes and then click Next to continue.

5. On the next page, you are asked to select the network connection that connects the server to the Internet (see Figure 17.5). Select the appropriate Local Area Connection, and then click Next to continue.

FIGURE 17.5
Select the net-
work interface
that connects
the server to
the Internet.

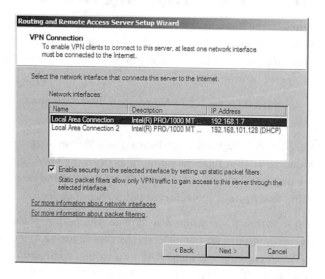

Routing and Remote Access Server Setup Wizard

VPN Connection
To enable VPN clients to connect to this server, at least one network interface
must be connected to the Internet.

Select the network interface that connects this server to the Internet.

Network interfaces:

Name	Description	IP Address
Local Area Connection	Intel(R) PRO/1000 MT ...	192.168.1.7
Local Area Connection 2	Intel(R) PRO/1000 MT ...	192.168.101.128 (DHCP)

☑ Enable security on the selected interface by setting up static packet filters.
Static packet filters allow only VPN traffic to gain access to this server through the
selected interface.

For more information about network interfaces.
For more information about packet filtering.

< Back   Next >   Cancel

6. On the next page, you are asked to choose how remote access clients will be assigned their IP addresses. You can choose Automatically, which uses the network DHCP server to assign addresses, or if you do not use DHCP, the RAS server assigns the addresses. You can also choose to have the addresses assigned from a specified range. After making your selection, click Next. If you select to use a specified range, the next screen asks you to supply that range. Then click Next.

7. The next page relates to how connection requests are authenticated. You can use the local Routing and Remote Access service to authenticate connection requests, or you can set up the RAS server to use a *RADIUS* (Remote Authentication Dial-In User Service) server for authentication. RADIUS (meaning a Network Policy Server) is discussed later in the hour; to get a feel for remote access, select the option No, Use Routing and Remote Access to Authenticate Connection Requests, and then click Next.

8. The wizard summary page appears. To finish the remote access installation, click Finish.

The Routing and Remote Access service starts on the server. You are returned to the Routing and Remote Access snap-in.

Configuring Modem Ports

When the RRAS service is started for the first time, it creates ports for any modems that are installed on the server. You must configure these modem ports to allow remote client connections.

To configure a modem port, follow these steps:

1. In the Routing and Remote Access snap-in, click the server icon in the tree to expand the node. Right-click the Ports icon and select Properties. The Ports Properties dialog box appears (see Figure 17.6).

2. Select the device (such as a modem) for which you want to configure the port, and click the Configure button. The Configure Device dialog box opens.

3. To configure the device for inbound connections, click the Remote Access Connections (Inbound Only) check box to select it. You must also supply a phone number if you are configuring a modem port, so enter the number in the appropriate box (see Figure 17.7). Then click OK.

4. You are returned to the Ports Properties dialog box. Click OK to close it.

The modem is added to the Ports list (seen in the Details pane when you select the Ports node). After the modem port has been enabled, the RAS server is ready to accept incoming calls. Another aspect of configuring dial-in remote access is determining the authentication protocol (or protocols) used to authenticate remote users. Authentication protocols are discussed in the next section.

Understanding Authentication Protocols

Windows Server 2008 supplies you with several protocol choices to authenticate remote users dialing into your RAS server. These protocols supply different "strengths" of authentication. You choose the protocol or protocols that you want to use for remote user authentication on the Security tab of your RAS server's Properties dialog box (which is covered after we sort out the different authentication protocols).

The authentication protocols available (in order of security strength) are the Extensible Authentication Protocol (EAP), Microsoft Encrypted Authentication Version 2 (MS-CHAP v2), Microsoft Encrypted Authentication (MS-CHAP), encrypted authentication (CHAP), Shiva Password Authentication Protocol (SPAP), unencrypted password (PAP), and unauthenticated access (meaning that no protocol is used to control authentication). The sections that follow briefly describe each of these protocols.

> By default, EAP, MS-CHAP v2, and MS-CHAP are the selected authentication protocols for remote access.

By the Way

Understanding the Extensible Authentication Protocol

The *Extensible Authentication Protocol* (EAP) was first introduced with the Windows 2000 Server operating system. EAP is actually an extension of the Point-to-Point Protocol and is designed to provide for the authentication of users through additional security devices. These additional security devices can take the form of a *smart card reader* attached to the computer that requires the user to place a smart card in the reader for authentication. EAP can also take advantage of authentication strategies such as one-time passwords and the use of certificates for authentication (using certificates is discussed in Hour 22. Because EAP is extensible (after all, it's part of the name), additional EAP authentication types will be added to the protocol.

Currently, EAP supports three EAP methods:

- ▶ **MD5-Challenge**—This EAP method is similar to CHAP, but it uses EAP messages when sending challenges and responses.

- ▶ **EAP-TLS**—This is a mutual authentication method, which means that both the client and the server prove their identities.

▶ **Smart card or other certificate**—This method requires a smart card reader or Certificate Authority to provide certificates for authentication. This method cannot be deployed on a standalone RAS server.

Understanding the Challenge Handshake Authentication Protocol

The *Challenge Handshake Authentication Protocol* (CHAP) is a more secure authentication scheme than PAP (which is discussed in a moment) because the username and password are not disclosed over the link as clear text. CHAP uses a three-way handshake scheme for authentication when the remote host requests a connection. The receiving server sends a challenge message that contains a random number and asks the dialing device to send its username and password. The host responds with an encrypted value that is unencrypted by the receiving device yielding the username and password. There are two Microsoft-proprietary versions of CHAP:

▶ **Microsoft Challenge Handshake Authentication Protocol (MS-CHAP)**—MS-CHAP is the Microsoft-proprietary version of CHAP and has been modified for the Windows environment. MS-CHAP uses a response packet specifically designed for computers running the Windows operating system.

▶ **Microsoft Challenge Handshake Authentication Protocol Version 2 (MS-CHAP v2)**—MS-CHAP v2 is a further modified version of CHAP that provides greater security than the premier version and provides for the use of separate cryptographic keys for sending and receiving data. Version 2 of MS-CHAP also supports mutual authentication. This means that both the remote host and the server must provide proof of their identities for the connection to be successful.

Understanding the Shiva Password Authentication Protocol

The *Shiva Password Authentication Protocol* (SPAP) is the authentication scheme for the Shiva-proprietary connectivity software that supplies client and server operability. If you are using a Shiva client to connect to a Windows RAS server, the server can use SPAP to validate the user's connection. Be advised that data encryption cannot be used with SPAP. SPAP also provides Windows clients with the capability to connect to Shiva servers.

Understanding the Password Authentication Protocol

The *Password Authentication Protocol* (PAP) uses a username and password in clear-text format. When the remote host creates the connection to the server, it sends a username and password; these are authenticated by the RAS server. If the username and password are not accepted, the connection is terminated. This type of password protection is referred to as a *two-way handshake*. The problem with PAP is that the clear-text username and password are susceptible to snooping, so the username and password could actually be captured with some sort of protocol analyzer.

Understanding Unauthenticated Access

The final alternative offered for authenticating users to the RAS server is to have no authentication. When you enable unauthenticated access, you are no longer requiring the remote host's username and password. You are also not requiring the host machine to be configured with the same authentication protocol that is configured on the RAS server.

Although unauthenticated access might be useful when end users have inappropriately configured remote hosts and you still want them to log on to the network, you are making it very easy for anyone with the phone number of the RAS server to attach to your network. Microsoft recommends "strong" authentication for securing your RAS environment. This means using authentication protocols such as EAP and the two flavors of CHAP.

Configuring Authentication

You can select the type of remote access authentication that you want to use on your RAS server. To configure the authentication protocol (or protocols) supported by the RAS server, follow these steps:

1. In the Routing and Remote Access snap-in, right-click the server icon in the tree and select Properties from the shortcut menu that appears. The Properties dialog box for the server appears.

2. Click the Security tab on the Properties dialog box. The Security tab lists the current authentication provider. To view the authentication methods, click the Authentication Methods button. The Authentication Methods dialog box appears.

3. Check boxes enable you to specify the authentication methods that will be supported by the RAS server (see Figure 17.8). Check the appropriate boxes (EAP, MS-CHAP, and MS-CHAPv2 are selected by default).

FIGURE 17.8
Choose authentication methods using a series of check boxes.

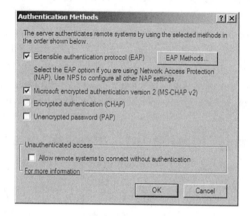

4. If you use EAP as an authentication method, you can select the EAP methods used. Click the EAP Methods button. The EAP Methods dialog box appears.

5. Select the EAP method. Then click OK to return to the Authentication Methods dialog box.

6. When you have completed selecting the authentication methods, click OK to close the Authentication Methods dialog box.

7. Click OK to close the server's Properties dialog box.

Your server is now configured with remote access authentication methods. For a client to attach to the server through a dial-in connection, it must support one of these authentication methods—that is, it must be configured for a particular authentication protocol or protocols.

Configuring Remote Access Clients

After the RAS server has been installed and configured, you must enable user accounts for remote access (or vice versa). You enable dial-in capabilities for your users in the Active Directory Users and Computers snap-in. To enable dial-in for users in the Active Directory, follow these steps:

1. Open the Active Directory Users and Computers snap-in (Start, Administrative Tools, Active Directory Users and Computers).

2. Expand the domain node and then click the Users folder. The domain users and groups appear in the Details pane.

3. At this point, you can add new users and then enable the account for dial-in or enable existing accounts (adding new domain users is discussed in Hour 8, "Understanding and Configuring Active Directory Domain Services"). To enable an existing account for dial-in, double-click the user account. The account's Properties dialog box appears.

4. Click the Dial-In tab of the user's Properties dialog box (see Figure 17.9).

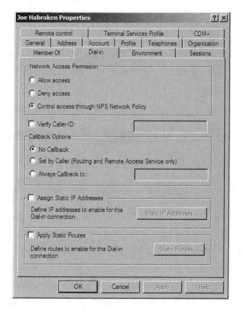

FIGURE 17.9
Set the remote access permission for dial-in or VPN.

5. Select the Allow Access option button to allow the account to use dial-in (or VPN) to connect to the network (or you can choose to control access through the Network Policy Server, discussed later in this hour).

6. If you want to limit the user to a dial-in connection that is initiated from a particular phone number, click the Verify Caller ID check box and enter the user's phone number in the accompanying box.

7. If you want to add callback security to the connection, click the Set by Caller option button or the Always Callback To option button. With the Set by Caller option, the caller dials into the server and then provides a number that the server will use to call the user back and provide a connection to the network. With the Always Callback To option, you provide the phone number that the server always uses to call the user back and set up the network connection.

8. You also have an option of specifying a static IP address for the connection. Click the Assign a Static IP Address check box and then type an IP address in the accompanying box.

9. After making your selections on the Dial-In tab, click OK to close the Properties dialog box.

You can now configure other user accounts for remote access. After you've installed your modem, enabled and configured the RAS server, and configured user accounts for dial-in access, you have completed the setup that is necessary on the server side of the RAS connection.

Obviously, an alternative to using dial-in for remote access is virtual private networking. When you enable a user account for remote access, you are enabling it for both dial-in and VPN. Let's switch gears and take a look at VPN and how it is configured on your RAS server.

Understanding Virtual Private Networks

Because most computer users either already have some type of connection to the Internet from any number of Internet service providers both at home and on the road (and often have a connection speed faster than a dial-up modem), you can take advantage of this in how you provide remote access to your remote clients. A *virtual private network* is a secure and private way for a remote user connected to the Internet to connect to your private corporate network. In effect, you are creating a private communication line over an otherwise public communication system. VPN is also useful in that users on business trips, for example, can use local phone connections to an ISP instead of using long-distance connections with an RAS dial-in server.

VPN uses a tunneling protocol that provides the secure connection over the Internet between the client and the VPN server. You can take advantage of VPNs for remote client connections and for connecting different Windows Server 2008 network sites into one seamless network.

The VPN Tunneling Protocols

VPN uses tunneling protocols to provide the secure "tunnel" through an unsecured, public network such as the Internet. In effect, a point-to-point connection is made between the client and the VPN server. Windows Server 2008 provides three tunneling protocols for VPN:

▶ **Secure Socket Tunneling Protocol** (SSTP)— SSTP is a new tunneling protocol available with Windows Server 2008 and Windows Vista and is an extension of PPP (the Point-to-Point Protocol used for many dial-up Internet connections). SSTP enables your remote access data traffic to pass through a firewall that blocks PPTP and L2TP traffic (see the following PPTP and L2TP definitions). SSTP encapsulates PPP traffic over the SSL (secure sockets layer) channel of the HTTPS protocol and provides an extremely secure connection between the VPN client and the RAS server, using encryption and key negotiation.

▶ **Point-to-Point Tunneling Protocol (PPTP)**—PPTP is an extension of PPP. This tunneling protocol encapsulates network data packets (such as IP or IPX) in encrypted PPP data packets. PPTP requires IP communication between the client and the server. Authentication protocols such as CHAP, MS-CHAP, and EAP are used to provide security to the connection. PPTP uses Microsoft Point-to-Point Encryption (MPPE) for data encryption.

▶ **Layer 2 Tunneling Protocol (L2TP)**—L2TP is an industry-standard tunneling protocol that can also be used to create VPN connections over the Internet. L2TP does not require IP communication between the client and the server as PPTP does. This means that L2TP can be used with other media than the Internet, such as X.25, Frame Relay, and Asynchronous Transfer Mode (ATM). Connections made with L2TP can be secured with IP Security Protocol (IPSec), discussed later in this hour.

SSTP, PPTP, and L2TP are automatically installed on computers running Windows Server 2008 and Windows Vista. PPTP and L2TP are installed on other Windows clients such as Windows XP and Windows 2000.

Creating a VPN Server

A VPN server is created and configured using the Windows Server 2008 Routing and Remote Access Service. The RRAS Setup Wizard walks you through the steps of enabling RRAS for VPN. To be configured as a VPN server, the server needs to contain two network cards. This makes it a multihomed computer (a fancy name for a computer with two or more network cards), which could also be configured as a router (discussed in Hour 18).

One network card provides the IP address that the VPN clients will use to connect to the VPN server (which can be a NIC that is configured with a public IP address for connection to the Internet); the other network card is the VPN server's connection to the local area network. If you look back at the section "Enabling and Configuring RRAS," both dial-up and VPN remote access were both added during the initial configuration of the RAS server.

If you did not add VPN to the RAS server's configuration in the Routing and Remote Access Server Setup Wizard, you can right-click the server node in the RRAS snap-in node tree and select Properties from the shortcut menu. On the General tab of the server's Properties dialog box, select the IPv4 remote access check box. This enables the RRAS server to function as both a VPN server and as a dial-in RAS server (if the server is configured with a modem or modem pool).

Understanding Virtual Private Network Ports

When you configure RRAS for VPN (as discussed earlier in the hour), ports are created that remote clients use to connect to the VPN server (or that the VPN server uses to connect to another server via an outbound connection). A *port* is a channel that provides a single point-to-point connection. Three types of ports are created: WAN Miniport (SSTP), WAN Miniport (PPTP), and WAN Miniport (L2TP). By default, 128 of each of these port types are created. So, you have many ports available for each of the tunneling protocols provided by the server's RRAS VPN feature.

You can view the ports created by the RRAS configuration for VPN; expand the local server node and then click the Ports icon in the RRAS snap-in tree. The VPN ports appear in the Details pane (see Figure 17.10).

FIGURE 17.10
Ports are created for the VPN connection.

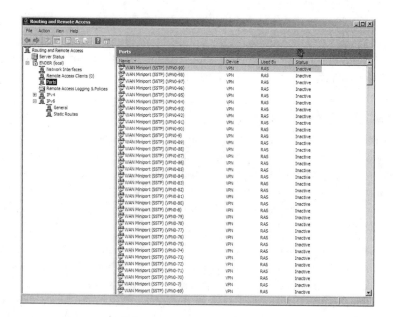

You can change the number of VPN ports that are available on the RRAS server (you might find the default of 128 for each tunneling protocol inadequate if you have a large number of potential VPN connections). Right-click the Ports node and select Properties. The Ports Properties dialog box appears (see Figure 17.11).

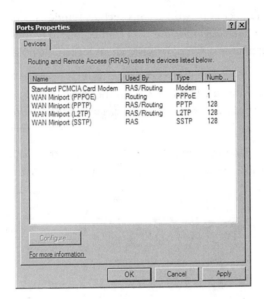

FIGURE 17.11
You can change the number of VPN ports.

Select WAN Miniport (SSTP), WAN Miniport (PPTP), or WAN Miniport (L2TP) in the Properties dialog box, and then click the Configure button. The Configure Device dialog box for the WAN Miniport type that you selected opens.

By default, the ports are configured for inbound connections and demand-dial routing (both inbound and outbound). You can change the number of ports available by using the Maximum Ports check box. The maximum number of ports that you can configure is 1,000.

Obviously, the number of ports that you decide to provide for incoming connections should depend on the amount of bandwidth that you have available on your server's Internet connection. If the server is using a T1 line or other high-speed service and has a great deal of bandwidth available, you can increase the number of calls—that is, you can provide a fairly large number of VPN ports for client connections.

Configuring the VPN Client

Configuring a VPN client is actually a two-step process. First, you must enable the user's domain account for VPN access (as discussed earlier in this hour in the section

"Configuring Remote Access Clients"). Second, you must configure the client computer for a remote connection. When the client computer attempts to connect via the VPN connection, the user's domain account is used to validate the remote access session.

Users running a number of network clients such as Windows 2000, Windows XP, and Windows Vista can take advantage of VPN connections to a domain. Let's look at how you would configure a Windows Vista client for remote access via VPN. Follow these steps:

1. Open the Control Panel and then open the Network and Sharing Center window (click View Network Status and Tasks under the Network and Internet group).

2. In the Network and Sharing Center, click Set up a connection or network in the Tasks list. The Set Up a Connection or Network Wizard opens (see Figure 17.12).

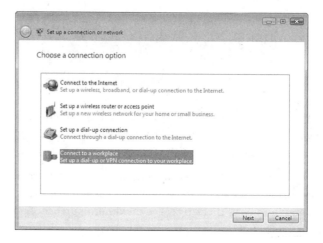

3. Click the Connect to a Workplace option and then click Next.

4. Click Next to continue. On the next screen, you are asked to specify the type of connection that will be used: dial-up or VPN. Select the Virtual Private Network connection option and then click Next to continue.

5. On the next page, select the Use My Internet Connection (VPN) option.

6. On the next page (see Figure 17.13), type the hostname or the IP address of the VPN server. You can also provide a destination name for the connection. You can also select other options at this point, such as the use of a smart card

for authentication or to allow other people (who use the computer) to also use the connection. After specifying the hostname or IP address and the other settings (as needed), click Next.

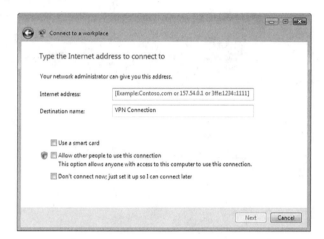

FIGURE 17.13
Provide the DNS name or public IP address of the RRAS server.

7. On the next page, provide the domain username and password for the connection. You can also supply the domain name (which is optional).

8. To connect, click the Connect button. The connection is made from the remote client to the VPN server. The wizard should provide a message: You are connected. You can click Close to close the wizard.

To connect to subsequent VPN sessions, open the Network and Sharing Center window and then click Connect to a Network in the Tasks list.

After the connection has been made, remote users can access any resources on the network that they could if they were directly connected to the local area network. Access levels are based on the permissions that you have assigned to the particular user account used for the remote connection. For more about protecting network data and using permissions, see Hour 13, "Using Share and NTFS Permissions."

Managing VPN or Dial-In Connections

You can manage (and troubleshoot) your remote connections by using the RRAS snap-in. For example, the number of remote access connections is displayed on the

Remote Access Clients node in the snap-in tree. If you want to view individual users, click this node. The currently connected users are then listed in the Details pane (see Figure 17.14).

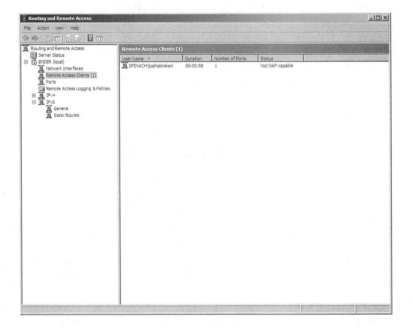

You can also view the properties associated with a particular user; double-click the user's connection in the Details pane. The Status box that appears provides the user's name, the duration of the connection, and other information related to the connection itself.

Not only can you view details related to an individual user connection, but you also can view the status of the modem and VPN ports provided by the server. In the snap-in tree, click the Ports node. The current ports available on the VPN server appear in the Details pane. Figure 17.15 shows an active VPN port connection on the RRAS server.

To view a particular port's status, double-click the port in the Details pane. A status box opens for the port. This status box is very similar to the status box for your remote users; it shows the connection time and other parameters related to the current connection. You can close the connection (basically cutting off the remote user) by clicking the Disconnect button.

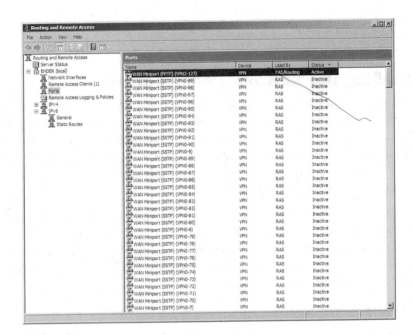

FIGURE 17.15
Click the Ports node to view the status of the server's VPN or dial-in ports.

We have been discussing using the RRAS snap-in for management of a local RRAS server, but you can also use it to manage a number of remote RRAS servers in the domain. This gives you an overall picture of RAS connections in the domain.

To add other servers to the RRAS snap-in, right-click the Routing and Remote Access icon in the snap-in tree and select Add Server. The Add Server dialog box appears. You can specify the addition of a particular server or add all Routing and Remote Access Servers in the domain by providing the domain name.

The Add Server dialog box also provides for the browsing of the Active Directory to enable you to find a particular RAS server and add it to the snap-in. After the server has been added to the snap-in, you can view its status and view the current connections to the server.

Understanding RADIUS and the Network Policy Server

A RADIUS (Remote Authentication Dial-In User Service) server provides authentication of remote access users and also provides an accounting system for tracking access to your RAS server. RADIUS servers are typically used by Internet service providers to authenticate and track remote users. The Windows Server 2008 RRAS implementation provides the Network Policy Server, which can use RADIUS for authentication.

Installing the Network Policy Server

RADIUS comes in a number of different third-party software vendor flavors and runs on various network operating system platforms. You can use RADIUS authentication in your domain without buying additional RADIUS software; the Windows Server 2008 Network Policy Server can be configured as a RADIUS server. This means that all RAS remote client requests for authentication in the domain are forwarded from the RRAS server to the server running NPS.

The Network Policy Server can be installed when you add the Network Policy and Access Services role (as discussed earlier in the hour). If you did not add the NPS during the installation of the role (say, for example, you installed only the Routing and Remote Access Services role), you can add the NPS service to the Network Policy and Access Service role from the Sever Manager.

Follow these steps:

1. In the Server Manager, expand the Roles node and then select the Network Policy and Access Services node.

2. In the Details pane click, Add Role Services. The Add Roles Services Wizard opens with a list of the services associated with the Network Policy and Access Services role (see Figure 17.16).

FIGURE 17.16
Select the Network Policy Server check box.

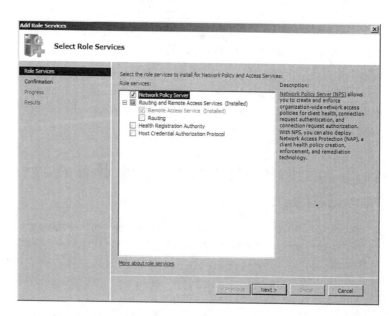

3. Select the Network Policy Server check box and then click Next.

4. The confirmation page opens. Click Install.

When the installation is complete, you can click Close to close the Add Role Services Wizard. After the NPS service is installed, you can then configure NPS for RADIUS authentication.

Configuring the NPS Server

To get NPS up and running as a RADIUS server, you must configure NPS; you can configure NPS from the Server Manager: Expand the Network Policy and Access Services node and then select the NPS node. You can also use the Network Policy Server snap-in in the MMC (Start, Administrative Tools, Network Policy Server) to configure your NPS settings. Follow these steps:

1. In the NPS snap-in (in the Server Manger or MMC), click the Standard Configuration drop-down list in the Details pane. Select Radius Server for Dial-Up or VPN Connections from the list.

2. Click Configure VPN or Dial-Up. The Configure VPN or Dial-Up Wizard opens (see Figure 17.17).

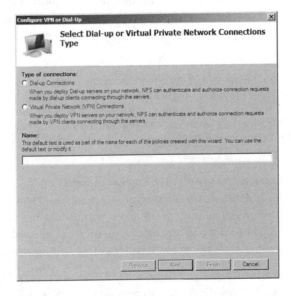

FIGURE 17.17
You can configure the NPS for VPN or dial-up.

3. For sake of discussion (and because VPN is now used more the dial-in) select the Virtual Private Network (VPN) Connections option button. This also places Virtual Private Network (VPN) Connections in the Name box. You can go with this default name or change the name as needed. Click Next.

4. On the next wizard page, you must specify the VPN (or dial-in) RAS servers that will use RADIUS for authentication. These servers would be designated as RADIUS clients. Click the Add button. The New Radius Client dialog box opens.

5. In the New Radius Client dialog box, specify the friendly name or the IP address of the server. You must also enter a shared secret password and confirm the shared secret. You also need to supply the shared secret when you configure the RAS server as a VPN server that uses RADIUS for authentication. Click OK to add the VPN server. You can add other VPN servers as needed. When you return to the Configure VPN or Dial-Up Wizard (after listing your VPN servers), click Next to continue.

By the Way

> The shared secret is used to verify the RAS VPN server to the NPS (RADIUS) Server. You need to enter the same shared secret password when you configure NPS (as we are doing in this section) and when you use the Routing and Remote Access Server Setup Wizard to configure the RAS server as a VPN server that will take advantage of RADIUS authentication.

6. On the next wizard page, you select the authentication methods for the server (see Figure 17.18). MS-CHAP v2 is the default. If you plan on using smart cards or certificates for client authentication, you should choose EAP. You can select more than one authentication method if necessary. Then click Next.

By the Way

> RADIUS embraces the same authentication protocols (such as EAP and CHAP) that can be set for the Windows authentication of remote clients. If you deploy NPS or have another RADIUS platform running on your network, select RADIUS as your authentication method when you use the Routing and Remote Access Server Setup Wizard to configure the RAS server.

7. On the next page, you are given the option of supplying the names of specific user groups (from the Active Directory) that are provided with remote access (or not), based on the network policy access permission. You can add groups as needed. If you do not add any groups, all users are allowed or denied remote access based on the network policy access permission. Click Next.

8. On the next wizard page, you can specify IP filters that control the type of IP packets (both IPv4 and IPv6) that are sent on the VPN server's network interface. You can also create filters that limit the type of IP packets received on the interface. IP filters are based on TCP/IP protocol stack transport protocols such as TCP, UDP, and ICMP. A filter for incoming packets would specify the

destination network by network IP address and subnet mask. The specific protocol would also be specified (or you can select Any for all transport protocols). After specifying IP filters, click Next.

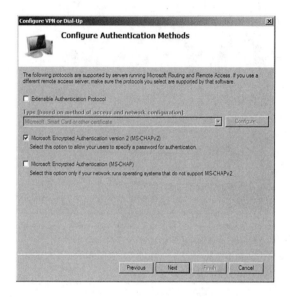

FIGURE 17.18
Select the authentication method to be used.

Using incoming filters could help protect the network against a Denial of Service attack where the RAS server is inundated with requests via a transport protocol such as UDP. For a primer on the TCP/IP protocol stack, see Hour 7, "Working with the TCP/IP Network Protocol."

By the Way

9. On the next wizard page, you can select the type of encryption that should be used for communication between the clients and the RAS server. By default (see Figure 17.19), three encryption methods are selected: Basic Encryption, Strong encryption, and Strongest Encryption. You can disable any or all of these encryption settings. The settings that you choose must match the encryption settings that you select when configuring your RAS server (in the RRAS snap-in). After selecting the encryption type or types, click Next.

10. On the next wizard page, you can specify your realm name (this is optional). The realm name is specified by your ISP, and is a portion of the username that has been assigned to your network by your ISP. The realm name is used to route traffic to your network. Enter the realm name (you do not have to enter a realm name if you have not been assigned one by your ISP) in the Realm Name box. Then click Next.

FIGURE 17.19
Select the encryption methods to be used.

11. The Completion page appears. You are ready to complete the setup of the NPS RADIUS settings. Click Finish.

Access to your RAS server is now authenticated by the NPS (RADIUS) server. The NPS and also the Network Access Protection provided by an NPS server are ultimately controlled by network policies. The network policies for your NPS server can be accessed via the Network Policies node in the NPS snap-in. Double-click a policy to open and edit that policy's properties.

Security and access are tightly wound with policies on your server. These policies, also known as Group Policy Objects (or GPOs), are configured in the Group Policy Object Editor (although you can access NPS policies from the NPS snap-in). Hour 11 provides an overview of both GPOs (such as the Network Policy Server GPO) and the new Network Access Protection feature provided by Windows Server 2008.

Summary

The Network Policy and Access Services role provides a number of remote access and network policy services including the Network Policy Server and Routing and Remote Access Services. RAS servers can provide dial-in remote access by using asynchronous modems and can also supply remote access via virtual private networks.

Remote access is enabled on the Routing and Remote Access service in the RRAS snap-in, which can be run in the Server Manager or the MMC.

RAS ports must be configured for dial-in service on the server's modem or other connectivity devices. The RAS server must also be configured for incoming calls. VPN ports are added by default to the RAS server when you configure the server for VPN.

A number of different authentication protocols, such as EAP, MS-CHAP, and Shiva, are used to authenticate remote users to the RAS server. The remote client must be configured with the same authentication protocol that is required by the RRAS server.

You can configure ports and monitor access to your RAS server in the RRAS snap-in. You can view the length of a VPN or dial-in remote connection and you can also terminate connections if needed.

RAS servers can embrace Windows authentication (via the RRAS server) or then can take advantage of RADIUS authentication, in which a dedicated RADIUS server provides authentication of remote users. The Windows Server 2008 Network Policy Server service can be configured as a RADIUS server.

Q&A

Q. *What two types of authentication can be used with an RAS server?*

A. Authentication can be handled by the local Routing and Remote Access service or by a server running the Network Policy Server service as a RADIUS server. If RADIUS authentication is used, the RAS server becomes a client of the NPS (RADIUS) server.

Q. *How are remote users authenticated when authentication is handled by the RAS server?*

A. A number of different authentication protocols are available to authenticate remote users to a dial-in RAS server. These protocols provide different strengths of authentication. The Extensible Authentication Protocol provides the strongest authentication and is followed by the MS-CHAP V2 and MS-CHAP protocols. The weakest form of authentication is to configure unauthenticated access, which means that no protocol is used to control authentication.

Q. *How are remote access clients configured in the domain?*

A. The Active Directory Users and Computers snap-in is used to configure user settings related to remote access.

Q. *What are the tunneling protocols used to provide a secure tunnel through the Internet for a client connection to your RAS server?*

A. Windows Server 2008 provides three tunneling protocols for VPN: Secure Socket Tunneling Protocol (SSTP), Point-to-Point Tunneling Protocol (PPTP), and Layer 2 Tunneling Protocol (L2TP).

Implementing Network Routing

What You'll Learn in This Hour:

▶ Windows Server 2008 and Routing
▶ Understanding Routed Networks
▶ Adding the Network Policy and Access Services Role
▶ Enabling Routing and Remote Access
▶ Configuring Network Interfaces
▶ Configuring IP Routing
▶ Configuring RIP Interfaces
▶ Monitoring IP Routing
▶ Understanding and Configuring the DHCP Relay Agent

A routed network or internetwork is actually a network of networks. An internetwork consists of different subnets; each subnet uses a router as its connection point to the other subnets in the internetwork. Windows Server 2008 provides the Routing and Remote Access Services (RRAS), which enable you to configure a server as a router.

Windows Server 2008 and Routing

When IP networks become large, they are typically segmented into subnets to keep local data traffic on each segment and to make the most out of available network bandwidth. Networks that are made up of multiple sites (geographic locations) also use subnets to divide the various parts of the network into one internetwork (a network of networks).

The device that joins separate segments (subnets in the case of a TCP/IP network) into one network is called a *router*. A router is an intelligent networking device that can determine whether data should stay on the local segment (subnet) or be forwarded to another subnet on the network.

Most internetworks use dedicated routers (a number of vendors provide routers, such as Cisco Systems, Juniper Networks, and 3Com). These routers provide a hardware solution to routing and switching data between subnets and have their own proprietary operating systems. Routers providing hardware routing are designed for medium- to large-sized networks.

Windows Server 2008 provides a software solution for routing as part of the Routing and Remote Access Services. The only extra hardware needed to deploy a server running Windows Server 2008 as a router is a second network interface. A server with multiple network interfaces (or a network interface and a modem) is referred to as a *multihomed* computer.

Windows Server 2008 routing is ideal in a situation where you don't need to deploy actual routing hardware (a router) but still want to subnet a network. For example, you might have a network where a segment consists of users that share sensitive information and you want to keep that data on that particular segment. Or you need to connect a small branch office to the main network using inexpensive Wide Area Network (WAN) technology (say broadband or DSL), and want to use a server running Windows Server 2008 as the connecting point (the router) between the two segments. Windows Server 2008 is basically a low-cost option in cases where the network segmentation doesn't require a dedicated device.

Windows Server 2008 also enables you to take advantage of a single Internet connection for the clients on a LAN. The Windows server basically functions as the gateway between the Internet and the LAN. Network Address Translation (NAT) can be used to assign the IP addresses to the clients on the LAN so only a single public IP address is needed for the server's connection to the Internet.

Let's take a quick look at some of the basics of how routing works on IP networks. We can then explore the various aspects of configuring a server running the Windows Server 2008 Routing and Remote Access Server as a router and then look at taking advantage of Network Address Translation.

To create subnets on an IP network, you need to have some understanding of how to determine the range of IP addresses for each of your subnets. See Hour 7, "Working with the TCP/IP Network Protocol," for information on configuring TCP/IP and working with subnets.

Understanding Routed Networks

Routers are responsible for determining the path of routed packets and for actually routing the packets to the appropriate subnet. Routers can have multiple LAN and WAN interfaces, and each interface is used as a connecting point to a different subnet on the network.

So, the routing process really involves the "intelligent" transfer of IP data packets from one segment to another. Depending on the number of network devices and the complexity of the network design (meaning the number of subnets), the actual implementation of routing can become very complicated. There may be many different paths that a packet can actually take to get to its final host destination. However, routers contain routing tables that list the possible routes by which packets delivered to the router can be sent.

By the Way

When you configure IP network clients with a default gateway setting (in the TCP/IP properties), you are usually entering the IP address of a router's LAN interface. Used in conjunction with the subnet mask assigned to the client (either entered statically or provided through DHCP), the default gateway instructs the local computer to send packets not destined for the local subnet to the router, which routes the packets to the appropriate subnet.

Routers can use either dynamic routing or static routing to route packets. *Dynamic routing* is handled by a routing protocol (RIP—the Routing Information Protocol—is an example of a routing protocol). Routing protocols build and maintain routing tables that determine the network topology for your internetwork. Dynamic routing is a good idea if your network topology may change. The routing protocol can respond to changes in the LAN or WAN connections and can update the routing table appropriately.

Static routing is handled by the network administrator (meaning you). Routes are actually manually entered on the router and are used to determine how packets are routed on the network. Static routing is fine when the network topology is very constant and consistent. Any change in network connections requires the administrator to re-enter the static routes.

The Routing and Remote Access Server (RRAS) provided by Windows Server 2008 can be configured for both dynamic and static routing. To take advantage of the RRAS features such as routing, you need to install the Network Policy and Access Services role and Routing and Remote Access Services.

Adding the Network Policy and Access Services Role

You can add the Network Policy and Access Services role from the Initial Configuration Tasks window or the Server Manager. Select the Add Roles link and then click Next to bypass the Add Roles Wizard's initial page.

On the next wizard page (see Figure 18.1), select the Routing and Remote Access Services check box. This adds the Remote Access Service and the Routing service. Click Next and then click Install to install Routing and Remote Access Services.

FIGURE 18.1
Add the Remote Access Services to the server's configuration.

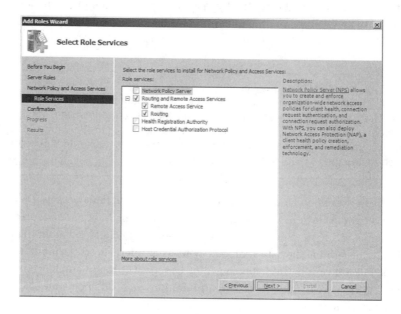

> **Did you Know?**
>
> You may have already added the Network Policy and Access Services role during your exploration of Hour 17. If you did not add the Routing and Remote Access Services when installing the role, you can add this service from the Server Manager. With the Network Policy and Access Services node selected in the node tree, click the Add Role Services link in the Details pane. The Add Role Services Wizard opens. Select the Routing and Remote Access Services check box and then click Install. The service is added to the server and the Routing and Remote Access node appears as a subnode of the Network Policy and Access Services node.

After RRAS is installed (as part of the Network Policy and Access Services role), the Routing and Remote Access snap-in is added to the Server Manager (as a subnode of the Network Policy and Access Services node). The Routing and Remote Access snap-in can also be started via an icon that is added to the Administrative Tools menu (on the Start menu). This enables you to run the Routing and Remote Access snap-in in the MMC (rather than in the Server Manager).

Enabling Routing and Remote Access

Before you can configure RRAS (more specifically, routing), you must enable the service. You can enable (and then configure) RRAS via the Server Manager or the RRAS snap-in running in the MMC.

Follow these steps:

1. In the Server Manager, expand the Roles and Network Policy and Access nodes and then click the Routing and Remote Access node to select it. In the Routing and Remote Access snap-in in the MMC, select the server node (the name of your server; see Figure 18.2).

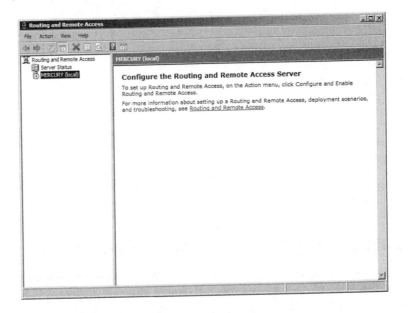

FIGURE 18.2
Select your server in the MMC's node tree.

2. Select Action, and then Configure and Enable Routing and Remote Access. The Routing and Remote access Server Setup Wizard opens. Click Next to bypass the wizard's initial page.

3. On the next wizard page, you are provided a number of options related to the RRAS feature (features such as VPN and VPN remote access were discussed in Hour 17). Because we are interested (at this point) only in enabling routing, click the Custom Configuration option button and then click Next.

4. On the Custom Configuration page, select LAN Routing (see Figure 18.3).

FIGURE 18.3
Select LAN
Routing.

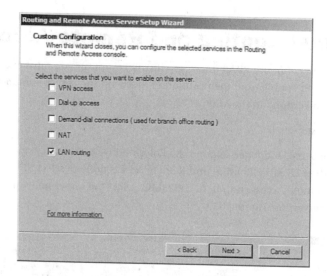

5. Click Next. A summary screen appears (LAN routing will be added to the RRAS configuration). Click Finish.

6. The Routing and Remote Access dialog box opens, asking whether you wish to start RRAS. Click Start Service.

RRAS starts on the server and the wizard closes. You are returned to the RRAS snap-in (MMC) or to the Server Manager.

Configuring Network Interfaces

Because the RRAS-enabled server is to serve as a router between two segments of the network, you need to configure the network interfaces on the server with the appropriate fixed IP addresses. The IP address for each network interface is dictated by the range of IP addresses that you are using for the subnet.

After you do the math to create your subnet (or use a subnet calculator), you have a range of addresses for each IP subnet that you plan to deploy on the network. The IP address that you use for a network interface needs to be taken from the IP address range to which the interface is to connect; meaning the interface will be the default gateway for that particular subnet. It makes sense to use the first address available in the subnet as the address for the network interface. That way each router interface is configured with an IP address that is consistent with the subnet it serves.

Creating subnets from an IP network address is discussed in Hour 7. Both IPv4 and IPv6 can be subnetted. If you don't want to do the math yourself, a number of subnet calculators are available on the Web that can help you figure out the address range when you subnet both IPv4 and IPv6 network addresses. Do a search on the Web for "IP subnet calculator." For a primer on working with IP addressing and the basics of subnetting, see Hour 7.

By the Way

To configure a network interface, click Start and then right-click Network and select Properties. This opens the Network Connections dialog box. Right-click a local area connection icon and then select Properties. The Properties dialog box for that interface opens (see Figure 18.4).

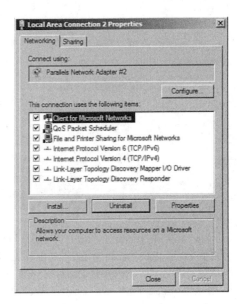

FIGURE 18.4
Open the Properties dialog box for a LAN interface.

You can configure both IPv4 and IPv6 addresses from the Properties dialog box. For example, if you have subnetted an IPv4 Class C network with the network address of 200.10.44.0, the range of node addresses for the two subnets is

Subnet 1 range: 200.10.44.65-200.10.44.126

Subnet 2 range: 200.10.44.129-200.10.44.190

You would then assign one interface with the address 200.10.44.65 (see Figure 18.5) and the other LAN interface with 200.10.44.129. The subnet mask for both subnet ranges would be 255.255.255.192 (again, the basics of subnetting are discussed in Hour 7).

To assign the IP address to the interface, select the appropriate Internet Protocol Version (in the discussion example, Internet Protocol Version 4—TCP/IPv4) and then click Properties. Enter the IP address information in the IP Properties dialog box and then click Close.

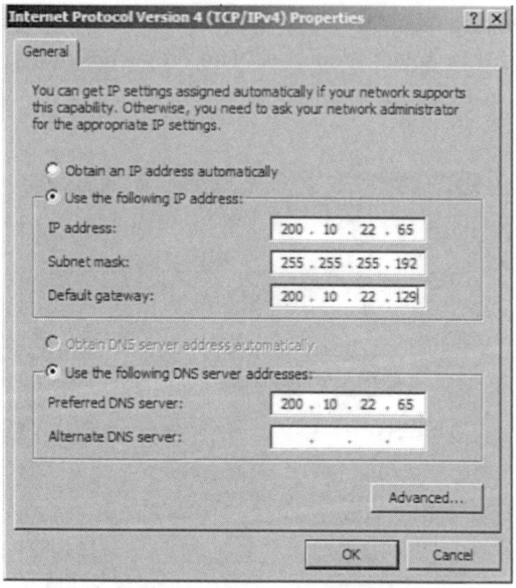

FIGURE 18.5
Configure the static IP address for the router interface.

You can view the IP address (and the incoming and outgoing bytes) for a LAN interface on the server/router. Expand the server name node (in the MMC) or the Routing and Remote Access node in the Server Manager. Expand the IPv4 node (for example) and then click the General node. The local area connection IP addresses and other statistics appear in the Details pane (see Figure 18.6).

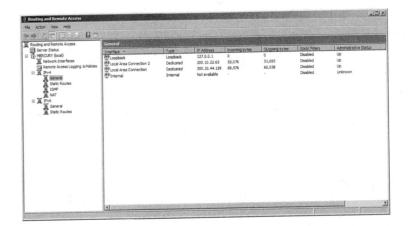

FIGURE 18.6
View the IP addresses and status of a LAN connection by IP version.

> If the RRAS snap-in is still showing the default IP addresses (the addresses assigned to the LAN interfaces before you made your changes), right-click in the Details pane and select Refresh to update the information.

Did you Know?

Configuring IP Routing

After you have your server's network interfaces configured with the appropriate IP addresses and RRAS is enabled, you can configure the server for routing IP. Routing can be handled in two different ways: static routing and dynamic routing.

As already mentioned earlier in the hour, static routing requires that routing information be entered by the administrator. The static route is fixed and cannot react to changes in the network topology.

Dynamic routing uses a routing protocol that builds and maintains the routing tables. The routing tables determine how data is then routed on the network. Windows Server 2008 uses RIP (Routing Information Protocol) as the routing protocol.

Let's take a look at how to configure static routing. We can then take a look at the alternative, dynamic routing, and look at how to add RIP to the RRAS configuration.

Configuring Static Routing

Static routing is configured in the RRAS snap-in. A static route configuration consists of an interface selection (one of the network interfaces on the routing server), a destination address, a gateway, and a metric.

In terms of routing, the *gateway* is the address of the device that provides the connection between the networks that will embrace the static route that you are creating. The gateway basically functions as a forwarding agent as the packets move to their final destination.

A *metric* is the number of hops (from router to router) that are required to move the packets from source to destination. You want to create routes with the fewest number of hops (also known as the cost of the route) and, thus, the lowest metric.

To configure a static route, follow these steps:

1. Expand the server node in the RRAS snap-in tree in the MMC (or the Routing and Remote Access node in the Server Manager). Then expand the appropriate IP routing node. (Because IPv4 routing is much more common than IPv6 routing, expand the IPv4 node.)

2. Right-click the Static Routes node, and select New Static Route. The Static Route dialog box appears (see Figure 18.7).

FIGURE 18.7
The Static
Route dialog
box.

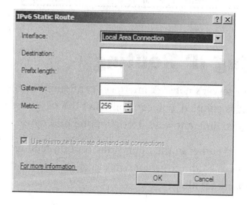

3. Use the Interface drop-down list to select the interface on the router (the RRAS server) that you want to configure with the static route.

4. Enter the destination IP address in the Destination box.

5. Enter the network mask (the net mask that you computed when you subnetted your network—this is discussed in Hour 7) for your network. If you want to make the route proprietary for packets with the destination address that you entered in the Destination box, use the mask of 255.255.2555.255. If you want to make the route available for any destination, enter the mask of 0.0.0.0.

6. In the Gateway box, enter the IP address of the forwarder for your network segment.

7. Enter the metric for the route in the Metric spin box. The default is the maximum 256.

8. Click OK to complete the creation of the static route.

Other static routes can be created as needed. You can edit any static route by right-clicking the route in the Details pane and then selecting Properties. Delete static routes by right-clicking the route and then selecting Delete.

If the number of hops or other network topology changes in relation to your static routes, you must reconfigure the routes. Because static routes are static (and require hands-on editing and management), the alternative of dynamic routing might be more to your liking. Dynamic routing is discussed in the next section.

Did you Know?

You can also create static routes at the command line by using the route command. Use the route print command to view the routing table.

Configuring Dynamic Routing

To configure dynamic routing, you must add the RIP routing protocol to the IP (routing) node of your server/router. RIP is a distance-vector routing protocol that uses hop count as its metric. RIP sends out routing update messages every 30 seconds to neighboring routers. Because RIP is a distance-vector routing protocol, it requires routers to share complete copies of their routing tables with other routers. RIP has a limit of 15 hops and, thus, is not appropriate for very large enterprise-size internetworks.

By the Way

Windows Server 2003, the previous version of Microsoft's network OS, also provided a second routing protocol OSPF (Open Shortest Path First) as an RRAS option and alternative to RIP. OSPF has been removed from the Windows Server 2008 RRAS configuration, so RIP is the only possibility.

To add RIP to your server/router, follow these steps:

1. Expand an IP node in the snap-in tree (such as the IPv4 node).

2. Right-click the General node and select New Routing Protocol from the shortcut menu. The New Routing Protocol dialog box opens (see Figure 18.8).

FIGURE 18.8
Adding a routing
protocol.

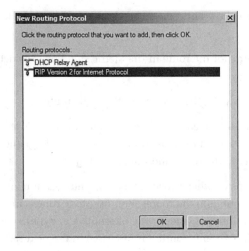

3. Select RIP Version 2 for Internet Protocol (the DHCP Relay Agent choice is discussed later in the hour).

4. After selecting RIP, click OK. RIP is added to the IP node as a subnode.

After you've added RIP to the RRAS IP Routing configuration, you need to create an interface for the routing protocol. Configuring RIP interfaces is discussed in the next section.

> Adding RIP to the IPv4 node does not automatically add RIP to the IPv6 node. So, if you are planning on routing IPv6 addresses, you need to add RIP to IPv6 as well.

Configuring RIP Interfaces

RIP interfaces are configured for a number of settings, including the protocol type used for outgoing packets and whether your router accepts routes from all its neighbors (other nearby routers). To configure an interface for RIP, follow these steps:

1. Right-click the RIP node (under the IP node in the snap-in tree) and select New Interface. The New Interface for RIP dialog box opens.

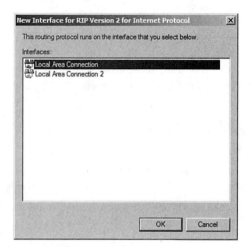

FIGURE 18.9
RIP runs on the interface you select.

2. In the New Interface for RIP Version 2 for Internet Protocol dialog box, select the interface for the protocol.

3. Click OK. The RIP Properties dialog box for the interface that you selected appears (see Figure 18.10).

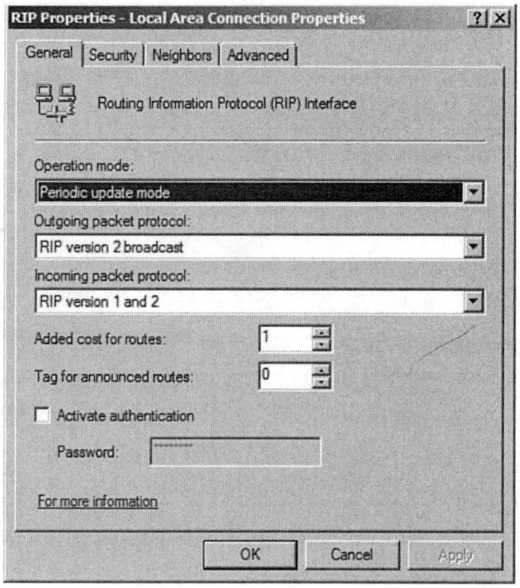

FIGURE 18.10
The RIP Properties dialog box for the interface.

4. On the General tab (see Figure 18.10), the operation mode is set to periodic update by default (and should be left as the default). You can change the RIP

version that is used for outgoing and incoming packets. RIP Version 2 broadcast is the default for outgoing packets, but you can use the drop-down list to select RIP Version 1 if this is running on other routers on the network. You can also choose to have the router listen to other routers (to build a routing table) but not advertise to its neighbors; this selection is Silent RIP.

5. The Incoming Packet Protocol drop-down list is used to specify the types of RIP packets that the interface accepts. You can choose to accept RIP Version 1, 2, or both types of packets.

6. To change security settings for the RIP interface, select the Security tab. You can see actions related to incoming and outgoing routes. You can choose to accept all routes, accept routes listed in a range, or ignore routes listed in a range.

7. To change settings related to the router's neighboring routers, click the Neighbors tab (see Figure 18.11).

FIGURE 18.11
How the router interacts with neighboring routers is configured on the Neighbors tab.

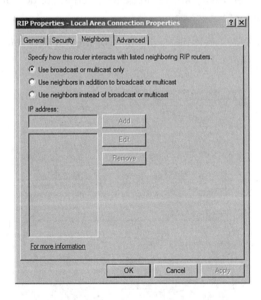

8. By default, the router uses broadcast multicast messages to contact its neighbors. You can specify that unicast messages go to certain routers, either in addition to or instead of broadcast or multicast messages. Select either the option Use Neighbors in Addition to Broadcast or Multicast or the option Use Neighbors Instead of Broadcast or Multicast. Then add the IP addresses of the neighbors to the IP Address box.

9. To set advanced features, select the Advanced tab on the dialog box. Most of these settings should remain the defaults, although you can change the periodic announcement interval for the router. Split-horizon processing, which is enabled by default, helps to negate routing loops on the network. Routing loops happen because certain routes become unavailable and the routers do not have updated routing tables; data just continues to loop around the internetwork. Poison-reverse processing "poisons" (marks for deletion) routes that have not been verified by a neighboring router.

10. When you have completed setting the configuration for the RIP interface, click OK.

The interface appears in the Details pane when you select the RIP node in the snap-in tree. You can add other interfaces as needed for RIP and configure them.

Monitoring IP Routing

Routing can be monitored in the RRAS snap-in. For example, to see a list of neighbor routers for the RIP protocol, click the RIP subnode (for one, the IP nodes such as IPv4) and then select Show Neighbors. A Neighbors dialog box opens that lists the addresses of neighboring routers.

To view the status of the router interfaces and other information, such as the incoming and outgoing bytes from the interface, expand the IP Routing node and then click the General node (see Figure 18.12).

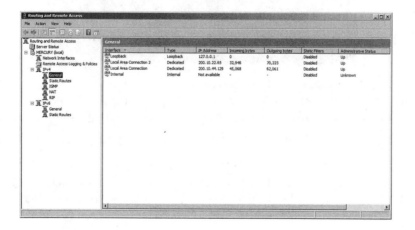

FIGURE 18.12
View the status of the router's interfaces.

To view the routing table for a router interface (using RIP), right-click one of the
interfaces and select Show IP Routing Table from the shortcut menu. The routing
table appears (see Figure 18.13).

FIGURE 18.13
View the dynam-
ic routing table
for an interface.

MERCURY - IP Routing Table		
Destination	Network mask	Gateway
0.0.0.0	0.0.0.0	0.0.0.0
127.0.0.0	255.0.0.0	127.0.0.1
127.0.0.1	255.255.255.255	127.0.0.1
200.10.22.64	255.255.255.192	0.0.0.0
200.10.22.65	255.255.255.255	0.0.0.0
200.10.22.127	255.255.255.255	0.0.0.0
200.10.44.128	255.255.255.192	0.0.0.0
200.10.44.129	255.255.255.255	0.0.0.0
200.10.44.191	255.255.255.255	0.0.0.0
224.0.0.0	240.0.0.0	0.0.0.0
255.255.255.255	255.255.255.255	0.0.0.0

A useful command-line utility for monitoring IP routes is the tracert command. It
provides you with the number of hops between a source and a destination IP
address. To use tracert, open a command prompt window. Type **tracert**, followed
by the IP address or name of the destination. Figure 18.14 shows a tracert result
that was four hops to the destination address.

FIGURE 18.14
tracert shows
the number of
hops between a
source and a
destination.

```
Administrator: Command Prompt

C:\Users\Administrator>tracert 192.168.1.3

Tracing route to GABBY [192.168.1.3]
over a maximum of 30 hops:

  1    <1 ms    <1 ms    1 ms  GABBY [192.168.1.3]

Trace complete.

C:\Users\Administrator>
```

Using tracert is actually a very good way to determine whether a router or route is
down on your internetwork. If the number of hops to the same destination changes
dramatically over time, there is a problem on the network.

Did you Know?

Another fast way to see whether an IP address is reachable or if a router interface
is up or down is to use the ping command. At the command line, type **ping *ip
address***, where *ip address* is the actual IP address of the node you are attempting to contact.

Understanding and Configuring the DHCP Relay Agent

Before we leave this discussion of routing, we should discuss issues related to running DHCP in environments where either remote clients (as discussed in the previous hour) receive their IP addresses from a DHCP server or you have a subnetted IP network that uses DCHP. Both these problem scenarios (in terms of getting IP addressing information to client computers) can be solved by deploying the DHCP Relay Agent.

In the case of routed networks, routers, by design, do not pass broadcast messages from one subnet to another, so this is a problem if you are using the DHCP service but do not have a DHCP server on each of the IP subnets. The DHCP Relay Agent can be configured so that it knows the location of a DHCP server or servers on other subnets of the network (that is, on the other side of the router). The Relay Agent takes the broadcast request from DHCP clients on the subnet (where both the client and the Relay Agent reside) and relays a point-to-point communication to the DHCP server that there has been a request for an IP address lease. (This type of communication is passed on by the router because it is not a broadcast message, but is directed to the specific IP address of the DHCP server.)

As already mentioned, the DHCP Relay Agent is also necessary when you are providing remote access clients with IP addresses from a DHCP server. The DHCP Relay Agent relays IP address requests from remote clients to the DHCP server.

You cannot set up the DHCP Relay Agent on a server that is a DHCP server, nor can you install it on a server that is running Network Address Translation (NAT is discussed in Hour 22, "Using Network Address Translation and Certificate Services").

The DHCP Relay Agent is added and configured in much the same way that you added and configured the RIP routing protocol. To configure a server as a DHCP Relay Agent, follow these steps:

1. In the Routing and Remote Access snap-in, expand your server node and then expand an IP Routing node (such as IPv4).

2. Right-click the General node and select New Routing Protocol. The New Routing Protocol dialog box appears (see Figure 18.15).

3. Select DHCP Relay Agent in the routing protocol list. Then click OK. DHCP Relay Agent appears as a subnode of the IP node.

FIGURE 18.15
Select DHCP
Relay Agent in
the New Routing
Protocol dialog
box.

4. To add an interface (or interfaces) for the DHCP Relay Agent, right-click the DHCP Relay Agent node and select New Interface. The New Interface dialog box opens. Select the interface from the list and then click OK. The DHCP Relay Properties dialog box for the connection opens.

5. By default, the interface relays DHCP packets. You can change the hop count threshold or boot threshold for the interface. The hop count threshold is the number of Relay Agents that can relay the DHCP requests. The maximum hop count is 16. The boot threshold is the number of seconds that the Relay Agent waits before it forwards DHCP messages. In both cases, the defaults generally suffice. Click OK to continue.

6. To complete the DHCP Relay Agent configuration, right-click the DHCP Relay Agent node and select Properties (see Figure 18.16).

7. Add the IP addresses of the DHCP servers to which the DHCP Relay Agent is to forward DHCP requests.

8. Click OK to close the dialog box.

The server now acts as a DHCP Relay Agent. Remember that it is necessary to configure the DHCP Relay Agent when you have multiple subnets but do not have a DHCP server on each subnet.

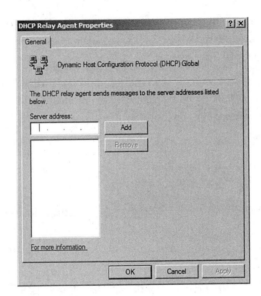

FIGURE 18.16
Configure the
Relay Agent with
the IP address-
es of the DHCP
servers.

Summary

A routed network consists of IP subnets that are connected by routers. A server running Windows Server 2008 and configured with multiple network cards can be configured as a router through the Routing and Remote Access Service.

The Routing and Remote Access Service is a service provided by the Windows Server
2008 Network Policy and Access Services role. This role is added via the Initial
Configuration Tasks window or the Server Manager.

After Routing and Remote Access Services is enabled in the RRAS snap-in (in the
MMC or the Server Manager), you can configure the server as a router. You need to
configure each of the server's interfaces with fixed IP addresses from the pool of
addresses used for each IP subnet.

To configure IP routing in RRAS, you can use static or dynamic routing. Static routing requires that you configure routing tables that provide the information needed
for packets to be routed on the network.

You can also take advantage of dynamic routing, which uses the RIP routing protocol. RIP builds the routing tables automatically and so can respond to changes in
your network topology.

You can monitor your router's status from the RRAS snap-in. You can also use command-line commands such as `tracert` and `ping` to determine whether IP addresses on the network are reachable.

The DHCP Relay Agent is on networks where you do not have a DHCP server on each subnet. The DHCP Relay Agent takes DHCP broadcasts and relays them as point-to-point communications so that they are forwarded by routers on the network.

Q&A

Q. *Routing and Remove Access Service, is part of what Windows Server 2008 role?*

A. RRAS is one set of services provided by the Network Policy and access Services role.

Q. *What types of routing can be configured on a Windows Server 2008 RRAS server?*

A. You can configure the RRAS server for static routing where you enter your own routing tables. You can also configure the RRAS server for dynamic routing where the RIP routing protocol builds dynamic routing tables automatically.

Q. *What is the DHCP Relay Agent?*

A. When you have a network with more than one subnet but do not have a DHCP server on each subnet, the DHCP Relay Agent takes broadcast requests from DHCP clients and relays them as point-to-point communications to DHCP servers on the network.

Q. *What are some ways to manage and troubleshoot router connections?*

A. The RRAS snap-in enables you to monitor whether or not your router interfaces are active. You can also use command-line tools such as `tracert` and `ping` to check the connectivity between routers and nodes on the network.

HOUR 19

Implementing Terminal Services

What You'll Learn in This Hour:

▶ Understanding Terminal Services
▶ Adding the Terminal Services Role
▶ Working with Terminal Services Licensing
▶ Configuring the Terminal Server and TS Connections
▶ Using the Terminal Services Manager
▶ Connecting to the Terminal Server

The typical notion of a network client computer is a desktop computer that not only has a Windows operating system installed on it but also has applications installed locally (say, Microsoft Office). However, you may have client computers on the network that do not supply the configuration (meaning installed software) that meets all the needs of all the users who may need to use that computer. The Windows Terminal Services enables you to supply "nonstandard" network clients with Windows-based applications on a Windows desktop environment.

Understanding Terminal Services

The concept of the network thin client has been around nearly as long as desktop computing. A *thin client* is software (although it is often used to refer to the computer itself) that enables a computer with a minimal hardware configuration to connect to an application server. The thin client computer, which normally would not be capable of running a full-blown copy of a particular desktop operating system or desktop applications, is "served" these items by the application server. In the Windows Server 2008 environment, Terminal Services provides the desktop OS and required applications to the network thin client.

Using Terminal Services to provide thin clients with a Windows desktop operating system and applications enables users to access network resources on older desktop computers or computers with minimal hardware configurations. All the application processing and data storage is handled by the server. In essence, the terminal server functions as an *application server,* providing applications that would not run as standalone software on the thin client. A server running Terminal Services is referred to as a *terminal server.*

By the Way

So, what's new with Terminal Services found in Windows Server 2008? First of all, the Terminal Services RemoteApp completely integrates applications running on a terminal server with users' desktops. This means that the remote applications behave as if they were running on the user's local computer. The new Terminal Services Web Access permits users to use applications via a web browser. So, Windows Server 2008 Terminal Services increases the ways that users can access the programs they need.

Terminal Services clients can access the applications provided over any TCP/IP connection. This means that users can connect via your local area network or can use remote access strategies such as dial-in or VPN to connect to the terminal server.

By the Way

Terminal Services clients are not necessarily limited to computers running different versions of the Windows operating system. These clients can include computers running the Macintosh OS. The Macintosh Remote Desktop client can be downloaded from the Microsoft Website (http://www.microsoft.com).

To take advantage of a terminal server on the network, you need to have a Licensing server on the network that provides and manages Terminal Services licenses. Each client that connects to the terminal server must have a license. These licenses are provided by the terminal server license server (TS license server). The TS license server can be the same server that is providing Terminal Services to network clients, or it can be another server on the network. If you are deploying Terminal Services on a very large network, it probably makes sense to allow a server other than the Terminal Services server to deal with the licenses to reduce some of the load on the Terminal Services server.

Any discussion of getting a terminal server up and running on the network is really a two-part story: You need to have a Terminal Services server to provide the applications and Windows desktop to the Terminal Services client, and a TS License server to take care of the licensing of clients requesting services from the Terminal Services server. On small networks one server can serve as both the Terminal Services server and the TS license server, and this is the approach used in the Terminal Services installation described in this hour.

Adding the Terminal Services Role

Terminal Services can be added to any domain member server. You can add the Terminal Server role to a Windows Server 2008, using the Add Roles Wizard.

1. From the Server Manager (with the Roles node selected) or the Initial Configuration Tasks window, select Add Roles. The Add Roles Wizard opens. Click Next to bypass the initial wizard page.

2. On the next wizard page, select the Terminal Services check box and then click Next.

3. An introduction to Terminal Services appears on the next page, which also includes a link to more information about Terminal Services. Click Next.

4. On the next page, you are provided a list of the services available as part of the Terminal Services role:

    ▶ **Terminal Server**—This service enables the server to host Windows applications or a complete Windows desktop.

    ▶ **TS Licensing**—This service is used to manage Terminal Services client access licenses. Each user or device that connects to a terminal server requires Terminal Services Licensing (TS Licensing).

    ▶ **TS Session Broker**—This service allows load balancing between Terminal Services servers in a domain. This service is not needed when only one Terminal Services server is being deployed on the network.

    ▶ **TS Gateway**—This service enables remote users to connect to the terminal server (or servers) on the network from any Internet-connected device.

    ▶ **TS Web Access**—This service enables users to access RemoteApp programs running on the terminal server via a Web browser.

Select the services you want to install (for discussion purposes in this hour, assume that you have added the terminal server and TS Licensing services; the

TS Gateway and TS Web Access services require an understanding of a number of other Windows Server 2008 services—see the tip that follows) and then click Next.

If you install the TS Gateway and/or the TS Web Access services, the IIS 7 (Internet Information Service) web server must also be installed on the server. When you click either TS Gateway or TS Web Access on the Select Role Services page, the Add Roles dialog box opens. It alerts you that IIS must be installed. In the dialog box, click Add Required Role Services to install IIS (during the terminal server installation). For more about IIS, see Hour 23, "Using the Internet Information Service." The Network Policy Server (NPS) is also installed when you select the web access–related Terminal Services. See Hour 17, "Remote Access and Virtual Private Networking," for more about NPS.

5. The next wizard page relates to application compatibility. If the server already has applications installed on it, you should remove them and then reinstall them after you install Terminal Services. Click Next.

6. The next wizard page relates to a new user authentication feature provided by Windows Server 2008. Users running Windows Vista (which can take advantage of this new authentication method) who connect to a Terminal Services server running Windows Server 2008 can be authenticated using Network Level Authentication. This authentication method authenticates the user before a Remote Desktop connection is established. This provides better security for the server and also doesn't initially require all that many resources to perform the authentication. Click Require Network Level Authentication to enable the feature. Otherwise, click Do Not Require Network Level Authentication (see Figure 19.1). Then click Next.

Windows Vista is currently (at the time this book was written) the only client OS that can take advantage of Network Level Authentication. If you are going to want clients running earlier versions of Windows to access the Terminal Services server, don't enable the Network Level Authentication feature on the server.

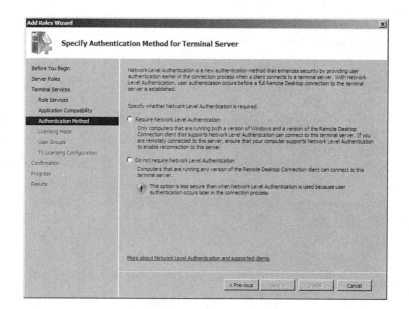

FIGURE 19.1
You can enable
(or disable) the
Network Level
Authentication
feature.

7. On the next page (if you chose to install the TS Licensing service on this
server), you must specify the TS Licensing mode you will use on the Terminal
Services server. You can select one of the following options: Configure Later
(you have 120 days to test Terminal Services), Per Device (each device must
have a TS license), or Per User (each user must have a TS license). Select an
option and then click Next.

8. On the next wizard page, you are asked to provide the user groups that will be
authorized to connect to this terminal server. The Administrators group has
been added by default; click the Add button to add other groups as needed.
After adding the groups, click Next.

9. The next page requires that you specify the discovery scope of the TS Licensing
server (see Figure 19.2): This Domain or The Forest. This Domain enables any
terminal servers in the domain to use the Licensing server, and the The Forest
option enables any terminal servers in the forest to use the Licensing server.
Select an option.

This page also enables you to specify the location of the TS licensing database
on the server. Use the Browse button to specify a path (other than the default
location provided). Then click Next.

FIGURE 19.2
Set options for
the TS
Licensing
service.

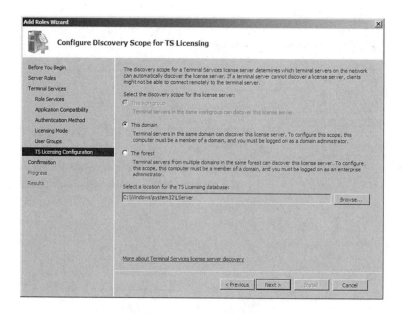

10. The Confirmation page for the Terminal Services installation appears. Click
Install.

When the installation is complete, you need to restart the server. Click Close and
then Yes. After the server has rebooted, you need to close the wizard window (click
Close).

Working with Terminal Services Licensing

An important aspect of providing Terminal Services to clients is licensing. Each
client that connects to the terminal server must have a license. Whether you install
the TS Licensing service on the terminal server (as we did in the previous section) or
on another server in the domain, you need to configure TS licensing and add licenses to the TS Licensing service. Terminal Services licenses are not the same as the
licenses that are used to license your Windows Server 2008 network clients. When a
Terminal Services client requests a connection to the terminal server, it is provided a
license by the license server. As discussed during installation of the sample terminal
server, the licensing mode can be per device or per user.

If you did not select a licensing mode (meaning you set licensing for the 120-day evaluation), during the installation of the TS Licensing service you can set the mode in the Terminal Services Configuration snap-in. In the Server Manager, expand the Terminal Services node (expand the Roles node first) and then select the Terminal Services Configuration node. In the Details pane is an Edit Settings area, and a subset of this Edit Settings area is designated as Licensing (see Figure 19.3).

Terminal servers that are not supported by a terminal server license server do not provide connections to clients beyond the 120-day evaluation period. So, you must configure a license server on the network (and purchase licenses) if you really plan to use a terminal server as a network connectivity option.

By the Way

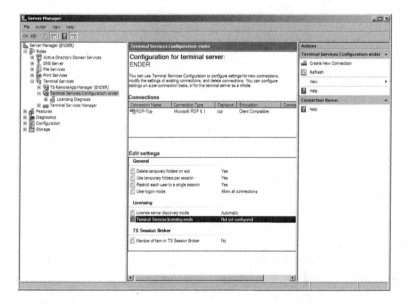

FIGURE 19.3
The Licensing settings in the Terminal Services Configuration Details pane.

Right-click the Terminal Services licensing mode and then select Properties. On the Licensing tab of the Properties dialog box, select Device or Per User. You can also specify the license server discovery mode on the Licensing tab. Select Automatically Discover a License Server if you want the terminal server to find a TS license server automatically. Or you can use the Use the Specified License Servers option. Selecting this option requires you to specify the name or names of the TS Licensing servers you will use.

When you have completed configuring the license mode, click OK. You will be returned to the Terminal Services Configuration snap-in.

Now you need to activate the TS Licensing server and then add licenses to the server. To activate the TS Licensing server, open the TS Licensing Manager as shown in Figure 19.4 (Start, Administrative Tools, Terminal Services, TS Licensing Manager).

FIGURE 19.4
Open the TS Licensing Manager.

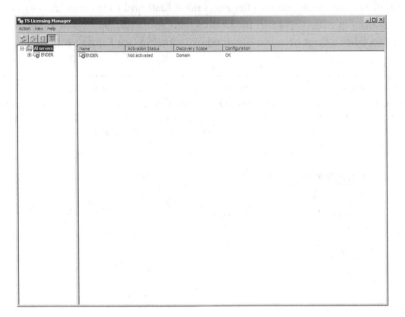

Right-click the server (your Licensing server) in the Details pane and select Active Server. The Active Server Wizard opens.

Click Next to bypass the first wizard page. On the next page, select the connection for license server activation. This connection mode is also used to contact the Microsoft Clearing House where TS licenses are stored. The connection possibilities are Automatic Connection, Web Browser, and Telephone. The Automatic Connection option is the recommended connection mode.

Select a connection (such as Automatic) and then click Next. On the next screen provide your name, company information, and country (or region). Then click Next. On the next page, you can provide optional information such as an email address and company address. Click Next. The server is activated.

When activation is complete, the Activate Server Wizard supplies a summary screen letting you know that the license server has been activated. It also provides you with the option of starting the Install Licenses Wizard (by default). Let's go ahead and look at how a TS license is installed. Click Next.

You can bypass the first wizard page by clicking Next. On the next page, select a license program in the drop-down list box provided (see Figure 19.5).

FIGURE 19.5
Select the license program.

Click Next. On the next page provide your license code and add the code to the License Codes Entered box. Click Next. On the next screen, you are asked to supply the product version for the license (such as Windows Server 2008) and whether the licenses are per device or per user. You also are asked to supply the number of licenses that you have purchased. After you supply this information, click Next to continue; the licenses are installed. Click Finish to close the wizard.

You are returned to the Terminal Server Licensing snap-in. You can add additional licenses at any time by right-clicking the Licensing Server icon and then selecting Install Licenses.

A new utility provided by the Terminal Server Configuration snap-in is the Licensing Diagnosis tool. You can click the Licensing Diagnosis node in the Terminal Server Configuration snap-in (in the MMC or the Server Manager). Any warnings related to problems with the Licensing server are displayed in the Details pane. Other information provided includes the licensing mode and the connection mode for the TS Licensing server.

By the Way

Configuring the Terminal Server and TS Connections

After you've activated the TS Licensing server and added TS licenses, you are ready to configure the terminal server and the connections provided by the server.

However, before you work with terminal server configuration and connection settings, you may want to install the Desktop Experience on the terminal server. When a user uses Remote Desktop Connection to connect to a terminal server, the desktop currently on the terminal server is reproduced for that user. The Desktop Experience feature provides applications found in Windows Vista, such as the Windows Media Player and the Windows Calendar; using Desktop Experience provides a somewhat more familiar and user-oriented desktop for the remote user.

Follow these steps:

1. In the Server Manager's node tree (if necessary open the Server Manager using the icon on the Quick Launch bar), click the Features node to select it.

2. In the Features Summary area, click Add Features. The Add Features Wizard opens.

3. Select the Desktop Experience check box (see Figure 19.6). Then click Next.

FIGURE 19.6
Select the
Desktop
Experience
feature.

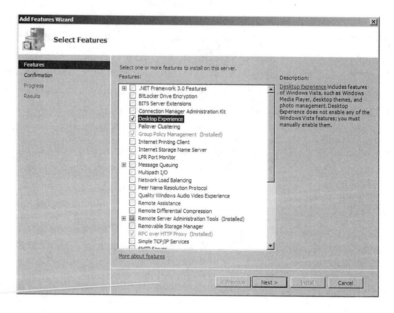

4. The Confirmation page appears. Click Install.

5. After the installation is complete, click the Close button and then click Yes to restart the server.

After your terminal server restarts, you are ready to work with terminal server tools. Let's look at server settings and then TS connection settings.

TS Server Settings

The Terminal Server settings can be accessed in the Terminal Services Configuration snap-in. You can access this snap-in in the Server Manager or the MMC (Start, Administrative Tools, Terminal Services, Terminal Services Configuration).

Click the Terminal Services Configuration node (in the snap-in). The TS server settings appear in the Details pane (see Figure 19.7).

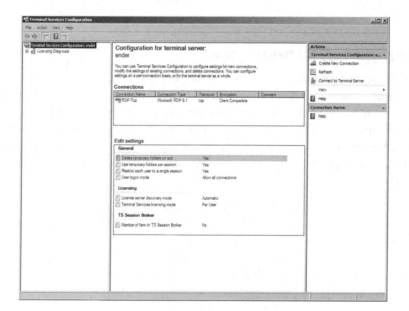

FIGURE 19.7
TS Server configuration settings.

These settings basically provide the environment that terminal server clients experience when connected. The settings also provide some housekeeping duties, such as cleaning up temporary folders created during terminal server sessions.

Many of these settings are Yes or No propositions; you are turning a particular server setting either on or off (or enabling or disabling the feature). The following are the Terminal Server settings available:

▶ **Delete Temporary Folders on Exit**—By default, temporary folders created during the Terminal Services session are deleted. If you want to save temporary folders created, you can disable this setting.

▶ **Use Temporary Folders Per Sessions**—By default, temporary folders are used during Terminal Services sessions. This setting can be disabled by accessing the setting's Properties dialog box.

▶ **License Server Discovery Mode**— The default discovery mode is Automatic; you can change this mode by specifying TS Licensing servers.

▶ **Terminal Services Licensing Mode**—Your selected mode (either Per Device or Per User) is listed.

You can change any of these settings as needed. Right-click the setting in the Details pane and select Properties. The Properties dialog box opens and you can edit the settings.

Configuring Connections

By default, a connection is created when you install the Terminal Services features on a server. The default connection is designated as RDP-tcp. This connection should be sufficient for all your remote connection users (although you can add additional connections if you feel that it is necessary). To view the properties for the default connection, right-click the connection in the Terminal Services Configuration snap-in Details pane and select Properties. The Properties dialog box for the connection opens (see Figure 19.8).

FIGURE 19.8
The connection's Properties dialog box.

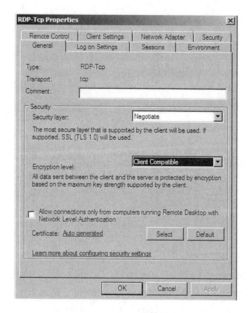

The Properties dialog box for a terminal server connection consists of a number of different tabs. These tabs are used to configure the connection as follows:

▶ **General**—This tab shows the connection type and the connection's transport protocol. You have the option of entering a comment related to the connection. This tab also enables you to set the encryption method used when data is sent between the Terminal Services server and the client. The Client Compatible setting uses encryption embraced by the client operating system used to make the connection.

▶ **Remote Control**—This tab (by default) enables you to control or observe a user's remote session. You control the session with the Terminal Service Manager (discussed later in the hour). This tab also provides the options of only shadowing users to observe their session.

▶ **Logon Settings**—This tab provides a default setting of having all terminal server users connect using client-provided logon information. This means that the user would provide a domain username and password to log on (when using the Remote Desktop Connection client, discussed later in the hour). The other option provided is to set up the connection so that only one username and password is used by all clients. This enables all users to log on with the same name and password.

▶ **Client Settings**—This tab enables you to configure the color depth used on the client monitor and the redirection settings related to the client, including the user's ability to map drives, connect to printers, and redirect audio.

▶ **Sessions**—This tab enables you to override user settings, such as setting time limits for ending a disconnected session, setting a time limit for connection sessions, or setting an idle session time limit. If you select the Override User Settings options, you set the time limits in a series of drop-down boxes.

▶ **Network Adapter**—This tab enables you to select the network adapter (or adapters) that you want to bind to the terminal server transport protocol. You can choose to have all adapters configured with the protocol or specify a single adapter to be configured with the protocol.

▶ **Environment**—This tab enables you to specify that a particular program start when users log on to the connection. This is particularly useful when you are using Terminal Services to provide access to an application such as Microsoft Word. Word could be started automatically when clients connect to the terminal server.

▶ **Security**—This tab is used to set the permission levels for groups or users that are to access the terminal server. Rather than set permissions in this tab, it is advised that you add users to the Remote Desktop Users group and edit permissions on the Remote tab of the System Properties dialog box.

After you have edited any connection settings, you can close the Properties dialog box. Click OK. This returns you to the Terminal Services Configuration snap-in.

Using the Terminal Services Manager

The Terminal Services Manager enables you to view information related to your terminal server or servers, such as users' sessions. This snap-in also provides you with the capability to end sessions, log off users, and send messages to users. You can run the Terminal Services Manager in the Server Manager or the MMC (Start, Administrative Tools, Terminal Services, Terminal Services Manager). When the snap-in opens, you receive a message that remote control and connect is not available if you are running the snap-in in a console session (meaning that you are using it to view the local server rather than to connect to a remote server). Figure 19.9 shows the Terminal Services Manager snap-in.

FIGURE 19.9
You can manage user connections in the Terminal Services Manager.

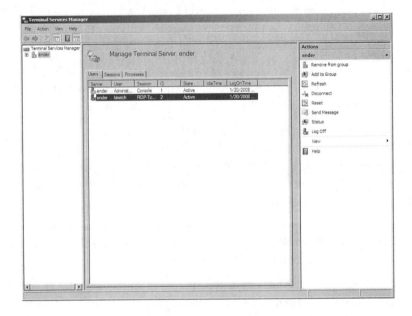

When you select the terminal server in the node tree, the users currently connected to the server are shown in the Details pane (as shown in Figure 19.9). You can disconnect sessions, log off users, and send messages to users. Each of these tasks is quickly accomplished in the Details pane.

For example, if you want to log off a particular user, select a user session and then select Logoff in the Actions pane. Click OK when the Logoff message box appears.

Logging a user off actually closes down the applications and other services that were being used by that particular user.

The Terminal Services Manager also makes it easy for you to quickly communicate with attached users. You can actually send messages to a user (or send a message to multiple connected users) on the network. Select a user or users and then click Send Message in the Actions pane. The Send Message window opens (see Figure 19.10).

FIGURE 19.10
You can send messages to users.

Type your message and then click OK. The message appears on the user's remote desktop connection window.

You can also view the status of a particular session. This enables you to view the bytes and frames sent and received between the client and the server, and also to view the number of bad frames that have passed between the two (many bad frames can be the indication of a problem). To view the status of a session, select the Session tab in the Details pane. Then right-click the session then select Status from the shortcut menu.

Did you Know?

When you have completed monitoring and managing the sessions on your terminal server, you can close the snap-in. Click the Close button in the upper right of the MMC (or select another role in the Server Manager).

Connecting to the Terminal Server

Terminal server clients use the Remote Desktop client to connect to a terminal server. This client is built into Windows clients such as Windows XP and Windows Vista, and is also available on server platforms such as Windows Server 2008. You can download and install the most recent version of Remote Desktop to client computers by searching http://www.microsoft.com for the latest update.

Connecting to a terminal server is really quite easy for your network users. Because they have a domain username and the appropriate password, they can open the Remote Desktop window and then log on to the terminal server. You can designate the terminal server by using the server name or the server's IP address. Let's look at connecting a Windows Vista Remote Desktop client to a Windows Server 2008 terminal server.

In Windows Vista, select Start, All Programs, Accessories, Remote Desktop Connection. The Remote Desktop Connection window opens (see Figure 19.11).

FIGURE 19.11
The Remote Desktop Connection client enables a user to connect to the terminal server.

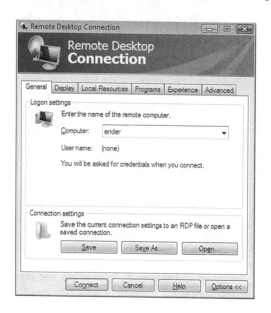

The Remote Desktop Connection client consists of six tabs:

▶ **General**—This tab (shown in Figure 19.11) enables you to specify the name (or IP address) of the terminal server. Save the connection settings by clicking the Save As button.

▶ **Display**—This tab enables you to set the display resolution and colors that will be provided by the terminal server. Colors can range from 256 to Highest Quality.

By the Way

The screen colors and resolution achieved by the client depend on the threshold that you set when you configured the terminal server settings.

▶ **Local Resources**—This tab is used to configure settings such as whether sounds should be played on the local computer or left on the server (when they are accessed, they are played locally on the client). Keyboard hotkeys such as Alt+Tab can also be configured to act locally or on the terminal server. Local devices and resources can also be enabled or disabled on this tab, such as Printers and the Clipboard.

▶ **Programs**—This tab enables you to specify an application (and path) to start automatically when the connection is made to the terminal server.

▶ **Experience**—This tab enables you to configure the connection experience for the client. A higher speed presents more features in the terminal server experience, such as presenting the desktop background and menu and window animation.

After the Remote Desktop Connection client is configured, it can connect to a terminal server. This is just a matter of clicking the Connect button (after the computer name has been entered on the General tab, which then must be followed by the entering of a username and password). Figure 19.12 shows a connection to a terminal server.

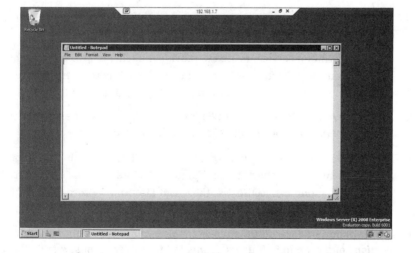

FIGURE 19.12
A connection to a terminal server.

The software resources that Remote Desktop Connection client can access depends on the applications that you have installed on your server. Remember to install applications on the terminal server after you have installed the Terminal Services role and configured the Terminal Server.

Summary

A terminal server provides a desktop environment and applications to thin clients. Windows Server 2008 Terminal services can provide remote connections to clients running Windows and the Macintosh operating system.

Windows Server 2008 Terminal Services provides the terminal server functionality that enables a server to function as an application server. For a terminal server to function, you must configure a TS Licensing server in the domain. The TS Licensing server can be the terminal server (configured with the TS Licensing service) or another server in the domain. TS licensing is configured and managed in the TS Licensing Manager.

Terminal server and connection settings are configured in the Terminal Services Configuration snap-in. The Terminal Services Manager enables you to monitor and control connections from remote users. Client computers need the Remote Access Connection client to connect to Terminal Services on the network. Users can log on with their domain usernames and passwords.

Q&A

Q. *What Windows Server 2008 service can be used to accommodate thin clients with a Windows desktop environment and user applications?*

A. Windows Terminal Services is used to provide thin clients with minimal hardware configurations with a desktop and application environment that keeps application processing and data storage on the terminal server.

Q. *Running Terminal Services on a Windows domain also requires what type of server to handle the licensing of Terminal Services clients?*

A. A terminal server license server holds the clients' licenses for the Terminal Services clients that connect to your domain terminal servers. Each client requires a client access license. Use the Client Licensing Wizard to record these licenses on the terminal server License server.

Q. *What Windows Server 2008 snap-in enables you to view and manage connections and even log off users connected to the terminal server?*

A. The Terminal Services Manager enables you to view connections to the terminal server and view user sessions. You can manage connections and sessions and even send messages to connected users with the Terminal Services Manager. The snap-in can also be used to monitor remote terminal servers on the network.

HOUR 20

Understanding WINS

What You'll Learn in This Hour:

▶ Understanding WINS and NetBIOS

▶ Installing and Configuring WINS

▶ WINS Configuration Issues

▶ Adding Replication Partners

▶ Managing the WINS Database

▶ Configuring WINS Clients

▶ Avoiding WINS Problems

▶ Using NBTSTAT

This hour looks at the Windows Internet Naming Service (WINS) and issues related to use of the NetBIOS interface, NetBIOS services, NetBIOS names, and NetBIOS name-to-IP-address resolution.

Understanding WINS and NetBIOS

The Network Basic Input/Output System (NetBIOS) was developed in 1983 and used by IBM as a way for computer applications to communicate over a network. NetBIOS is also firmly ingrained into all Microsoft operating systems that have come before the Windows 2000 series. Legacy software applications may also rely on NetBIOS for locating resources on the network.

NetBIOS provides a way for identifying resources on a network (such as a printer, file server, and so on). All devices running on the network are assigned a unique 16-byte name that defines the particular computer or printer to the network (or a service on a computer—this means that a single computer may provide services identified by different NetBIOS names). NetBIOS names are typically assigned when you install a particular operating system on a computer. Down-level operating systems such as Windows NT all request that a unique, 15-character NetBIOS name be entered for the computer during the installation process of the OS. When you install Windows on a computer, a computer name is created for that computer. If you change the hostname and the name is fewer than 15 characters, it also becomes the NetBIOS name for the computer (otherwise, the hostname is truncated to a 15-character NetBIOS name).

In fact, NetBIOS names are 16 characters long. The last character is used by the computer's operating system to specify the special functions of certain computers such as domain controllers and browsers.

Even though the default networking protocol for Windows Server 2008 is TCP/IP and the primary name-resolution strategy is DNS, an important issue related to NetBIOS names rears its head on your Windows Server 2008 domain. Applications that still use NetBIOS for identifying other computers and resources on the network must have a way of resolving these NetBIOS names to IP addresses. This process is cleverly called *NetBIOS name resolution*. NetBIOS is also required in the networking environment for NetBIOS-dependent applications.

NetBIOS Broadcasts

When a computer seeks to resolve a NetBIOS name to an IP address, it sends a NetBIOS broadcast. Because the name-resolution request takes the form of a broadcast message, it is sent to all nodes on the local subnet (the subnet being a particular segment on a routed network).

For example, imagine a computer named Kirk wants to send data to a computer named Spock. Kirk broadcasts that it would like to send data to Spock but does not know Spock's IP address. When Spock hears this broadcast (as do all nodes on the subnet), Spock sends a response providing Kirk with the IP address. Kirk can now proceed with establishing a network session with Spock and transferring data as needed.

Two obvious problems plague the use of broadcasts for NetBIOS name resolution. First, the broadcast messages clog your network with broadcast traffic, which sucks up your bandwidth. Another problem is that broadcast messages are not typically forwarded by routers on the network (unless the router has also been configured as a bridge). So, if a computer on one subnet uses a broadcast message to resolve a NetBIOS name for a computer that is on another subnet, the broadcast message is never forwarded to the intended target.

One strategy that has been worked out to cut down on the number of broadcast messages is as follows: After a computer has discovered the IP addresses of other computers on the segment through the use of broadcasts, these IP addresses are kept in a NetBIOS name cache on that computer. This cuts down on broadcasts in the case of "repeat" business with a particular computer or computers on the network.

You can view the NetBIOS name cache on a computer running Windows Server 2008 by using the NBTSTAT command. We discuss this command-line tool later in the hour.

Working with LMHOSTS Files

Another alternative for NetBIOS name resolution is to use an LMHOSTS file. The LMHOSTS file is a text file that lists the IP addresses of computers on the network followed by their NetBIOS name. LMHOSTS files are static and must be updated by the network administrator (that means you). And although they provide the computer with a quick way to look up an IP address based on a NetBIOS name, you must place them on each computer on the network (and whenever you add computers to the network, you also have to update all the LMHOSTS files on all the computers).

Some network administrators still use LMHOSTS files to resolve NetBIOS names to IP addresses on their networks. On a server running Windows Server 2008, the LMHOSTS file is kept in the \Windows\system32\drivers\etc folder. The basic structure of an LMHOSTS file is a two-column text file:

```
IP address   NetBIOS name
```

Windows 2008 actually provides a sample LMHOSTS file in the \windows\system32\drivers\etc folder. You can open it using Windows Notepad or another text editor.

Included in the Windows 2008 LMHOSTS file are explicit directions for building your own LMHOSTS lists. Pay special attention to the fact that descriptive entries in the file are always followed by the number sign (#). All other entries are read as mapping records.

> The major problem with LMHOSTS files is that they represent a fairly labor-intensive way to manage NetBIOS name resolution. If LMHOSTS files have been used on the network in the past, however, they can be integrated into the WINS database on your WINS server. An Import LMHOSTS File command is available on the WINS snap-in Action menu. We discuss the WINS snap-in later in the hour.

By the Way

Understanding NetBIOS Node Types

Before concentrating on the Windows Server 2008 WINS service and its installation and configuration, it is important to discuss the different node types that can exist in the NetBIOS environment. A node type simply refers to the way that a computer on the network registers with a NetBIOS name server (such as WINS) and seeks to resolve NetBIOS names to IP addresses. There are four node types, as described in Table 20.1.

TABLE 20.1   Node Types

Node Type	Description
B	The client uses broadcast messages for name registration and name resolution.
P	The client uses unicast (directly to the server's IP address) messages to a NetBIOS name server for both name registration and NetBIOS name resolution.
H	A hybrid node type, these clients use unicast messages to the NetBIOS name server for registration and resolution. If they cannot find a NetBIOS name server (a WINS server), the client resorts to broadcast messages for registration and resolution.
M	Clients use broadcasts for name registration and for name resolution. However, if the name cannot be resolved by broadcast, the client attempts to contact a NetBIOS name server.

Windows 2008 WINS clients (those configured for WINS) act as H nodes. They attempts to resolve names by using the WINS server first, and then they resort to broadcasts if a WINS server is not available. As a last resort, these clients consult their LMHOSTS file if one is available locally.

Deploying a WINS Server

The most foolproof method for dealing with NetBIOS naming issues is to deploy a WINS server (or servers) on your network. WINS provides the greatest amount of efficiency in terms of your network bandwidth. The series of steps that allows a WINS client to take advantage of the WINS server for NetBIOS name resolution is very straightforward:

   1. When a WINS client computer boots up, it registers its NetBIOS name and IP address with the WINS server.

2. When a WINS client on the network wants to communicate with a network resource designated by a particular NetBIOS name, it communicates with the WINS server to handle the NetBIOS name resolution of its intended target, rather than sending out a broadcast to all nodes on the segment.

3. The WINS server finds the appropriate mapping of NetBIOS-name-to-IP-address in its database and returns the IP address to the WINS client.

4. If the WINS client cannot contact the primary WINS server, the client makes two more attempts to contact the primary WINS server. Then it attempts to contact the secondary WINS server if one has been designated in the TCP/IP properties for the client (or if the client is a DHCP client with multiple WINS servers configured).

5. If the secondary WINS server (or other WINS server because the client attempts to contact WINS servers in the order designated in the TCP/IP properties) can handle the request, no problem. However, if the client cannot contact any designated WINS server, the client resorts to a network broadcast. If a number of WINS servers are available on the network, the chances of the client having to resort to a broadcast message are slim.

The great thing about WINS is that the database compiled by the server is dynamic. The WINS clients actually register with the server, supplying the entries in the WINS database. This is similar to the way that Dynamic DNS (DDNS) works, however WINS does not provide a mechanism for secure updates as DDNS does. Any computer configured to use a WINS server can register itself in the WINS database.

By the Way

A WINS client is actually a network client running any Windows operating system that has the IP address of the primary WINS server configured as part of its TCP/IP properties. A WINS client can also be set up when you use a DHCP server and configure the WINS server IP address with the other DHCP client information. (DHCP is discussed in Hour 16, "Using the Dynamic Host Configuration Protocol.") WINS client configuration is discussed later in the hour.

Installing and Configuring WINS

WINS can be installed on any computer that runs Windows Server 2008 (but you might not want to overburden your domain controllers by placing WINS on them). Before you install the WINS component, make sure that the server is configured with static IP address and a default gateway. (TCP/IP settings for a server are discussed in Hour 2, "Installing and Configuring Windows Server 2008.")

WINS is installed as a feature. You can open the Add Features from the Initial Configuration Tasks window or the Server Manager.

To install WINS, follow these steps:

1. In the Initial Configuration Tasks window (or with the Features node selected in Server Manager), click the Add Features link. The Add Features Wizard opens (see Figure 20.1).

FIGURE 20.1
WINS is added via the Add Features Wizard.

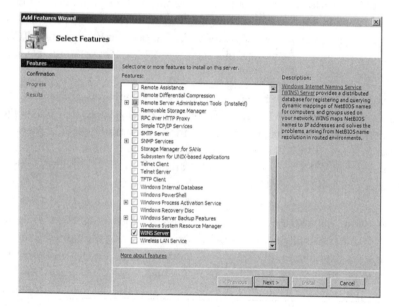

2. Select WINS Server in the features list. Then click Next to continue.

3. The next screen confirms that WINS Server will be installed. Click Install.

4. The final wizard screen lists the features that were installed, in this case WINS Server, and whether or not the installation succeeded. Click Close to close the wizard window.

After the WINS installation is complete, the WINS Server feature is listed in the Customize This Server area of the Initial Configuration Tasks window. You can also view the features installed on the server in the Server Manager (Start, Administrative Tools, Server Manager).

Expand the Features node in the Server Manager Node pane. WINs is listed as a feature. Select WINS in the node tree and the Active Registrations and Replication Partners folders appears (see Figure 20.2).

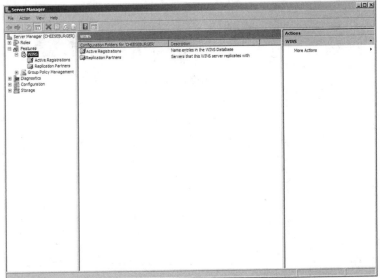

FIGURE 20.2
The WINS feature can be managed via the Server Manager window.

You can manage WINS from the WINS Server Manager snap-in. You can also run the WINS snap-in in the Microsoft Management Console. The WINS configuration discussion that follows uses the WINS snap-in in the MMC.

> The WINS snap-ins provided in the Server Manager and the MMC respectively differ slightly in the nodes and icons that appear in the Node pane. The WINS snap-in in the MMC actually requires a little less overhead to run because it does not track events and multiple roles and features (as well as installed services) as the Server Manager does.

By the Way

WINS Configuration Issues

After you add the WINS Server feature to your Windows Server installation, you can view the status of the service and configure various WINS features.

You start the WINS snap-in (in the MMC) by selecting Start, Administrative Tools, WINS. Figure 20.3 shows the WINS snap-in in the MMC.

When you select the Server Status icon in the Node pane (on the left of the window), the server status is displayed in the Details pane (refer to Figure 20.3). The status of the server is updated every five minutes. If you wish to change the update status, right-click the Server Status icon and then click Properties on the shortcut menu. Change the time interval in the Update status box and then click OK.

FIGURE 20.3
WINS is managed in the WINS snap-in.

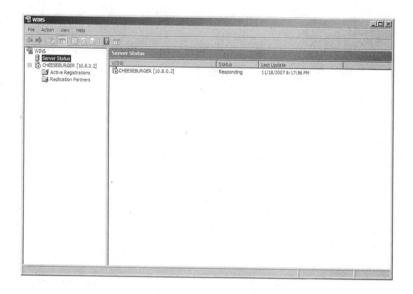

The WINS snap-in also enables you to configure replication partners (which are other WINS servers on the network) and manage WINS records. You can also manually add static mappings (NetBIOS-to-IP mappings) or delete records in the WINS database.

Settings related to the operation of the WINS server can also be configured in the WINS snap-in. Select the WINS Server node (identified by the name you gave your server when you installed Windows) in the node list of the snap-in. Then right-click the Server icon and select Properties. The Properties dialog box for the server opens.

The WINS server's Properties dialog box has four tabs:

- ▶ **General**—On this tab, you can set the time interval for when to update the WINS statistics. The default is set at every 10 minutes. You can also specify the default path that you want to use for backing up the WINS server.

- ▶ **Intervals**—This tab (see Figure 20.4) is where you control the time interval for settings related to how records in the database are handled. Settings include Renew Interval, Extinction Interval, Extinction Timeout, and Verification Interval.

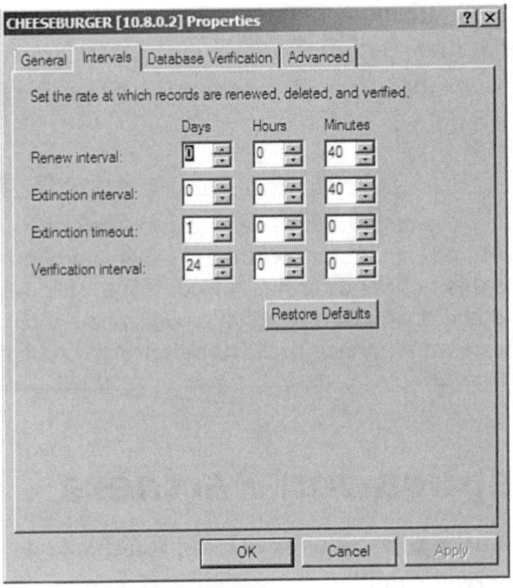

FIGURE 20.4
The Intervals
tab is used to
set renew,
extinction, and
verification inter-
vals for the
WINS server.

▶ Renew Interval controls how often a WINS client renews its registration
of its name. Increasing this interval lessens the performance load on a
WINS server.

▶ Extinction Interval specifies the time interval between when an entry is
marked as Released and when it is marked as Extinct in the WINS database.

▶ Extinction Timeout determines when a record that has been marked as
Extinct is actually removed (also known as scavenging) from the database.

▶ Verification Interval specifies when the WINS server must verify the
names in the database that it has received from other WINS servers during replication.

▶ **Database Verification**—This tab allows you to enable the WINS server to
periodically verify its database with a remote WINS server. This setting basically allows you to check the consistency of a WINS server on a large network.

▶ **Advanced**—This tab allows you to enable event logging of WINS events to
the Windows system log (accessed through the Event Viewer, discussed in Hour
24, "Monitoring Server Performance and Network Connections"). You can also
change the setting for the Enable Burst Handling feature. This feature, which
can be configured as Low, Medium, High, or a custom setting, sets the number
of requests that the WINS server can handle at one time. The default setting is
Medium.

Although you can configure many of these parameters in the WINS snap-in, Microsoft recommends that you attempt to run your WINS implementation with the default settings. This provides you with a performance baseline for WINS, which you can then fine-tune if required.

Did you Know?

> To determine whether the default WINS settings work best for your network, use the Reliability and Performance Monitor (the Reliability and Performance Monitor is discussed briefly in this hour and further in Hour 24) to take a look at parameters such as CPU usage and disk I/O. Upgrading server memory or using a RAID stripe set can often enhance performance of WINS better than changing WINS settings.

Adding Replication Partners

On large networks that require the WINS service, you should deploy more than one WINS server. These servers can then share the WINS database information as replication partners. This provides load balancing for the WINS database and also helps conserve bandwidth across slower WAN connections. (A single WINS server would tie up bandwidth when communicating with NetBIOS clients.)

Designating replication partners for your WINS server and then synchronizing the databases is a very straightforward process. Follow these steps:

1. In the WINS snap-in, expand the node icon that represents your WINS server. Then right-click the Replication Partners subfolder in the node pane. Point at New on the shortcut menu that appears, and select New Replication Partner.

2. The New Replication Partner dialog box opens (see Figure 20.5). Enter the name or IP address of the server that you want to add as a partner (you can also use the Browse button to locate the server on the network).

3. Click OK to designate the partner. Repeat the process as needed to add replication partners.

To view the replication partners, double-click the Replication Partners icon. A list of all added partners appears in the Details pane, as shown in Figure 20.6.

FIGURE 20.5
Replication partners can be added for your WINS server.

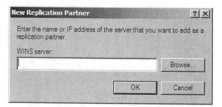

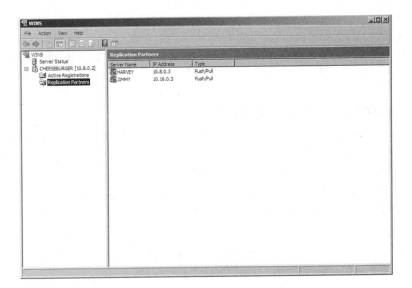

To start the replication between your WINS server and its partners on the network, right-click the Replication Partners icon and then point at All Tasks on the shortcut menu. Select Replicate Now. You are asked whether you want to replicate the WINS database. Click Yes to continue.

You are told that the replication request has been queued on the server. You can check to see when the replication actually takes place, using the Windows Event Viewer (which, again, is discussed in Hour 24).

> By default, a persistent connection is set up between WINS replication partners. This means that replication partners maintain an open line of communication between them on the network. This negates the need for setting up and closing a connection during replication, which can use up network bandwidth.

Managing the WINS Database

The WINS snap-in provides you with a monitoring tool that can be used to view the mappings that are dynamically placed in the WINS database by communication between WINS clients and the WINS server. In the WINS snap-in, double-click the Active Registrations folder. The current mappings in the database appear in the Details pane.

The WINS snap-in also provides you with the management tools that enable you to manipulate the WINS database and keep it healthy. You can use the WINS snap-in to add static records to the database, delete records, and even back up the WINS database.

Creating Static Mappings

You can add static WINS records to the WINS database. This is useful when you need to support non-WINS clients (computers running operating systems that you cannot configure to take advantage of WINS).

In the WINS snap-in, right-click Active Registrations and select New Static Mapping from the shortcut menu. In the Static Mapping dialog box (see Figure 20.7), provide the name and IP address of the computer.

Use the Type drop-down list to select the type of static mapping you are creating. Table 20.2 defines the different static mapping types available.

TABLE 20.2 Node Types

Mapping Type	Description
Unique	Used to associate a single IP address with a computer name.
Group	Used to include a computer that is already specified in a static mapping as part of a Windows workgroup.
Domain Name	Used to map a domain name to a Windows NT domain controller IP addresses.
Internet Group	Used to group resources on the network under a group name. IP addresses are mapped to resource IP addresses in the static mapping.
Multihomed	Used to create a static mapping of multiple IP addresses (up to 25) to one NetBIOS name.

After specifying the static mapping type, click OK. The mapping becomes part of the WINS database.

By the Way

> The NetBIOS name can be up to 15 characters, but a sixteenth character in hexadecimal format indicates the resource type. For example, when the Unique type is used to create a static mapping, actually three records are added to the WINS database: [00h] WorkStation, 03hMessenger, and 20h File Server.

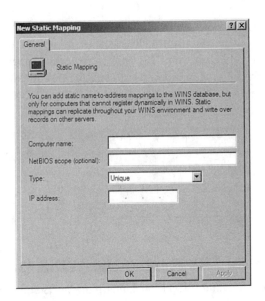

FIGURE 20.7
You can create static mappings in the WINS snap-in.

Deleting or Tombstoning Mappings

You can view the active registrations for the WINS server. Click the Active Registrations folder (in the Node pane) and the active registrations appear in the Details window (see Figure 20.8). You can delete or tombstone records from the WINS database. When you tombstone a record, it is removed from all replication partners the next time the databases are synchronized.

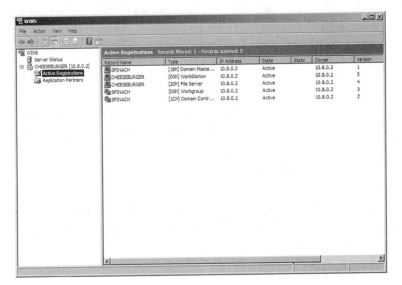

FIGURE 20.8
You can view the current records in the Active Registrations folder.

Right-click a particular record in the database (in the Details pane) and then select Delete (see Figure 20.9). If you want to delete the record on just this server, select the option Delete the Record Only from This Server. If you want to remove the record from all WINS servers on the network, select Replicate Deletion of the Record to Other Servers (Tombstone). After making your selection, click OK.

Backing Up and Restoring the WINS Database

Another aspect of managing WINS is backing up the WINS database. Because the WINS database is constantly changing as a result of the dynamic registration process (WINS clients communicate with the server to set up their records), there can be file corruption. So, it makes sense to back up the WINS database periodically. Then if you are experiencing difficulties with the WINS service, you can restore the database file.

The backup of the WINS server is automatic after you specify a location for the database. To configure the backup of the WINS database, follow these steps:

1. In the WINS snap-in, right-click the WINS Server node icon and then select Properties from the shortcut menu that appears. The Properties dialog box appears (see Figure 20.10).

2. Specify a path for the backup (you can use the Browse button) in the Default Backup Path box.

3. If you want, you can select the option Back Up Database During Server Shutdown. This backs up the WINS database whenever you shut down the WINS server.

4. Click OK to close the Properties dialog box.

The WINS database is backed up by default every three hours. The WINS database, wins.mdb, is placed in a \wins_back\new folder that is created in the path that you specified for the backup.

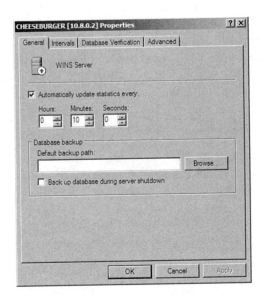

FIGURE 20.10
Specify a location for the WINS backup.

> To manually back up the server, right-click your WINS Server icon and select Back Up Database. The Browse for Folder dialog box opens; use it to specify the folder for the backup. Then click to back up the WINS database.

Did you Know?

Now that you have a backup of your WINS server, when you begin to have problems with the service and suspect database corruption, you can restore the WINS database. First you must stop the WINS service. Right-click your WINS Server icon in the snap-in tree, point at the All Tasks selection on the shortcut menu, and then select Stop. This stops the WINS service (the green icon turns red).

To restore the database, right-click your WINS Server icon and select Restore Database. The Browse for Folder dialog box appears. Specify the folder that holds the backup file; then click OK. The database file is restored and the WINS service restarts.

Configuring WINS Clients

Another aspect of WINS is configuring WINS clients so that they use the service for NetBIOS name-to-IP resolution. Any Microsoft Windows client or server can be configured as a WINS client. And although each client operating system is configured for WINS in a slightly different way, you are basically providing the client with the IP address of your WINS server so that it will use it as a mapping resource of NetBIOS name to IP address rather than send broadcasts onto the network.

Figure 20.11 shows the WINS tab of the Advanced TCP/IP settings for Windows Server 2008. To add the IP addresses of WINS servers, click the Add button and then supply the IP address of the WINS server (repeat if several WINS servers reside on the network). The WINS tab on a Windows Server 2008 is very similar to the tab that you find on Windows Vista, Windows XP, and Windows 2000 clients.

FIGURE 20.11
Both client computers and servers, such as this Windows server, can be configured as WINS clients.

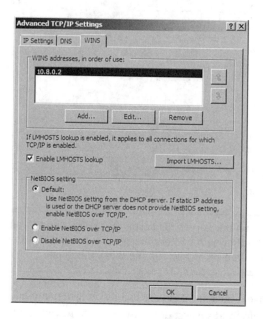

Remember that a WINS client is merely a computer that has been configured to take its NetBIOS name requests to the WINS server. DHCP clients can also be set up to use a specific WINS server and the IP address of the preferred WINS server can be broadcast to the DHCP client when the client renews its IP address.

By the Way

> WINS server information as well as preferred DNS settings can be configured for your DHCP clients in the DHCP snap-in. See Hour 16.

Avoiding WINS Problems

One way to avoid WINS-related problems (according to Microsoft) is to use the pre-configured WINS settings on a newly established WINS server. These settings should serve you well in most situations.

Microsoft also advises against using static WINS entries in the WINS database, although using static entries can protect you from conflicts related to the NetBIOS names of key servers on the network. You would not want an incorrectly configured client (as far as NetBIOS name goes) to come online on the network and register with the WINS database, negating the important resource server from using its configured name (which computers on the network use to get at resources on the server).

As far as an upper threshold goes for a WINS server, Microsoft says that one WINS server can accommodate around 10,000 WINS clients on a network. And if you are having problems with client connectivity, make sure that the client's TCP/IP properties have been configured so that the use of WINS servers has been enabled.

If you find that the best practices discussed in this hour still don't provide you with a smooth-running WINS deployment, you can monitor WINS performance and server performance by using the Reliability and Performance Monitor (which can be accessed in the Computer Management window; Start, Administrative Tools, Computer Management).

You may also want to log events related to the WINS service if you are troubleshooting a problematic WINS installation. To log detailed events related to WINS, right-click the WINS server node icon (it's the one with the server name and IP address) in the Node pane of the WINS snap-in. On the shortcut menu, select Properties.

Click the Advanced tab of the WINS server's Properties dialog box. Then select Log Detailed Events to Windows Event Log (see Figure 20.12).

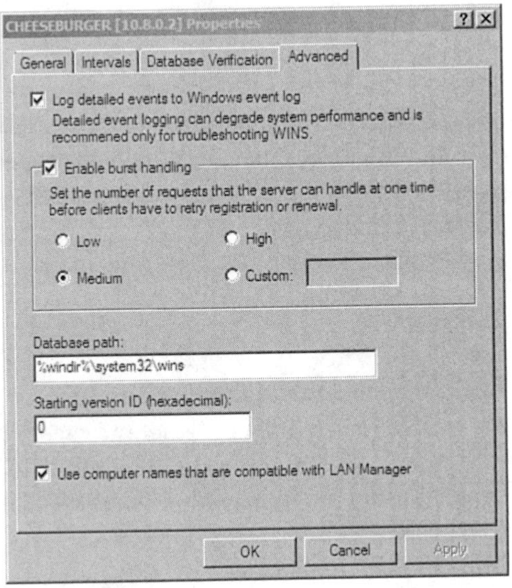

FIGURE 20.12
Select the Log Detailed Event to Windows Event Log check box.

This detailed logging can degrade the server's performance (as it says on the Advanced tab). So, you want to use this detailed logging only in cases where you are having problems with the WINS server and want to use the Event Viewer to ferret out the issues.

To start the Event Viewer select Start, Administrative Tools, and then Event Viewer. Expand the Windows Logs node and then select the System events folder. Figure 20.13 shows WINS-related errors in the System Log for a WINS server. (The log has been filtered for WINS; more about filtering logs in Hour 24.)

FIGURE 20.13
The Event Viewer can help you track down problems with your WINS server.

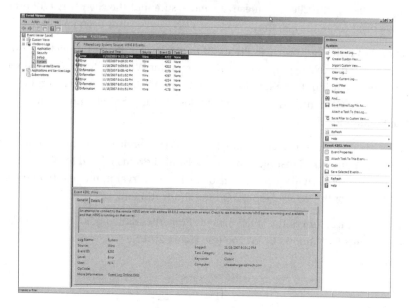

Both the Reliability and Performance Monitor and the Event Viewer are discussed in more detail in Hour 24. Also remember that a backup of the WINS database can be very useful when you are having problems with a single WINS server implementation if the database has become corrupt.

Using NBTSTAT

A useful command-line tool related to this discussion of NetBIOS and WINS is NBTSTAT. NBTSTAT can be used to determine whether the client's NetBIOS names are registered in the WINS database. It can also be used to release and renew a computer's NetBIOS names registered with the name server and to show a computer's current NetBIOS sessions.

To use NBTSTAT, follow these steps:

1. Open a command prompt window (Start, Command Prompt).

2. To view the local computer's locally registered NetBIOS names, type **nbtstat -n**.

3. Press Enter.

The NetBIOS local name table for the computer appears. Note that in Figure 20.14, two tables of NetBIOS names are provided: a table for each IP address assigned to the server.

FIGURE 20.14
NBTSTAT can be used to view the local NetBIOS names.

As already mentioned, NBTSTAT provides a number of different command extensions that enable you to view NetBIOS information and even renew name registrations or purge the computer's NetBIOS cache. Some of the more useful forms of the NBTSTAT command are as follows:

▶ NBTSTAT -c—Shows the name-to-address mapping for other computers found in the NetBIOS name cache.

▶ NBTSTAT -rr—Enables you to release the NetBIOS names of a client computer registered with a WINS server and renew the client computer's registration.

▶ NBTSTAT -s—Lists the current NetBIOS sessions (for the local computer and connected computers) and their status.

Other switches also are available for NBTSTAT. You can view all the different switches for the command; at the command line, type **nbtstat/help** and then press Enter.

Summary

In this hour, you learned how to install and configure the WINS service. NetBIOS is used by legacy Windows client operating systems and legacy applications to identify resources on the network. NetBIOS names must be resolved to IP addresses by these clients, which use broadcast messages for the resolution.

The Windows Internet Naming Service provides an environment in which a dynamic database is built that resolves NetBIOS names to IP addresses. WINS clients can then query the database for name resolution to identify resources on the network. Larger networks might require more than one WINS server, and these servers can be set up as replication partners, enabling them to share WINS database records. A WINS client is any computer that has been configured to use the WINS server for resolution of NetBIOS names to IP addresses. Windows clients and servers must have their TCP/IP properties configured so that they point at the WINS server or servers on the network. This configuration makes them WINS clients.

Q&A

Q. *What are three strategies available for resolving NetBIOS names to IP addresses?*

A. Resolving NetBIOS names to IP addresses can be handled by NetBIOS broadcasts and the storage of mappings in a computer's local cache. LMHOSTS files can also be deployed on computers to provide a static database of mappings of names to IP addresses. A dynamic database of mappings of NetBIOS names to IP addresses can be created if a WINS server is deployed in the domain.

Q. *What is required to implement WINS in a Windows domain?*

A. A server running WINS needs to be deployed in the domain. The client computers on the network must also be configured with the IP address of the WINS server. This makes them WINS clients. They then query the WINS server when they need to resolve a NetBIOS name to an IP address.

Q. *What is the best way to deploy WINS on a larger network that might use some WAN connections?*

A. It is a good practice to deploy more than one WINS server on the network. These WINS servers function as replication partners and share their databases. This cuts down on clients using slow WAN connections to reach a single WINS server in a domain. The presence of multiple WINS servers enables client computers to connect to the closest WINS server for name-resolution queries.

Q. *What tool is used to add static records to the WINS database, delete records, and back up the WINS database?*

A. The WINS snap-in enables you to both monitor and manage the WINS database.

PART IV

Network Security, Web Services, and Performance Monitoring

HOUR 21

Working with the Windows Firewall and IPSec

Protecting your network from outside attack is extremely important; particularly in situations where your private network is connected to a public network—the Internet. Windows Server 2008 provides a number of strategies for protecting your network data and this hour takes a look at the basics of working with the Windows Firewall and IPSec (IP Security Protocol).

Understanding the Windows Firewall

A firewall is best defined as hardware or software (or both) that is designed to sit between your computer (or network) and the Internet and protect the computer (or network) from outside attack. Firewalls examine data entering and leaving the internal network and can filter (meaning block or drop) the data traveling in both directions.

If data packets do not meet a particular rule that has been configured on the firewall, the data is not allowed to enter the internal network. Firewalls can also filter outgoing data and prevent data from leaving the internal network (meaning connections to the Internet via certain software can be controlled with a firewall).

Depending on the complexity of your network, you may already deploy a hardware firewall that sits as an intermediary device between your internal network and the Internet. Software firewalls, such as the Windows Firewall, are designed to provide security at the computer level. The "new" Windows Firewall available on servers running Windows Server 2008 and network clients running Windows Vista is a host-based solution for data filtering and protection from attacks both inside and outside the network.

The Windows Firewall is a stateful firewall, meaning it keeps track of the state of a computer's network connections as it examines both incoming and outgoing data packets. In terms of incoming data traffic, data that is considered unsolicited (meaning it is not the result of a request from the local computer for that data) is dropped by the firewall and so protects the host. The Windows Firewall can be configured with exceptions that allow some data traffic to be received by the host, based on an exception rule that is configured for particular software and ports.

In terms of outgoing data traffic, the Windows Firewall rules can also be configured to block specific outgoing traffic based on software and ports. This enables the network administrator to limit network communication to certain software. By default the Windows Firewall is configured to allow all outgoing connections.

The Windows Firewall can be configured locally on the host and you can also control its configuration by using policies via Group Policy, which provides a network administrator with a way to make the Windows Firewall configuration for network clients consistent throughout the network. Both Group Policy and Network Access Protection (both of which have settings related to the required use of Windows Firewall on clients and actual firewall settings) are covered in Hour 11, "Deploying Group Policy and Network Access Protection." This hour concentrates on firewall settings as they would be configured on the host (for example, a server running Windows Server 2008).

Configuring the Windows Firewall

Two different utilities are used to configure the Windows Firewall on a server running Windows Server 2008: the Windows Firewall Settings dialog box and the Windows Firewall with Advanced Security snap-in. Let's look at the Windows Firewall Settings dialog box first.

The Windows Firewall Settings dialog box provides access to only a somewhat basic collection of settings. For example, you can quickly turn the firewall on or off and set basic exceptions (in relation to software that allowed through the firewall). You can also select the network connections (if the server has multiple network adapters) that are protected by the firewall and specify the network connections you want protected by the firewall.

To open the Windows Firewall Settings dialog box, open the Control Panel (Start, Control Panel). Then select the Allow a Program Through the Windows Firewall link under the Security group. This opens the Windows Firewall Settings dialog box with the Exceptions tab selected (see Figure 21.1).

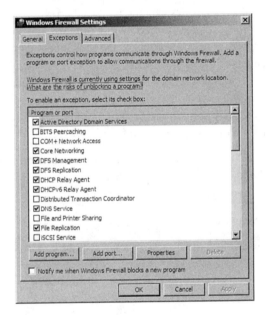

The Windows Firewall Settings dialog box.

The Windows Firewall Settings dialog box has three tabs:

- **General**—This tab enables you to turn the Firewall on or off (via the On and Off option buttons, respectively) and also provides a Block All Incoming Connections check box, which blocks all incoming connections (designed for connections to unsecured, public networks) and also ignores all exceptions that you have specified (discussed in a moment).

- **Exceptions**—This tab enables you to select from a list of default program exceptions. You can select a program from the list to add that exception. You can also add a program to the exceptions list by using the Add Program button. You can also open a port in the firewall with the Add Port button.

- **Advanced**—This tab enables you to select (or deselect) the network connection or connections (on the computer) that are protected by the firewall.

If you edited the exceptions for the Window Firewall and would like to return to your default settings, click Restore Defaults on the Advanced tab of the Windows Firewall Settings dialog box.

The Windows Firewall Settings dialog box provides you with a quick way to open a port or allow a particular application through the firewall. However, it is more of an end-user tool and is not designed for access to more advanced firewall settings.

In terms of working with the more advanced settings (basically meaning rules, which are really full-blown policies when taken together), you need use the Windows Firewall with Advanced Security, which can be configured for the Windows Firewall snap-in. This snap-in enables you to manage inbound and outbound rules that are preconfigured for the firewall. You can also create new inbound and outbound rules with the snap-in. You also have the option of creating connection security rules that enable you to restrict connections to a server, based on authentication requirements that include domain membership or other criteria such as health policies (health policies are discussed in Hour 11).

To open the Windows Firewall with Advanced Security, select Start, Administrative Tools, and then Windows Firewall with Advanced Security. The MMC opens, containing the snap-in (see Figure 21.2).

FIGURE 21.2
The Windows Firewall with Advanced Security snap-in.

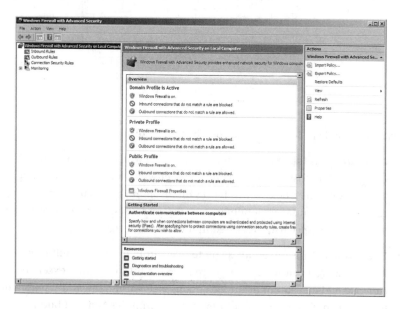

In the Details pane (when the Windows Firewall with Advanced Security on Local Computer node is selected) an Overview box provides a list of three firewall profiles: Domain, Public, and Private. These profiles relate to network connection types (and so have different settings based on the connection risks related to those network connection types) and are defined as follows:

- **Domain**—Computers running Windows Server 2008 and Windows Vista can recognize physical networks that are part of a domain. The domain connection profile on the firewall requires that computers be authenticated (in the domain) to access the domain controller. The domain network connection (or profile, if you prefer) is special in that it refers to a logical network rather than a physical network such as the public and private profiles that defined in a moment.

- **Public**—The public profile is used by the firewall to protect the computer when it is on a public network. A public network connection would be any connection that you make in a public place (via Wi-Fi). Because a server running Windows Server 2008 is typically not a device that you take on the road with you, the public connection refers to any connection that is not on your local and secure network, meaning the network that sits behind your perimeter firewall.

- **Private**—The private profile is used by the firewall to protect the computer when it uses a private connection, meaning a network protected by a hardware firewall.

As the network administrator (or at least the server administrator), you determine whether or not a new connection is public or private, and Windows Server 2008 asks you to identify the network as such (public or private) when you use the Connect to a Network task in the Network and Sharing Center. When the type of network to which the computer is connected is identified, Windows can optimize some of its configuration, especially its firewall configuration, for the specified network location type.

Because you have three potential profiles to work with (domain, public, and private) and each profile can have different settings in terms of firewall rules, you are provided a great deal of flexibility in terms of configuring the Windows Firewall. For example, any connections to a public network use the public network profile, which can be configured with a more robust and protective set of rules, whereas the private network profile could contain less restrictive rules related to such things as file and print sharing. Because the Windows Firewall on domain servers and on Windows network clients can ultimately be configured based on Group Policy (which is discussed in Hour 11), the overall flexibility of the firewall settings makes it easier for you to protect individual hosts on the network by using group policies that dictate specific firewall rules.

Before you consider how to configure the Windows Firewall and work with inbound or outbound rules, you need to understand how the connection type profiles are applied when the firewall examines network traffic. For computers that are part of a domain (both servers and clients), the domain profile is applied first (which really protects the domain controllers in the domain because authentication is required).

It then comes down to whether you apply the public or private profile. If the computer's network interface (or interfaces) is authenticated to a domain controller, the private profile is applied because the connection to the domain controller itself dictates that a trusted private network is in place. If the computer's interface is not authenticated to a domain controller, the public profile is applied.

Each of these network connection profiles can be configured separately. Let's look at the Windows Firewall Properties dialog box and then at firewall rules.

Configuring the Windows Firewall Properties

To open the Windows Firewall with Advanced Security properties dialog box, click the Windows Firewall Properties link in the Details pane (near the bottom of the Overview box). The Windows Firewall with Advanced Security (for the local computer) properties dialog box opens (see Figure 21.3).

FIGURE 21.3
The Windows Firewall properties dialog box.

The Windows Firewall with Advanced Security properties dialog box has a tab for each of the firewall profile types (or connection types, if you prefer) discussed in the previous section. As shown in Figure 21.3, you can see that the Domain Profile tab is currently configured with the firewall state for the profile set to On. Inbound connections are configured to be blocked by default, as specified by the Block setting (unless a firewall rule states otherwise). The Outbound connections are configured to be allowed, as specified by the Allow setting (again, unless you have a firewall rule that states otherwise).

The Private Profile and Public Profile tabs are configured exactly the same (by default) as the Domain Profile tab. You can see that the trick to strengthening a particular profile depends on the rules that you specify (or create) for that profile (as discussed in the next section).

A fourth tab, the IPSec Settings tab, is included on the Windows Firewall with Advanced Security properties dialog box. IPSec, or the IP Security Protocol, is discussed later in the hour.

Understanding Windows Firewall Rules

The Windows Firewall allows or denies network traffic based on the rules that have been created and configured for the firewall. You can create three types of rules: inbound rules, outbound rules, and connection security rules. Let's look at inbound and outbound rules and then at connection security rules, which are a slightly different animal.

Inbound rules are designed to "unblock" inbound traffic (connections) as defined by the rule. Remember that the default Inbound Connections setting for the three profile types (Domain, Private, and Public) is Block. Outbound rules are designed to "block" outbound connections as defined by a specific rule. The default setting for Outbound Connections is Allow, and so it makes sense that Outbound rules would need to negate this completely open doorway (in terms of outbound connections) by blocking the application or port traffic.

You can create four types of inbound or outbound rules. (The next section walks you through the actual steps of creating a rule.) These rule types are

▶ **Program**—This rule type allows a connection based on a program. You specify the program that needs the inbound or outbound connection (depending on whether you are creating an inbound or outbound rule) by specifying the path to the application's executable file (.exe).

▶ **Port**—This rule type allows a connection based on a port number (or a range of port numbers). You also specify the TCP/IP transport protocol, TCP or UDP, for the connection.

▶ **Predefined**—This rule type allows a connection based on one of the programs or services available on your computer (as provided by the Windows operating system you are using, such as Windows Server 2008). For example, you can create a rule (inbound or outbound) related to a Windows service, such as file and print sharing or the remote desktop.

▶ **Custom**—This rule type provides the greatest flexibility in creating a rule where you want to specify the application, services, port numbers, and protocols for a new rule. It also requires that you supply more information to create the rule than the other rule types available such as a program or port only rule.

It becomes fairly obvious when you open the Windows Firewall with Advanced Security snap-in and select either the Inbound Rules or the Outbound Rules node that a number of both inbound and outbound preconfigured rules are available by default. You can filter the rules list (for inbound or outbound) in the Details pane, making it easier to concentrate on rules that are for a certain connection profile or rules that are in a certain state (enabled or disabled).

With either the Inbound Rules or the Outbound Rules node selected, click Filter by Profile (Domain, Public, or Private) to filter the rules by one of the connection profiles. You can also filter the rules by state (Filter by Enabled or Filter by Disabled). Figure 21.4 shows the inbound rules filtered by the Enabled state.

You can also filter the selected rule type (inbound or outbound) by the Windows service or program with which the rule is associated; each service or program is referred to as a *group*. For example, you can filter the rules by Remote Desktop (select Filter by Group and then Filter by Remote Desktop) and find that there is only one default rule (inbound rule) related to the Remote Desktop feature (or group if you prefer). When you have finished viewing the rules that meet the criteria of a specific filter, click the Clear All Filters action in the Actions pane to view all the rules.

You can open an existing rule's properties from the Details pane (whether the list is filtered or not). Double-click a rule (inbound or outbound) and the Properties dialog box for that rule opens (see Figure 21.5).

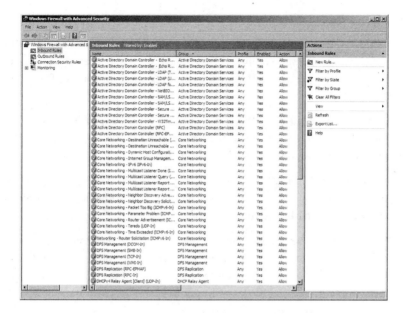

FIGURE 21.4
You can filter the rules list in the Details pane.

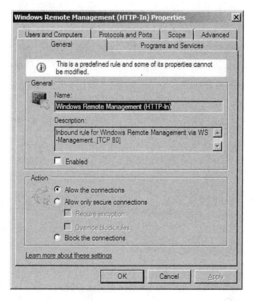

FIGURE 21.5
A firewall inbound rule's Properties dialog box.

You cannot edit all the properties of a predefined rule; in many cases the program associated with the rule cannot be changed, and the ports and protocols set for the rule cannot be changed. Both of these make sense because rules are often associated with a particular Windows service or program that then uses specific ports and protocols for communication.

By the Way

A rule's Properties dialog box contains six tabs:

▶ **General**—This tab provides the name and description of the rule and enables you to change the state of the rule (enabled or not) and select the action for the rule: Allow the Connections, Allow on Secure Connections, or Block the Connections.

▶ **Users and Computers**—This tab enables you to specify the computers or users (using groups if you wish) who can connect to the local computer (in relation to the service or program that the rule is associated with).

▶ **Protocols and Ports**—This tab enables you to specify the ports (by number) and protocols (for example, TCP or UDP) that are required for communication with the computer by the rule.

▶ **Programs and Services**—This tab specifies the Windows program or service that is sending data packets to the remote computer. You can set this tab to All Programs (using the All programs option button) or specify a program by executable file by using the Browse button.

▶ **Scope**—This tab enables you to specify a scope of local or remote IP addresses that are required for communication with the host.

▶ **Advanced**—This tab enables you to specify the profile with which the rule is associated (all profiles, domain, public, or private). You can also specify the network adapter (connection) with which the rule is associated.

You can modify existing rules as needed (although some predefined rule settings cannot be changed). If you need to create a new rule, follow the steps in the section that follows.

Creating Windows Firewall Rules

You can create new inbound or outbound rules as needed. The New Inbound (or Outbound) Rule Wizard walks you through the steps of creating your new rule. Follow these steps:

1. Select the Inbound Rules or Outbound Rules node in the Windows Firewall with Advanced Security snap-in.

2. In the Actions pane, click New Rule. The New Rule Wizard (Inbound or Outbound) opens.

3. On the first wizard page, select the rule type: Program, Port, Predefined, or Custom. (These rule types were discussed in the previous section; select Custom for sake of discussion.) Click Next.

4. Depending on the rule type you selected, you need to specify the program (by executable) or the port (you must specify TCP or UDP as the transport protocol and then the actual port numbers) or the predefined service (for a predefined rule). For sake of discussion, let's look at a custom rule, which requires that you specify a number of these settings.

   Specify the programs for the rule (you can specify all programs) by providing the path for the program (see Figure 21.6). You can also use the Customize button to specify the services that are to be associated with the rule. Click Next.

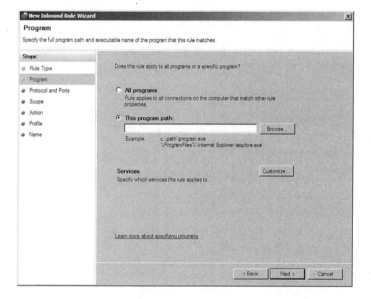

FIGURE 21.6
Specify the program for the rule.

5. On the next wizard page, use the Protocol drop-down list to specify the protocol associated with the rule. You can set local port and remote port numbers as needed. Then click Next.

6. On the next wizard page, you can specify a specific scope of local and remote IP addresses for the rule (the default is any local IP addresses and any remote IP addresses). Click the These IP Addresses option for local or remote IP address ranges, and then use the Add button to specify the range (by subnet) of IP addresses. Then click Next.

7. On the next wizard page, you specify the action that will be taken when a connection matches the rule's conditions. The actions are Allow the Connection, Allow the Connection If It Is Secure, and Block the Connection. After setting the action, click Next.

8. On the next wizard page, you specify the profile or profiles that are associated with the rule (see Figure 21.7). Use the check boxes as needed to associate the rule with a profile or profiles (Domain, Private, and/or Public). Then click Next.

FIGURE 21.7
Specify the profile or profiles for the rule.

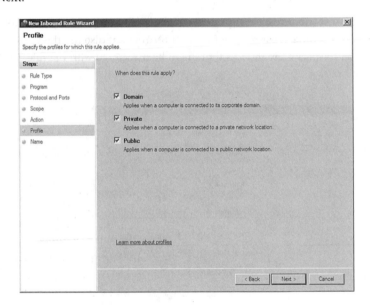

9. On the last wizard page, supply a name and an optional description for the rule. You can then click Finish.

The new rule is created and placed in the rule list (either inbound or outbound). You can edit the properties for the rule by double-clicking the rule in the Details pane.

Working with Connection Security Rules

Inbound and outbound rules control the movement of data to and from a particular computer (say a server) on the network (as already discussed). The Windows Firewall also offers connection security rules, which are used to control authentication between two computers (say two network servers) so that any connection established between these two network nodes is secure. Connection security rules use authentication methods such as certificates (discussed in Hour 22, "Using Network Address Translation and Certificate Services") and IPSec to secure these computer-to-computer connections (IPSec is discussed later in the hour) .

There are no default connection security rules (when you select the Connection Security Rules node in the Windows Firewall and Advanced Security snap-in). You can create your own connection security rules, and there are five types of connection security rules:

- ▶ **Isolation**—This rule restricts connections to a computer (meaning it isolates them) based on authentication criteria such as domain membership or other policies, such as health policies, as defined in the domain's group policies (which is discussed in Hour 11).

- ▶ **Authentication exemption**—You can create a rule that allows unauthenticated connections to the local computer. The computers allowed to connect are designated by IP address or an IP address range.

- ▶ **Server to server**—This type of rule is used to make the connection between two servers secure. You specify the servers that will be involved in the connection and you design what type of authentication is to be used to secure the connection.

- ▶ **Tunnel**—This type of rule is perfect for setting the parameters for a connection over a public network between two perimeter or gateway servers on your network. You specify the endpoints (the server's) for the connection rule and you also specify how the connection is to be authenticated.

- ▶ **Custom**—This type of connection security rule gives you complete flexibility in terms of selecting the properties, such as authentication and endpoints (the computers involved) for the rule.

You create connection security rules by using the New Connection Security Rule Wizard. Let's create a custom rule that enables you to look at the information that you have to provide to create the other connection security rule types (isolation, authentication exemption, and so on); follow these steps:

1. Select the Connection Security Rules node in the Windows Firewall with Advanced Security snap-in.

2. In the Actions pane, click New Rule. The New Connection Security Rule Wizard opens.

3. On the first wizard page, select the connection rule type, such as Custom. Then click Next to continue.

4. On the next wizard page (see Figure 21.8) you specify the endpoints for the connection: Endpoint 1 can be the local computer or a subnet of IP addresses available to the local computer, and endpoint 2 would be the other side of the connection, specified by an IP address or range of IP addresses. After specifying the endpoints, click Next.

FIGURE 21.8
Specify endpoints for the connection security rule.

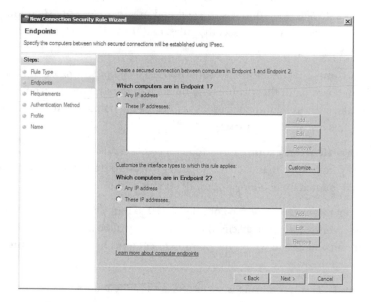

5. On the next wizard page, you select the type of authentication to be used:

> ▶ **Request Authentication For inbound and Outbound Connections**—Authentication is not required by this option but is the preferred setting (meaning inbound or outbound authentication is not really required but you might want to use it anyhow).

> ▶ **Require Authentication for Inbound Connections and Request Authentication for Outbound Connections**—Inbound connection must be authenticated; however, outbound connection authentication is not required.

> ▶ **Require Authentication for Inbound and Outbound Connections**—Both inbound and outbound connections must be authenticated or the data traffic is blocked by the rule.

> ▶ **Do Not Authenticate**—No authentication is required by this connection rule.

After specifying the authentication type for the rule, click Next.

6. On the next wizard page, you select the authentication method to be used by the rule (see Figure 21.9). The default option uses the authentication method selected for the profile (the method with which the rule will be associated. You can also select to authenticate based on both the user and computer (requiring domain membership), the computer only, or use a computer certificate (certificates are discussed in Hour 22). After making your selection, click Next to continue.

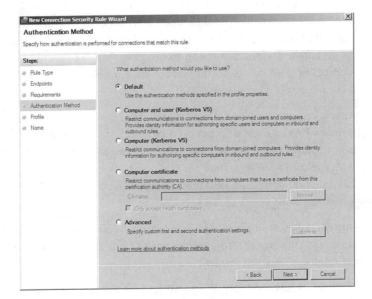

FIGURE 21.9
Specify the authentication method for the connection security rule.

You can also specify a first and second authentication method for a connection security rule by using the Advanced option on the Authentication Method page of the New Connection Security Rule Wizard.

By the Way

7. On the next page, select the profile with which the connection rule will be associated (Domain, Private, Public). All the profiles are selected by default. Then click Next.

8. On the last wizard page, provide the name and an optional description for the rule. Then click Finish.

The new connection security rule appears in the rules list in the Details pane. You can edit the settings for a connection security rule by double-clicking that rule. The Properties dialog box for the rule opens, enabling you to edit any of the settings that you specified for the rule when you created the rule using the New Connection Security Rule Wizard.

Understanding IPSec

The *IP Security Protocol* (IPSec) is a suite of cryptography-based protection services and security protocols that can be used to secure internal networks and can also be used to secure remote access connections such as a VPN. IPSec secures the data even if the routers and other devices involved in moving the data from sender to receiver do not support IPSec. IPSec can be used to secure the movement of data on LANs, WANs, and remote access connections.

IPSec uses strong cryptography and provides protection for network data because it protects the data while en route and can even be used to protect private network data that is transmitted across public network environments such as the Internet. The biggest plus related to IPSec is that it can be used to protect data inside the network and eliminate snooping and hacking by employees, contractors, or attackers that have actually gained access to the network.

IP packets are encrypted on a packet-by-packet basis. IPSec can also make use of authentication keys such as certificates (discussed in Hour 22) as a way of establishing a trust relationship between the sending and receiving computers.

Windows Server 2008 has combined IPSec settings with the Windows Firewall. So, this means that you can configure IPSec settings for the firewall in the Windows Firewall with Advanced Security properties dialog box.

To open the Windows Firewall with Advanced Security Properties dialog box for the local computer, right-click the Windows Firewall with Advanced Security node in the snap-in node tree and select Properties. The Properties dialog box opens. IPSec settings for the firewall can be accessed via the IPSec Settings tab (see Figure 21.10).

The IPSec Settings tab provides a Customize button that enables you to access the IPSec defaults for the firewall. The IPsec settings that you select apply to all the connection security rules that you create.

To access the Customize IPsec Settings dialog box, click the Customize button (see Figure 21.11). The IPSec settings fall into three categories: key exchange, data protection, and authentication method. You can customize the settings for any of these IPSec categories.

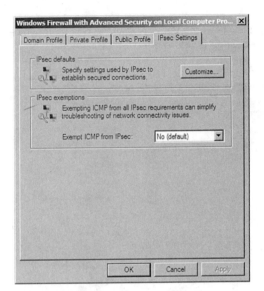

FIGURE 21.10
The IPSec tab of the Windows Firewall properties dialog box.

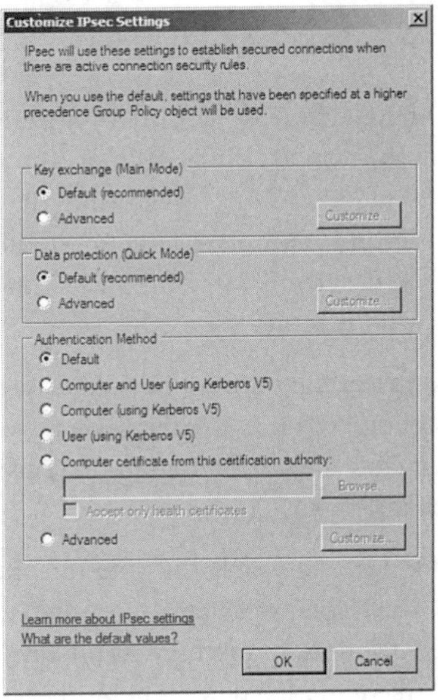

FIGURE 21.11
The Customize IPSec Settings dialog box.

The key exchange default settings relate to the integrity and encryption methods that are selected. To view the key exchange settings available, click the Advanced option button under Key Exchange. Then click the Customize button. The Customize Advanced Key Exchange Settings dialog box opens (see Figure 21.12). By default the key exchange settings use the Diffie-Hellman Group 2 key exchange algorithm (which uses a public and a private key to encrypt the data).

Diffie and Hellman invented the public key encryption methodology in 1976 and so this encryption method is referred to by their names.

FIGURE 21.12
The IPSec key exchange settings.

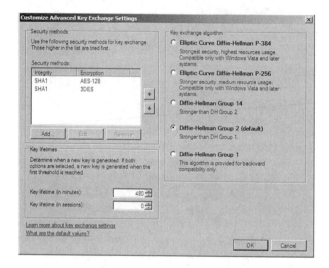

If you want, you can strengthen the IPSec security by selecting a key exchange algorithm that is stronger than the default (Diffie-Hellman Group 2) such as the Elliptic Curve Diffie-Hellman P-384 algorithm. However, using this algorithm restricts your client base to Windows Vista and your server base to Windows Server 2008. You can also edit the key lifetime settings if you wish. The shorter the lifetime for the key the more secure the connection (in theory).

You can also edit the data protection settings. In the Customize IPsec Settings dialog box, click the Advanced option button in the the Data Protection (Quick Mode) area of the dialog box and then click the Customize button. This opens the Customize Data Protection Settings dialog box.

By default, two protocols are used to supply the data integrity and encryption algorithms for IPSec: ESP and AH. The Encapsulating Security Payload (ESP) protocol provides data origin authentication, connectionless integrity, and an anti-replay service for the IP payload (meaning the data). The Authentication Header (AH) protocol provides security for the IP header. You can edit the settings in the Customize Data Protection Settings dialog box, but the defaults should work well in most circumstances.

The Customize IPSec Settings dialog also enables you to select the authentication method to be used to make secure connections between computers (look back at Figure 21.11). The choices are

▶ **Computer and User (Using Kerberos V5)**—This option requires both computer and user authentication.

> Kerberos V5 is an authentication method that uses a key or ticket, which is assigned to users and computers within the domain. Messages sent by a user or computer are then identified by the ticket, which is embedded in data sent by the user or computer.

▶ **Computer (Using Kerberos V5)**—This option requires that the computer be authenticated.

▶ **User (Using Kerberos V5)**—This option requires that the user be authenticated.

▶ **Computer Certificate from This Certification Authority**—This option enables you to use a certificate for authentication. Certificates can be assigned to both users and computers. For more about certificates and certification authorities, see Hour 22.

When you have finished working with the Customize IPSec Settings dialog box, click OK (or Cancel). You can then close the Windows Firewall with Advanced Security dialog box to return to the firewall snap-in.

The full possibilities of IPSec are certainly beyond the scope of this book. However, you can manage IPSec using IPSec policies. These policies are a set of filters and filter actions that are used to determine how IP packets are treated by a particular computer or group of computers. IPSec policies are integrated with the Windows Server 2008 Group Policy, and IPSec policies can be assigned to individual computers, Organizational Units, and domains. This makes it easy for you to design (and lowers the management overhead of) a domain- or enterprise-level plan for IPSec deployment. For more about the basics of working with Group Policy, see Hour 11.

Summary

The Windows Firewall monitors the state of the computer's network connections and examines incoming and outgoing data traffic. Basic settings for the Windows Firewall can be configured in the Windows Firewall Settings dialog box, which is accessed via the Windows Control Panel.

More advanced settings for the Firewall, including the creation of inbound, outbound, and connection security rules are configured via the Windows Firewall with

Advanced Security snap-in. The snap-in provides access to the Windows Firewall properties dialog box, which enables you to set the state of firewall profiles and configure other settings such as the IPSec settings.

You can use a wizard to create rules (each rule type—inbound, outbound and connection security—has a specific wizard). You can then view rules in the Windows Firewall with Advanced Security snap-in by selecting the appropriate rule node. You can view the properties (and edit those properties) for a particular rule by double-clicking the rule in the Details pane.

IPSec provides security for IP traffic on internal and remote network connections. IPSec encrypts IP packets and uses authentication keys to establish a trust between the sending and receiving computers. You can configure IPSec settings for your Windows Firewall by using the IPSec Settings dialog box (which is accessed via the Windows Firewall with Advanced Settings dialog box).

Q&A

Q. What type of firewall is the Windows Firewall?

A. The Windows Firewall is a stateful firewall, meaning it keeps track of the state of a computer's network connections as it examines both incoming and outgoing data packets.

Q. What are firewall profiles?

A. Windows Firewall profiles relate to connection types. There are three firewall profiles: domain, public, and private. Each profile is responsible for a connection type, and so has different rules to manage the security for that particular network connection type.

Q. What mechanism does the Windows Firewall use to allow or deny incoming or outgoing data traffic?

A. The Windows Firewall uses rules to allow or deny network traffic. Inbound rules control inbound connections and outbound rules are used to control outbound traffic. Connection security rules are used to secure point-to-point connections between nodes on the network, such as a server-to-server connection.

Q. What protocol suite provides a method to secure both internal and external IP traffic?

A. IPSec is a suite of protocols that provides cryptographic and security protocols that can secure IP traffic on both internal networks and on remote connections.

Using Network Address Translation and Certificate Services

What You'll Learn in This Hour:

▶ Using Network Address Translation

▶ Configuring NAT on the Server

▶ Understanding the Active Directory Certificate Services

▶ Adding the Active Directory Certificate Services

▶ Configuring the Certificate Authority

▶ Requesting Certificates

▶ Managing the CA

Hour 17, "Remote Access and Virtual Private Networking," took a look at some of the features provided by the Routing and Remote Access Service, and then Hour 18, "Implementing Network Routing", continued this discussion in relation to routing. This hour looks at how you can use Network Address Translation (NAT) to "hide" a group of computers behind one public IP address. This enables a small network or branch office to take advantage of one Internet connection provided by a server running Windows Server 2008.

Another important issue related to networking with Windows Server 2008 is security. As discussed briefly in Hour 21, "Working with the Windows Firewall and IPSec," protecting data on your network is extremely important, particularly when data exchange occurs between private and public networks. The public key infrastructure embraced by Windows Server 2008 provides a method of authenticating users involved in data transactions. One aspect of creating an environment in which the identity of users involved in transactions is known is using the digital certificate. This hour looks at how you install and use the Windows Server 2008 Active Directory Certificate Services.

Using Network Address Translation

Network Address Translation (enables you to hide a group of computers (such as a network) behind one IP address. In the good old days of computing, which weren't that good and certainly weren't that long ago, this was known as *IP masquerading*. Basically, your network sits behind the NAT server, meaning that you need only one "legal," or public, IP address for the server running the NAT software. The IP addressing scheme that you use on the computer network behind the NAT server is really up to you (although ranges of IP addresses are reserved for this purpose).

When the Internet Assigned Numbers Authority (IANA) developed the IPv4 address classes (A, B, and C), it designated a range in each class to serve as private addresses. So, a private address is an IP address taken from one of the private ranges designated by IANA.

These addresses are meant to be used, as their name suggests, on private networks. They are not to be used as legitimate IP addresses for connecting to the Internet. These private addresses provide a means of assigning unique IP addresses to an internal network that then uses Network Address Translation to actually connect to the public Internet.

There are Class A, B, and C private ranges:

- ► Class A: 10.0.0.0 to 10.255.255.255, with a subnet mask of 255.0.0.0

- ► Class B: 172.16.0.0 to 172.31.255.255, with a subnet mask of 255.255.0.0

- ► Class C: 192.168.0.0 to 192.168.255.255, with a subnet mask of 255.255.255.0

The great thing about using NAT is that you can use as many IP addresses as required internally. For example, you can treat your internal network as if it were a Class A or a Class B network, which provides a huge number of addresses. Remember, NAT requires only one "official" IP address for the NAT server that sits between your network and the Internet.

A server with multiple network interfaces (such as the router configuration discussed in this hour) can sit between your private network and a public network and, using RRAS and NAT, provide a connection between the two networks. This enables you to take advantage of a single broadband or DSL connection when you want to connect a small office to the Internet.

Before configuring NAT as part of RRAS, configure one of the LAN interfaces with the IP address provided by your Internet service provider (or connect the interface to the broadband or DSL devices that connect to your ISP so that the device can receive the public address via DHCP from your provider).

Configure the other LAN interface with a fixed IP address from one of the IPv4 private ranges (a Class A, B, or C private range address). You can then set up NAT to provide private IP addresses using NAT's DHCP allocator (discussed shortly).

Configuring NAT on the Server

As mentioned in Hour 18, the Routing and Remote Access Services (RRAS) are added to a server when you add the RRAS role in the Add Roles Wizard. (Open the Add Roles Wizard via the Initial Configuration Tasks window or the Server Manager.) When RRAS is enabled in the Routing and Remote Access snap-in, you can add NAT in the Routing and Remote Access Server Setup Wizard (discussed in Hour 18).

If you did not add NAT in the Routing and Remote Access Server Setup Wizard, you can add NAT as a routing protocol: In the RRAS snap-in, right-click the General node (in the node tree) and select New Routing Protocol from the shortcut menu. Select NAT in the New Routing Protocol dialog box. Then click OK.

NAT is configured as a protocol. After NAT has been added to the RRAS configuration, you then add an interface for the protocol and then provide configuration information for the protocol—in this case NAT. Let's take a look at adding NAT Interfaces and then look at additional configuration information related to NAT.

You cannot run the DHCP Relay Agent and NAT on the same RRAS server. So if you are using the server as a router (multihomed) computer, you need to deploy NAT on another server (that is also configured with at least two network interfaces)

By the Way

When you add the NAT interfaces to the RRAS configuration, you need to add one private interface (this is connected to the private network) and an interface that will serve as the public interface. It is this interface that will be connected to the Internet.

To create a new NAT interface in the RRAS snap-in, right-click the NAT node in the IPv4 node (expand the IPV4 node) and select New Interface from the shortcut menu. The New Interface for IPNAT dialog box opens (see Figure 22.1).

Select an interface in the New Interface for IPNAT dialog box. Then click OK. As already mentioned, you configure one interface as public and the other interface as private. Let's take a look at creating a public interface and then a private interface.

In the Network Address Translation Properties dialog box (for the currently selected interface), select the Private Interface Connected to Private Network option button. Then click OK.

FIGURE 22.1
Add the new
NAT interface.

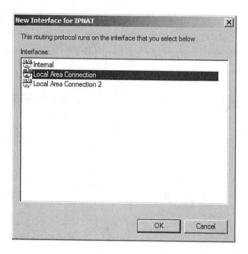

Repeat the process of creating a new NAT interface (select the interface in the IPNAT dialog box, and then click OK to open the NAT Properties dialog box for the interface). To create the public interface, click the Public Interface Connected to the Internet option button. Then click Enable NAT on This Interface (see Figure 22.2).

FIGURE 22.2
Enable NAT on
the public
interface.

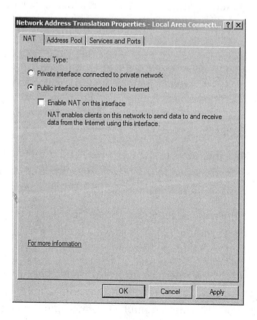

You can now set the other properties for this NAT public interface. Click the Service and Ports tab of the Properties dialog box.

You can select Internet-related services requested on your private network that are redirected to the public interface (and Internet nodes). For example (see Figure 22.3), you can enable the FTP Server service, the Post Office Protocol Version 3 (POP3) email service, and the Web Server (HTTP) service.

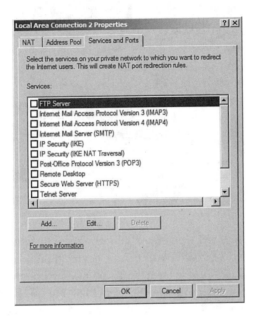

FIGURE 22.3
Select the services you want to redirect from the private network to the public interface.

After you have finished making your selections you can close the dialog box. Click OK.

The only thing that you still need to configure related to NAT (and your private and public interfaces) is NAT's capability to assign private IP addresses to the clients on your private network. Right-click the NAT node in the RRAS snap-in. Select Properties.

In the NAT Properties dialog box, click the Address Assignment tab. Then click the Automatically Assign IP Addresses by Using the DHCP Allocator check box (see Figure 22.4).

By default a private Class B subnet network address is provided and the appropriate subnet mask. You can use the IP address range provided or you can use any of the private networks (Class A, B, or C) to create your own subnet and mask. If you need to add exclusion to the IP address pool (for computers that need a fixed IP address from the pool), click the Exclude button and add reserved addresses as needed. When you have completed configuring the Address Assignment settings, click OK to close the NAT Properties dialog box.

FIGURE 22.4
Configure the
address assign-
ment settings in
the NAT
Properties
dialog box.

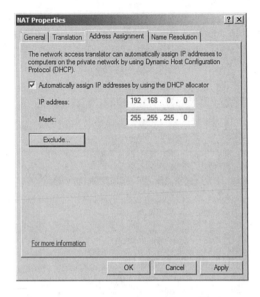

If you have configured the NAT interfaces correctly, the NAT server should operate
without errors. If computers on the network are having trouble communicating with
the Internet or computers outside the network are have trouble communicating with
computers on the private network, use the Event Viewer to check NAT-related log
files. These should provide some insight into configuration errors that might have
occurred when NAT was implemented on the server.

Understanding the Active Directory Certificate Services

Certificates play an important role in the public key infrastructure that Microsoft
has developed to protect network data. A *certificate* (also known as a digital certificate) is used to identify an entity on the network. The holder of a certificate (how
the certificate is obtained is discussed in a moment) is trusted by the network.

The public key infrastructure actually uses both secret keys and public keys when
data is exchanged. The secret key provides the security for the exchange and is often
generated just for the session when the data moves from sender to receiver. The
secret key (which is encrypted) is shared between the users in the data exchange session; each user is identified by a public key.

A certificate, then, is used to identify a public key user. Certificates are provided by a
Certificate Authority, which is basically a trusted third party that authenticates a

user's public key with a certificate (somewhat like a certificate of authenticity that you receive for expensive jewelry or an antique). A number of public Certificate Authorities, such as Verisign, provide digital certificates. If a user who wants to send data is identified by a certificate, the receiver of the data has no problem accepting the data because it is from a "trusted and certified" user. A number of applications can use certificates for secure data exchange such as Microsoft Outlook and Microsoft Internet Explorer.

Although a number of Certificate Authorities can be used to purchase certificates, you might want to take advantage of certificates as another level of security on your Windows Server 2008 domain (or enterprise network). A server running Windows Server 2008 can be configured for Active Directory Certificate Services. The server can then act as your own internal Certificate Authority.

Adding the Active Directory Certificate Services

Microsoft's Certificate Services enables you to issue, renew, and revoke digital certificates. Certificate Services is added to Windows Server 2008 via the Add Roles Wizard.

1. From the Initial Configuration Tasks window or the Server Manager (with the Roles node selected), click Add Roles. The Add Roles Wizard opens.

2. In the Roles list, select Active Directory Certificate Services (see Figure 22.5). Then click Next.

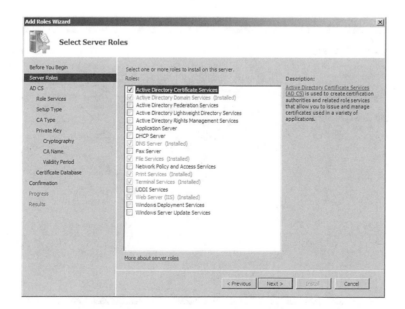

FIGURE 22.5
Add Active Directory Certificate Services to the server.

3. On the next wizard page, a short description of Active Directory Certificate Services (AD CS) is provided. Links to additional information on AD CS are also included. After taking advantage of the links, click Next to continue.

4. On the next page, the services associated with AD CS are listed. Click the Certification Authority check box (other optional services are also available; see the By the Way that follows). Click Next to continue.

> AD CS has other services (other than the Certification Authority) associated with it. The Certification Authority Web Enrollment service provides a web interface where users can request and renew certificates. This service requires that you install the Internet Information Service (IIS) on the server (see Hour 23, "Using the Internet Information Services," for more about IIS). The Online Responder allows users to access certificate revocation data. This service also requires IIS. The Network Device Enrollment Service allows you to assign certificates to network devices such as routers that are secured by domain accounts.

5. On the next screen (see Figure 22.6), you must specify the type of Certificate Authority (CA) that you want to set up: Enterprise or Standalone. An Enterprise CA requires the Active Directory (and Group Policy) and issues certificates based on domain membership. An Enterprise CA can be installed on a domain controller or a domain member server. A Standalone CA does not require the Active Directory and users are authenticated to the server based on other identifying information (other than a domain account). For sake of discussion, select Enterprise and then click Next.

FIGURE 22.6
Select the CA type: Enterprise or Standalone.

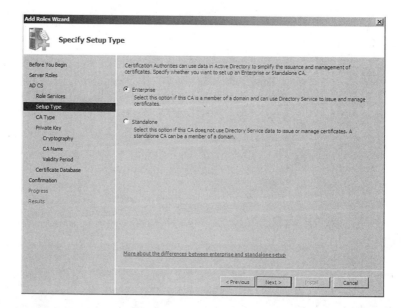

6. On the next page, select one of the following:

   ▶ **Root CA**—This CA becomes the root certificate server for your network. Active Directory is required to create an enterprise root because the CA serves your entire domain tree.

   ▶ **Subordinate CA**—If you already have an enterprise root CA established, you can create subordinate CAs. A subordinate CA is actually verified by a certificate from the enterprise root CA.

   Click Next to continue.

7. Each CA must be configured with a private key. You have the option of creating a new key for the CA or using an existing key. Again, for the sake of discussion, let's create a new private key. Select the Create a New Private Key option and then click Next.

8. On the next wizard page, you must select the cryptographic service provider (CSP), the key character length, and the hash algorithm for the key (see Figure 22.7). Use the drop-down list to select a CSP (you can go with the default). Also select a hash and adjust the key character length if you wish. Then click Next.

9. On the next wizard page, you must configure the CA name. By default the name is provided and is in the following format: *domain-server name*-CA. CA names cannot be more than 64 characters. If you are going to deploy a root CA and additional subordinate CAs, you may want to establish your own hierarchical naming convention, taking into account that the subordinate CAs are dependent on the root CA. After entering the CA name (or going with the default), click Next.

FIGURE 22.7
Select the CSP,
hash, and key
character
length.

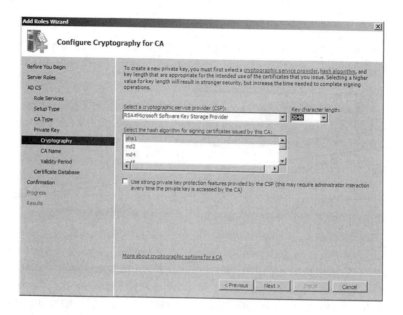

> **By the Way**
>
> The name that you create on the CA server becomes the common name for the server and is included with every certificate that the CA issues. After you name the CA server, you can't change the name unless you remove the AD CS role and then reinstall it.

10. On the next page, you set the validity period for the certificate that will be generated, which allows communication between this root CA and any other CAs you may deploy on the network. The validity period can be in years, months, weeks, or days. Specify a number (the default is 5) and the interval (the default is Years) and then click Next.

11. On the next page, you set the path for the certificate database (CertLog) and the certificate log location. By default the path for both is Windows\System32\CertLog. You can go with the default or use the Browse button to set the certificate data location and the certificate log location. Click Next.

12. The Confirmation page provides a list of the selections that you made to add the CA to the server. Click Install.

When the installation is completed, you can click Close (to close the Add Roles Wizard). After you have installed AD CS, you will find that the Active Directory Certificate Services role has been added to the Server Manager (see Figure 22.8).

Clicking the role provides you with a quick look at any events that have been logged related to the service, and you can also view what services associated with the role are running.

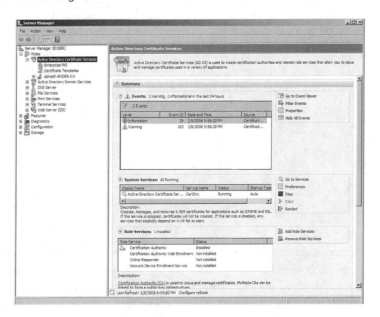

FIGURE 22.8
The AD CS role is added to the Server Manager.

When you expand the Active Directory Certificate Services node, you are provided access to the Certification Authority (by clicking the name of your CA server in the node tree) and other tools related to AD CS, such as the Certificate Templates snap-in.

You will also find that the Certification Authority (CA) snap-in has been added to the server's administrative tools (Start, Administrative Tools, Certification Authority). So, you can configure and manage your CA server from either the Server Manager or the Certification Authority snap-in in the MMC.

Configuring the Certificate Authority

The Certification Authority snap-in is used, either in the Server Manager or the MMC, to configure and manage the CA. To open the Certification Authority snap-in running in the MMC, click Start, Administrative Tools, Certification Authority. Figure 22.9 shows the Certification Authority snap-in running in the MMC.

FIGURE 22.9
The Certification
Authority
snap-in.

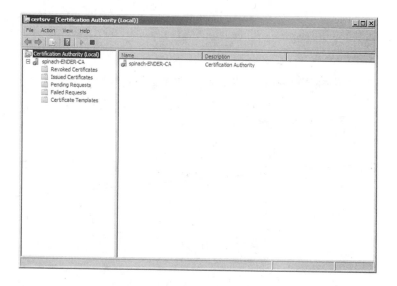

The Certification Authority snap-in provides you with access to the certificate server's properties and enables you to view certificates that have been revoked or issued, certificates that are pending, and certificate requests that have failed. These different certificate nodes in the snap-in can be used to view actual certificates and manage certificates (such as revoking certificates, as discussed later in the hour).

The snap-in also enables you to list and view the default certificate templates that are provided. These certificate templates include Domain Controller, Web Server, Computer, and User certificate templates. Certificates can be assigned to users, computers, and even computer services.

> Certificate Services is an advanced Windows Server 2008 feature that is usually used in conjunction with Group Policy and other Windows security features, such as IPSec, to secure the domain. Manipulating certificate templates is beyond the scope of this book. However, to get your feet wet working with certificate templates, open the Certificate Templates snap-in by expanding the CA server node in the Server Manager. You can duplicate any of the existing templates and change the properties of the copies as you require. You can then delete any of these copies after you are finished experimenting with them.

To view (and edit, if necessary) the properties for your certificate server, right-click the CA icon in the tree of the snap-in and select Properties from the shortcut menu. The CA Properties dialog box opens (see Figure 22.10).

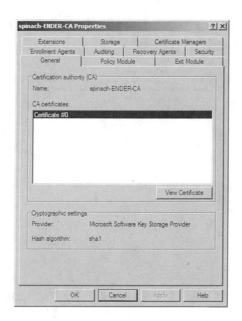

FIGURE 22.10
The CA
Properties
dialog box.

The Properties dialog box consists of 10 tabs:

▶ **General**—This tab (see Figure 22.10) is provided mainly for information. It lists the name and the cryptographic settings for the CA. These settings cannot be changed. The tab also shows the CA's certificate, which grants it the capability to assign certificates within the domain. To view the details of the CA certificate, click the View Certificate button. Figure 22.11 shows the CA certificate for an enterprise root CA. To close the certificate, click OK.

▶ **Storage**—Shows the paths that you selected for the CA to keep its certificate database and request log. These settings cannot be changed.

▶ **Policy Module**—Shows the current policy that is used to determine how the CA handles certificate requests. The default policy module is the Windows default. Unless you have access to a third-party module (or write your own), the default (Windows) is the only possibility when you click the Select button. If you want to adjust the properties of the default policy module, select the Properties buttons. Two option buttons are provided related to request handling. You can set certificate requests to Pending so that the administrator must issue the certificate, or you can choose to follow the default certificate template for the type of certificate being requested. If no template exists, the certificate is issued automatically. This is the default (and best practice) setting.

FIGURE 22.11
You can view the CA certificate details.

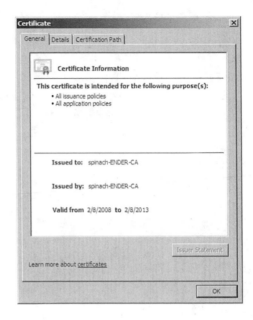

▶ **Auditing**—Enables you to select the types of CA events that you want to audit. Audited events appear in the security log of the Event Viewer (enabling auditing in Group Policy is discussed in Hour 11, "Deploying Group Policy and Network Access Protection"). You can audit any backup or restore of the CA database, changes made to the CA configuration, and other events related to various CA activities (see Figure 22.12).

FIGURE 22.12
You can audit CA events.

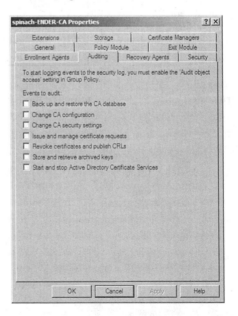

▶ **Exit Module**—Shows the current exit module selected for the CA. A Windows default exit module is available (set as the default); unless you have access to additional custom exit modules, it is the only possibility.

▶ **Security**—Enables you to set the permissions for the certificates generated by the CA (see Figure 22.13). The permissions include Read, Issue and Manage Certificates, Manage CA, and Request Certificates. By default, all authenticated users can request certificates. You can add or remove groups or users from the list by using the Add or Remove buttons. Permission settings for the CA and its certificates are similar to the permissions that can be applied to any number of services and resources in the Windows domain.

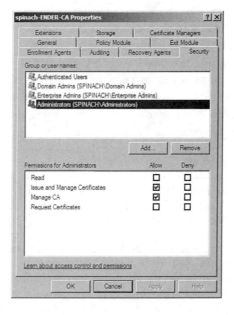

FIGURE 23.13
Permissions can be set for CA objects.

▶ **Extensions**—Enables you to configure where the certification-revocation list (CRL) is published on the CA (the path, which can be a URL). You can also configure the path for the Authority Information Access Points (AIAs), which specify the location where users can get the CA's certificate. Default paths are set for both of these parameters (and, in most cases, the defaults are probably what you will want to go with).

▶ **Enrollment Agents**—Enables you to specify enrollment agents. An *enrollment agent* is a user who can request or "enroll for" a certificate for another client. Unlike a certificate manager, an enrollment agent can only process the enrollment request and cannot approve pending requests or revoke issued certificates. Bottom line: You create enrollment agents to enroll for certificates for other users, computers, or services based on group membership. For example, you may have a user group for which you want to create an enrollment agent, and then this enrollment agent basically handles the negotiation for the certificates that the group needs with the Certification Authority. You can limit enrollment agents to certain certificates based on selected templates.

▶ **Certificate Managers**—Certificate managers are specified on the Security tab of the CA's Properties dialog box. You can choose to restrict certificate managers to specific certificate templates and also add or remove permissions related to those certificate templates.

▶ **Recovery Agents**—*Recovery agents* are designated users that can recover certificates for users in the domain. Recovery agents are actually created on the Security tab and a recovery agent (meaning a user) must be added to the Security tab. This user or recovery agent is then assigned a duplicate of the key recovery agent certificate template (see the By the Way that follows related to duplicating certificate templates). The duplicate key recovery agent certificate template must also be added to the CA (in the snap-in) and then the recovery agent can request recovery certificates for users, computers, or services.

By the Way

The various certificate templates provided in the Certificate Templates snap-in (open in the Server Manager by expanding the AD CS node) can easily be duplicated. In fact, it's a good idea to work with duplicates because it enables you to fine-tune the settings for that particular certificate template (by accessing the Properties for that template). You must then add any "new" templates that you create (by duplicating provided templates and changing the properties) to the CA. In the CA snap-in (in the Server Manger or the MMC), right-click the Certificate Templates node. On the shortcut menu, point at New and then click Certificate Template to Issue. The Enable Certificate Templates dialog box opens. Select the certificate template you want.

When you have completed viewing and editing the configuration settings for the CA, click OK. You are returned to the Certification Authority snap-in.

Requesting Certificates

Any user in the domain can request a certificate. Certificates can be granted to a user or another object in the domain, such as a computer. Although certificates are often added to a computer when certain software is installed, domain users can request certificates directly from the enterprise or another CA.

Utilities for requesting certificates are available to the various Windows domain clients: Windows 2000, Windows XP, Windows Vista, and Windows Server 2008 computers. Windows 2000. Windows XP, and Windows Server 2008 use the MMC with the Certificates snap-in. You use the Certificates snap-in to manage and request certificates on the local computer (for the domain user).

To create an MMC snap-in for certificates (in Windows Server 2008 or Windows XP), follow these steps:

1. Select Start. In the Start Search box, type **mmc**. Then click mmc in the Programs list (above the Start Search box). A blank MMC console opens. To add the Certificates snap-in, select File and then Add/Remove Snap-In. The Add or Remove Snap-ins dialog box opens (see Figure 22.14).

If you are creating a MMC snap-in for Certificates on Windows Server 2003 or Windows XP, use the Run box in step 1 (rather than the Start Search box). You can then follow the other steps as listed.

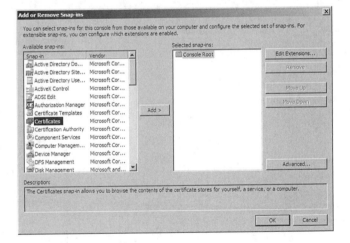

FIGURE 22.14
Add the Certificates snap-in to the MMC.

2. In the Add or Remove Snap-ins dialog box, select Certificates in the snap-in list and then click the Add button. A Certificates Snap-In box opens with option buttons that dictate which certificates the snap-in is to manage.

3. Select My User Account (the default), Service Account, or Computer Account to select the certificate type that the snap-in is to manage. Then click Finish.

By the Way

> If you select Computer Account, you need to specify the computer for which the snap-in is to manage the certificates. If you select Service Account, you need to specify the local or other computer and then specify the service such as Active Directory Domain Services, DNS Server, or DHCP client (there are a number of different service accounts related to the various services that the domain can provide).

4. Click Close to close the Add Standalone Snap-in dialog box, and click OK to close the Add/Remove Snap-In dialog box.

For example, if you chose to add the Certificates snap-in to manage the certificates related to the current user, the Certificates-Current User snap-in appears (see Figure 22.15). This snap-in enables you to manage certificates assigned to the local user and also enables you to request a new certificate for the local user (yourself). As with any snap-in created with the MMC command, you can save the snap-in by using File and then Save. The snap-in in Figure 23.8 was saved as usercertmgr.

FIGURE 22.15
Use the Certificates snap-in to manage certificates locally.

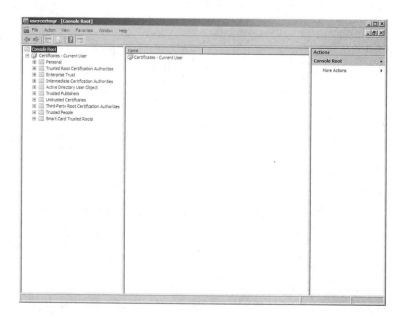

You can view personal certificates assigned to the current user. Expand the Personal node and then click the Certificates folder to view the certificates in the Details pane. To view certificates related to trusted root CAs, select the Trusted Root Certification Authorities node and then select the Certificates folder that it contains. Certificates for trusted CAs are displayed in the Details pane.

1. pertinet

> Use the File menu and the Save command to save the MMC containing the Certificates snap-in. This enables you to quickly open the Certificates snap-in from any MMC session (using the File, Open command).

The Certificates snap-in is also used to request certificates from the CA (which is more germane to our discussion of a user requesting a certificate).

1. In the snap-in tree, expand the Certificates–Current User node so that you can see the Personal node in the tree.

2. Right-click the Personal node and then point at All Tasks on the shortcut menu that appears.

3. Select Request New Certificate.

4. The Certificate Request Wizard opens. Click Next to bypass the initial screen.

5. On the next screen, you are asked to select the type of certificate you want to request (see Figure 22.16). You can request an Administrator certificate (if you are logged on as an Administrator) or a User certificate. Other certificate types are related to the Encrypting File System (EFS). (They are the Basic EFS and EFS Recovery Agent certificates.)

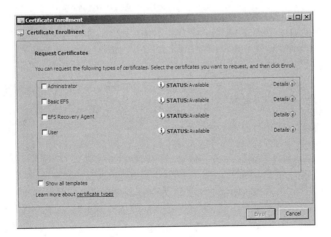

FIGURE 22.16
The Certificate Request Wizard provides a list of certificates that you can request.

6. Select the type of certificate you want to request and then click Next to continue. On the next screen, you are asked to type a friendly name and an optional description for the certificate. After doing so, click Next. A summary screen appears for the new certificate, including information on the type of certificate and the friendly name for the certificate. Click Finish.

7. A message appears letting you know that that certificate request was successful. Click OK to close the message box. Certificates added to the snap-in appear in the Certificates folder of the Personal node.

By the Way

> The types of certificates available to a user depend on the certificate templates that are active on the CA (through the Active Directory and Group Policy for the domain). The certificates available are also related to the services running on a server; for example, when Internet Information Service is available, certificates related to this web service can be requested. The use of certificates can also be tied to security and hardware devices such as smart card devices on computers. The interaction of certificates and other domain security measures, and all the ins and outs of Group Policy, are certainly beyond the scope of this book. However, you can get started with Group Policy by checking out Hour 11.

Managing the CA

If your users (and you, the administrator) can request certificates from your CA and receive them successfully, this means that your CA has been configured correctly and is up and running. Managing the CA and its certificates is done in the Certification Authority snap-in (which can be run in the Server Manager or the MMC: Start, Administrative Tools, Certification Authority).

You can view certificates that the CA has issued by expanding the CA node (in this case, a root CA) and then selecting the Issued Certificates node (see Figure 22.17).

FIGURE 22.17
You can view issued certificates.

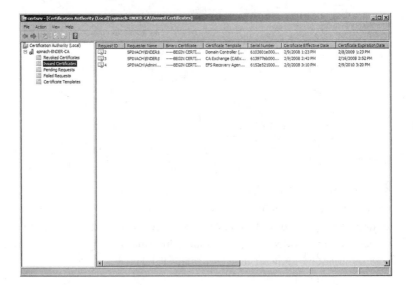

You also can view pending requests and failed requests for certificates by selecting the appropriate folder in the snap-in tree. That brings us to revoked certificates. Revoked certificates are issued certificates that you revoke for a particular reason. For example, the key of the certificate might have been compromised, or the CA itself might have been compromised (meaning that you are going to revoke a lot of bad certificates). In some cases, you might also want to put a hold on a certificate by temporarily revoking it. This type of revocation can be reversed later so that the certificate can again be used by the assignee.

To revoke a particular certificate, follow these steps:

1. Click the Issued Certificates node to view all issued certificates in the Details pane. Right-click a certificate in the Details pane, point at All Tasks and then Revoke Certificate. The Certificate Revocation dialog box opens.

2. To select a reason for revoking the certificate, click the Reason code drop-down box and select a listed reason. If you plan to take the revocation off the certificate at a later time, you must select the Certificate Hold reason code.

3. After selecting the reason code, click Yes to revoke the certificate.

You can view revoked certificates by selecting the Revoked Certificates folder in the snap-in tree (see Figure 22.18). The revocation date and other specifics related to the revoked certificates are displayed in the Details pane.

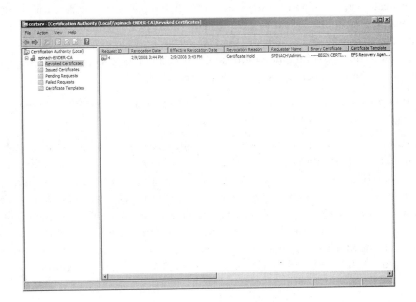

FIGURE 22.18
Revoked certificates can be viewed in the snap-in.

You can unrevoke certificates that have been placed on hold. Certificate Hold then appears in the Revocation Reason column of the Details pane for these certificates. To unrevoke a certificate, right-click the certificate, point at All Tasks, and then select Unrevoke Certificate. The certificate is removed from the Revoked Certificates folder and placed in the Issued Certificates folder. When you have completed working with the Certification Authority snap-in, you can close it by clicking its Close button in the upper-right corner.

Summary

Network Address Translation (NAT) enables you to automatically assign a range of private IP addresses to a group of computers. This way you can "hide" the computers behind the NAT server, which can be connected to a public network via a public IP address. To use NAT on a server running Windows Server 2008, you need two network interfaces on the server.

One network interface connects to the group of computers that is to use the private IP addressing range. The other network interface can be connected to a public network connection, such as a DSL or broadband connection. Using NAT in this way enables you to provide an Internet connection to several computers with only one public IP address. NAT is one of the services available on a server configured with the Routing and Remote Access Services role.

Certificate Services provides a method of identifying public key holders with digital certificates. A number of public Certificate Authorities are available that can provide digital certificates for network services and security signing of software applications. You can also configure a Certificate Authority for your domain or enterprise network, using a server running Windows Server 2008.

You make a server a CA by adding Certificate Services to the server's configuration, using the Add or Remove Programs applet.

After Certificates Services has been added to the server, you can fine-tune the settings for the certificate server, using the Certification Authority snap-in. When a CA is up and running on the network, users can request certificates. Clients such as Windows XP (and Windows Server 2008) use the Certificates snap-in to manage and request certificates for the local computer (and local users). Certificate requests are handled by the Certificate Request Wizard. This wizard enables you to select the type of certificate that is being requested and specify a friendly name for the certificate. When the certificate is received, it is added to the local computer certificates store.

Q&A

Q. *What IP address ranges should be used when NAT is configured on a server running the RRAS role?*

A. IANA has reserved IPv4 address ranges for NAT as follows: Class A: 10.0.0.0 to 10.255.255.255, with a subnet mask of 255.0.0.0; Class B: 172.16.0.0 to 172.31.255.255, with a subnet mask of 255.255.0.0; and Class C: 192.168.0.0 to 192.168.255.255, with a subnet mask of 255.255.255.0. By default, Windows 2008 NAT uses a private Class B subnet and mask, but you can change this as needed in the NAT Properties dialog box (on the Address Assignment tab).

Q. *How do you specify the network interface that will be used for Network Address Translation?*

A. After NAT has been added to the RRAS configuration, you add a new interface in the RRAS snap-in and specify the network interface that is to be connected to the computers that will take advantage of NAT.

Q. *What purpose do certificates play in the public key infrastructure used to protect network data?*

A. Certificates identify an entity on a network, such as a user or a computer. The holder of a certificate, which is granted by a Certificate Authority, is trusted by the network.

Q. *When you install the Certificate Services on a server running Windows Server 2008, what types of Certificate Authorities can be created?*

A. When you install Certificate Services on a server running Windows Server 2008, you can create an enterprise root CA, an enterprise subordinate CA, a standalone root CA, or a standalone subordinate CA. An enterprise root CA requires the Active Directory; a standalone root CA does not require the Active Directory on the network.

Q. *How is a Certificate Authority configured and managed?*

A. The Certification Authority snap-in is used to configure and manage the Certificate Authority. It can be used to set properties for the Certificate Authority and to view and manage issued, revoked, and pending certificates.

HOUR 23

Using the Internet Information Service

What You'll Learn in This Hour:

▶ New IIS 7.0 Features

▶ Installing Internet Information Service 7.0

▶ Adding a Website

▶ Configuring IIS Defaults

▶ Configuring Site Features

▶ Configuring Virtual Directories

▶ Creating FTP Sites

Communication and marketing strategies for most of today's businesses and institutions include the use of the World Wide Web. In many cases, businesses use the Web because they feel compelled to have a corporate presence on the Web.

This hour looks at the Internet Information Service, IIS 7.0. This latest version of IIS provides both a web server and application server platform that provides a stable and secure platform for delivering web content. It also looks at adding the FTP service to an IIS server.

New IIS 7.0 Features

The IIS 7.0 services provided by Windows Server 2008 integrates a number of content delivery platforms, including IIS (web services), ASP.NET, and SharePoint services, into one easy-to-manage web platform. IIS 7.0 provides all the security enhancements developed for IIS 6.0 and also enables you to remotely administer websites via a web browser.

IIS 7.0 also provides new features (when compared to IIS 6.0). These new features include a new IIS management tool and other improvements to IIS that are transparent to the IIS administrator. Some of the new IIS 7.0 enhancements are

▶ **New administration tools**—IIS 7.0 provides a new management snap-in—the Internet Information Service (IIS) Manager. This snap-in provides a more task-based approach to managing the IIS components. A new command-line tool, <u>appcmd, enables you to add and configure sites from the command line</u> (see Figure 23.1).

FIGURE 23.1
New IIS features include the appcmd command-line tool.

▶ **Modular architecture**—IIS 7.0 is made up of <u>a number of modules,</u> enabling the IIS administrator to install only the modules that are needed. This reduces the hardware requirements for an IIS installation and also makes it easier to secure the IIS server.

▶ **Increased diagnostic capabilities**—Administrators can configure IIS to collect run-time data such as what requests are currently running and how long they have been running. IIS can also be configured to track trace events related to failed requests.

In a nutshell, IIS 7.0 provides a scalable, easily managed, and secure web server and application server environment. This means that a single IIS application server can provide the home for a number of websites and application platforms. You can use IIS 7.0 to serve both internal and external content to users.

Installing Internet Information Service 7.0

Before you install IIS on a server, you should keep in mind a couple of security-related issues. First, you should definitely install IIS on an NTFS volume, which enables you to secure IIS resource files with the stronger permissions provided by NTFS. You might also consider installing IIS on a standalone member server that does not provide any other services. This helps control the workload placed on the server if it is receiving a large number of web hits and then also has to provide other important network services. Running other services on the IIS server can also potentially lead to security leaks on the server that could compromise the web server and the entire network.

IIS 7.0 can be quickly added to a Windows server's configuration when you use the Add Roles Wizard. To configure a computer as a web server, follow these steps:

1. From the Server Manager (with the Roles node selected) or the Initial Configuration Tasks window, select Add Roles. The Add Roles Wizard opens. Click Next to bypass the initial wizard page.

2. On the next wizard page, select the Web Server (IIS) check box (see Figure 23.2) and then click Next.

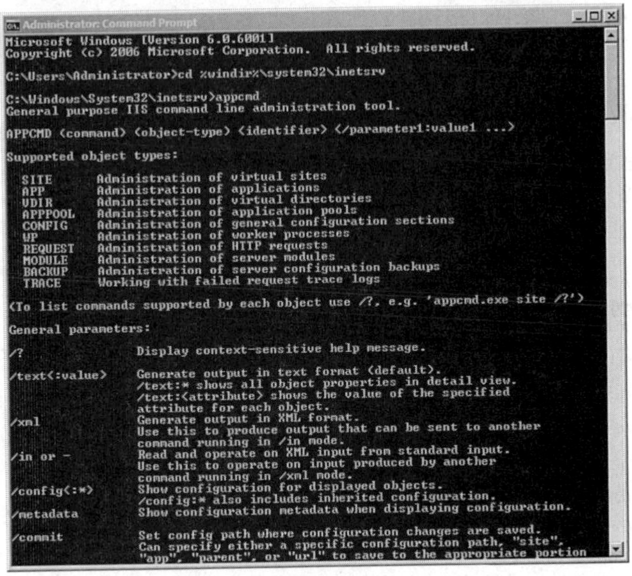

FIGURE 23.2
Select the Web Server (IIS) role.

3. On the next wizard page, you are provided an overview of the Web Server (IIS) role and provided links to more information about IIS. After taking advantage of the links, click Next to continue.

4. On the next page you are provided a list of the IIS services that can be installed as part of the Web Server role (see Figure 23.3). For now, install the default services (services such as the FTP service are added later in the hour). Click Next.

FIGURE 23.3
Select the Web Server role services.

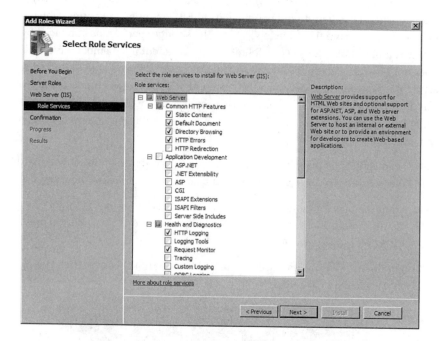

5. The Confirmation page lists the roles and services to be installed. Click Install.

6. When the installation is complete, click Close to close the wizard.

By the Way

Other services can be added to the Web Server role in the Server Manager through use of the Add Role Services Wizard.

After IIS is installed on the server, the Web Server (IIS) node is added to the Server Manager (see Figure 23.4). You can select the Web Server (IIS) node to view events related to the IIS installation and view the status of the system services. The role services installed are listed in the Role Services area of the Details pane.

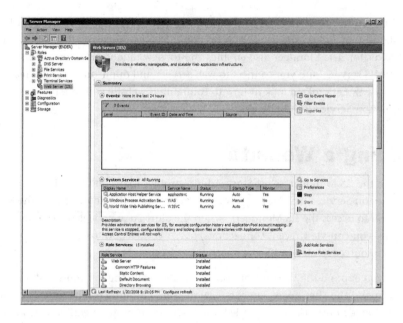

FIGURE 23.4
View system
events and
service status
related to IIS.

Your IIS platforms such as your web server are configured in the new Internet
Information Service (IIS) Manager. This tool is run as a snap-in in the Server
Manager or the MMC (see Figure 23.5).

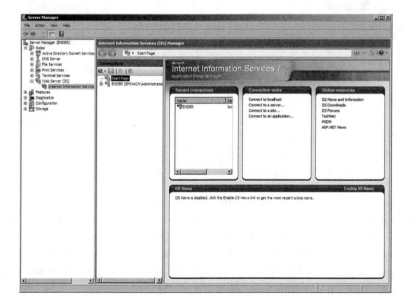

FIGURE 23.5
The Internet
Information
Service (IIS)
Manager is
used to manage
your IIS
platforms.

The Internet Information Service (IIS) Manager enables you to configure your IIS installation, including site delegation (to non-administrators who need to add content to a site). The Manager also enables you to view diagnostic information related to your IIS servers, and you connect to web servers and application servers using a web browser. Let's take a look at how to configure a website with the Internet Information Service (IIS) Manager.

Adding a Website

To open the IIS Manager, select Start, Administrative Tools, and then Internet Information Services (IIS) Manager (or you can expand the Roles node in the Server Manager to access the IIS Manager). When the Start Page node is selected in the snap-in, you can view recent connections, access connection tasks, and also access online resources related to IIS.

When you expand the Web Server node (which is really the localhost node) and then expand the Sites node, you can view the sites currently on the server. If you haven't added any sites (or upgraded a web server running an earlier version of Windows server such as Windows Server 2003), only the new Default Web Site is listed in the Sites pane (see Figure 23.6).

FIGURE 23.6
List the sites currently on the web server.

You can use the Default Web Site as the site on the web server if you wish. You can rename the site as needed (right-click the site and select Rename). When you install the IIS services on your server, a default folder, \Inetpub\Wwwroot, is created on your system drive for the Default Web Site. You can use this folder as the location for your published web content or you can create another location for your web content (you can specify a different drive and folder on the server for the Default Web Site).

An alternative to using the Default Web Site is to create a new site, which we do in a moment. In terms of configuration websites (site configuration is discussed later in the hour), there are really two configuration layers related to your websites. There are settings that affect all the websites created on the IIS server, and then there are configuration settings for each website that you create.

Let's take a look at adding a website, and then we can examine the configuration options provided by the IIS Manager. To add a website to the server, follow these steps:

1. In the IIS Manager (in the MMC or Server Manager), click the Sites node in the node tree and then click Add Web Site in the Actions pane. The Add Web Site dialog box opens (see Figure 23.7).

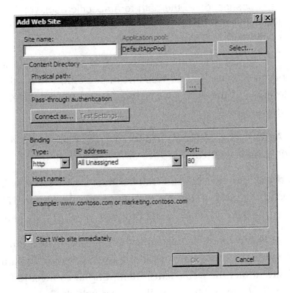

FIGURE 23.7
Add a website to the IIS server.

2. In the Site Name box type a unique, friendly name for the site. As you type the name, an application pool for the site is created with the same name as the site (the pool name uses a maximum of 64 characters). The application pool is configured to use the .NET Framework by default and can be edited after the site has been created.

You can change site settings after you create the site. This includes the site friendly name, the content path, and other site settings.

Did you Know?

3. In the Physical Path box, type the path where you want to store the site content. The path can be on the local server or you can specify a remote share, using the UNC naming connections \\Server\Share. If you wish to browse for the path, click the Browse for Folder button.

✔ 4. By default the server uses pass-through authentication as the connection method to the physical path that you supplied in step 3. This means that the server uses the credentials of the requesting user to access the physical path. This authentication type provides access to both credentialed users and anonymous requests. You can test your connection settings (to the physical path) by clicking the Test Settings button.

By the Way

> If you want to limit connection to the path to a specific user, you can click the Connect As button. You can then use the Connect As dialog box to specify that username and password.

5. In the Binding area of the Add Web Site dialog box, you set the protocol type, the IP address, and the port. For the Type, set HTTP (the default) or HTTPS in the drop-down box.

6. In the IP Address box, select an IP address for the site in the drop-down list or type an IP address. You can use IPv4 or IPv6 addressing.

7. In the Port box, provide the port number that the IIS server will use to listen for connection requests to the site. Port 80 is the default for HTTP (HTTPS uses port 443 as the default). You should probably go with the defaults.

8. If you want to have web clients connect to the site by hostname (domain name), provide the hostname for the site (such as www.sitename.com). If you specify a site name, the web clients attempting to connect to the site need to use the hostname rather than the IP address (which makes sense for public sites available on the Web).

9. When you have supplied all the information for the new site in the Add Web Site dialog box, click OK. The Add Web Site dialog closes.

The new site will be added to the Sites list in the IIS Manager. You will get an error when you attempt to connect to the site until a default document is configured for the site. Adding pages to a site is discussed later in the hour.

By the Way

You can also provide access to the path for a site that does not contain a default document by enabling directory browsing on the IIS server. The directory browsing settings can be set on the Features page for the site. Click the site in the Connections node tree and then double-click Directory Browsing to open the Directory Browsing settings. We discuss setting features for a site later in the hour.

After you have created a new site or sites (this includes the default site if you plan on using it), you can set the configuration settings for all your sites and also fine-tune settings for specific sites. The following section discusses setting "global" settings for all the sites on your IIS server.

Configuring IIS Defaults

You can configure the default settings for the IIS server. These settings affect all the sites on the server. This enables you to specify settings such as the physical path credentials, connection limits, and enabled protocols. After the defaults for sites are established, you can fine-tune these settings on each of your sites as needed.

To set the defaults for all your websites, select the Sites node in the Connections plane if the IIS Manager. In the Action pane click Set Web Site Defaults. This opens the Web Site Defaults dialog box (see Figure 23.8).

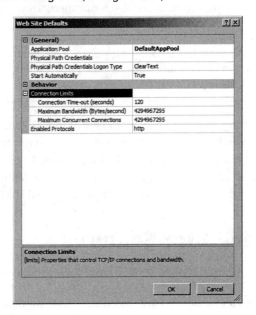

FIGURE 23.8
Web Site Defaults dialog box.

The Web Site Defaults dialog box enables you to quickly set some of the defaults for your IIS server, and these defaults will be applied to each of the sites on the server. The following are the default settings:

▶ **Application Pool**—This setting dictates the application platforms available on the server. The default application pool is DefaultAppPool, which is actually the .NET Framework. Go with the default setting.

▶ **Physical Path Credentials**—This setting enables you to use pass-through authentication (as discussed in the previous section) or you can specify a user for the path credentials.

▶ **Physical Path Credentials Logon Type**—This setting enables you to specify the logon type to access the physical path mapped to a virtual directory. ClearText is the default, but you can also select other options such as Interactive and Network. Virtual directories are discussed later in the hour.

▶ **Start Automatically**—This setting is set to True by default, meaning the website starts automatically when the IIS server comes online.

▶ **Connection Limits**—Under the Behavior node, this setting enables you to specify the connection time-out, the Maximum Bandwidth (Bytes/Second), and the Maximum Concurrent Connections.

▶ **Enabled Protocols**—This setting includes protocols (such as HTTP and/or HTTPS) that you want to have enabled for connections to the site.

By the Way

> Settings made in the Web Site Default dialog box are inherited by each website that you create on the server. Each site can then be fine-tuned as needed (as discussed in the next section).

These advanced settings (which are discussed here as global settings for all sites on the IIS server) can also be set for each of the sites on the server. To access these same settings for a specific site, select the site in the Connections tree (expand the Sites node) and then click Advanced Settings in the Actions pane. Settings you make for a specific site override the settings that you made at the global level (the server level).

Configuring Site Features

When you select a site in the Connection tree of the IIS Manager, you are provided a set of icons in the Details pane (see Figure 23.9). This is (by default) the Features View. The Features View provides a task-based system for configuring specific settings required for a particular website.

FIGURE 23.9
The Setting icons for a website.

> If you want to deploy sites that use extremely consistent settings (across all the sites on the server), you can access the Features View (and the subsequent settings that it provides) for the IIS server itself. Click the name of your IIS server in the Connections node tree. IIS and Management features are available.

By the Way

The settings available for a site (when you are in the Features view) range from authentication to directory browsing to the SSL settings for sites that use the HTTPS protocol for client access. Some of these settings are quite straightforward and are basically enabled by default. You can disable a particular setting or fine-tune the settings as needed.

> When you access the features page for a particular site, you can quickly access the folder that contains the site content, meaning the site folder. Click the Explore link in the Actions pane.

Did you Know?

To access a settings page (such as Compression or Directory Browsing) double-click the icon in the Features view). Settings that are extremely straightforward in terms of their configuration include

▶ **Compression**—By default, compression is enabled for static content on the site. This allows you to take better advantage of network bandwidth in terms of content delivery and helps improve server performance. To disable static compression, clear the Enable Static Content Compression check box on the Compression page. You can also compress dynamic content (which can affect CPU performance and actually make the site run slower because of caching issues). You need to add the Dynamic Content Compression services to the IIS role (if you did not add it during the initial installation of IIS) via the Add Services Wizard. When you make changes to the compression settings, make sure that you click Apply in the Actions pane.

▶ **Default Document Page**—This page enables you to configure the list of default documents that are used when a user accesses the site without specifying a document name. For example, a user accessing www.popeye.com is directed to the first default document in the list (such as default.htm), which is actually contained in the folder that holds the site's content. You can add or remove pages from the Default Document page and you can also use the Move Up and Move Down buttons to re-order the list of documents.

▶ **Directory Browsing**—This page is used to specify the information displayed when a user browses a directory on the web server (see Figure 23.10). By default, the time, size, extension, and date are shown. You can clear any of the setting check boxes (such as Time or Date) if you do not want these settings to appear.

FIGURE 23.10
The Directory Browsing settings for a site.

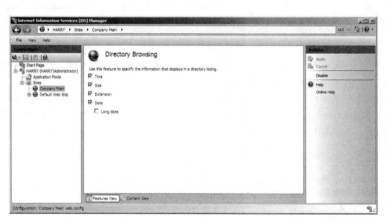

▶ **Error Pages**—This page enables you to specify custom error messages. When content that is requested cannot be accessed, a custom error message appears in the visitor's web browser. A number of custom messages are provided in the Error Pages list by default. To edit an error page, select a page on the Error Pages page and then click Edit in the Action pane. You can use the Edit Custom Error Page dialog box to specify the file path to a static file, specify a URL to execute on the site, or to respond with a 302 redirect where you specify the URL for the response. You can also add custom error pages as needed to the error page list (click Add in the Tasks pane.

▶ **Handler Mappings**—Handlers process the requests that are made to the sites and applications on your IIS server. IIS determines the handler to be used for a client browser request, based on the order of handler mappings found on the list in the Handler Mapping page. The StaticFile mapping is used by default. You can add managed handlers in the Add Managed Hander dialog box. It enables you to set the request path and specify the handler type. Mappings can also be edited. However, in most cases (although this depends on the content of your website) you do not need to edit or add handlers.

▶ **HTTP Response Headers**—When a user's browser requests a web page, a response header HTTP header is returned, which includes the HTTP version date and the content type. By default, IIS provides no custom response headers. However, you can create custom headers that pass information to the client browser when a particular page is requested. For example, you may want a custom header that provides information about a web page such as its status (under construction). To create a custom header, click the Add button. Type a name and provide a value for the header. The value is a path statement specifying the location of the header value.

✓ ▶ **MIME Types**—This page provides a list of the file extensions (MIME) that can be served from the site. IIS provides a list of default MIME extensions such as .avi (Microsoft video extension), .doc (Microsoft Word extension) and .gif (image extension). You can delete the MIME extensions that you do not need on the site (because the site serves up only certain content). If necessary, you can add other MIME types as needed (click the Add button in the Actions pane).

▶ **Modules**—IIS uses modules to handle the requests made to your website. By default, modules are provided by IIS based on the choices that you made during the addition of the IIS role to the server. Additional modules can be added to extend the capabilities of the site. These modules can be either DLLs or C++ APIs. The default modules installed provide you with all the capabilities needed for a typical website. Custom modules are required only for specific resources not accessed by the provided, default modules.

▶ **Output Caching**—This page enables you to configure caching rules that control how server content is cached (in the Output cache, meaning part of the server's memory). Output caching can improve server performance in cases where a page is accessed regulary by a client. Caching the page in the server's memory returns the page faster to the requesting client. To create an output cache rule, click Add in the Actions pane. In the Add Cache Rule dialog box (see Figure 23.11), provide the filename extension and then click User-Mode

Caching. The file is removed when the output cache is updated. You can also set a time interval so that the cache is cleared at a specific time interval. When you have completed the cache rule, click OK.

FIGURE 23.11
Create a cache rule.

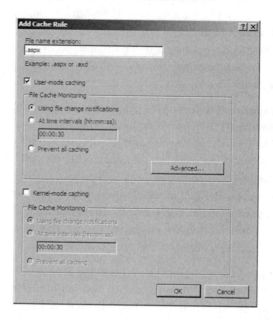

 If your server runs low on memory, the cached items will be dumped. They are then reloaded the next time a user requests that particular page.

▶ **SSL Settings**—If you are using HTTPS on the site, you can require Secure Sockets Layer encryption to be used between your server and the site's clients. If you select Require SSL on the SSL Settings page, the 40-bit data encryption method is used to secure the data as it is sent between the site and the client. You can require 128-bit encryption (select Require 128-Bit SSL). You can also specify that certificates are used by clients to access the server by selecting the Require option under the Client Certificates heading. (Certificates and the Windows Certificate Services are covered in Hour 22, "Using Network Address Translation and Certificate Services").

All the settings that we have discussed in relation to a specific site can also be set at the server level. These settings are then inherited by each site on the server. To set these various settings at the server level, click the server name in the Connections pane and then use the icons discussed in this section to access those specific settings.

1. Transmitting

Two of the available settings for a site (or the server itself, propagating all the settings to each and every site on the server), Authentication and Logging, require a little more explanation in terms of their configuration. Let's take a look at Authentication and then Logging.

Authentication

By default, the authentication for a site is set to anonymous authentication. This allows any user to access the public content on the site (which makes sense for sites available on the Web). Anonymous authentication does not require a username or password for the client's web browser to connect to the site.

To view the setting status, double-click the Authentication icon in the Features pane. The Authentication details appear (see Figure 23.12).

FIGURE 23.12
Authentication details.

Anonymous authentication is enabled by default (as shown in Figure 23.12). To edit the authentication setting, click Anonymous Authentication in the Details pane and then click Edit in the Actions pane. The Edit Anonymous Authentication Credentials dialog box opens.

To set specific user credentials (other than the default IUSR, which is created when you install IIS), click the Set button and provide the username and password for anonymous authentication. You can choose to select the Application Pool Identity option button, but the use of this setting gives anonymous users internal network access associated with the Network Service account.

Did you Know?

It is best to use the default IUSR account for anonymous access. Specifying an account or using the Application Pool Identity setting gives anonymous users any administrative rights that the account you choose might have. This can ultimately be a security risk to the server itself.

When you have completed setting the options in the Edit Anonymous Authentication Credentials dialog box, click OK. You are returned to the IIS Manager.

By the Way

If you need to disable the Anonymous Authentication as you work on a website, right-click Anonymous Authentication in the Authentication Details pane and then click Disable on the shortcut menu.

Logging

The Logging page enables you to configure how requests to the site (or to the entire server if you set this parameter at the server level) are logged (see Figure 23.14). This setting enables you to specify the format of the log file, the directory where the log file should be stored, and the log file rollover schedule.

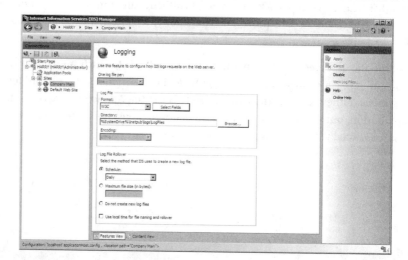

The default logging file format is W3C, which is an ASCII text file format. You can change the file format to other types such as IIS; this format does not allow you to customize the fields that are logged, however.

If you use the default W3C format, you can also select the fields that are logged (by clicking the Select Fields button). The default fields that are logged include information such as the date, time, client IP address, and the server port (see Figure 23.15).

FIGURE 23.15
Select the fields to be logged for the site.

You can clear the check boxes for logging fields to preclude the information from being included in the log file. You can also specify additional logging fields such as Server Name and Bytes Sent or Received if you wish. When you have finished editing the logging fields, click OK to close the dialog box and return to the Logging settings.

You can specify when a new log should be created for the site (or all the sites on the IIS server if you are configuring the Logging settings globally). Specify an interval such as Hourly, Daily, Weekly, or Monthly, using the Schedule drop-down list. To specify a maximum file size for the log (the required minimum size is 1048576 bytes), use the Maximum File Size (in Bytes) option button and associated text box.

You need to apply any changes you made to the Logging settings. Click Apply. After you configure the logging for the site, you can view the log file from the IIS Manager snap-in. With the Logging page open (double-click the Logging icon), click the View Log Files link.

> If you need to disable logging, click the Disable link in the Actions pane. You can then enable the logging service in the Actions pane as needed.

Configuring Virtual Directories

You may want to include content on a web server that is not contained in a local folder. You can create a website that takes advantage of a virtual directory. A virtual directory is a pointer to an actual physical directory. This physical directory can be local but it can also be a remote directory, meaning you can point to the remote content rather than actually copying it to a physical folder on the local server.

To create a virtual directory, follow these steps:

1. With a site selected in the Connections tree, click View Virtual Directories in the Actions pane. The Virtual Directories page appears.

2. In the Actions pane, click the Add Virtual Directory link. The Add Virtual Directory dialog box appears (see Figure 23.16).

FIGURE 23.16
The Add Virtual Directory dialog box.

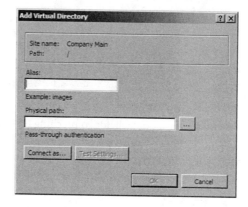

3. Type an alias for the virtual directory in the Alias box.

4. Type the physical path for the virtual directory in the Physical Path box. You can use the Browse button to locate the folder (locally or remotely) that will serve as the physical path for the virtual directory.

5. The default authentication is pass-through. You can (if you wish, but anonymous authentication works just fine) specify to connect as a specific user in the Connect As dialog box—click Connect As.

6. When you have finished configuring the virtual directory, click OK.

The new virtual directory appears in the virtual directory list (see Figure 23.17). You can edit the virtual directory by selecting it and then clicking Basic Settings.

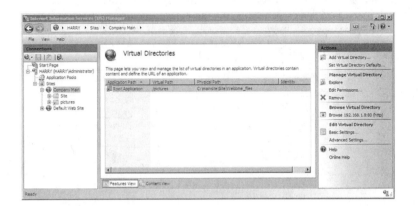

FIGURE 23.17
Virtual directories can be edited or removed.

You have access to the virtual directory items as if they were saved locally. To view the virtual directory (in Internet Explorer), click the Browse link in the Actions pane. To explore the content of the virtual directory, click Explore. You can also edit the permissions for a virtual directory by clicking the directory to select it and then click Edit Permissions. (Permissions are discussed in Hour 13, "Using Share and NTFS Permissions.")

Bottom line: The use of virtual directories makes it easier to keep track of content and configure content access. This is true whether the virtual directory points to a local folder or a remote folder.

Creating FTP Sites

Hosting an FTP site on your IIS server can be a great way to provide the users on your network with either files that they need or a place to store files that are shared as part of a particular project. Supplying a repository of downloadable files might also be important to your company as a service that you provide to your public web users. As with the web server service of IIS, the FTP service can be used on the public Internet or for your private corporate intranet.

The FTP service can be added when you install the Web Server (IIS) role. If you need to add FTP to an existing server configured for IIS, follow these steps:

1. Expand the Roles node in the Server Manager (Start, Administrative Tools, Server Manager).

2. In the Add Role Services window, click the FTP Publishing Service check box (see Figure 23.18). If the Add Roles Services Required for FTP Publishing Service dialog box opens, click Add Required Role Services. Then click Next.

FIGURE 23.18
Add the FTP
Publishing
Service.

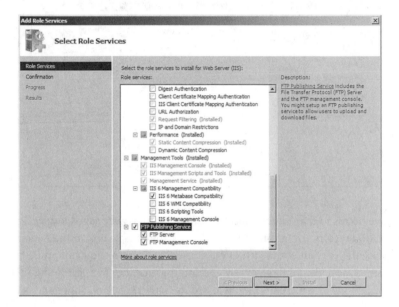

3. Click Install to add the FTP services.

4. When the installation is complete, click Close.

Expand the IIS Server node (in the IIS Manager or the Server Manager) and you can see that an FTP Sites node has been added to the node tree. However, the FTP service is actually managed in the IIS 6.0 Manager snap-in (originally provided in Windows Server 2003). To open the IIS 6.0 Manager, click the Click Here to Launch link in the IIS Manager or the Server Manager when the FTP Sites node is selected (you can also start IIS 6.0 Manager from the Start menu (Start, Administrative Tools, and then IIS 6.0 Manager).

The first thing that you should do is start the Default FTP Site. (You can use the default site or create additional sites as needed.) Expand the FTP Sites node in the IIS 6.0 Manager (see Figure 23.19).

Right-click the Default FTP Site node (or, in the future, any FTP site you want to start). On the shortcut menu, select Start. An IIS6 Manager dialog box opens. Click Yes to start the site.

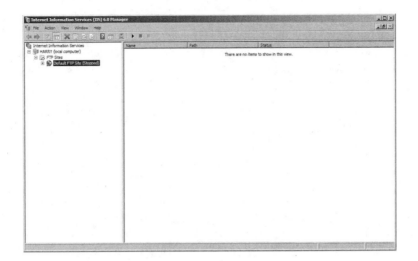

FIGURE 23.19
The IIS 6.0
Manager
snap-in.

Although you are using a snap-in from a previous version of IIS, you can set global settings for FTP sites or settings for each FTP site, using the FTP Sites Properties dialog box or the Properties dialog box for a specific site. To access the Properties dialog box, either right-click the FTP Sites node or a FTP site node and then select Properties from the shortcut menu.

As already mentioned, a default FTP site is created when you install the FTP service. Table 23.1 provides an overview of the tabs found on the Properties dialog boxes for both the global and specific settings (the tabs are very similar on the two different Properties dialog boxes).

TABLE 23.1 FTP Properties

Property Dialog Box Tab	Settings
FTP Site	Enables you to set the description for the site, the IP address, and the TCP port. It also enables you to set the number of site connections and the log format.
Security Accounts	Allows you to enable or disable anonymous logon and select the user account used for anonymous logon.
Messages	Enables you to set the banner, welcome, and exit messages displayed when users log on to the FTP site.
Home Directory	Used to specify the content directory, the local path for the FTP directory, and permissions (Read, Write, Log visits) for the site. You can also specify whether directory listings should be in UNIX or MS-DOS format.
Directory Security	Enables you to deny or permit access based on IP addresses. By default, all computers are granted access.

You can use Windows Explorer to quickly populate the FTP site. The FTP root folder is c:\inetpub\ftproot. Any files placed in this folder (just copy them to the folder, using Windows Explorer, from anywhere on your network) are available to your users. The default permission, Read, gives them the capability to download files from the site.

If you also want to enable users to upload files to the site using their web browser or an FTP client, you must enable the Write permission on the site. You can do this in the FTP site's Properties dialog box.

Right-click the site in the Details pane and then select Properties. Select the Home Directory tab (see Figure 23.20).

FIGURE 23.20
Enable Write capabilities on the FTP site.

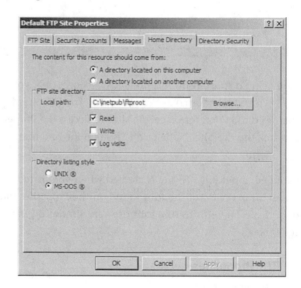

On the tab, select the Write check box. Then click OK.

After the FTP site is up and running (and has been populated with files), links to the FTP site can be placed on web pages provided by the IIS server, making it easy for users to download files from or upload them to the FTP server.

Summary

In this hour, you learned how to install and configure IIS 7 on a server running Windows Server 2008. You configured both global and specific settings for websites using the IIS Manager (7.0) snap-in, which provides a task-based access to IIS and website settings. You became familiar with installing the FTP service. You also used the IIS 6.0 Manager to view and configure FTP site settings.

Q&A

Q. *What changes have been made to the IIS 7.0 Management snap-in when compared to the previous IIS 6.0 snap-in?*

A. The IIS 7.0 Management snap-in provides a more task-oriented interface for managing the IIS server and the specific websites found on the server. The Features view in the snap-in provides quick access to settings related to authentication, authorization rules, directory browsing, and a number of other settings.

Q. *How do you set "global settings" that will affect all the websites hosted on an IIS server?*

A. Select the server name in the IIS Manager node tree and make sure that the Features view is selected. You can double-click any of the feature icons such as Authentication, Compression, or Error Pages to configure the settings for that particular set of features.

Q. *How do you add the FTP service to the IIS server?*

A. Use the Add Role Services window to add additional components to your IIS server, such as the FTP service.

Q. *How is FTP managed on your server running Windows Server 2008?*

A. The FTP service is actually managed by the previous version of the IIS Manager, IIS 6.0 Manager. When you install the FTP service, the 6.0 Manager snap-in is added to the server. You can launch the IIS 6.0 Manager from the Start menu.

Monitoring Server Performance and Network Connections

What You'll Learn in This Hour:

▶ Using the Reliability and Performance Monitor
▶ Exploring the Performance Monitor
▶ Adding Objects to the Monitor
▶ Viewing Performance Data
▶ Selecting and Understanding Counters
▶ Creating Data Collector Sets
▶ Using the Reliability Monitor
▶ Working with the Event Viewer
▶ Clearing and Saving Log Events
▶ Using the Network and Sharing Center

An important aspect of administering a Windows Server 2008 network is keeping tabs on the performance of the servers on your network and monitoring network traffic. Windows Server 2008 provides you with the capability of monitoring server performance using the Reliability and Performance Monitor. The Reliability and Performance Monitor snap-in includes the new Reliability Monitor and also access to the Performance Monitor, which has been an essential part of the Windows network operating system since its early incarnation in Windows NT Server.

Another tool, the Event Viewer, provides you with the capability of monitoring a number of different log files that can be used to identify problems and troubleshoot server and network issues. Windows Server 2008 also includes the Network and Sharing Center, which can provide real-time information related to your network. This includes the type of connection the server has to the network and also provides capabilities for troubleshooting connection problems. We look at all three of these tools in this hour.

Using the Reliability and Performance Monitor

The Reliability and Performance Monitor snap-in enables you to monitor server performance in real time. You can monitor hardware and application performance and create threshold alerts and performance reports. In terms of defining performance and reliability, *performance* describes how quickly the server completes the tasks it must accomplish. *Reliability*, on the other hand, is more a measure of how often the server performs exactly as you would expect in relation to its configuration.

The Reliability and Performance Monitor snap-in also provides access to the Performance Monitor, which was available in Windows Server 2003, and the new Reliability Monitor. The Performance Monitor enables you to add counters to quickly view real-time hardware information such as the percent processor time and also view information related to system services such as HTTP (on a web server).

The Reliability Monitor provides a System Stability chart that can be used to quickly view specific information about hardware, application, and Windows failures. You can click on a chart date, which runs along the x-axis of the chart and then view various system stability reports related to alerts and failures. The Reliability Monitor, which, in effect, provides some of the same type of information that you could glean from the Event Viewer, is discussed later in the hour.

Obviously, the Reliability and Performance Monitor provides a lot of potential information related to how a server is performing in terms of both hardware and software (including the operating system). What you are really trying to do when you monitor server performance is identify potential performance bottlenecks (say the CPU or the hard drive). When you measure reliability, you are looking for such things as device drivers that failed to initialize or services that had to stop and restart. Reliability often relates to the server configuration rather than hardware configuration, as performance does.

You can open the Reliability and Performance Monitor in the Server Manager (Start, Administrative Tools, Reliability and Performance Monitor). Expand the Diagnostic node and then select the Reliability and Performance node.

You can also run the Reliability and Performance Monitor snap-in in the MMC (Start, Administrative Tools, Reliability and Performance Monitor). Figure 24.1 shows the Reliability and Performance Monitor in the MMC.

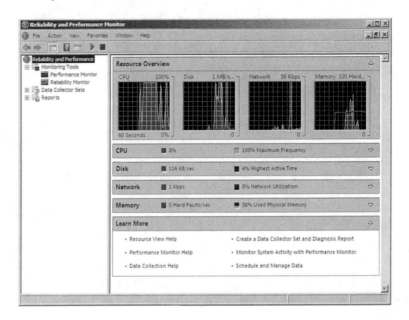

FIGURE 24.1
The Reliability and Performance Snap-in.

The Resource View pane of the Reliability and Performance Monitor provides you with a quick look at CPU, Disk, Network, and Memory usage on the server. Real-time counters at the top of the window show you how each of these resources is currently affected by demand on the server from such things as user access, resources served to users, and other processes running on the server that are related to the various roles you have assigned the server.

Below the Resource View graphs is the Resource View details area. By default, all the Resource details are closed and show a counter that provides the running data points that are shown in the associated graph.

You can expand each of the Resource views to view the details related to a particular resource such as the CPU resource, which measures the total percentage of CPU capacity currently in use. When you expand the CPU resource, you are in the Resource Oveview details (for CPU capacity), which provides a detail table (see Figure 24.2).

FIGURE 24.2
The Resource
Overview details
for CPU usage.

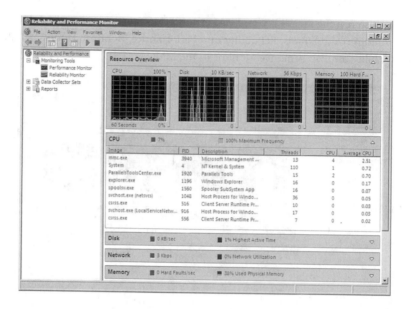

Let's look at each of the resources measured in the Reliability and Performance Monitor and what kind of details are provided when you look at the expanded view details for a particular resource. The Resource view provides the following information:

▶ **CPU**—The total percentage of CPU use is displayed in green. The CPU Maximum Frequency is displayed in blue. The details table contains the following:

  ▶ **Image**—Application using the CPU

  ▶ **PID**—The application instance's process ID

  ▶ **Description**—The application name

  ▶ **Threads**—Active threads from the application instance

  ▶ **CPU**—CPU cycles active from the application instance

  ▶ **Average CPU**—Average CPU load (over the last 60 seconds) from the application instance

By the Way

The *PID* or process *identifier* is the unique number the operating system assigns to a process. A *thread* is part of an application that can execute independently.

- **Disk**—The total input/output (current) is displayed in green. The percentage for the highest active time is displayed in blue. The details table contains the following:

  - **Image**—Application using the disk

  - **PID**—The application instance's process ID

  - **File**—The file read/written by an application

  - **Read**—The current read speed (in bytes/minute) for the data by an application

  - **Write**—The speed (bytes/minute) at which the application is writing data

  - **IO Priority**—The I/O task priority for the application

  - **Response Time**—Disk response time in milliseconds

- **Network**—Displays the total network traffic (Kbps) in green and the network capacity percentage currently in use in blue. The details table contains the following:

  - **Image**—Application using the network resources

  - **PID**—The application instance's process ID

  - **Description**—The application name

  - **Address**—The network address (IP address, FQDN name, or computer name) with which the local computer is exchanging information

  - **Send**—The data currently being sent from the local computer (as sent by the application named in the Image line)

  - **Receive**—The amount of data currently being received (bytes/minute)

  - **Total**—Total bandwidth used (that is, sent and received) in bytes/minute by the application

- **Memory**—Displays the hard faults per second in green and the physical memory currently in use percentage in blue. The details table contains the following:

A hard fault or page fault is basically when data requested by the application instance is not in real memory and so must be retrieved from the paging file and loaded into memory.

By the Way

▶ **Image**—Application using the network resources

▶ **PID**—The application instance's process ID

▶ **Description**—The application name

▶ **Hard Faults/Min**—Hard faults (per minute) resulting from the application instance; a lot of hard faults would indicate that your server's memory is becoming a performance bottleneck

▶ **Working Set (KB)**—The amount of memory (in kilobytes) currently being used by the application instance

▶ **Shareable (KB)**—The amount of memory in the working set that may be available to other applications.

▶ **Private (KB)**—The amount of memory in the working set reserved for the application instance

Obviously, the Resource view details provide a lot of information. But the key to using this information really lies in the fact that server performance can be affected in a negative way by two things: hardware problems and software problems.

The typical hardware bottlenecks for a server are the CPU, disks, network adapter (or adapters), and memory. The Reliability and Performance Monitor provides graphs for these hardware components because they can often be the reason the server is underperforming.

If the problem isn't directly related to a hardware malfunction, the problem can be a software issue that is monopolizing one of the key server hardware components, such as the CPU or the network adapter. Having quick access to the information related to the application instance enables you to potentially identify a malfunctioning software entity.

So, although you can gain more specific real-time data using the various counters available in the Performance Monitor (discussed in the next section) and more details related to server hardware and software events that are logged in the Event Viewer (discussed later in the hour), the Reliability and Performance Monitor is definitely a quick way to survey a server's health.

By the
Way

The Reliability Monitor, a new tool provided by the Reliability and Performance Monitor snap-in, provides a system stability chart that enables you to view events related to software, application, and hardware failures. It provides quick access to "bad" events in a timeline, making it a useful addition to server troubleshooting, particularly when used with Event Viewer data. The Reliability Monitor is discussed later in this hour.

Exploring the Performance Monitor

The Windows Server 2008 Performance Monitor provides you with a visual tool for measuring the performance of your Windows server (you can also monitor other computers on the network). Performance Monitor looks at such hardware performance parameters as processor utilization, drive performance, and memory usage. Each item (such as the processor) that can be analyzed with the Performance Monitor is referred to as an *object*.

A performance data item that can be measured for a particular object is called a *counter*. For example, the processor (an object) has a number of counters that you can view, including the % Processor Time and the Interrupts/Sec counters.

Using counters to analyze the various performance aspects of a particular hardware component (an object) enables you to determine whether a piece of hardware on a server (such as the processor or hard drive) has become a bottleneck in terms of server performance.

The Performance Monitor can display the data as a graph (see Figure 24.3), a histogram (a horizontal or vertical bar graph format), or a report. You set the performance counters that are viewed in the Performance Monitor Details pane.

You select a particular object and then add the counters related to the object you want to monitor. The following section examines adding object counters.

FIGURE 24.3
The
Performance
Monitor displays
data as a
graph.

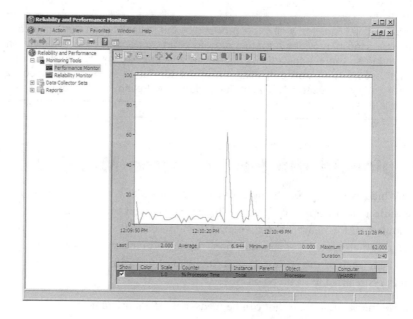

Adding Objects to the Monitor

Use the Add button (+) on the Monitor toolbar to add objects to the Performance
Monitor. Click the Add button; the Add Counters dialog box appears (see Figure 24.4).

FIGURE 24.4
The Add
Counters dialog
box is used to
add counters to
the System
Monitor.

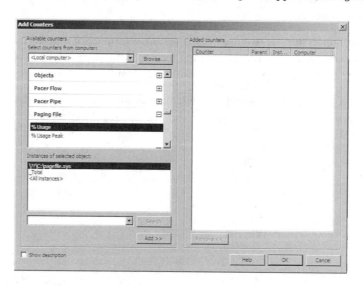

You can also open the Add Counters dialog box by right-clicking the graph or the legend at the bottom of the graph and selecting Add Counters from the shortcut menu.

The dialog box enables you to select where the counters are located (on the local computer or other computer on the network) and for which performance object you want to add a counter. Each performance object, such as a Processor, has a number of performance counters. Each of these counters uses different parameters to measure the object's performance.

By default, % Processor Time (monitoring the processor) is the only counter that appears in the Performance Monitor.

A number of different options are available in the Add Counters dialog box (almost too many). For clarity, some of these options are listed and defined in Table 24.1.

TABLE 24.1   Add Counters Dialog Box Options

Available Counters	Provides categories of counters for the currently monitored computer. Expand a category to view individual counters for a particular object.
Select Counters from Computer	A drop-down box is used to select the computer to be monitored.
Show Description	A check box that, when selected, shows a description of the currently selected counter group or counter.
Instances of Selected Object	When you select a group or a specific counter, a list is provided of the process instances for that group or object. Click a process in the Instances of Selected Object list and then click Add to add it to the counter. Adding all instances for a particular group such as PhysicalDisk provides aggregate drive performance rather than performance for a particular drive.
Search	You can highlight a counter group and then type a process name in the Search box. Click Search to find a particular process counter in the group. You can re-use search names that you enter in the Search box by using the Search drop-down list.

You can add a particular counter from the expanded counter group by selecting it or by selecting a particular instance of the selected object in the Instances of Select Object box. You then click the Add button. You can add any number of counters; however, remember that in Graph view, a large number of counters can give rise to a very busy (and confusing) graph.

When you have finished adding the appropriate counters, click the OK button. You are returned to the Performance Monitor. Your new counters appear on the graph.

Each counter that you add to the graph is assigned a different graph color. This enables you to monitor multiple counters on the graph.

By the Way

> Remote performance monitoring is nothing more than selecting performance objects and counters that are on a remote server on the network. Selecting the computer to be monitored is handled in the Add Counters dialog box.

The graph provides a visual representation of your counters, but you can view statistics for a particular counter by selecting the counter name in the legend at the bottom of the graph. The last instance measured (Instance), an average, a minimum, a maximum, and the duration (monitoring time) are provided directly below the graph for the selected counter.

Did you Know?

> You can highlight a particular counter by selecting the counter in the legend and then clicking the Highlight button on the toolbar (or pressing Ctrl-H). This turns the graph lines white so that they are easily viewed. Click the Highlight button a second time to turn off highlighting.

You can also delete counters from the graph. Select the counter in the legend area and then click the Delete (Delete key) button on the Graph toolbar. If you want to remove all the counters on the graph, right-click on the Counter list and then select Remove All Counters from the shortcut menu.

Did you Know?

> To clear the current activity on the chart in the Details pane (but not remove the current counters), right-click on the Counter list and then select Clear from the shortcut menu.

Adding counters is a simple process, but understanding what the various counters mean is another story. We'll look at some of the counters that you might want to use in the Performance Monitor and how the values that they provide give you insight into the performance of a particular object (coming up later in this hour).

Viewing Performance Data

The default view for the System Monitor is Graph view. It provides real-time data, using a line graph plotted to an x-axis of time and a y-axis that relates to the particular counter that you are using (such as %use, where the chart would plot from 0 to 100%). Two other views are available: Histogram view and Report view.

Using the Histogram View

The Histogram bar view provides a bar-graph view of each counter that you add to the chart. To switch to Histogram view, click the Change Graph Type drop-down list on the toolbar and select Histogram Bar.

This view is useful for comparing different objects and their overall affect on computer performance. Figure 24.5 shows a histogram displaying the default System Monitor counters.

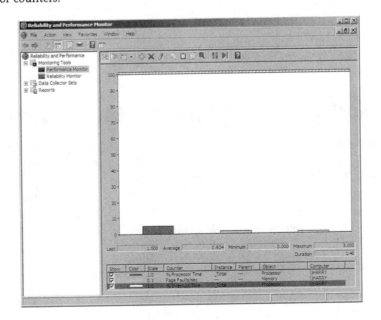

FIGURE 24.5
The histogram bar is useful for comparing overall performance effects.

Using the Report View

Report view enables you to see the various counter statistics (in real time) as a text report that lists each counter. To switch to Report view, click the Change Graph Type drop-down list on the toolbar. The Chart and Histogram view give you a visual look at your performance counters, but Report view provides actual running statistics (see Figure 24.6).

FIGURE 24.6
Report view provides running statistics for the counters.

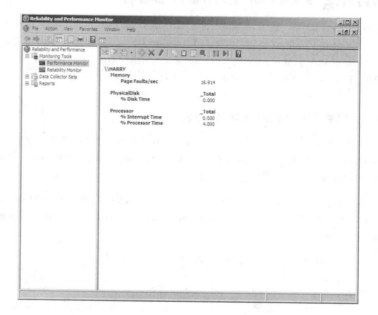

Selecting and Understanding Counters

Selecting counters that will actually tell you something about the performance of your servers and help you understand what they are telling you is an extremely important aspect of using the System Monitor. As already mentioned, the System Monitor provides counters for hardware objects such as hard drives and processors, and includes counters for services that you have installed such as DNS and WINS. Counters are also available to track protocol performance such as IPv4 and NWlink.

Because hardware can often be a limiting factor in server performance, let's look at some of the counters that you will want to watch as you assess the performance of a server's processor, hard drives, and memory.

Useful Processor Counters

A potential bottleneck on a server is the processor. That is why high-end servers support multiple processors. The bottleneck arises because the processor can't keep up with all the system calls that it gets from different software processes running on the server.

Counters that can help you track processor performance are listed here:

- **%Processor Time**—This counter (found under the Processor object or counter group) is a measure of the time that the processor is executing a nonidle thread. If it is consistently around 75–80%, you might need to upgrade the processor on the server (or add another processor if the motherboard allows for dual processing).

- **Interrupts/Sec**—If this counter (found under the Processor object or counter group) increases beyond 3,500 (it's the average number of interrupt calls that the processor is receiving from hardware devices, such as a network card or modem) and the %Processor Time counter does not increase comparatively, your problem might not be your processor, but a device that is sending spurious interrupts to the processor (such as a bad network card or SCSI card). This can be caused by the device itself or by the driver you are using for the device.

Make sure you are using the most up-to-date drivers for hardware devices on a server. This can negate issues with interrupt overload.

- **Processor Queue Length**—This counter, found under the System object or counter group, measures the number of threads waiting to be processed. If it reaches a value of 10 or more, the processor might be a bottleneck. This means that you need either a faster processor or you need to go even further and upgrade to a multiprocessor motherboard on the server.

Useful Disk Counters

Another hardware device that can be a potential bottleneck on a server is the computer's physical drives. Not only is the available space important, but the drive's read/write speed is also an issue. Counters that you might want to monitor related to disk performance are listed here (the object type precedes the counter name):

- **%Disk Time**—This counter (found under the PhysicalDisk counter group) shows the percentage of elapsed time that the drive is busy with read/write functions. If the counter consistently reads around 90%, the drive is having problems. You can defragment the drive, replace the drive, or configure a volume stripe to replace the drive (stripe sets are faster than a single disk).

▶ **Disk Reads/Sec or Disk Writes/Sec**—These counters are found under the PhysicalDisk counter group. Check the manufacturer's specifications for the drive. If the I/O operations shown by this counter are lower than the specifications, the drive is having problems. Defragmenting might help remedy the problem.

▶ **%Free Space**—This counter, found under the Logical Disk counter group, indicates free space on a volume. If this counter goes below 20%, you need to increase the volume size or put a larger drive in the system.

▶ **Current Disk Queue Length**—This counter, found under the Logical Disk counter group, measures the number of outstanding or queued requests for the volume at a particular moment in time (when the measurement is taken). If the average value is more than 2, disk waits are slowing down access to the volume. You can install a faster drive or consider using a stripe set or using a volume on another server.

Useful Memory Counters

Another key resource on network servers is memory (RAM). More memory (above the Windows Server 2008 minimum memory specification of 512MB) is always better. Remember that when a Windows server uses its entire RAM, it resorts to the paging file on the hard drive (what we sometimes call *virtual memory*); this means that data dropped to the paging file must be reloaded into RAM to be used. To track memory issues, use these counters in the Memory counter group:

▶ **Available Bytes**—This counter is a measure of the physical memory available to running processes. If it consistently falls to less than 4MB, you need more memory on the server.

▶ **Pages/Sec**—This counter measures the number of times the computer must rely on the paging file (dumping items in RAM to the hard drive temporarily). This event is known as a *page fault*. If this counter consistently reads at 20 on the System Monitor, you should add more RAM. Excessive page faults can cause systemwide delays in terms of server access.

▶ **Committed Bytes**—This counter shows the amount of RAM being used and the amount of space that will be needed for the paging file if the data had to be moved to the disk. You should see a value on this counter that is less than the RAM installed on the server. If the value is more than the RAM, you are using the paging file too often; add more memory.

Creating Data Collector Sets

Windows Server 2008 puts a new spin on the concept of collecting server performance data with the data collector set. A *data collector set* is basically a grouping of
data collectors. These data collectors can be performance counters (such as the
counters discussed in the previous sections), Event trace data, and even system configuration information such as Registry key values. So, in its most basic terms, a
data collector set is just a convenient container that enables you to group different
performance and system data collection entities. You can then quickly review the
different data points in the data collector set, using the Performance Monitor, log
files, or reports.

> **By the Way**
>
> Data collector sets basically replace the counter and trace logs that you needed
> to create in previous versions of the Windows network operating system.

To create data collector sets, you can use the Performance Monitor, use a data collector set template, or create one from scratch. Creating a data collector set via the
Performance Monitor is extremely straightforward.

> **Did you Know?**
>
> Windows Server 2008 provides three premade data collector sets that can be
> found when you expand the System node (under the Data Collector Sets node) in
> the Reliability and Performance Monitor node tree. These data collector sets are
> LAN Diagnostics, System Diagnostics, and System Performances. Click on one of
> the data collector sets to view the trace, performance counter, and configuration
> events that make up that particular set. You can right-click any of the data points
> in the Details pane and the select Properties to view the specifics related to that
> performance counter, key value, or event trace. These data collector sets are not
> running (stopped) by default. If you want to experiment with a particular data col-
> lector set or all the sets, right-click the set node in the node tree and select Start
> from the shortcut menu.

Add the counters that you want to include in the data collector set to the
Performance Monitor (as discussed in the previous sections) and then right-click the
Performance Monitor node in the Reliability and Performance Monitor, point at
New, and then click Data Collector Set. The Create New Data Collector Set Wizard
opens. Supply a name for the data collector set in the Name box and then click
Next.

On the next wizard screen, you are asked to provide a location where the data is to
be collected. By default the data is kept on your system drive as a subfolder in the
Perflogs\Admin path (see Figure 24.7).

FIGURE 24.7
Specify the path
where the data
is to be saved.

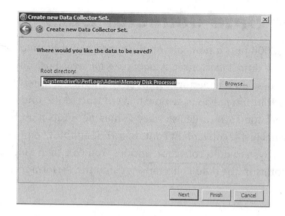

You can use the default folder supplied or use the Browse button to specify another path. After specifying the path, click Next.

On the next wizard page, you specify whether you want to run the data collector set under the default username (the user currently logged on to the server) or another username (you can delegate ownership of this data collector set by using the Change button). You can also specify whether you want to start the collector set by selecting the Start This Data Collector Set Now option button. The default option is Save and Close (which for discussion purposes we use for this set). Click Finish to create and save the new data collector set.

The new data collector set appears as a new subnode when you expand the User Defined node in the Reliability and Performance Monitor node tree. To start the new data collector set, right-click the set's node and then click Start. The various data collectors that you added to the data collector set (in this case all Performance Monitor Counters) begin collecting data.

You can easily add data collectors to this (or any) data collector set. Right-click the data collector set, point at New, and select Data Collector. The Create New Data Collector Wizard opens. After naming the data collector, you can select an event trace to add to the data collector via the Event Trace Providers dialog box, as shown in Figure 24.8 (click the Add button to open the dialog box).

As already mentioned, you can create data collector sets based on a template. Windows Server 2008 provides three templates: Basic, System Diagnostics, and System Performance.

The Basic template is designed for modification, meaning you will want to add additional data collectors to the set after you've created it. A data collector set based on the Basic template includes, by default, the Processor performance counters, the Windows Registry key (HKEY_LOCAL_Machine\SOFTWARE\Microsoft\Windows NT\Current), and the Windows Kernel Trace (a trace event related to the Windows kernel).

The System Diagnostics template is designed to create a data collector set that enables you to maximize system performance. The report generated by this data collector set looks at hardware resources and system response times. A data collector set based on this template includes performance counters for the processor, physical disk, memory, and network interfaces. In terms of trace events, the Windows Kernel Trace is included. A number of Configuration data collectors, including those for the operating system, BIOS, and NTFS performance are included in a data collector set based on this template.

To create a new data collector set based on a template, right-click the User Defined node in the node tree, point at New, and then select Data Collector Set. By default, selecting the Create New Data Collector Set option creates the new collector set from a template (see Figure 24.9).

All you have to do is name the new data collector set and then choose one of the templates (Basic, System Diagnostics, or System Performance). After creating the new data collector set based on a template, you can add addition data collectors to the new data collector as needed.

FIGURE 24.9
Create a new
collector set
based on a
template.

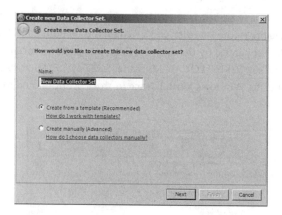

Did you Know?

You can add or remove data collectors (trace events, performance counters, and configuration collectors) from any of the performance counter sets that you create. It doesn't matter whether you create the data collector set from counters on the Performance Monitor, the data collectors provided by a template, or a data collector set that you have created from scratch.

Creating a Data Collector Set from Scratch

Probably the best way to start your exploration of data collector sets is to create a data collector set from scratch. The only real difference between creating a data collector set from scratch and using a data collector set based on a template is that you don't inherit all the data collectors that would be provided by the template. This enables you to think through the process of what kind of data you would want to the data collector set to collect and then report.

To create a data collector set from scratch, follow these steps:

1. In the Reliability and Performance Monitor snap-in, right-click the User Defined node (under the Data Collector Sets node), point at New, and then select Data Collector Set. The Create New Data Collector Set wizard opens.

2. On the first wizard page, type a name for the data collector set in the Name box.

3. Click the Create Manually (Advanced) option button and then click Next.

4. On the next wizard page (see Figure 24.10), select the type of data collectors (data logs) you want to create. You can select to include data collectors from the performance counter, event trace data, and system configuration

information by selecting the appropriate check boxes (let's assume that you selected all three for this discussion's sake). Click Next.

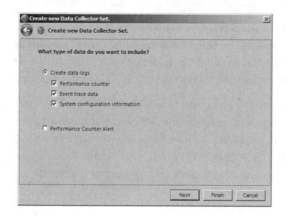

FIGURE 24.10
Select the data collector types you want to include in the set.

5. On the next wizard page, add the performance counters you want to include in the data collector set. Click the Add button and select counters from the counter groups (exactly as you would when adding counters to the Performance Monitor). Click OK. The Performance counters you selected will be listed. Click Next to continue.

6. On the next wizard page, you select the event trace providers to be included in the data collector set. Click the Add button; the Event Trace Providers dialog box opens. Select the trace providers you want to include and then click OK. Repeat the process to add other event trace providers. The event trace providers that you have selected appear on the wizard page (see Figure 24.11). Click Next.

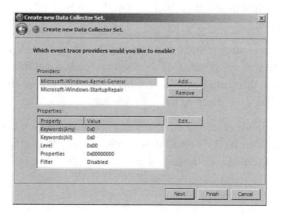

FIGURE 24.11
Add the event trace providers you want to include in the data collector set.

7. On the next wizard page, you can add the Windows software Registry key to the data collector set (if you want to include it). Click Add and the software Registry key is added to the Registry keys list. Click Next.

8. On the next wizard page, you supply the directory where you would like the data to be saved. The default is a subfolder (based on your data collector set's name) in the PerfLogs\Admin folder on your system drive. You can use the Browse button to specify another path if you want. Click Next.

9. On the last wizard page, you can delegate the data collector set to another user by using the Change button. By default it is owned by the user currently logged on to the server. To save and close (the default setting) the new data collector set, click Finish. You are returned to the Reliability and Performance Monitor. The new data collector set appears as a subnode of the User Defined node in the node tree.

After you have created the new data collector set, you can open the Properties dialog box for that set. The Properties dialog box for a data collector set enables you to set the directory for the set on the Directory tab (if you want to change it) and you can also set the security settings for the set (user permissions) on the Security tab.

You can actually save a template based on a data collector set that you have created. You can then connect to other servers on the network and create a data collector set for that server based on your own template. Right-click the data collector set you have created and choose Save Template from the shortcut menu.

Two important settings that you can configure on the set's Properties dialog box are the schedule for the set and whether you want a stop condition. To set a schedule for the set, click the Schedule tab and then click Add. The Folder action dialog box opens (see Figure 24.12).

Configure the active range to include a beginning date and an expiration date (if you want to include the expiration date). Then, in the Launch area of the dialog box, specify a start time and the days on which you want the set to run. Click OK to close the dialog box and return to the Schedule tab.

To create a stop condition for the data collector set, click the Stop Condition tab (see Figure 24.13). You can set the overall duration for the set or specify limits based on duration or maximum size of the log file.

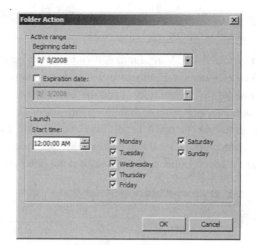

FIGURE 24.12
You can create a schedule for the data collector set.

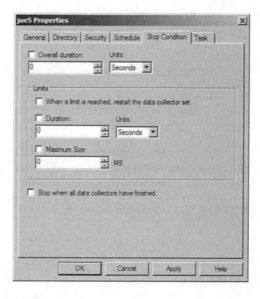

FIGURE 24.13
You can set a stop condition for the data collector set.

After you have specified the stop condition for the data collector set, click OK. This closes the Properties dialog box for the set and returns you to the Reliability and Performance Monitor.

Viewing Data Collector Set Reports

After you have created a data collector set (or sets) and then started a particular data collector set (either manually by right-clicking a set and selecting Start or using a set schedule), the data collector set collects data. After the data has been collected, you can view this data in a report.

The Reliability and Performance Monitor makes it very easy for you to view the data collected by your data collector set. In the node tree under the Reports node, expand the User Defined node (or the System node if you are using one of the predefined data collector sets such as LAN Diagnostics or System Performance). Expand a specific User Defined (or System) data collector set. A Report icon appears under the expanded node (there are multiple Report icons if you have run the set more than once). Select the Report icon and the report appears in the Details pane (see Figure 24.14).

FIGURE 24.14
You can set view a report generated for a data collector set.

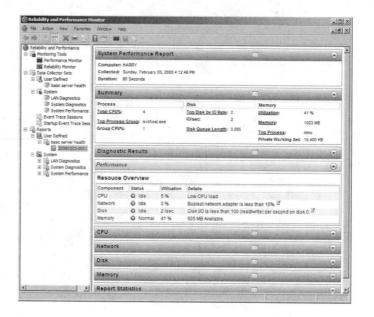

The report provides summary information based on the data collectors that you included in the set. For example, a data set collector that includes data collectors related to the CPU, disk usage, and memory (such as the one shown in Figure 24.14) provides summary data related to CPU, disk, and memory usage. A diagnostic results area contains performance information (if you included performance counters in the set).

You can see additional information by expanding a particular resource area such as CPU or Memory (again depending on the data collectors you included in the set). To view the statistics related to the report itself, expand the Report Statistics area. This data includes the start time and end time for the data collection and the number of processed events. It also tells you the files that are involved in the data collection.

Because performance counters are typically part of a data collection set, you can switch from the Report view (the default view for the data collector set report) to the Performance Monitor. This places a snapshot of the same data available in the report into the Performance Monitor (see Figure 24.15).

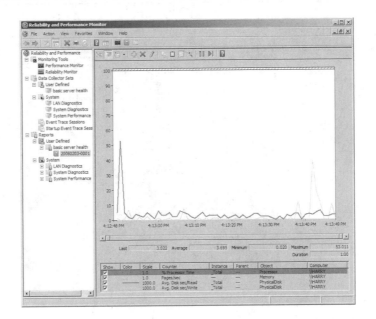

FIGURE 24.15
View the report
data in the
Performance
Monitor.

Click View Data in Performance Monitor on the Reliability and Performance Monitor toolbar. You can use the timeline scrollbar to move around the timeline to view the data. To return to the report, right-click the report icon in the node tree, point at View, and then select Report.

Data collector sets enable you to capture the data that you find the most important in terms of monitoring server hardware and software performance. As you collect data over time in your data collector set reports, you can compare these reports to see whether server performance is degrading or whether a change in the server configuration (such as the addition of a role) is causing performance issues.

Using the Reliability Monitor

The Reliability Monitor is a new tool provided by Windows Server 2008. The Reliability Monitor is designed to enable you to monitor (over time) the relative stability (relative to the initial benchmark set when you start the Reliability Monitor for the first time) of your server.

The Reliability Monitor actually calculates a system stability index that is viewed as the System Stability Chart (see Figure 24.16). The x-axis of the chart is time and the stability indicators (providing the y-axis) are software installs (and uninstalls), application failures, hardware failures, Windows failures, and miscellaneous failures.

FIGURE 24.16
The Reliability
Monitor tracks
system stability
over time.

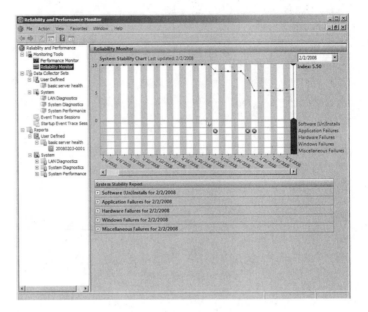

The System Stability Chart enables you to select actual event markers on the on the chart and then view the data related to that event in the System Stability Report area of the Reliability Monitor. Different types of markers on the chart provide different kinds of report information. For example, an information icon when selected (in a date column) shows what took place successfully on that date. For example, you might have installed a driver or other software successfully on the date.

The failure icons (the x in the red circle) show when a failure has taken place. For example, a particular application might have failed. Figure 24.17 shows an application failure. In the Application Failures report area, the information provided notes that Internet Explorer stopped working on that date.

The Reliability Monitor provides another avenue for quickly diagnosing problems with your server. The high end for the stability index is 10. When you see the chart dip below this number, you will find that an associated failure or failures has occurred on the server. Viewing the details of a failure enables you to remedy software installation issues, bad drivers, or even Windows installation issues.

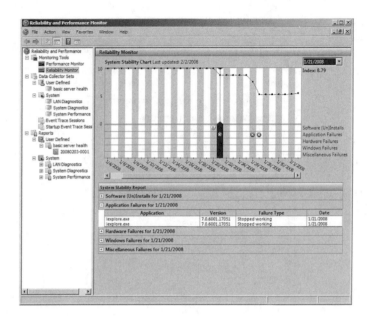

EVENT VIEWER

Working with the Event Viewer   *PERFORMANCE MONITOR*

A huge number of things are happening at any one time on a server: Users are logging in and accessing files, drives are spinning away, and processors are trying to   ✓
make sense of it all. Each of these instances is considered an *event*. Being able to
monitor these events and use them to interpret the health of your servers is an
important aspect of administering a Windows Server 2008 network.

As its name suggests, the Event Viewer is used to view events. Although it is more of
a passive tool (it doesn't supply you with the real-time data that you see in the
Performance Monitor), it does give you access to a great deal of information.

As you have already seen as we have explored the various Windows Server 2008
server roles throughout this book, you can view the events related to a particular
role by selecting that role node in the Server Manager. For example, you can view
the events related to file services on a file server by clicking the File Services node in
the Server Manager node tree (see Figure 24.18).

Although the Server Manager provides quick access to events related to a role, let's
take a closer look at the Event Viewer, which can be opened as a separate snap-in.
The Event Viewer accumulates events in a number of log files: Event Viewer can help
you monitor hardware, application, service, and security issues.

FIGURE 24.18
View events related to a particular role in the Server Manager.

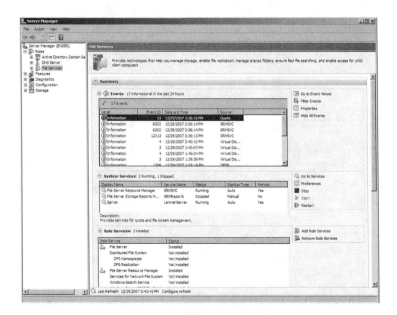

The Event Viewer (Start, Administrative Tools, Event Viewer) provides two main categories of logs: Windows logs and Applications and Services logs. The Windows logs include the following:

▶ **Application log**—This log records events about the various applications running on the system. The developer typically presets these events in the software. The application log also records alerts configured in the System Monitor.

▶ **Security log**—This log records events related to the audit policies that you configure in Group Policy (Group Policy is discussed in Hour 11, "Deploying Group Policy and Network Access Protection"), such as the auditing of file access or the logon of a particular user or group of users. This log also tracks events related to resource use (such as files) on the network shares.

▶ **Setup log**—This log records events related to application installation and setup. This includes events regarding the adding or removal of server roles, information events when a role is added successfully, and warning events when a restart is necessary to finalize the addition of a role.

▶ **System log**—This log provides log entries based on a number of Windows Server 2008 presets. This includes information on things such as driver failures and services that fail to load. Anything to do with services or system resources can show up in this log.

A new set of logs, the Applications and Services logs, provide event logging for individual applications and server components. The default Application and Services logs include the Hardware Events (events related to hardware installation and failure), Internet Explorer (Internet Explorer–specific events) and Key Management Service (which is related to the use of encryption keys when sending and receiving data to other computers on the network). Other logs available in this category depend on the software and roles installed on the server.

A system of icons is used to classify the type of event that has been recorded in a particular event log. In the System log and the Application log, you can find the following event categories (each represented by a different icon in the Event Viewer):

▶ **The Information icon**—Denotes the logging of successful system events and other processes

▶ **The Warning icon**—Shows a noncritical error on the system

▶ **The Error icon**—Indicates the failure of a major function (such as a driver failure)

To view a specific log in the Event Monitor, select the log's node in the node tree. The events recorded in that log appear in the Details pane. Figure 24.19 shows Information, Warning, and Error icons in the System log.

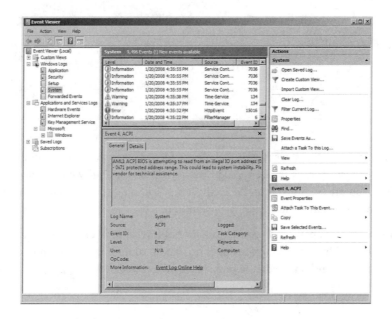

FIGURE 24.19
Different icons are used to identify the type of event recorded in a log file.

Two additional icons are found in the Security log:

▶ **The Success Audit icon**—Shows that a security access event was successful (such as the access of a certain folder or file on the network)

▶ **The Failure Audit icon**—Shows that an audited security event failed (such as the failure of a user logon)

To view the properties of a particular event in a log, double-click on the event's icon in the Details pane. For example, you may want to see the details related to an Error event logged in the System log. Figure 24.20 shows the event properties (from the Service Control Manager Eventlog provider) specifying that the parallel port driver service failed to start.

FIGURE 24.20
You can view the properties of a logged event.

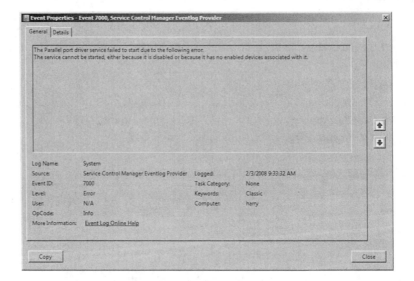

Microsoft now provides event-specific help for logged events. For more information on a logged event, click the Event Log Online Help link in the event's Properties dialog box. You are informed that the Event Viewer will send the information related to the event over the Internet. Click Yes to continue.

Internet Explorer opens and provides additional information on the event (see Figure 24.21). This information includes an explanation of the event and possible actions to be taken to remedy the problem related to the event.

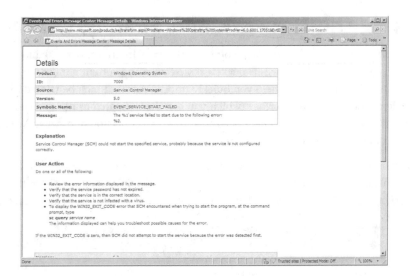

FIGURE 24.21
You quickly get
additional infor-
mation on a par-
ticular event.

Clearing and Saving Log Events

Over time, a number of events build up in the various log files. You can clear the
events from a particular log and (if you want) save the log events to a file for later
inspection or reference.

In the Event Viewer snap-in, right-click any of the log icons in the tree pane. Select
Clear Log from the shortcut menu. A message box appears asking whether you
want to save the particular log before clearing or just clear the log. If you want to
save the log file, click Save and Clear. The Save As dialog box for the log appears
and enables you to designate a filename and path in which to save the log file.
Then click Save.

You can also save the events in a log without clearing the log contents. Right-click a
log icon and then select Save Events As. The Save As dialog box appears. Provide a
name and a path for the new log file, and then click Save. You can then load the
saved event log file into the Event Viewer for later reference (right-click a log icon
and select Open Log File).

Using the Event Viewer on a regular basis helps you keep your server and your network up and running. Becoming familiar with the different types of events that are
logged helps you get a handle on potential server problems before they become a
major meltdown.

Using the Network and Sharing Center

The Performance Monitor can help you track real-time information related to a server's network interface such as packets sent/second and current bandwidth. And the Reliability Monitor can help you quickly track events that may be related to a problem with a network interface (which you can then research using the Event Viewer), the quickest way to check a server's network connection and network settings is to use the Network and Sharing Center.

To open the Network and Sharing Center, click Start and then Control Panel. In the Control Panel, click the View Network Status and Tasks link under the Network and Internet Group. The Network and Sharing Center window opens (see Figure 24.22).

FIGURE 24.22
The Network and Sharing Center.

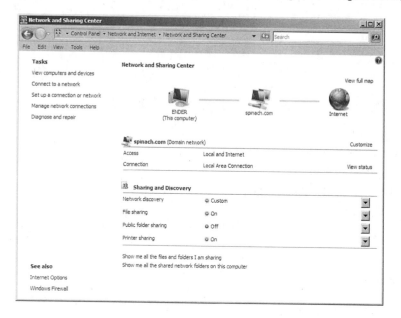

At the top of the Network and Sharing Center, a map of the server's network connection is provided. In the case of Figure 24.22, the map shows that the server named Ender is connected to the spinach.com domain and also has a connection that provides access to the public Internet.

To view the full map in the Network and Sharing Center, you must enable mapping on the local Group Policy (this can be done on a computer running Windows Server 2008 or Windows Vista). Click Start and type **MMC** in the Start Search box. Click MMC in the Search Results and the MMC opens. Click File, and then Add/Remove Snap-ins. Select the Group Policy Object Editor and then click Add. The Group Policy Object Wizard opens; make sure that Local Computer appears in the Group Policy Object box and then click Finish. The GPO Editor for the Local Computer opens in the MMC. In the node tree, expand Administrative Templates and then Network, and then click the Link-Layer Topology Discovery node. In the Details pane, enable the Turn on Mapper I/O (LLTDIO) Driver policy and the Turn on Responder (RSPNDR) Driver policy (double-click the policies and then enable them in their Properties dialog boxes).

Did you Know?

You can view a more complete map of the network by clicking the View Full Map link (see Figure 24.23). The number of devices shown on the map depends on how the network is configured and also depends on whether the mapping and responder drivers are configured on the computer's network interface (see preceding Did You Know?).

FIGURE 24.23
You can view a more detailed map of the network.

The Network and Sharing Center also provides quick access to the Sharing and Discovery settings for the server. You can use any of the toggle switches on the right to focus on the settings for a particular Sharing and Discovery item such as Network Discovery. Click the toggle switch again to view all the sharing and discovery settings.

More importantly, the Network and Sharing Center provides quick access to your network adapter settings and also provides a quick fix tool when you are experiencing connectivity problems. For example, if you see a red X through any of the connections on the network map, you can click the Diagnose and Repair task. Windows Server 2008 attempts to remedy any connectivity problems automatically.

To access the server's network connections, click the Manage Network Connections task. The Network Connections window opens, displaying the network adapters on the server (see Figure 24.24).

FIGURE 24.24
View network adapters on the server.

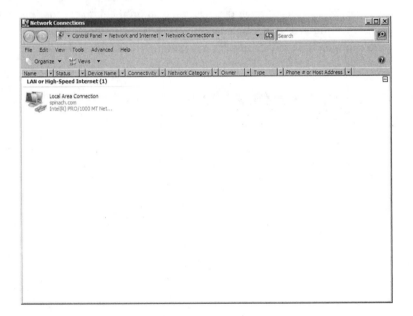

To view the properties for an adapter, right-click the adapter and then select Properties. The Local Area Connections Properties dialog box for the adapter appears (see Figure 24.25).

You can access the properties for any of the network protocols or other items in the adapter's Properties dialog box; select an item and then click Properties. TCP/IP and IP addressing are discussed in detail in Hour 7, "Working with the TCP/IP Network Protocol." Many connectivity problems can be associated with improper IP settings.

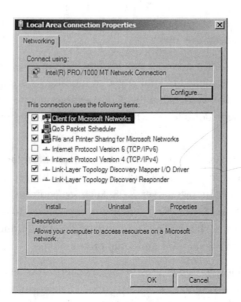

FIGURE 24.25
Network adapter problems may be associated with protocol settings in the adapter's Properties dialog box.

Although the Network and Sharing Center provides only a simple set of tools for dealing with network adapter issues, it is a good place to start when you are experiencing problems with server network connectivity. If Windows Server 2008 is unable to repair a problem network interface, your next step is to explore the adapter driver that is currently installed; this can be done using the Device Manager, which is discussed in Hour 3, "Configuring Windows Server 2008 Basic Settings."

Summary

The new Reliability and Performance Monitor provided by Windows Server 2008 provides you with an immediate look at CPU, disk, network, and memory usage on the server, using real-time counters, when you open this snap-in. The Reliability and Performance Monitor also provides two tools for quickly accessing server performance and the reliability of the server: the Performance Monitor and the Reliability Monitor.

The Performance Monitor enables you to monitor server hardware and services, using any number of performance objects and counters. Counters can be viewed as a graph, histogram, or report. A number of useful counters are provided, enabling you to monitor processor performance, disk usage, and memory usage.

Data collector sets enable you to add a number of performance collectors to a set and then view the data collector set data in the Reliability and Performance Monitor snap-in. Data collector sets can include performance monitors, trace events, and Registry key information.

The Reliability Monitor is a new tool provided by Windows Server 2008. The Reliability Monitor is designed to enable you to monitor (over time) the relative stability of your server. The System Stability Chart enables you to select event markers on the chart for specific dates to see what events have affected the overall reliability of the server system.

The Event Viewer enables you to view events that have been logged in the System, Application, and Security logs, or other logs that apply to specific services that you have installed on the Windows Server 2008. Each log contains entries with a specific theme; for example, the Security log contains events related to audit policies and resource use on network shares. The Setup log, on the other hand, contains events related to application installation and setup on the server.

The Network and Sharing Center provides a quick look at a server's network connectivity status to both private and public networks. The Network and Sharing Center also gives you quick access to Sharing and Discovery Settings for your server. You can also quickly access network adapters and their local area network connections Properties dialog boxes through the Network and Sharing Center tasks.

Q&A

Q. *How does the Performance Monitor provide performance data?*

A. You must set object counters in the Performance Monitor to view performance data. After a counter such as a processor or a memory counter has been added to the System Monitor, the data can be viewed as a graph, as a histogram, or in a report format.

Q. *How can you collect counter data, trace events, and information related to Registry settings in the Reliability and Performance Monitor?*

A. You can create data collector sets, which can include counter data, trace events, and Registry settings all in one convenient container. You can then view a report of the data collector set data in the Reliability and Performance Monitor snap-in.

Q. *How does the Reliability Monitor provide your server's relative stability?*

A. The Reliability Monitor calculates a system stability index, which is shown on the System Stability Chart. This chart provides dates on the x-axis and you can access event markers for a particular date (that has affected the overall stability of the server) to view what event took place.

Q. *What type of log events can be viewed in the Event Viewer?*

A. The Event Viewer maintains a number of logs, including the Application log, a Security log, and a System log. These log files contain events related to system and application processes on the server. Additional logs might also be available on the server, depending on the services that you have installed on the server. Events found in the log files are identified by icons, including the Information icon, the Warning icon, and the Error icon.

Q. *How can you quickly check the connection status of your server?*

A. The Network and Sharing Center provided by Windows Server 2008 enables you to quickly view the status of your server's private and public network connections. It also provides access to the server's network sharing settings and enables you to quickly access the properties for network adapters installed on the server.

Index

Computer certificate from this certification authority option (Customize IPSec Settings dialog box), **487**

Computer Configuration section (Group Policy Objects Editor), **222-224**

Computer folder, managing share permissions, **280**

Computer Management snap-in, **200-201**

Computer Name Changes dialog box, Member of Domain option, **207**

Computer Name dialog box (New Object-Computer dialog box), **198**

Computer Name/Domain Changes dialog box

  Active Directory Users and Computer snap-in, 204

  System Properties dialog box, 211

Computer window, Properties dialog box, **105-107**

computers

  accounts

    deleting, 200

    moving between domains, 200

    remote administration, 201

    viewing properties, 202-203

  client computers

    adding to domains, 195-199, 204-208

    allowing remote administration through firewalls, 201

    managing accounts, 200-203

    viewing network settings, 208-209

    Volume Shadow Copy Services, 265

    workgroups, 212-213

  web server configuration, 515

Configuration icon (Server Manager), 47

Configuration snap-in (Terminal Services)

  Licensing Diagnosis tool, 435

  TS Licensing service, 433

Configure VPN or Dial-Up Wizard, 401

Configure Your Server Wizard, 310

configuring

  Active Directory sites, 185-188

  AD DS, 148

  backups, 111

  CA, 497-504

  computers as web servers, 515

  data collector sets, 556

  DHCP

    clients, 372

    Relay Agent, 423-424

    scopes, 358-361

  DNS clients, 345-346

  DNS servers, 335

    cache-only servers, 346

    forward lookup zones, 336-339

    reverse lookup zones, 339-341

  file servers

    disk quotas, 250-254

    file services role assignments, 246-249

  GPO, 226-227

  hardware, standardizing configurations, 196

  IIS 7.0, 518

  IP routing

    dynamic routing, 417-418

    static routing, 415-416

  IPv4 addressing, 135

    ipconfig command, 137

    ping command, 138

  IPv6 addressing, 135

    ipconfig command, 137

    ping command, 138

  modem ports, RRAS configurations, 385

  NAT, 491-493

  network interfaces, 413-414

  NPS servers, 401-404

  paging file settings, 45

  RIP interfaces, 418-421

  routing

    dynamic routing, 417-418

    RIP interfaces, 418-421

    static routing, 415-416

  RRAS, 383-385

  scopes (IP addresses), 358-361

W - X - Y - Z

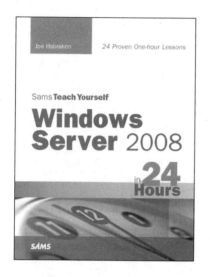